FROM BRITTANY
TO THE REICH

FROM BRITTANY TO THE REICH

The 29th Infantry Division in Germany, September–November 1944

Joseph Balkoski

STACKPOLE
BOOKS

Published by
STACKPOLE BOOKS
5067 Ritter Road
Mechanicsburg, PA 17055
www.stackpolebooks.com

Printed in the United States of America

10 9 8 7 6 5 4 3 2 1

FIRST EDITION

Library of Congress Cataloging-in-Publication Data

Balkoski, Joseph.
   From Brittany to the Reich : the 29th Infantry Division in Germany, September–November 1944 / Joseph Balkoski.
      pages cm
   Includes bibliographical references and index.
   ISBN 978-0-8117-1168-5
   1. United States. Army. Infantry Division, 29th. 2. World War, 1939–1945—Regimental histories—United States. 3. World War, 1939–1945—Campaigns—Germany. I. Title.

   D769.329th .B35 2012
   940.54'1273—dc23
                                                    2012015910

For

Melvin Sherr

104th Medical Battalion, 29th Infantry Division

1941–1945

Faithful soldier, devoted father, brilliant violinist, and loyal friend

Contents

Maps

Maps continued

Introduction
"29, Let's Go!"

From Brittany to the Reich is the third volume of what I anticipate will be a five-volume history of the 29th Infantry Division from its mobilization in February 1941 until its return to the States in January 1946. The first volume, *Beyond the Beachhead*, published in 1989 and updated in 2005, chronicles the division's activities from its call-up at Maryland, Virginia, and District of Columbia National Guard armories through the end of the Normandy campaign in August 1944, including the monumental Omaha Beach invasion and the titanic battle for the key Norman cities of St. Lô and Vire. *From Beachhead to Brittany* relates the story of the 29th Division's transfer from Normandy to the crucial Breton city of Brest, occupied by a formidable enemy garrison of more than 40,000 men, and whose massive harbor Generals Eisenhower and Bradley craved as an immediate solution to the Allies' mounting logistical predicament in the aftermath of the Normandy breakout. The top brass expected Brest to be in Allied hands by the end of August. Instead, savage fighting endured until mid-September, by which time the situation on the Western Front had changed so profoundly that Eisenhower ultimately decided against restoring Brest's devastated harbor.

In little more than three months of nearly continuous combat, the 14,000-man 29th Division had suffered close to 15,000 battle casualties, an unspeakable ordeal that completely turned over personnel—in some cases two or three times—in nearly all of the division's eighty-one rifle platoons, each comprised of forty-one men. Almost all of the 29th Division's original Maryland and Virginia guardsmen had become casualties, their places filled by thousands of anxious and lonely replacements who knew little about the 29th and even less about their new comrades-in-arms. In a matter of days at the front, those replacements quickly discovered the implicit truth in the muttering of shell-shocked veterans: over time, and short of final victory, all riflemen would eventually be removed from the front line on a stretcher. The lucky ones would still be breathing, recipients of tender care from medics and rear-echelon doctors and nurses; the unlucky ones would be dead, cared for not by doctors and nurses, but by graves registration personnel.

Why five volumes to recount the history of just one of nearly one hundred U.S. Army and Marine Corps divisions that participated in World War II, especially one whose period in combat endured only eleven months? The immediate answer to that question is that such a comprehensive story is a fitting and valuable acknowledgment of the service of all of the American divisions that waged war against ruthless enemies from 1942 to 1945. True, my narrative may cover only a single unit, but the descriptions of battle and life out of the line should be familiar to all who served in ground combat units in World War II, particularly those members of the many storied divisions that bore the brunt of the fighting in the European and Mediterranean theaters from the November 1942 invasion of North Africa until V-E Day in May 1945.

The 29th Division's harrowing combat period was obviously not unique. Indeed, it is astonishing to note that the 32,000 battle deaths suffered by only seven U.S. Army units—the 1st, 3rd, 4th, 9th, 29th, 45th, and 90th Infantry Divisions—amounted to 11 percent of the 291,000 Americans killed in action throughout World War II in all branches of military service, despite the fact that at any given time, those seven divisions totaled fewer than 100,000 men and represented but a tiny fraction of the nearly 12 million American men in uniform in 1944. If there is one prevailing theme to the 29th Division's story, therefore, it is that ordinary American riflemen—the pitiable "dogfaces"—carried America to victory in World War II and, in so doing, suffered an inordinate quantity of casualties in relation to their number as a whole. That story is at once inspirational and extraordinarily sobering.

In a more personal sense, when I first interacted with 29th Division veterans more than thirty years ago, I was profoundly touched from the start by the realization that I had been drawn into the same sort of poignant human history that had entranced me in my youth during exploration of battlefields alongside my long-suffering parents during the Civil War centennial. Out of the bonds forged with 29th Division veterans over many years, there emerged a rare opportunity any good historian would gladly accept, one that I was privileged to stumble upon. Assuming I possessed the requisite patience and persistence—and I harbored acute doubt that I did—that chance could eventually yield not only a detailed chronicle of American men at war that would contribute materially to our understanding of U.S. Army combat operations in World War II, but also relate a story that the ex-warriors themselves for the most part had refrained from articulating after the war, either to family or friends, for fear of receiving an uncomprehending or unsympathetic audience.

Just as important as my enduring friendships with countless 29ers across three decades was my introduction to, and later management of, the Maryland National Guard's marvelous collection of original 29th Division records and photographs held in the Fifth Regiment Armory in Baltimore. For more than a quarter of a century, I have benefited immeasurably from having the freedom to study and learn at my leisure from this priceless archive, and when ultimately the State of Maryland Military Department hired me as a historian to preserve, catalogue, and enhance that collection, I benefited still more. It was both chilling and thrilling to hold responsibility for the 29th Division's official papers, brought home in their entirety in 1946 by the diligent Lt. Col. William Witte, the 29th's wartime operations officer. Most of these documents had lain unexamined in boxes for decades. Over time, this collection has been significantly augmented with daily morning reports from almost every 29th Division company or battery; unpublished memoirs of more than a hundred 29ers; a voluminous collection of my correspondence with and biographical information on some 1,600 members of the division; and rare combat film footage of 29th Division troops during World War II. Supplementing all of these precious historical resources has been the undeniably spellbinding work environment of the Fifth Regiment Armory, in which one can perform research while sitting in the same room as invaluable 29th Division artifacts, such as General Gerhardt's jeep, *Vixen Tor*; various regimental colors and company guidons carried overseas during World War II; and the general's "war room" guestbook, signed by the likes of Dwight Eisenhower, Bernard Montgomery, Omar Bradley, and Bill Mauldin.

That the 29th Infantry Division was and remains a family becomes obvious to anyone who attends an annual reunion, a D-Day anniversary dinner, or the funeral of a faithful World War II 29er. One cannot deny, however, that during World War II the 29th Division family was at times dysfunctional, ruled with an iron hand by an old-school martinet. Nevertheless, the principal sentiment holding the family together, then and now, is the somber comprehension shared by wartime 29ers of the extraordinary number of comrades who died in battle in a time period amounting to a mere snippet of world history and the far greater number of men physically or spiritually traumatized by the experience.

I suppose I could have approached the 29th Division story dispassionately, detailing the military operations undertaken by the division using the straightforward academic methods by which professional historians are trained. For me, however, the old adage adhered to by veteran authors—"know your audience"—precluded that technique. These 29th Division narratives are written not for a scholarly audience, but for all those men, regardless of unit, who endured the World War II ground combat experience, as well as for the multitude of their increasingly curious progeny who crave to understand their forebears' role in a global cataclysm of which fewer and fewer Americans have direct memories. Indeed, one of the most common themes expressed to me by 29ers over the years has been their near-total ignorance of the monumental events in which they were direct participants. Aside from knowing where they were fighting—and even that perception was astonishingly imprecise—the proverbial fog of war and the dual desire to survive and follow orders prevented almost every American soldier below general officer rank from distinguishing the "big picture" and, in fact, from comprehending any event taking place beyond their field of vision.

Ultimately, if readers of this volume and its companions gain a modest awareness of the abnormal and deadly world populated by American fighting men during World War II and an appreciation of the context of the great events in which those men participated, I consider my effort worthwhile.

29TH INFANTRY DIVISION ORGANIZATION

In fall 1944, the 29th Infantry Division, at least on paper, consisted of about 14,300 men. Typically, however, battle and non-battle casualties reduced that number by a considerable factor. Several non-divisional units attached on a semi-permanent basis, including tank, tank destroyer, and antiaircraft battalions, augmented the division's manpower and combat strength. The heart of the 29th Division's military muscle was its three 3,100-man infantry regiments: the 115th (1st Maryland), the 116th (Stonewall Brigade), and the 175th (5th Maryland). (According to a venerable U.S. Army custom, the word "regiment" is considered superfluous when referring to units of regimental size, and references such as "115th Infantry" always imply regiments.)

A regiment was configured into three 870-man battalions, designated simply 1st, 2nd, and 3rd and typically commanded by a major or lieutenant colonel. Battalions in turn were broken down into companies: A, B, C, and D in the 1st; E, F, G, and H in the 2nd; I, K, L, and M in the 3rd. (By convention, no U.S. Army regiment contained a J Company.) Companies D, H, and M were heavy-weapons companies, armed with six 81-millimeter mortars and eight .30-caliber water-cooled machine guns. All other lettered companies were rifle companies.

Rifle companies were organized into three forty-one-man rifle platoons and a single thirty-five-man weapons platoon, equipped with three 60-millimeter mortars and two .30-caliber air-cooled machine guns. In turn, each rifle platoon was broken down into three twelve-man rifle squads and a five-man platoon headquarters. Led by a staff sergeant, a rifle squad was equipped with eleven M1 rifles and a single Browning automatic rifle.

The 29th Division also included thousands of non-infantry soldiers, among them artillerymen, engineers, cavalrymen, military policemen, signalmen, and medical, ordnance, and quartermaster personnel.

29TH INFANTRY DIVISION, SEPTEMBER 18, 1944

Division Headquarters

Commanding General	Maj. Gen. Charles Gerhardt, Jr.
Assistant Division Commander	Col. Leroy Watson

Division Staff

Chief of Staff	Col. Edward McDaniel
G-1 (Personnel)	Lt. Col. Cooper Rhodes
G-2 (Intelligence)	Lt. Col. Paul Krznarich
G-3 (Operations)	Lt. Col. William Witte
G-4 (Supply)	Lt. Col. Louis Gosorn

Division Artillery

Commanding General	Brig. Gen. William Sands
Executive Officer	Col. H. Ridgely Warfield
110th Field Artillery Battalion	Lt. Col. John P. Cooper
111th Field Artillery Battalion	Lt. Col. David McIntosh
224th Field Artillery Battalion	Lt. Col. Clinton Thurston
227th Field Artillery Battalion	Lt. Col. Neal Harper

Division Troops

121st Engineer Combat Battalion	Lt. Col. Robert Ploger
104th Medical Battalion	Lt. Col. Arthur Eriksen

Division Special Troops

29th Cavalry Reconnaissance Troop	Capt. Edward Jones
29th Military Police Platoon	Maj. Vern Johnson
29th Quartermaster Company	Capt. Frank Hines
729th Ordnance Company	Capt. Harold Price
29th Signal Company	Capt. Arba Williamson
29th Division Band	CWO William Fisher

115th Infantry

Commanding Officer	Lt. Col. Louis Smith
Executive Officer	Maj. Harold Perkins
S-3 (Operations)	Maj. William Bruning
1st Battalion	Maj. Glover Johns
2nd Battalion	Lt. Col. Anthony Miller
3rd Battalion	Maj. Randolph Millholland

116th Infantry

Commanding Officer	Col. Philip Dwyer
Executive Officer	Lt. Col. Harold Cassell
S-3 (Operations)	Maj. Maurice Clift
1st Battalion	Maj. Thomas Dallas
2nd Battalion	Maj. Charles Cawthon
3rd Battalion	Maj. William Puntenney

175th Infantry

Commanding Officer	Lt. Col. William Purnell
Executive Officer	Lt. Col. Arthur Sheppe
S-3 (Operations)	Capt. Henry Reed
1st Battalion	Maj. Miles Shorey
2nd Battalion	Maj. Claude Melancon
3rd Battalion	Lt. Col. William Blandford

ONE

An American Art of War

1. HOLD OR DIE

They emerged into the sunlight by the thousands. The forlorn hordes hobbled out of their subterranean hiding places and gathered in ragged lines on the cratered esplanade outside the submarine pens, looking like pitiable immigrants thronging Ellis Island after a rough trans-Atlantic voyage. They carried dilapidated suitcases, rolled-up overcoats, and brown fur-lined knapsacks filled with personal items, most of which would soon end up on a trash heap. Then they waited patiently, just as they always had, hoping that someone in authority would tell them what to do. For them, the war was over; given the intensity of the recent battle, which had endured for more than six appalling weeks, surely they were lucky to be alive. Perhaps the American propaganda leaflets that had fluttered down on the Germans had been right: an honorable surrender was indeed the only way to depart this wretched city alive so that when the war reached its inevitable conclusion, they could return home and reunite with their families.

The victors heard them coming long before they came into view. It began with the muffled *clomp-clomp-clomp* of trudging feet, growing in resonance by the minute as the glum columns of German captives climbed the harborside's steep hills to the prisoner of war camps in the interior. Only when the multitudes finally crested the hills did the magnitude of the

1

enemy's capitulation dawn on the triumphant Americans. The days of goose-stepping automatons marching with the pounding beat of a jack-hammer at a Nazi rally in Nuremberg were over. Instead, the astonishingly long procession of prisoners, including a few disconsolate Frenchwomen who had unwisely cast their hearts with the enemy, shuffled pathetically past their subjugators in a manner that was decidedly unmilitary. One American observer noted "the sorry plight of Hitler's supermen" and added that the prisoners all had "a filthy, mole-like color from continuous existence in holes in the ground." The shabby appearance and despondent behavior of the Germans were indisputably a direct reflection of the totality of their defeat.

The fog of war had dissipated for a moment, and the attentive American onlookers could not fail to be impressed at the unfolding spectacle. The enemy came on and on, passing endless rows of bombed-out buildings and the all-pervading wreckage of pulverized stone, shattered glass, and smashed furniture, piled up so haphazardly in the street that it would take days to clear a path, not to mention the years required to restore vitality to neighborhoods that had suffered the worst of war's many misfortunes. In the current conflict, modern weapons had demonstrated time and again their power to wreak havoc on vibrant urban areas representing centuries of human labor. But this renowned seafaring city of Brest, on the western tip of France's Brittany peninsula in the picturesque region known as Finistère, was something altogether different. The absolute level of destruction here exceeded virtually anything that had come before in World War II—on any front, from St. Lô to Kiev.

That the Americans had brought about such a devastating defeat to their reviled enemy yielded grim satisfaction, for that was the task millions of GIs had crossed the Atlantic to fulfill. True, if the achievement of that task could only be defined by the seizure of Berlin and the death of Hitler, the road home could still be long and arduous. But on September 18, 1944, the day the Germans surrendered Brest, even the lowliest private in the European theater could perceive that the long journey was much closer to its end than its beginning.

Would the Nazis meet their demise by Christmas 1944? Many in the highest reaches of the Anglo-American command thought so, and their record of uninterrupted success since the Normandy breakout in late July seemingly corroborated that presumption. The enemy's smash-up at Falaise, the exhilarating liberation of Paris, the blitzkrieg across France, the invasion of the French Riviera, and the first thrusts into Germany all had triggered blaring headlines in newspapers across the free world, and to them now could be added the Americans' noteworthy triumph at Brest, one of France's most impressive ports. When added to the list of other sizeable harbors under Allied control—Antwerp, Marseille, Le Havre, Cherbourg—the Allies apparently now possessed the facilities they would need to supply their armies with materiel and extend their assault across the Rhine River and beyond, all the way to Berlin.

Ultimately, when an experienced military leader tallied up those accomplishments and carried them to their logical conclusion, he could reasonably deduce that Germany would be finished before the start of the new year. The commander of the U.S. Twelfth Army Group, Lt. Gen. Omar Bradley, later confessed, "I thought they might quit." This attitude had been fostered by highly optimistic Allied estimates of the enemy's will to resist, such as the one generated on September 5 by Col. Benjamin Dickson, the First Army's chief intelligence officer. "The [German] retrograde movement has now developed in some instances into a complete rout," Dickson wrote. "The overall picture represents a scene of defeat, chaos, and collapse of morale far beyond that of the early days of November 1918."

Of the Allies' senior military leaders, none had more experience fighting the Germans than Field Marshal Sir Bernard Montgomery, the celebrated hero of El Alamein. In mid-September, Monty wrote to his boss Eisenhower and professed similar confidence, tempered by the assertion that "the vital factor is time: what we have to do, we must do quickly." On September 17, only one day before the surrender at Brest, Montgomery followed through on that contention by launching the combined ground offensive and airborne assault known as Operation Market-Garden. If that ambitious plan succeeded, the Allies would soon have a bridgehead over the Rhine in Holland at Arnhem and be situated one giant step closer to their essential objective, Berlin.

Meanwhile, on the Eastern Front, the Soviets' summer offensive had shattered the German defenses, and Marshal Georgy Zhukov's troops surged into Poland all the way to the outskirts of Warsaw, only 350 miles from Berlin—roughly the same distance currently separating Eisenhower's spearheads from the German capital. Even more positive from the Allies' perspective was that the Soviet triumph had caused the number of Nazi Germany's few remaining allies to diminish. By the fall of 1944,

Finland had surrendered, and Romania and Bulgaria had changed sides, just as Italy had the previous year.

The optimism of the moment within the Allied camp was so contagious that it swept into the conference rooms of Quebec's renowned Chateau Frontenac, where President Franklin Roosevelt and Prime Minister Winston Churchill had come together with their staffs on September 11, 1944, for the eleventh time since the start of the war to discuss Anglo-American global strategy. "The affairs of the United Nations have taken a revolutionary turn for the good," a buoyant Churchill announced at a September 13 meeting at the historic Citadel. "Everything we have touched has turned to gold, and during the last seven weeks, there has been an unbroken run of military successes."

Ordinarily, such summits focused heavily on Anglo-American strategy in Europe, but this time, with Hitler's ruin apparently at hand, Roosevelt and Churchill had shifted their scrutiny to postwar Germany. Communicating their approval of Eisenhower's achievements in Europe in a memorandum to Ike only five sentences in length, the senior American and British military chiefs turned their attention to the Pacific and the inevitable redeployment of Allied forces to that theater. For the most part, the subject of Germany was limited to its postwar occupation and the policies the Allies must carry out to ensure German militarism would never rise again. Every soldier who had engaged in combat against the Germans agreed with Churchill that the Allies must follow up their inevitable victory with harsh peace terms: "The German working man should be allowed sufficient food for his bare need and work, but no more," Churchill grumbled to Roosevelt.

It was perhaps a little premature to make sweeping judgments of that kind, for the Nazis were not yet finished, a point highlighted by Roosevelt on September 13 when he observed that it was "still not quite possible to forecast the date of the end of the war with Germany." Only five days previously, the Germans had launched a bombardment against southern England with their remarkable secret weapon, the V-2, a forty-six-foot rocket that ultimately descended to earth from sixty miles high to impact the ground at an incredible 2,500 miles per hour with a warhead weighing more than a ton. No feasible means of early warning or defense against these rockets existed short of destroying or overrunning their launch sites. So far, the Germans had managed to launch only three or four V-2s per day, so for the moment, the threat to England was tolerable. Nevertheless, as Churchill noted in his war memoirs, the British War Cabinet "considered proposals . . . which would have involved evacuating about a million people from London." If the Germans continued to bring forth significant numbers of secret weapons of such deadly effectiveness, they could temporarily gain the upper hand tactically and delay defeat indefinitely.

Another factor of potential significance on the Western Front had just surfaced, one that Anglo-American commanders could not possibly gauge because Allied soldiers had never before experienced it in either twentieth-century war against Germany. Presently, the enemy was about to fight in defense of its homeland: whether that state of affairs would provide sufficient incentive to rejuvenate the Germans' military effort was anyone's guess. History could provide little guidance, for no foreign power had crossed the Rhine in wartime since the Napoleonic Wars. If that notable historical record were to be perpetuated, Hitler must simultaneously provide inducement to the German people to maintain faith in the war effort while bestowing on his senior commanders the manpower and materiel they would need to halt the Allies on the German frontier.

Three weeks after Dickson's confident September 5 intelligence estimate noting the Germans' apparent "collapse of morale," he issued a new report with an entirely different tone. "The decline in morale following the defeats in France has been checked by fighting on home soil," he wrote. "The situation before the German today is comparable to that faced by the Englishman in 1940; and if the prose of the Gauleiters lacks the majesty of [Churchill's] 'We shall defend our island whatever the cost may be' . . . the meaning to most Germans is the same."

If extraordinary measures would be required to salvage Nazi Germany's ruinous situation on the Western Front, an extraordinary man must be selected to manage that effort. Hitler's military acumen was notoriously erratic, but this time, he did the right thing and chose the perfect man for the job, a selection tantamount to a rare admission of error because he had fired that man from the same post little more than two months before. Field Marshal Gerd von Rundstedt had spent fifty-two of his sixty-eight years in the German Army, and by the fall of 1944, his stature among the German people was so lofty that even Hitler had to admit that he was far above petty politics. The elderly field marshal accepted the post despite the observation by his former chief of staff, Gen. Günther Blumentritt, that "[he] knew that from the military point of view the war was lost." Shortly thereafter, Rundstedt bluntly related to

Blumentritt: "It was my duty as a soldier not to refuse at a moment of the greatest danger."

Some German soldiers, however, viewed loyalty practiced at such extremes as a wholly foolhardy trait, given the calamitous fate toward which Germany rolled like a runaway train, thanks to the Nazis' abhorrent practices over the past decade. Proof of Rundstedt's blind obedience to the Nazi regime emerged when Hitler reacted to the July 20, 1944, assassination attempt against his own life by appointing Rundstedt as president of a "Court of Honor" aiming to rid the German Army of all those soldiers who participated or knew of the plot so they could be tried and subsequently executed by Nazi judges. Field Marshal Rundstedt's participation on that entirely distasteful court led some to view him somewhat more irreverently. When Hitler soon thereafter reappointed Rundstedt as commander-in-chief on the Western Front, some maintain that the field marshal's true inner devotion emerged when he supposedly declared, "My Führer, whatever you order I shall do to my last breath."

The Nazis would of course insist that the fight continue regardless of who was in command. Hitler's infamous minister of propaganda, Dr. Joseph Goebbels, had stated that intent bluntly: "Germany will go on fighting because there is nothing else to do." Holding to that attitude, the Nazi military machine had been able to field more than half a million new soldiers since the debacles of July 1944 by reducing the conscription age to sixteen years, transferring troops from support to combat branches, and calling up workers by the tens of thousands from war industries. Many of those fresh troops, ready or not, would be ordered up to the Western Front in the fall of 1944 to hold back the Allied tide. According to Colonel Dickson, "The appointment of Field Marshal von Rundstedt of the Wehrmacht and not of the SS as Commander-in-Chief West further unifies the nation in the face of invasion."

On September 16, 1944, Hitler wrote, "In the west, fighting has advanced onto German soil along a broad front. . . . All we can do now is to hold our positions or die." Could the Nazis succeed in forcing the German people to fight on? And even if they did, could the Western Front possibly hold? Field Marshal Rundstedt may have routinely suppressed his innermost political feelings, but he did not conceal military opinions. As he took over his old command at Koblenz on September 5 and carefully scrutinized the situation, he reported to Hitler: "The whole organization takes time. All our own troops are committed, are being heavily

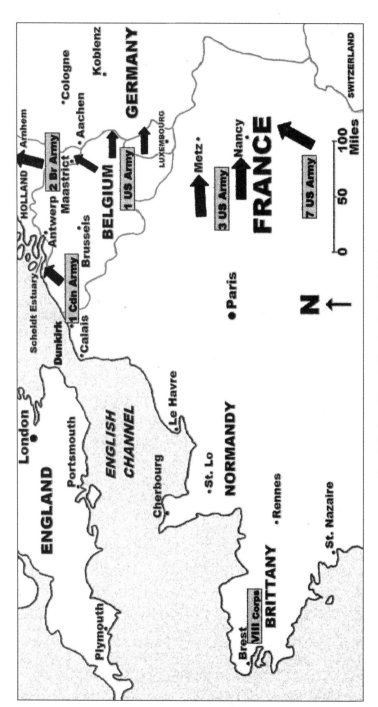

The Western Front, September 18, 1944.

attacked, and are becoming exhausted. There are no reserves worth mentioning. . . . If I am to command with any possibility of success, I again request that, regardless of the consequences elsewhere, all available tanks be sent forward at once."

If Germany could hold on until winter, then Rundstedt could, as one of Hitler's senior generals advised, use "fog, night, and snow" to his advantage. Hitler agreed: "That's the best chance."

Meanwhile, nearly 600 miles west of Rundstedt's Koblenz headquarters, the 70,000 or so U.S. Army soldiers who had overcome the German defenders of Brest on September 18, 1944, began what they hoped would be a lengthy rest period along the stunning Finistère coastline. Having lost 10,000 comrades in the protracted siege of that great port city, the GIs were ready for an interval away from combat, and there was no better place to do it than Brittany, which was about as far as one could get from the front in the European theater of operations. It was indeed a lucky break—but the GIs had earned it.

So far, almost no one in the Allied camp had criticized the high command's decision to make such a major effort to capture Brest. For now, the victorious troops could rest on their remarkably impressive laurels. Ike had never wavered in his stipulation that Brest was an essential pillar of the Overlord plan, and now it and its enormous harbor were finally in Allied hands. It was regrettable that the Americans had taken six weeks longer to capture it than the planners had foreseen, but even so, the GIs had forcibly removed more than 40,000 names from the rolls of the German Army. Even if that number could not offset the throngs of fresh German troops reporting to the Western Front daily in defense of the Fatherland, Eisenhower would appreciate that the victors at Brest had completely eradicated one of Hitler's most elite combat outfits, the 2nd Parachute Division, and had dispatched its redoubtable Nazi general, Hermann Bernhard Ramcke, to a prisoner of war camp.

In those giddy last days of summer, the GIs in Brittany enjoyed a respite from the incessant crash of the guns, desperately craving to believe in the positive articles that had recently appeared with regularity in *Stars and Stripes*. Somehow, spending several glorious days on a serene Finistère beach, gazing at the vast Atlantic or, even better, at the local girls, made it easier to accept that agreeable news as the truth. The war could be over soon, and dreams of crammed troopships heading into New York harbor danced in the minds of thousands. As one soldier at

Brest recalled, "The men had somehow or other gotten the idea they had fought their last fight."

But could the vast distance separating Brest from the front magnify one's confidence out of all proportion from reality? Any GI who had battled the enemy since D-Day knew with certainty that the Germans were not quitters, even when their cause appeared hopeless. The recent lesson of Brest proved that point. Ramcke and his fanatical garrison had fought on for six terrible weeks despite the obvious detail that their fate had been sealed the moment the Americans surrounded the city.

One's ability to believe in imminent Allied victory was directly related to how close and how long one had engaged the enemy: the closer a GI had witnessed the Germans' amazing ability to persevere and the more time he had spent in the front line, the more likely he would be to scoff at the idea that the Nazis were ready to quit. True, he lacked the top brass's broad perspective on strategy, and he was not privy to the Allies' impressive secret intelligence. Still—he would have been right.

2. SOUND OFF

At the moment the German garrison of Brest was emerging from its hideouts and marching morosely into captivity, 5,000 miles to the west, a dignified four-star general approached the podium, glanced over the vast audience, and began his speech. From every corner of the United States, middle-aged men wearing dark sport jackets and military-style garrison caps had assembled in a Chicago convention hall for the annual national gathering of the American Legion, an organization of World War I veterans of the American Expeditionary Force founded in Paris in 1919. The silver-haired general was about to give a keynote address considered so weighty that the Mutual Broadcasting System would air it live on radio.

Sixty-three-year-old Gen. George C. Marshall, himself a proud Great War veteran and Legion member, would now speak in his capacity as the U.S. Army's leading soldier, its chief of staff, a position he had held for more than five years in an environment of unimaginable complexity. Marshall's military career was still going strong after forty-three years, a longevity that could be traced in part to his unadulterated frankness. Only seven months before, during a February 1944 Legion speech in Washington, D.C., that frankness had emerged with startling clarity: "I speak with an emphasis that I believe is pardonable in one who has a terrible responsibility for the lives of many men, because I feel that here at home we are not yet facing the realities of war, the savage desperate conditions of the battle fronts," he observed. "Vehement protests I am receiving against our use of flamethrowers do not indicate an understanding of the meaning of our dead on the beaches of Tarawa. Objections to this or that restriction are inconsistent with the devoted sacrifices of our troops."

Since that earlier speech, however, the Allies had successfully carried out the monumental D-Day invasion and liberated France; American heavy bombers were preparing to pound Japanese cities mercilessly from the recently liberated Mariana Islands. Accordingly, the throng of Legionnaires in Chicago expected to hear a speech from General Marshall that would be considerably more upbeat.

> During recent months, our great advantage over the Germans lay in the quality and training of our men, the abundance and excellence of their equipment, and the skill displayed by higher commanders and staffs in the handling of divisions, corps, and armies. Of the ground Army, more than sixty divisions have reached the front, thoroughly trained, equipped, and most of them already battle-tested. . . . A conspicuous factor in the sustained successes of the past six weeks has been the steady flow of well-trained men to replace combat losses. Our divisions are kept at full strength from day to day. The losses suffered by battle casualties are usually made good within twenty-four hours and the missing materiel in trucks, tanks, and guns is being replaced at the same rate. On the German side of the line, divisions dwindling in strength and gradually losing the bulk of their heavy equipment, always find themselves beset by full American teams whose strength never seems to vary and whose numbers are constantly increasing. . . . [U.S. Army soldiers] are about to introduce the American art of war into Germany so that any doubts the enemy may have had regarding our military competence or willingness to fight will be dispelled in an unmistakable and final manner.

One of those sixty U.S. Army divisions spoken of so glowingly by Marshall was at that moment concluding its mission at Brest, its fighting men eagerly looking forward to a well-deserved break from combat, one that the division commander had hinted would last as long as two weeks and might even include furloughs to faraway England for some lucky souls. The 29th Infantry Division had indeed demonstrated to the enemy "the American art of war," a display of American manpower and muscle that had carried on almost continuously for fifteen weeks. Even the enemy would have to agree that the Americans waged war uniquely, if somewhat clumsily; every job they carried out was founded on that incredible abundance of men and materiel to which Marshall so proudly referred. Such a vast quantitative advantage over the enemy had obviously been decisive, for the 29th Division had not once failed to take an objective the top brass had assigned to it, including such deadly locales as Omaha Beach, St. Lô, Vire—and now Brest.

But for the 29th, nicknamed the "Blue and Gray Division," the process of achieving those objectives had been far tougher than Marshall's speech had implied. In those fifteen appalling weeks, the price of teaching the enemy the American art of war had been nearly 15,000 casualties, including 3,000 dead, a devastating loss rate that at times had come dangerously close to demoralizing the entire division. If that was the way the Americans waged war, one could hardly classify it as an "art."

It had all begun on Omaha Beach on D-Day, June 6, 1944, when the long-awaited assault on Hitler's Atlantic Wall had resulted in 1,300 29th Division casualties in eighteen hours. The path through Normandy was no easier, and by the time the high command mercifully pulled the 29th out of the line for a few days in mid-August, almost every 200-man rifle company in the division had suffered an almost complete turnover of personnel. Even worse, Brest had nearly equaled the physical and spiritual shock of Omaha Beach. What was supposed to have been a painless mop-up campaign against an encircled and demoralized enemy developed into a grueling monthlong slugfest, leading to a subtraction of 3,000 more 29ers from the division's rolls. As the division's chief of staff, Col. Edward McDaniel, observed a few months later, "The operation at Brest was, I believe, the most rugged slugging match that any American troops have been engaged in over a long period of time in this war. . . . Someday the operation at Brest will be written up in its true perspective."

The anguish of Brest was considerably accentuated when the men soon learned that the Allies did not possess the resources to restore Brest's vast harbor and would therefore gain no strategic value for it for the rest of the war. Could all that effort have been for nothing? Not a single person in the 29th Division could answer that question, so there was no point pondering it, at least for the moment. A far more vital question to contemplate was the impact of 15,000 casualties on a military organization that at any given time amounted to only 14,000 men: after losses of that magnitude—a number that exceeded the casualties in any other U.S. Army division since D-Day—could the 29th fight on and maintain the high standards it had established in training at Camp A. P. Hill, on the bleak English moors, and on the battlefields of France? Or was it finished as an effective fighting force?

That the 29th Division was most assuredly not finished was evident to any observer who managed to get a close look at the men in their rest camps in the beautiful Le Conquet peninsula, just west of Brest. For the past several weeks, 29th Division infantrymen had executed frontal attacks against an entrenched and tenacious enemy, day after day—a military situation that permitted no subtlety and was decided overwhelmingly by the brutal kind of fighting the Army euphemistically defined as "close combat." When the siege ended, those 29ers who had engaged the enemy closely at Brest had every reason for disillusionment, particularly those lucky few who had survived since Omaha Beach, but remarkably, most of them retained a modicum of cheer through the GIs' fatalistic attachment to the philosophy of living for the moment. What better place to spend those rare moments out of combat than the magnificent beaches and secluded coves of Le Conquet? There it would be easy to forget the war. Besides, the U.S. Army was not a democracy: why worry about what Eisenhower and Bradley had planned for the 29th Division next week? That was so far in the future that it was not worth a thought.

A more powerful influence on the 29ers' attitudes, however, stemmed from the division itself: its history, its social make-up, its commanding general, its traditions, and its essential way of doing things. All eighty-nine U.S. Army divisions possessed their own unique traits, but most 29ers, particularly those whose career in the division dated back before D-Day, professed the firm belief that the 29th was particularly special. That sentiment was not entirely positive. One of the division's most distinguishing characteristics was its uncanny knack for finding itself in some of the toughest fighting in the European theater for fifteen weeks running, a detail confirmed not only on Omaha Beach, but during its four-week struggle at Brest, a period when most other U.S. Army divisions in the theater were racing gloriously across France against little opposition all the way to the German frontier.

From his lofty perch as U.S. Army chief of staff, General Marshall surely did not have the time to give the 29th Division any thought. If he did, the detail he would have evoked was its National Guard origins. In the immediate aftermath of the Germans' devastating June 1940 blitzkrieg against the British and French armies, Marshall had urged President Roosevelt to mobilize the entire National Guard of the United States for a period of twelve months. By the stroke of FDR's pen that September, the part-time soldiers were called incrementally into full-time federal service, an act that eventually swelled the U.S. Army by more than 200,000 men. In actuality, however, a sizeable portion of those soldiers could not contribute much to the cutting-edge army Marshall strove to craft because they were over-age or physically unfit. Still, as the 29th Division would learn on the battlefields of Normandy and Brittany, many of the guardsmen who survived the weeding-out process ultimately developed into first-rate soldiers.

The 29th's turn came on February 3, 1941, when its constituent units from the Maryland, Virginia, and District of Columbia National Guard assembled at their home armories and, soon thereafter, at Fort Meade, Maryland. There the men would begin their twelve-month spell as full-time members of the U.S. Army. Then came Pearl Harbor, and everything changed. Forty-three months later, the 29th Division was still in active service, 3,000 miles from home, with no end in sight. By the time Brest fell, the 29th could no longer be regarded as a National Guard division since probably less than 5 percent of its personnel had Guard origins. Furthermore, in the units withstanding the worst of combat, the rifle companies, that percentage was close to zero. Actually, the 29th Division's transformation had begun only weeks after its 1941 mobilization when thousands of green draftees arrived at Fort Meade to bring the understrength division up to the manpower numbers prescribed by the U.S. Army's tables of organization. After its arrival in England, the division absorbed thousands more new men to replace those who had transferred to other units or could not endure the division's hellishly tough training in preparation for D-Day. But the largest infusion of fresh soldiers into the 29th Division occurred because of combat, for the casualties inflicted by the Germans at Omaha Beach, St. Lô, Vire, and Brest were far higher than anyone had foreseen.

At the end of the siege of Brest, one could depict the 29th as a typical U.S. Army division representing the great American melting pot. A closer examination, however, revealed that there was still something different, something exceptional, about the 29th Division. It had been in continuous active service for three-and-a-half years, and throughout that period, it had been either training or fighting with remarkable intensity. The judgmental division commander had long since weeded out weak and mediocre leaders. As of September 1944, a majority of his three regimental commanders and thirteen infantry and artillery battalion commanders were Maryland or Virginia guardsmen who had been affiliated with the 29th Division since the 1930s and, in some cases, the 1920s and had learned the art of war in fifteen weeks of some of the most severe combat any American unit would experience in World War II. If anyone grasped the realities of modern combat, it was these veteran guardsmen. Furthermore, many of the 29th's key staff positions were manned by soldiers with at least five and up to ten years of solid military experience dating back to their days in the National Guard.

Compared to several of the eighteen National Guard divisions federalized in 1940 and 1941, the 29th was exceptionally fortunate to retain a solid core of its best enlisted men and officers prior to overseas deployment. The division had not only a deep pool of qualified combat leaders, but also an evident solidarity that was the product of a common regional affiliation, shared military backgrounds, and the incredibly close camaraderie produced by years of serving together in the same units.

In due course, the World War II incarnation of the 29th Division that had been born on February 3, 1941, became legendary for the seriousness with which it carried out the minutia of military life, a trait that derived initially from the guardsmen's unwavering loyalty to their historic units and their familiarity with the Army's rigid codes of behavior. Two years later, when a new commanding general arrived to take over the division in July 1943, one of his highest priorities was to enforce old-school Army discipline, but by then, the 29th had been flooded by hordes of draftees who failed to appreciate the sometimes irrational methods the Army used to turn civilians into soldiers. Rational or not, the new general applied those methods with an iron will.

Maj. Gen. Charles Hunter Gerhardt, Jr., West Point class of 1917, held a solidly ingrained conviction that as long as the current war persisted, every member of the 29th Division, regardless of origins, must be wholly committed to the soldierly profession. It was Gerhardt's ceaseless devotion to that point that established the 29th's distinctive character. Like it or not, every 29er had to adhere to the countless rules the general concocted in his drive to make the division a model of American efficiency, strength, and spirit. The U.S. Army paid its two-star generals to be tough, and subordinates of any rank who did not follow Gerhardt's rules to the letter would swiftly find themselves in the general's doghouse—or much worse.

One of Gerhardt's strictest imperatives was his notorious "chinstrap rule," which dictated that 29ers must always buckle their helmet chin straps just above the point of their chins, as the U.S. Army prescribed. The general insisted that such a practice would prevent the helmet from falling off in combat, but he also believed that a

Maj. Gen. Charles Hunter Gerhardt, Jr.

buckled strap gave off a fine soldierly appearance. The men grumbled somewhat groundlessly that wearing the strap in combat could lead to a broken neck from the concussion of a nearby shell, but Gerhardt repeatedly refuted that argument.

Another Gerhardt essential was the division's battle cry, "29, Let's Go," which he ordered the troops to use in training, on official reports, on signposts, in ceremonies, and even in combat. As Joseph Ewing, the 29th Division's eminent official historian, wrote, however, "To most of the men, a battle cry and the rah-rah spirit it sought to create didn't seem to fit with their sober combat mood." Nevertheless, as Gerhardt intended, it eventually stuck, and one had to admit that hearing "29, Let's Go!" bellowed by hundreds of men was inspiring. Indeed, the slogan stuck so hard that Ewing titled his 1948 division history *29 Let's Go*, noting, "Nothing typified more the aggregate spirit of the Blue and Gray Division."

If, as Gerhardt insisted, the 29th Division's spirit was a reflection of its appearance and conduct, then every 29er must not only look like a first-class soldier, but act like one as well. Given the diverse background of the

division's members and their high turnover rate, fulfilling that resolve
would be a challenge, but somehow it worked. Starting with Gerhardt's
arrival, word filtered down from the top with a finality no one could doubt
that slovenly appearance, unhygienic habits, and failure to follow military
protocol would spark the general's wrath. Accordingly, when out of the
line, 29ers took care to dress properly and shave daily, and the general
himself routinely checked when his men needed to bathe. Even in the
front line, Gerhardt was known to bawl out a particularly sloppy soldier.
There would be hell to pay if he found an officer who did not wear his
rank insignia or had obscured the vertical officer's stripe on the back of
his helmet for fear of attracting a German sniper. As one 29th Division
soldier observed when he encountered a disheveled and unshaven GI at
Brest, "I knew he could not be a 29er."

One could hardly accuse the 29th Division of being purely a spit-and-
polish outfit. Gerhardt's 29ers were fighting soldiers, with a deadly job to
fulfill and a healthy skepticism of military claptrap. Even so, the general
strove to instill in them the idea that soldierly behavior yielded not only
dignity to the individual, but also pride to the division as a whole. "It is
those superficial things that you are judged by," Gerhardt asserted. In public places, therefore, 29ers walked around with their hands in their pockets at their peril. If the general caught them doing so, they would be forced
to carry bricks in both hands for an entire day as a punishment. They practiced military courtesy and ceremony by the book, offering snappy salutes
to their superiors when required; standing at attention facing the flag when
the stirring U.S. Army bugle call "To the Color" sounded; and marching
the way real soldiers were supposed to.

The general's exacting decrees, none of which evidently had anything
to do with boosting the 29th Division's combat skills, bewildered those
thousands of 29ers who had joined the division from replacement depots
since D-Day. By the time Brest fell, those replacements outnumbered by a
considerable margin the men who had trained with the 29th Division in
the States and in England, and if Gerhardt's prized esprit de corps were to
be preserved, each replacement would quickly have to learn the peculiar
ways of their new general. But in those spiritless "repple depple" camps,
where thousands of itinerant and jaded U.S. Army replacements waited to
enter combat, a transfer to the 29th would be an uplifting change for many
because, at long last, they felt attached to a genuine military organization,
one that radiated palpable pride and competence.

True, Gerhardt's multitude of rules were difficult to master and every so often seemed grotesquely illogical, but no American soldier, from his first days in basic training, ever expected military life to be completely rational. Moreover, the fresh arrivals could not ignore the ominous detail that wherever the 29th Division went, severe combat ensued, but according to Gerhardt, pride and proficiency provided the best chance for surviving that maelstrom and emerging from it not only in one piece, but victorious. To mold a man into an expert soldier was a complex task, but the general could boil it down to only three simple words: "March, Shoot, Obey." "The ones who have those characteristics," insisted Gerhardt, "perform well; the ones without them get into trouble."

And so division signposts blared some of Gerhardt's ground rules designed to enhance the 29ers' spirits: "Personnel must have chin strap buckled on point of chin; pants in leggings; have hair cut; be clean-shaven; carry weapons loaded and locked; maintain fifteen yards between individuals. Visitors are always welcome if they obey above rules." No 29th Division outfit could set up a command post inside a building, regardless of the weather; it had to be under a tent, in a dugout, or simply under a tree. Vehicles could not be driven with their canvas rain hoods deployed, and woe to the driver whose jeep had mud on its fender. The men had to know by heart the Army manual's prescribed "correct sight picture" for aiming a rifle: "Top of the front sight in the center of the peep sight." And when they marched, the general, who revered Army traditions, commonly insisted to young officers that their men chant time-honored cadences as they plodded along the roads of England and France in perfect step. The general regularly stood on the side of the road and watched with a mixture of pride and joy as the men passed: "You had a good home but you left—you're right! Your baby was home when you left—you're right! Sound off—one, two! Sound off—three, four! Cadence count!"

Like it or not, this was the 29th Infantry Division.

3. A VERY DANGEROUS PLACE TO BE

Old-timers knew that no wholly pleasurable interval in the Army could last long. The abrupt termination of the 29th Division's idyllic rest period in the Le Conquet peninsula established this beyond doubt. Lamentably, what the commanding general had promised would last ten days and perhaps even two weeks ended up lasting less than half that time. Furthermore, there would be no furloughs to England—except for the general himself, who had departed the division so hastily, only thirty-six hours after the fall of Brest, that he missed the critical decree emerging from General Bradley's headquarters on September 20, 1944, specifying that no 29ers would be permitted to take such a delightful excursion. The situation on the Western Front was now apparently too volatile to allow it.

The 29ers had only settled into their bivouacs for a single day before those officers running the division in Gerhardt's absence learned the astonishing news that the military situation at the front was indeed so instable that Bradley expected the division to re-enter the fight as soon as possible. That expectation was confirmed by a glum 29th Division staff officer who reported the upshot of a high-level planning meeting on September 21: "The rush seems to be to get us moving." When that news slowly filtered down the 29th's chain of command, it was received with widespread disappointment. What the 29ers could not grasp, however, was how unexpectedly Allied fortunes on the Western Front had changed. From Bradley's perspective, his demand to bring the 29th Division back to the front immediately was entirely justifiable. On the same day the 29th received orders to prepare to move east, Bradley's aide noted: "The general is now beginning to look tired. Today he showed the strain of days of worry. . . . Resistance on the line has stiffened and is now considered severe and rigorous. . . . It is the official opinion here that the German will continue to fight, that there will be no mass surrender [*sic*] as in the last war, but reduction of armies and smaller units piece by piece—which should make Germany a very dangerous place to be." Within two weeks, the 29ers would discover that Bradley's aide was entirely correct.

Meanwhile, the 29th Division had to prepare to shift to a new locale 500 miles away. Formulating a movement plan to cover that distance for an outfit of 14,000 men and thousands of pieces of heavy equipment was an extraordinary challenge that kept staffs constantly busy for days with the painstaking particulars that no one would notice unless something went wrong: organize truck convoys, assemble hundreds of train cars, plan routes, delineate schedules, pinpoint assembly areas upon arrival, and implement dozens of other more trivial details that only well-trained soldiers could sort out. Happily, by this stage of the war, the 29th Division was filled with plenty of soldiers of that kind, foremost among them its brilliant chief of staff, Col. Edward McDaniel, and arrangements of such magnitude rarely went awry. Still, many factors in the impending move were beyond the 29th's control, such as the weather, the derelict French rail and road network, and those imponderables that the great Prussian military thinker Carl von Clausewitz so aptly summed up as "friction." At the height of the frantic rush to transport the 29th Division back to the front, McDaniel would surely have agreed with Clausewitz's well-known but apparently contradictory adage, "Everything is very simple in war, but the simplest thing is difficult."

The difficulty had one beneficial result that delighted all 29ers: the arrangements to get moving were evidently so complex that the plan could not possibly be put in motion on the date initially prescribed by Bradley— September 22—but would have to wait until at least the twenty-fourth. At a minimum, that delay would give the 29ers two more days to enjoy themselves on the serene Le Conquet, an entirely agreeable development that would help alleviate the near-mutinous mindset that had developed when they were deprived of their promised ten-day break and furloughs to England.

Even so, the men had a great deal work to do and little time to do it. Troops had to gather personal belongings, replace missing and damaged equipment, and, most important, pack up all the items of military paraphernalia that made a U.S. Army infantry division a formidable fighting force. Regrettably, that kind of work would consume some the remaining blissful hours on the Le Conquet, but when a company first sergeant, the omnipotent "top kick," ordered it done, none but the most foolish soldiers would question his word.

Every 29er fully understood that their outfit's classification as an infantry division signified one salient truth: under normal circumstances, wherever the 29th Division had to go, most of its infantrymen would walk. Marching 500 miles from Brest to the main battle front, however, would not satisfy Bradley's need to have the division back in combat rapidly. Therefore, troop trains would have to do, assuming sufficient locomotives and freight cars could be assembled quickly and the French rail network could handle the traffic. Frantic staff officers devised plans to transport the division's twenty-seven rifle and nine heavy-weapons companies comprising its three infantry regiments to its destination by rail.

The U.S. Army had first learned the science of large-scale troop movements by rail during the Civil War. Eighty years later, that knowledge had changed little, but it still pertained vitally to the Army's wartime mission. McDaniel comprehended that science well, and it would be up to him to transport approximately 7,200 men by rail on a journey of more than 500 miles. Most of those men were infantrymen, the troops who had carried out the bulk of the toughest fighting in this war, and had so far suffered close to 95 percent of the division's casualties. McDaniel decided the job could be done with six trains: two for each of the division's three infantry regiments (115th, 116th, and 175th). According to the book McDaniel and his staff regarded as a bible, *FM 101-10*, the *Staff Officers' Field Manual*, a U.S. Army troop train should carry no more than 1,200 men in thirty-four cars, a mix of boxcars and one or two conventional passenger coaches. Advance parties would determine the optimal routes and choose a few suitable spots along the way for breaks.

The 29th may have been an infantry division, but as the product of the most industrialized and mobile society in the world, it still possessed plenty of motor vehicles—so many, in fact, that any German soldier who examined the U.S. Army's tables of organization must have immediately grasped why Germany was losing the war. Those tables indicated that the 29th Division had at its disposal nearly 1,500 vehicles, the vast majority of which were the legendary "Truck, $1/2$-ton," known universally and affectionately as the jeep, and the equally renowned "Truck, $2^1/2$-ton, cargo," identified by its nickname, the "deuce and a half." Every non-infantry unit in the division was so abundantly equipped with those two types of vehicles—and many more—that they were capable of transporting every member and piece of equipment by motor. Even an infantry regiment possessed 65 trucks and 161 jeeps, enough to move at least a small part of the unit by road. Moreover, American vehicles were celebrated for their reliability and durability, two factors that contributed mightily to the U.S. Army's reputation as the world's most mobile fighting force. In contrast, the primary mode of conveyance in German infantry divisions was one that the U.S. Army had discarded: the horse.

McDaniel organized those 29th Division units capable of moving under their own power into four groups, with departure times staggered over two days to avoid traffic jams. Nothing in France in 1944 resembled a modern American highway, so by necessity, speeds would be slow. More importantly, division MPs would man key checkpoints along the route to guarantee that no one got lost, an event McDaniel strove anxiously to avoid, for such a mistake would surely attract Bradley's attention and cast negative light on the division's ability to get things done. Bradley's order to get the 29th Division back in the fight swiftly was emphasized by Lt. Col. Louis Gosorn, the 29th's chief supply officer (G-4), who reported to McDaniel that a cardinal rule routinely followed by the division's truck drivers would be loosened: "[Trucks] can drive with lights [at night]. Eagle [Bradley's Twelfth Army Group headquarters] sent in an urgent call for that today."

McDaniel further subdivided each of the division's four vehicle groups into serials based on speed. Naturally, the slowest serials would depart Brittany last so that they would not clog the route, a problem that the division's ponderous 227th Field Artillery Battalion, equipped with twelve 155-millimeter howitzers, was sure to create if it was positioned ahead of a more mobile unit. The 155s were so hefty that the cannoneers had to transport them by slow-moving thirteen-ton tractors rather than the lighter deuce and a halfs. Additionally, the 227th possessed a single "heavy wrecker," a huge ten-ton truck used to tow damaged or broken-down vehicles. Members of the 227th who wished to extend their break from combat had the satisfaction of knowing that their unit would definitely be the last outfit to reach Holland.

The first 29ers to reach the division's destination traveled neither by truck nor train, but by air, thanks to one of the division's most unusual and little-known organizations, known as the "29th Division Air Force." This close-knit group of pilots and ground crews, led by Maj. Elmore Swenson, had at their disposal ten L-4 Cub aircraft, a diminutive observation plane so nimble that it required nothing more than a small pasture to take off and land. Those 29ers who knew what it could do prized it more highly than a P-51 Mustang. No church steeple or hill could match the aerial observation post the L-4s provided, and although they carried no weapons, they instilled fear in the enemy, for whenever one of them *putt-putt-putt*ed overhead a deadly American artillery barrage, called in by the aircraft's SCR-610 radio, would soon follow.

On September 24, one of Swenson's pilots gave the 29th Division's chief operations officer (G-3), Lt. Col. William Witte, a lift in an L-4 to Holland so he could prepare assembly areas close behind the front. Witte's trip, however, was not as easy as he had hoped. With a top speed of only 85 miles per hour and a range of only 200 miles on a full gas tank, a Cub was not an optimal aircraft for a journey of more than 500 miles. Witte's plane had to make at least two stops along the way for fuel; even worse, his L-4 had engine trouble and had to land at Rennes for repairs, forcing him to wait for a replacement. He finally made it, the first man among 14,000 to get a feel for the new locale that would be the 29th Division's battle arena for the next five months.

If the 29th had to return to the front, every 29er harbored the hope that this time the division would be deployed to a quiet sector, assuming such a place existed in a theater that was undergoing profound changes daily. From the Allies' perspective, those changes were decidedly negative, and in late September 1944, as the 29ers prepared to board trains and trucks for the long eastward journey, even an amateur military strategist could discern the enemy's remarkable comeback. Along the American sector of the line, the Germans were again resisting with their customary fanaticism, particularly at Aachen and the bleak locale nearby known as the Hürtgen Forest, as well as in Lorraine, 125 miles to the south, near the fortress city of Metz.

When the 29ers discovered in their Le Conquet rest camps that their destination would be the Dutch city of Valkenburg, located in that part of southern Holland known as Limburg, those who grasped the military situation on the Western Front must have sneered at the high command's insensitivity yet again. Valkenburg was just a few miles northwest of Aachen, close to a stretch of Nazi Germany's frontier defenses known as the West Wall, erroneously labeled the "Siegfried Line" in the American press. If the 29th Division transferred to that sector, would it be sucked into the swelling battle for Aachen, a place of symbolic significance to both sides since it was the first substantive German city to face imminent capture by the Allies? If the enemy was so obviously determined to hold Aachen, the 29th's future could be little different from Normandy and Brest.

In contrast, the 29ers could not help being amazed that their partners in the siege of Brest, the 2nd and 8th Infantry Divisions, would soon transfer to that inhospitable region of Belgium and Luxembourg known as the Ardennes, a place of comparative quiet that both sides, at least for the moment, seemed entirely willing to ignore. Meanwhile, VIII Corps headquarters, commanded by Maj. Gen. Troy Middleton, under whom the 29th Division had served at Brest, held orders to set up shop in the picturesque Belgian town of Bastogne in the heart of the Ardennes. Could there be a better place on the Western Front to get a meaningful break from the conflict? The inexplicable fortunes of war had yet again dealt the 29th Division a cruel blow.

At the northernmost American sector on the western front, where the 29th Division was headed, the U.S. Army currently faced a glaring dilemma, one with potentially ruinous consequences. That predicament could be ascribed to one man, a soldier whose name was familiar to every 29er, and in fact to all Allied fighting men. Field Marshal Sir Bernard Law Montgomery, the commander of the 21st Army Group, had first been introduced to the 29th Division during an inspection on January 15, 1944, in the course of the D-Day build-up. That episode was little more than eight months in the past but now seemed part of an entirely different epoch. Old hands in the division readily recalled Monty's self-confident, sometimes bombastic attitude, which in their view was wholly forgivable if he could bring them the same sort of victories he had achieved in the past. After the inspection, a delighted Gerhardt, who had endeavored to make his division a flawless representation of the U.S. Army, received a hand-written note from Monty stating "how very impressed I was by the soldierly bearing and general standard of your troops. . . . I regard it as a great honor to have such a fine body of men under my command. I have complete confidence that the 29th Division will earn great renown in battle." (After the war, an anonymous 29er penned a two-word postscript to the note: "WE DID!")

Unfortunately, in the last week of September 1944, there was hardly a soldier in the U.S. Army who held a favorable opinion of Montgomery. He had lately been involved in a testy exchange with Eisenhower on the future of Allied strategy in northwest Europe, a debate that had been considerably intensified by the failure of Monty's Market-Garden operation to gain a bridgehead over the Rhine at Arnhem. Market-Garden was undeniably a bold plan that had nearly worked, but in its aftermath, the Allied front in Holland was in chaos, with a fifty-two-mile protrusion into enemy lines that soon would be the object of the Germans' inevitable counterattacks. Had that narrow bulge brought the Allies any closer to a vital strategic objective, all of Monty's efforts would have been worth it. The Market-Garden scheme, however, created more problems than it solved, for the Allied bulge into enemy lines pointed like a finger—to nowhere.

Operation Market-Garden would profoundly influence everything the 29th Division was about to do. Triggered by Monty's foray, the military situation into which Gerhardt's men innocently marched was a staff officer's nightmare. Since early September, the Americans had been pushing toward Aachen and the Rhine on an easterly axis, the most direct route to Berlin, but Monty had made his Market-Garden thrust in a northerly direction. The U.S. Army's left flank had once tied neatly into Monty's right, but now the Americans and British were separated by a vast nine-mile gap, a situation any German general would jump to exploit. Paradoxically, the closer the Americans approached their immediate objective, the Rhine, the wider the gap became.

The commander of the corps that the 29th Division was about to join, Maj. Gen. Charles Corlett, was a petulant man who revealed that trait in a postwar observation: "The English started on their ill-advised jaunt to end the war over a single good road to Arnhem. Without a word of notice to me, they pulled out and opened my left flank for fifty [actually nine] miles. No change in boundary had been made and no provision whatever arranged for covering that gap. . . . It was not my responsibility, but I began to yell to high heaven about the situation."

Bradley heeded Corlett's yell, agreeing that the gap was a "damned nuisance," such a nuisance, in fact, that he issued immediate orders to Gerhardt's 29th Division to move up from Brest and deploy to cover as much of it as possible. Bradley's relationship with Monty during the Normandy campaign had been reasonably congenial, but the Market-Garden affair and its impact on American forces set the relationship on a downward spiral that would later trigger Bradley's acerbic remark to an aide that Monty was "one of the most arrogant and egotistical men I think I've ever known, and I don't think he ever respected anybody else's views that were different than his."

Disagreements between fellow generals rarely worked out well for the common soldier, and unfortunately, the situation into which the 29th was about to plunge was ripe for major divergences of military opinion. The Allies' essential problem was geography, which Eisenhower forcefully drove home in an October 13 letter to Monty: "This is no longer a Normandy beachhead! . . . We have a battlefront extending from Switzerland to the North Sea." He had a point. The Normandy front at its peak was no longer than about 75 miles; the new battle line along the German frontier in October 1944 was greater than 400 miles. Although several fresh Allied divisions had joined the campaign since Normandy, there were bound to be gaps in a front of such great length, and filling those gaps would be made even more difficult by Monty's 50-mile deep salient in Holland.

For the moment, Ike simply did not possess enough divisions to cover the front adequately, an argument he had made in an earlier note to Montgomery when he observed, "[We] may get a nasty little 'Kasserine' if the enemy chooses at any place to concentrate a bit of strength"—a reference to the defeat the Americans had suffered in Tunisia in February 1943 when the enemy unexpectedly counterattacked a vulnerable seam in the line with devastating effect. The 29th Division had seen enough of the German Army to respect its military proficiency; wherever there were gaps in the American line, the 29ers figured, German panzers would be near. If so, Gerhardt would have to watch out carefully that his own organization did not become the victim of a second Kasserine.

The enemy's resolve to fight markedly increased as a consequence of a major news story broken by the *New York Times* on September 24, just as the 29ers were boarding trains and trucks for the trip from Brest to Holland. It was undeniably a bombshell, revealing inner workings of the Roosevelt administration that the president would assuredly have preferred to keep secret. The scoop promptly swept across the United States and Europe, and within a few days, such Nazi stalwarts as Joseph Goebbels and Heinrich Himmler were learning of Secretary of the Treasury Henry Morgenthau's plan for "completely destroying Germany as a modern state and converting it into an agricultural country of small farms."

His fellow cabinet member, Secretary of War Henry Stimson, described Morgenthau, who was Jewish, as, "not unnaturally, very bitter" toward the Nazi regime—an anger that emerged in his scheme to eliminate the possibility that Germany could ever again trigger a world war. In a paper to Roosevelt, Morgenthau wrote: "All industrial plants not destroyed by military action shall either be completely dismantled and removed from the area or completely destroyed. All equipment shall be removed from the mines, and the mines shall be thoroughly wrecked." In a paper presented to the president on September 4, 1944, Morgenthau bluntly put forth his overall object: "The standard of living of the German population shall be held down to subsistence levels." Morgenthau also specified the provision that "All schools and universities will be closed until an Allied Commission of Education has formulated an effective reorganization program. [It] may require a considerable period of time before any institutions of higher education are reopened." To this was added the petty detail: "No person in Germany shall be permitted to wear any military insignia of rank or branch of service, service ribbons, or military medals."

That month, at the Quebec Conference, both Roosevelt and Churchill penned an "OK" and their initials under a four-paragraph summary of Morgenthau's policy, specifying that they "were in agreement with this program." Thanks to the *Times*, the world knew of Morgenthau's plan only eight days after Roosevelt and Churchill had approved it, and the headline, "Secretary of Treasury Would Convert Country to Small Agricultural Holdings," provided an opportunity that a propagandist as skilled as Goebbels could not pass up. Nazi radio was soon blaring the message that "the Jew Morgenthau sings the same tune as the Jews in the Kremlin," accompanied by calls for the German people to fight on as the only course of action left short of a humiliating submission to an invading army that would set Germany back hundreds of years. Although Morgenthau's plan shortly came under attack by veteran American and British diplomats, the damage was done. As the British official history of the campaign in northwest Europe later observed, "A stronger weapon for use by the German propaganda machine could scarcely be imagined."

Evidently, military affairs on the Western Front would soon become much more volatile, and for that reason, the top brass needed the 29th Division badly. When Bradley's decision to commit the 29th to the XIX Corps reached Corlett's immediate boss, the First Army's commander, Lt. Gen. Courtney Hodges, Maj. William Sylvan, Hodges's aide, noted on September 18: "Perhaps the most important news of the day is that the 29th Infantry Division reverts to First Army command and will be assigned to XIX Corps, probably arriving there four days from now. [It actually arrived eleven days later.] [General Hodges] has confidence in the drive and push of the 29th, which has set up for itself a fine record of aggressiveness in this war." The fact that Hodges was conscious of the 29th Division's fighting prowess would certainly have pleased Gerhardt, but its lofty reputation hinted that Hodges would throw the division into the proverbial breach where the battle was fiercest.

The 29ers could live without that reputation.

TWO

A Place Called Limburg

1. HOMMES 40—CHEVAUX 8

Saving wear and tear on the feet was a good thing, but when the 29ers got their first look at the implausibly diminutive French railroad boxcars known as "forty-and-eights," they knew the forthcoming journey from Brittany to Holland would be an unsettling experience. A forty-and-eight referred to the prominent label stenciled on the sides of each boxcar: *Hommes 40—Chevaux 8* ("40 men—8 horses"). As that tag implied, the occupants' comfort level on a long trip would be considerably less than in a stateside Pullman coach. The forty-and-eights had been stamped forever into the minds of the soldiers' fathers in World War I, almost all of whom would rather have forgotten them. Indeed, something about equating forty men to eight animals struck many cynical soldiers as a callous yet entirely typical military practice. Had not Wilfred Owen supplied such a metaphor in his touching Great War poem "Anthem for Doomed Youth": "What passing bells for those who die as cattle?"

One could scarcely imagine a more spartan mode of travel than a cramped and malodorous cattle car. If the 29th Division scrupulously adhered to the French edict and shoved forty men into each boxcar for a journey of 500 or more miles, carried out at a remarkably sluggish pace, the inevitable discomfort among the occupants would surely produce thousands of irritable and dispirited men. A few days in a forty-and-eight would make the travelers yearn for their destination, even though arrival in Holland would presage deadly combat.

Colonel McDaniel cut the orders on the afternoon of September 23:

> Entraining point: Landerneau [twelve miles east of Brest]; Detraining point: Liege, Belgium [eventually pushed forward ten miles to Visé, Belgium]. There will be six trains. The first train leaves at 0600, 25 September. Subsequent trains leave at three-hour intervals thereafter. It is estimated that the length of time of the train movement is 36 hours. [The trips actually lasted more than twice that.] Approximately 1,200 officers and men will be carried on each train. There will also be one carload of equipment, records, and so forth.

Normally, the Army's standard practice of "hurry up and wait" infuriated the GIs. But at Landerneau, Brittany, on Sunday, September 24, the Army's typical disorganization worked to the 29ers' advantage. The 115th Infantry and personnel from its supporting artillery outfit, the 110th Field Artillery Battalion, were scheduled to set out for Holland first. Early that morning, the rested 29ers packed up their meager belongings and prepared to board the trucks that would shuttle them from their beautiful Le Conquet rest camps to Landerneau. As usual, company-grade officers and NCOs professed ignorance of the design, and as for the horde of ordinary riflemen, had they realized their arrival at Landerneau would be eighteen hours prior to the first train's departure, they would have complained that they would have much preferred to spend those last hours on one final excursion to the serene Brittany shore.

Surprisingly, Landerneau turned out to be just as pleasurable as the beach. It was an ancient and quaint town, known for its Pont de Rohan, a unique 400-year-old bridge spanning the Élorn River and featuring several sturdy stone houses built directly atop the bridge's six arches, similar to Florence's celebrated Ponte Vecchio. The first batch of 29ers arrived in time to hear Landerneau's church bells ringing for Sunday mass, a particularly joyful toll to the locals, for this would be the first service celebrated since the surrender of the reviled Germans just six days ago. Moreover, according to the 115th Infantry's official history,

The Red Cross had set up a Clubmobile near the area where the troops were concentrated, and all day long the strains of popular tunes resounded through the woods where the men had placed their equipment. In Landerneau a few of the bistros were open and drinks could be obtained for a price. . . . Smoke from over a hundred small bonfires filled the crisp air as the men heated cans of meat and beans and vegetable hash. As the afternoon drew to a close, and the shadows lengthened in the woods, the men began straggling back from the town and drew close to the campfires, some talking or singing, and others just sitting quietly waiting for the time to pass.

Screeching whistles announced the imminent departure of a train, and top kicks gathered their companies for the movement down to the tracks. That procession was hardly carried out with the precision for which the 29th Division was renowned, for the men, burdened by all their worldly possessions, plodded rather than marched. With combat about to resume after a glorious six-day reprieve, the men's innermost thoughts again began to turn back to war and all its associated brutality.

Embarkation into the forty-and-eights was reasonably orderly, if somewhat depressing. Twenty-five or more boxcars, coupled in a chain of immense length, sat on the tracks with their doors wide open waiting to take on passengers, but fitting forty men and all their paraphernalia inside each car seemed unachievable. Fortunately, no 29th Division infantry outfit was even close to full strength. Therefore, as Maj. Charles Cawthon, commander of the 116th Infantry's 2nd Battalion, observed: "It was possible to shade the ratio of forty men per car. [Each car typically embarked about thirty.] The few extra feet of space was the only luxury available." The Army certainly did not believe in America's creed that all men were created equal, so just behind the locomotive and coal tender, French railroad workers attached a few passenger coaches, divided into enclosed compartments according to the European custom and strictly reserved for officers. Enlisted men were restricted to the far more austere boxcars, although a few ailing privates and NCOs were permitted to ride in the coaches.

Evidence that each troop train would shortly be entering an active war zone appeared when the passengers observed three gondola cars dispersed among the chain of forty-and-eights, each equipped with a pair of fixed

29ers on a "forty-and-eight."

.50-caliber machine guns for defense against the Luftwaffe. One car was placed just in front of the passenger coaches, the second in the middle of the train, and the last just in front of the caboose. The eight 29ers assigned to each gondola to operate the machine guns were lucky men, for they had the luxury of breathing space and an infinitely more pleasing view of the passing scenery. One of them, PFC Allen Levin of the 115th Infantry's Cannon Company, picked up some nails in Landerneau, and he and his buddies proceeded to fasten their shelter halves to their flatcar to provide shade and cover throughout the long journey. The machine-gun teams worked shifts: four men manned the guns while four men slept. The Luftwaffe, however, never made an appearance, so the 29ers never fired a shot.

Each of the six trains departed on time or, in some cases, early. But to the 29ers cooped up inside the forty-and-eights, the contrast between their recent freedom and the constricted boxcars was stark. Who would provide food? Where could one answer the calls of nature? How long would the journey take? As 29th Division historian Joe Ewing later noted based on personal experience, the immediate problem was establishing proprietary rights over a tiny spot on the boxcar floor so that one could pass the time in tolerable comfort. Ewing remembered:

The boxcar riders settled themselves in a half-sitting, half-lying position along the car walls and fell asleep in the slow, steady rumble and clicking of the wheels. But it was a fitful, pushing, cramped sleep, and you woke often in the pitch darkness of the car to shift and squirm into a new position or to disengage yourself from the knot of soldier legs that were twisted into incredible entanglements. When the floor of the car became too hard, or the air too close, you struggled to your feet, stretched and lit a cigarette, and worked your way to the partly opened door to breathe deeply and watch the shadowy French towns disappear in the dark.

The trains *click-clacked* down the track, conveying the division inexorably back into the main theater of war from which it had now been absent for well over a month. They passed into unknown regions of France, through towns few 29ers had ever heard of: Morlaix, Guingamp, St. Bieuc, Lamballe. McDaniel's advance parties had done their homework, and their designated first-day rest stops at Rennes and Le Mans provided a welcome opportunity for the GIs to exit the overcrowded forty-and-eights, relieve themselves, heat some food, and bargain with the locals, many of whom were happy to trade fresh baguettes, fruit, and vegetables for a couple of cans of C-rations. According to Cpl. Arthur Plaut of the 115th Infantry, the bystanders included "little children who asked for candy and *cigarette pour papa*."

Brittany was nothing but a memory now, although the men harbored a faint hope that something better lay ahead. If the top brass held any sympathy at all for the battered 29th Division, perhaps the troops would soon enjoy a stroll through a city that much luckier U.S. Army outfits had already passed through: Paris. But it was not to be. After a short break at a siding just outside Chartres, during which the 29ers could see the double spires of the renowned twelfth-century Chartres Cathedral looming over the town's petite red-roofed houses, the trains rolled on toward the sprawling French capital, liberated only a month earlier. The pace slowed to an agonizing crawl, and soon the men could see little except seemingly endless rail yards devastated by months of Allied bombing and more recent German demolitions. As Plaut remarked: "Paris from the railroad yards was not a particularly inspiring site."

What a waste . . .

On the morning of the third day, the lead train, carrying a substantial portion of the 115th Infantry, chugged unhurriedly out of the yards, leaving the tantalizing Parisian pleasures in its wake and provoking Plaut to remark sardonically that, in the end, the men of the 115th saw Paris "only in their dreams."

Not quite. Against orders, a small number of adventurous but foolhardy soldiers quietly slipped away from their boxcars while their trains lingered in the yards, made their way across a multitude of tracks, and vanished into the great metropolis. Most of them probably intended only to drift aimlessly among the Parisians for a while and then return, maybe even with a handful of souvenirs in hand, before their train's departure. Although the risks to one's military career greatly outweighed the fleeting pleasures of a short escapade in Paris, a few fortunate and fast-moving soldiers may have successfully accomplished their mission. Eventually, they could laugh about the fun and spin some yarns to their buddies or, in their old age, to their grandchildren. Most men who snuck off from the trains, however, would not find any humor in their actions: when they returned to the yard to find their train gone, the consequences of their foolish mistake would shoot through their minds with appalling abruptness.

The enticements of Paris proved irresistible for a sergeant and a private from Cannon Company, 115th Infantry. They snuck into the City of Light, bartered for some bottles of wine, and got drunk. Military policemen from the Seine Base Section used to dealing with soldiers of that kind arrested them, although not before one of the 29ers reportedly had intercourse with a Parisian woman of the evening. Both men were shipped back to the 29th under confinement, hoping that Uncle Charlie would be too busy settling into Holland to notice their transgression. The general surely noticed.

Many of the men who failed to make it back to their trains in Paris were guilty of no offense except exiting their idle boxcar for a few moments to answer a call of nature or heat up some of their K-rations.

Ordinarily, the engineer provided ample warning of his train's departure by giving a short blast on his whistle, but as related by Sgt. Don Van Roosen, a member of the 115th Infantry's Company H who had been a prisoner of the Germans at Brest little more than a week ago, "I was heating a cup of coffee beside our train when there was a stronger [than usual] toot, and the train began to immediately move out. I dumped my coffee and grabbed the first handle I could see. I looked back and there was some of my platoon with a horrified look on their faces watching us disappear. They were able to rejoin us several weeks later after being arrested by the military police, put behind barbed wire, and generally mistreated."

When the 115th Infantry finally arrived in Holland, the irate first sergeant of Company G called roll and noted on his morning report that sixteen company members—almost 10 percent of the unit—had gone AWOL, including a senior non-commissioned officer, T/Sgt. Maynard O'Dell. In the first few days of October, Company G, now at the front and involved in fierce combat, received all sixteen men. Gerhardt himself took interest in those "heroes who left the train in Paris"—as he sarcastically referred to them—and occasionally phoned the 115th Infantry's command post to inquire of their fates. The determination of a meaningful punishment, however, was difficult. Every sentence short of a firing squad for members of a rifle company seemed trivial in comparison with combat, a detail that may have triggered in some of those despondent riflemen who had gone AWOL a secret hope that they would be transferred unceremoniously to an obscure Services of Supply unit. But riflemen who fantasized about that brand of punishment deluded themselves, for the type of soldier Eisenhower currently needed desperately was the one the Army referred to somewhat inscrutably as MOS (Military Occupational Specialty) 745, the ordinary rifleman. The only practical punishment was reduction in rank and reassignment to a twelve-man rifle squad, but even that meant little: most of the offenders already held the Army's lowest rank, private, and were at present rifle squad members. All of the others save O'Dell were privates first class—just one small step above private—and most of them, too, already belonged to rifle squads. The salient detail on which all agreed was that if the wrongdoers remained in rifle squads long enough and combat as intense as Normandy and Brittany resumed, they would eventually get hurt. That point was proven when one of the Company G men who had gone AWOL, Pvt. Lemuel Garner, was killed in action less than two months later.

For those more dependable 29ers packed inside the forty-and-eights in the Paris yards, the scenery changed abruptly as their trains accelerated northward into the verdant farmland of Île de France and, shortly thereafter, Picardy. The passing place names should have been familiar to any soldier intimately involved in a war against Germany, past or present: Compiègne, the Somme, St. Quentin, Le Cateau, Maubeuge, and many other noteworthy battlefields upon which the German Army had established its fearsome reputation in this war and the last against less capable foes. Not many current 29ers cared anything for the past, however. The only factor worth contemplating was the future: would the 29th Division enter the names of new battlefields into the history books?

By September 28, far behind schedule, the trains rolled into Belgium, crawling through the manufacturing cities of Charleroi, Namur, and Liège, chugging along the north bank of a scenic river known as the Meuse, the waterway across which the Germans had shattered the Allied line in 1940 as they burst out of the Ardennes. During breaks, cheerful locals appeared alongside the boxcars in force; as Cpl. Jean Lowenthal, the editor of the 29th Division's cherished newsletter, *29 Let's Go*, observed: "The *bonjour* changed to *ha-lo*." The trains were close to their destination now, and standing patiently at a siding on the afternoon of September 29, a few miles up the track from Liège at the Belgian town of Visé, was Lt. Col. Bill Witte, the 29th Division G-3 whom Gerhardt called "his Napoleon." The men thankfully piled out of the stuffy forty-and-eights for the last time, as Witte and his staff provided guidance to officers concerning the next and final leg of the journey. Just about everyone had an overwhelming desire to stretch and get blood flowing again to stiff limbs and sore backs. No one could ever claim that five days in a forty-and-eight had been fun, but in a matter of days, when the 29ers would perceive how fiercely the rejuvenated Germans would defend their own frontier, they would look back on their time in those gloomy boxcars in a different light.

Those 7,500 29ers who traveled to Holland in 400 trucks and 700 jeeps experienced a vastly different kind of journey than the men who moved in forty-and-eights. The first of four huge vehicle convoys gathered at St. Renan, about six miles northwest of Brest, and set out on the morning of September 24. That the upcoming voyage was not a pleasure trip was made plain by a division order: "All practicable amounts of ammunition will be carried by motor [vehicles] in addition to basic load." Hundreds of trucks and jeeps roared eastward, rarely exceeding twenty-five miles per hour, bouncing along the rutted roads of Brittany in tightly packed streams that never would have been tolerated by Gerhardt had there been a chance the Luftwaffe would make an appearance. Whenever drivers came upon a perplexing road junction—a common occurrence in France—29th Division MPs gestured toward the proper route, occasionally pumping their right arm high in the air as a signal to pick up speed or extending it horizontally to slow down.

To adhere to McDaniel's schedule, the troops had to be in Holland by the evening of the fourth day, averaging about 160 miles every twenty-four hours. They would bid farewell to Brittany on the morning of the second day and enter the entirely unfamiliar countryside of the ancient provinces of Maine, Orléanais, and Île de France, passing through many of the same towns Patton's Third Army had liberated nearly two months ago in its now-famous blitzkrieg across France. On the 29th Division's thoroughly precise movement order, McDaniel had listed those towns by the dozens in the order the convoys would reach them: Chateaubourg, Vitré, La Gravelle, Laval, Vaiges, St. Denis d'Orques. Those names were unremarkable, of course, but one place, listed early on the third day's timetable between the insignificant towns of Trappes and Louvres, caused the passengers to sit up and take notice: Paris.

Packing twenty-five soldiers into a deuce-and-a-half, as field manuals prescribed, was hardly a pleasant way to travel; as all 29ers already knew, France's war-ravaged roads produced so much jostling and bouncing that no one could get any rest on the hard wooden benches. Even so, riding in U.S. Army motor vehicles was much more pleasant than forty-and-eights. Soldiers in trucks and jeeps never lacked for fresh air, especially given Gerhardt's edict that no 29th Division vehicle carrying personnel could deploy its bulky canvas rain hood, regardless of the weather. Vehicle convoys also stopped more frequently than trains, and breaks lasted longer—so much so that units issued passes to portions of their personnel at each evening stop so they could walk into a nearby town and enjoy a leisurely meal at a restaurant. As Lt. Col. John Cooper, commanding officer of the 110th Field Artillery Battalion, observed, those repasts included "the first beer which [we] had been able to obtain in France."

Those 29ers riding in deuce-and-a-halves and jeeps also had a much greater chance of interacting closely with the locals than those unlucky men in forty-and-eights. According to Cooper,

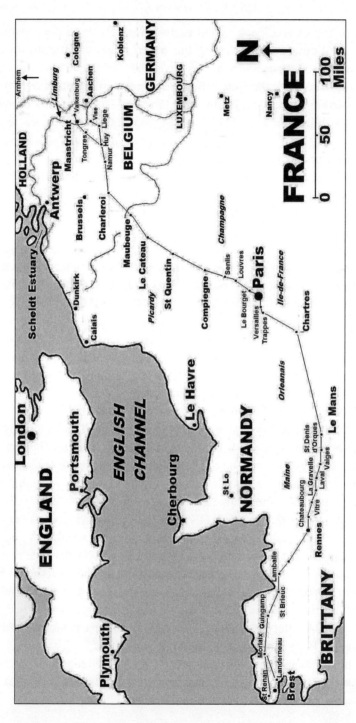

The 29th Division: From Brittany to the Reich.

Lining the road for miles at a stretch, the people tossed all sorts of gifts—including much-appreciated apples and tomatoes—into the passing vehicles. [In Charleroi] a middle-aged woman walked up and looked long and earnestly at M/Sgt. [Paul] Ritter [the 110th's sergeant-major] as though to assure herself that he actually was an American. Then she thrust a paper bag into his hands and hurriedly left. The bag was full of excellent grapes, which probably were valuable to the giver.

And then there was Paris, a city truckborne 29ers would see in its true glory, unlike those in boxcars, who mostly glimpsed dingy railroad yards. The vehicles missed the Champs Élysées by a wide margin, and the men caught only a distant glimpse of the Eiffel Tower, but Paris was Paris, and despite four years of a heartless German occupation that had deadened the city's spirit, the Parisians' notable *joie de vivre* had recently returned with remarkable intensity, the result of years of lost time that had to be made up with as much exuberance as possible. Most 29ers would never again have such an opportunity to see Paris; in fact, in this cruel war, who could predict with certainty that they would even be alive a few months into the future? Compassionate convoy commanders therefore allowed at least a few hours for their men to experience the two things about Paris they craved most: Parisian women and Parisian food.

And so, on the morning of the third day, when the convoys rolled out of Chartres, every 29er finally had something to look forward to. Less than three hours later, the trucks roared past Versailles, home of the renowned seventeenth-century palace and hunting grounds of the Sun King, Louis XIV, but currently the site of Ike's SHAEF headquarters. More relevant to the current conflict was the treaty signed in that palace's Hall of Mirrors twenty-five years before by the likes of Woodrow Wilson, Georges Clemenceau, and David Lloyd-George, a document that, according to Adolf Hitler, had brought Germany to its knees and justified all his appalling acts of revenge over the past decade.

"The Blue and Gray cavalcade sweeps on," wrote Lowenthal in *29 Let's Go.* "Out on the highway, into the endless stream of one-horse-powered vehicles chugging along toward Paris. Everyone is going to Paris. The cyclists are pumping their hearts out. The Blue and Gray goes droning into the night-wind, another campaign ahead." Paris was close now, but the city's sprawling suburbs bewildered the pent-up drivers, who could only follow the lead jeep in the hope that its occupants knew where they were going. Fortunately, they did, and the drivers eventually navigated onto the Paris ring road, named after Napoleon's marshals, enveloping the city roughly along the lines of its ancient walls. They crossed over a bridge spanning one of the great bends in the River Seine; past the largest open space in Paris, the vast Bois de Vincennes; and finally into the working-class district of eastern Paris known as the 20th Arrondissement. It was, as Lowenthal noted, "A city of beauty and glamour—girls with style."

The convoys finally halted, and the 29ers cheerfully tumbled out of the deuce-and-a-halves on the Boulevard Mortier for a few carefree moments of mingling, bartering, eating, and sightseeing. By now, GIs were so common on the streets of Paris that the fervor displayed by the Parisians upon liberation had diminished. Nevertheless, as Cooper related, "Children and adults flocked around and gave the soldiers many extras in the way of food and drink." Holbrook Bradley, a *Baltimore Sun* reporter who had been with the 29th since D-Day, observed: "Paris may not be the Paris she was before the war, but she is one of the most attractive spots most of us have seen since leaving home. London, which offered a good deal to Americans in the service stationed in the British Isles, seems drab in comparison. . . . Paris has just come out from under four years of occupation by the enemy and yet seems hardly to have been touched."

Since D-Day, the 29th Division had occupied a place in the front line, or very close to it, and its members had therefore never laid eyes on the vast horde of GIs employed by the U.S. Army in rear areas to keep the gigantic military machine operating. But that changed quickly in Paris, where the 29ers glimpsed thousands of American soldiers wearing the unfamiliar shoulder patch of the U.S. Army's Communications Zone, known universally as "COM-Z." Those men hauled supplies, pumped gasoline, managed finances, did laundry, ran trains, handled the mail, baked bread, laid telephone wire, and performed countless other tasks that the 29ers hardly noticed except for the passing thought that the soldiers performing them had a reasonably high expectation of surviving the war and were therefore exceptionally lucky.

To fighting men who had been taught that military etiquette was sacred and who had gained a fierce pride in unit cohesion as a direct result of combat, the sight of rear-echelon troops could be a shock. Less than two weeks in the past, Ike had written a scathing message to Lt. Gen. John

C. H. Lee, COM-Z's commander, noting, "I am informed that the dress, discipline, and conduct of American personnel in Paris is little short of disgraceful. Military police must be required to do their duty, and do it promptly and efficiently. . . . [You will] send away from there everyone whose presence is *not* necessary. Where these individuals have entered Paris without proper authority and merely for their own convenience, you will use every type of transport available to get them out."

The problem was infinitely more difficult to solve than Eisenhower realized. According to Roland Ruppenthal, COM-Z's historian, "Efforts to break the 'Paris fever,' which had seized Americans of all ranks, did not meet with spectacular success." Even worse, a handful of soldiers risked their futures by giving in to the temptations of the local black market and selling cigarettes and occasionally much more precious U.S. Army commodities like gasoline, food, cold-weather gear, and shoes to unscrupulous French civilians. As Eisenhower noted about the most blatant of those cases in his postwar memoir, *Crusade in Europe*, "It appeared that practically an entire unit [actually less than one-quarter of a COM-Z railway operating battalion] had organized itself into an efficient gang of racketeers and was selling these articles in truck- and carload lots." The reaction to such fraudulent practices by American combat soldiers, who had a pressing need for those items, greatly troubled Ike, who understated the case when he later wrote, "I was thoroughly angry."

That all was not right with the U.S. Army in Paris was first revealed to the 29ers when military policemen arrived to escort their trucks out of the city. As Cooper related, this was "partly because of the need for guides, but, according to [a] military police captain, mainly to forestall an ugly practice that had cropped up—particularly on the 'Red Ball' supply route from Cherbourg to the front—of drivers simply dropping out of sight to sell loads of food, clothing, gasoline, and even the vehicles to Parisian black marketeers."

An interval of a few hours was hardly enough time to experience Paris, but neither was a week—so why complain? The somewhat satiated 29ers gradually made their way back to their trucks, hopped up over the lowered tailgates, sat down sorrowfully on the unforgiving benches, and waited for the engines to start up. The collective growl of dozens of revving motors provided the depressing signal that the troops' momentary pleasure had come to an end, soon to be replaced by the much more familiar strains of life in a war zone. The MP escorts, on motorcycles, guided the convoys through the unfathomable streets and, as orders demanded, kept a sharp eye out for straying trucks. If there was a suitable way for the 29ers to remember Paris, it was the spectacular view just before the MPs peeled off and directed the convoys out of the city onto the Avenue Jean Jaurès. Dead ahead, only a mile away on Montmartre's dominating hill, was the stunning Basilica of Sacré-Coeur, whose three gleaming white domes stood out in the distance like a fairyland castle.

The trucks roared out of Paris on the Senlis road. In just a few miles, on the left, they passed a site all 29ers knew from their childhoods. It was Le Bourget Airport, where on May 21, 1927, the legendary aviator Charles "Lucky Lindy" Lindbergh had landed his *Spirit of St. Louis* to the cheers of 100,000 frenzied Frenchmen after the first solo flight across the Atlantic. Under its former occupants, the Luftwaffe, Le Bourget had been the target of several Allied bombing raids, and now its hangars and terminals were in ruins. Its new owner, the U.S. Army Air Force, was restoring the airfield and was daily demonstrating in the skies over Europe the astonishing advances aviation had undergone since Lindbergh's historic flight only seventeen years earlier. As any 29th Division combat veteran could attest, all of those advances had profoundly changed the way nations fought wars.

The break in Paris had put the 29ers a little behind schedule, and if the truck serials were to reach their third-day objective at St. Quentin by nightfall, the drivers would have to make up some time. The convoys sped up. As Cooper remembered, "The ever-changing countryside became practically level, grain fields were larger and woods were fewer," but in a *29 Let's Go* article, Lowenthal observed, "The church steeples on the horizon remind you that you are still in France." The French government had not invested in the high-speed motorways for which Nazi Germany was renowned, and 29th Division drivers had to apply their brakes and slow down considerably as they proceeded through the ancient villages of Picardy, where, as Lowenthal perceived, "The men, women, and children stroll with great loaves of bread under their arms." That the division had now left a great deal of its history behind as it plunged into an unfamiliar region of France was obvious to Lowenthal, who wrote with a twinge of melancholy that "the little, frail, white native hats worn by the women of Brittany are back there many miles behind. Perhaps one day the Blue and Gray will revisit the place of the savage battle, the place of pastoral romance."

How much farther? The interminable journey brought the 29th Division through the valley of the River Somme, the site of Great War battles more savage than what the division had just experienced at Brest. Evidence of that savagery lingered in the fields around St. Quentin, still severely scarred by shellfire. Most 29ers failed to notice, however, as the lengthy time for contemplation had drawn their minds elsewhere: to their family back in the States; to a girlfriend in England; to a buddy lost in combat in Normandy or Brittany; to their uncertain future.

On the fourth day, the convoys turned left at the little village of La Capelle and headed north toward the Belgian border, just beyond Maubeuge. No more border checkpoints, and in fact, since the Belgian locals also spoke French, there was little evidence that the 29ers, for the first time since D-Day, had departed France. One minor detail of the new surroundings was noticeably different from France: "[We] felt at home on seeing numerous signs advertising such American products as Coca-Cola and Ford automobiles," Cooper observed.

The 29th Division had spent 113 consecutive days in France, most of them in combat. It would spend less than one in Belgium, during which virtually no time was made available for the men to set foot on Belgian soil. The convoys' destination a few miles beyond Maastricht, Holland, was not far away now, and the First Army expected the 29th Division's arrival within the next twenty-four hours. That deadline was tight, so for the first and only time in the journey, the 29ers deviated from McDaniel's carefully scripted travel plan by following a shortcut from the Belgian village of Huy. The 175th Infantry and 224th Field Artillery Battalion were in the forefront of the division's motor procession, and convoy serial commanders agreed that avoiding the big-city road network of Liège, Belgium, congested with supply vehicles supporting the First Army's advance toward Aachen, would be prudent. The convoys therefore turned north out of Huy on a comparatively empty country road, heading toward Tongres, a quaint market town featuring ancient Roman walls—more than 1,800 years old, built by order of the Emperor Hadrian—and a beautiful Gothic basilica dating to the thirteenth century.

The shortcut would definitely shave some time off the final leg of the journey to Maastricht, but since the decision to take it was made spontaneously, those 29th Division convoys behind the leading serial had to be told. The 175th sent back an officer in a jeep to find the follow-on column, comprised of the 115th Infantry and 110th Field Artillery Battalion, and inform its commander of the route change. To make sure, the 175th left guides behind in Huy at appropriate road junctions. A major change in plans of that kind easily could have triggered a colossal snafu, but for the most part, the drivers followed the new route flawlessly. Such an accomplishment reflected well on the division's proficiency at large-scale troop movements, which it had been perfecting since the Carolina Maneuvers in September 1941.

Only nine more miles to Holland, but the hardest part of the journey lay ahead, particularly for those convoys still on the road after dark. "Drivers began to encounter numerous detours due to blown-up bridges and often could not see the soldiers acting as road markers over the latter part of the route," Cooper noted. "Following the faint, tiny tail lights used in blackouts became almost impossible, and in the rain and inky darkness a few vehicles missed critical turns."

This time, the international border was clearly delineated by an impressive manmade terrain feature, the Albert Canal, which the 29th Division convoys crossed courtesy of a XIX Corps engineer outfit and its recently constructed Bailey bridge. A short distance ahead was Maastricht, one of the oldest cities in Holland, tracing its origins to a Roman army camp in the epoch of Julius Caesar. The location of that Roman camp made perfect sense to twentieth-century generals, for Maastricht sits astride the Maas River (known as the Meuse in Belgium and France) at a pivotal western European crossroads through which countless armies had passed over the centuries, now including the U.S. Army and its 29th Infantry Division.

The Maas had been the last great water barrier standing between the Allies and the Rhine, and the Germans had done everything in their power to prevent the Americans from crossing it. In the end, however, that effort had not amounted to much. Two weeks before the 29th's arrival, the 30th Infantry Division had carried out an adroit flanking maneuver, capturing the city from the rear. The Germans had managed to blow up Maastricht's three Maas River bridges, but when the 29ers pulled into town, the 247th Engineer Combat Battalion was putting the finishing touches on a spectacular 600-foot Bailey bridge, which in three separate segments connected the wrecked spans of the historic St. Servaas bridge. It was one of the longest Bailey bridges ever constructed during World War II.

Almost there. The drivers plunged through the dense urban setting of Maastricht, guided by alert MPs through city streets that otherwise would have been unfathomable. On the far side of the Maas, Colonel Witte's guides were waiting to lead the serials to their final destinations, seven miles to the east in the Dutch countryside. The units would bivouac there for a day or two before joining Corlett's XIX Corps at the front. What would happen after that was anyone's guess.

Just a few miles beyond the division's new campground was the place which all Allied soldiers had been yearning to reach for years: Germany. For the 29ers, signs that the war was close once again were palpable. "The continual flashes and glimmers of artillery firing . . . weirdly lighted the black and cloudy night," Cooper wrote. "Above the intermittent rumble of gunfire the deadly drone of enemy aircraft steadily sounded. Rest and pleasant travel were finished."

As the diverse elements of the 29th Division closed up to the front, one vital component was missing—the division's commander. Gerhardt had departed Brest only two days after its liberation for a furlough in southwestern England, where 29ers had made many close friends during the division's lengthy training period before D-Day. Only hours after the general's departure, however, General Bradley had abruptly revoked all 29th Division furloughs and ordered Gerhardt to return posthaste. Unfortunately, it took the U.S. Army more than five days to locate him, and by that time, the 29th's leading elements were already beyond Paris. Gerhardt and his driver, T/3 Bob Cuff, hitched an airplane ride to France and caught up with the 29th Division on the morning of September 26. McDaniel promptly brought him up to speed on the division's movement back to the front.

Early on September 27, Gerhardt and Cuff, along with the general's aide, Capt. Bob Wallis, and his beloved spaniel, D-Day, settled into their familiar seats in Gerhardt's command jeep, *Vixen Tor*, and joined the enormous procession of vehicles snaking east. Gerhardt took position in the lead, the only place he knew. Around midday, just north of Maubeuge, the general ordered Cuff to pull over near the Belgian border so he could inspect his division as it passed. For Gerhardt, a man whose nearly fifty years of life had revolved almost entirely around the U.S. Army, watching his men go by surely was emotional. As he remarked to reporter Lou Azrael of the *Baltimore News-Post*, "Our division got its elementary education during training. The Normandy campaign was a college course in warfare. In Brittany we had a post-graduate course—and have come through with honors. We are now about to face the facts of life. Where that will be I cannot tell you now."

Gerhardt was pleased to note that many of the vehicles passing him were brimming with symbols of the unit pride the general had worked so hard to create. The 29th Division's blue-and-gray insignia was everywhere: jeeps, trucks, howitzers, helmets—and, of course, on the left shoulders of every 29er. The division's many hardfought battles since D-Day were also emblazoned on engine hoods, gun shields, truck doors, and jeep windshields: Omaha Beach, St. Lô, Percy, Villebaudon, Vire, and Brest. (The paint used to spell out Brest was still noticeably fresh.) Artillerymen wore scarves—one of Gerhardt's pet ideas—dyed red in honor of the gunners' traditional color. On the division's vehicles, the motto "29 Let's Go!" was ubiquitous, but somewhat more personally, several drivers had also added the names of their girls back home, some with a remarkably artistic flair. Those who cared deeply about unit pride had their chin straps buckled at the point of their chins and snapped perfect salutes as they passed their commanding general, who returned them with equal stylishness.

General Gerhardt in his jeep, *Vixen Tor*.

As Cooper remarked in a 1947 letter to Joe Ewing, these kinds of displays

> pleased the old man tremendously. Back in England, before General Gerhardt took over, if a driver in a moment of affection, painted 'Nellie' or some such name on his vehicle, he would have likely been court-martialed. But Gerhardt insisted that vehicle names and divisional symbols encouraged pride and ordered that it be done—neatly. In France, he ordered that names of battles should be added, and places where vehicles had been hit by enemy fire should be marked. [Gerhardt's own jeep, Vixen Tor, had all those features, including a yellow mark where the jeep had been hit by German fire at Villebaudon on July 29, 1944.] These things did add tremendously to pride in equipment and general ésprit. U.S. Army regulations were against it, and probably still are, but I heard General Gerhardt expound one day when questioned on this. He said that nobody would ever pick on a successful, hard-fighting outfit over details like these as long as it was winning. The general was absolutely right.

So far, the 29th Division had always won, but victory could not be complete until it reached Berlin. There, as Lowenthal noted in the division newsletter, "You have another rendezvous. On to it! For you there is only one road. 29 LET'S GO!"

2. EITHER YOU GET IT OR YOU DON'T

The 29th Infantry Division was in one piece again.

It was the morning of Saturday, September 30, 1944, somewhere in the Dutch countryside a few miles east of Maastricht, near a handsome old town known as Valkenburg. According to the division's daily operations summary, the day was "cloudy with intermittent light rains; visibility poor"—a type of weather the 29ers had to get used to soon.

The men awoke that bleak morning, keen to take in their new surroundings. But what little they could see was entirely surprising. Could this be Holland? It certainly was not the Holland of the 29ers' elementary school geography books: the eternal land of earthen dikes, holding back the surging waves of the North Sea; the endless tracts of green, moist earth known as polder, as flat as a billiard table; the maze of inland waterways;

the glorious and picturesque cities that were living reminders of the Dutch Golden Age; the colorful tulip fields, interspersed with scenic windmills; the local peasants in wooden clogs. Wherever the 29ers were, they could see none of these classic attributes of the Netherlands.

Officers examined maps freshly issued by S-2s and determined at a glance that this corner of Limburg could hardly be categorized as typical Dutch countryside. They were now in an area labeled by outsiders as the "Dutch Panhandle" or the "Maastricht Appendix," a narrow finger of Dutch land cutting a swath between Belgium to the west and Germany to the east. In a nation defined by its relationship to water, there was no place in Holland farther from the sea than Limburg. No flat polderland here: Valkenburg sits in the valley of the Geul River, which flows to the Maas through a sharply undulating landscape more evocative of the foothills of the Blue Ridge than the reclaimed lands adjacent to the Ijsselmeer. Their first panoramic view of south Limburg demonstrated to the 29ers how the region had gained the nickname "The Dutch Alps," for some of the lofty elevations south of Valkenburg could truly be classified as mountains, a type of terrain the GIs never expected to see in Holland. The Americans had supposed that much of Holland was near sea level, or even below it, but ironically, a glimpse at the contour lines on their maps indicated that the division was now at a higher elevation than almost any other place it had passed through in Normandy or Brittany since D-Day.

Springs rich in minerals gushed fresh water out of the Limburg hills, just as they did twenty-five miles to the south in the Ardennes, where a provincial Belgian town named Spa had become synonymous for medicinal water treatments. Generations of Limburgers had tapped rich seams of coal under this land, and for centuries before even that, dating back to Roman times, the locals had dug deep into the hills to mine marl, a form of limestone containing clay that was ideal building material and was used in the construction of dozens of historic local structures, most prominently a 900-year-old castle on a hilltop in Valkenburg. The excavation of marl-stone over the years had resulted in an impressive chain of caves and underground passageways in the Valkenburg area that seemed like a modern version of the legendary Labyrinth on Crete that housed King Minos's Minotaur in Greek mythology. Inside one of those caves was a chapel, established by a local priest in 1797 as a secret gathering place for local Roman Catholics in the aftermath of the French Revolution, which had swept into nearby Holland with its antireligious fervor.

Limburg, Holland.

Regrettably, the dull reverberation of nearby artillery fire and the frequent low-level passes of Allied fighter-bombers reminded the 29ers that the increasingly difficult situation at the front, just a few miles distant, would soon require the division to move forward into the line. Therefore, the chances of enjoying a few days in this idyllic locale were slim. So far, the troops' first tentative contacts with the Valkenburg locals had been entirely positive, but according to rumor, the division's next stop would be across the border in Germany, where the natives promised to be surlier. What the 29ers could not possibly realize, however, was that for the next five months, the division would be trapped in a seemingly endless phase of stagnant warfare, during which it would not stray more than a dozen miles from the Dutch border. Until late February 1945, most of the 29th's rear-echelon facilities, including rest camps for weary combat troops, would remain in and around the quaint villages of Limburg, where the 29ers would have a much better opportunity to get to know the Dutch locals than they ever had with the Normans and Bretons in the more than three months following D-Day.

One immediate obstacle was the Dutch language, which, at least in the Limburgers' dialect, sounded much more alien than French and, indeed, seemed as if it had nothing in common with English. One astonished American remarked after an encounter with a Dutch merchant that "she [spoke] in some strange tongue that isn't a language at all." Even the American melting pot that was the 29th Division contained hardly any speakers of fluent Dutch. The surprised 29ers would eventually learn that English, which in truth is much more closely related to Dutch than French, drew countless words from Old Dutch. When the local language was viewed in written form, entire sentences occasionally jumped out as wholly comprehensible to American troops. Furthermore, as Gerhardt noted, "Almost everyone [in Holland] was able to speak at least three languages"—one of which was usually English.

Then there was the problem of money. Limburg was adjacent to three European countries beyond Holland—Belgium, Germany, and France—each of which had its own national currency that exchanged with the others at varying rates. A few weeks after arriving in Holland, many perplexed 29ers reached into their pockets to discover wads of different kinds of paper money: French francs, Dutch guilders, German marks, Belgian francs, even some British pounds. (Ironically, the U.S. Army did not permit its soldiers to carry American dollars when deployed overseas.) "We've got money troubles," reporter Lou Azrael lamented in an October 1944 *Baltimore News-Post* article. "They make life very complicated."

Azrael related how he had once attempted to buy an item in a Dutch shop for seventy-five cents. (One hundred Dutch cents equaled one guilder.) He lacked Dutch currency, but he did have German, French, and Belgian money on hand. He eventually tried the French: "One 20-franc note and two 10-franc notes. That required some mathematics on my part. A franc is worth two cents. So I was giving her 80 cents, and she could give me five cents change. But the girl looked at me as if I were somewhat dim-wit. She didn't take the 20-franc note at all, and she gave me change from the two 10-franc ones. There was no use trying to get an explanation there." Azrael's mistake was equating a French franc with two *American* cents, but since a Dutch guilder was worth much less than an American dollar, a French franc was actually equal to about five *Dutch* cents. As Azrael concluded, "Either you get it or you don't"—and apparently neither he nor most 29ers ever got it.

One part of Azrael's interaction with the Dutch sales girl was telling. He had first tried to use German marks in the exchange, but she replied: "German! French—yes. Belgian—yes. German—no!" Such an attitude might have surprised Azrael, since American troops had been warned at first to be cautious around Dutch locals since it was assumed that townspeople so close to the German border might have been contaminated by Nazism over the years. The Germans, however, had applied their brutal occupation methods in Holland with an intensity the Dutch would never forget. More than 100,000 Dutch Jews, about 1.2 percent of Holland's prewar population, were deported to Germany to meet an unspeakable fate. Furthermore, for more than four years, the Nazis had exploited Holland's renowned agricultural productivity at the expense of the natives. Even worse, imminent liberation by the Allies ultimately drove the Germans to destroy Dutch farming by demolishing dikes and shutting down the conveyance of food by canal boat. The impact of that kind of cruelty was principally felt in the vast regions of northern and western Holland remaining under German occupation until the war's last days. Those areas included the cities of Amsterdam, Rotterdam, and The Hague, whose residents would endure seven more months of terrible privation after the Allies had first entered Holland in September 1944. The Dutch would later categorize that bleak period as the "hunger winter," during which 16,000 citizens perished from malnourishment.

The Limburgers had indeed been fortunate to be unchained from the Nazi yoke in the initial onrush of Allied troops across northwest Europe that began with the Normandy breakout in July. Free at last to speak their minds, they would soon demonstrate their hatred for everything Nazi to their new visitors from the 29th Division in much more meaningful ways than caustic remarks about Germans by shopkeepers. Ultimate proof of the Dutch people's odium for their former occupiers abruptly appeared in the 29th's rear-echelon zone a few days after the division's arrival in Holland. Three companies of Royal Netherlands *Stoottroepen* offered their services to Gerhardt. Organized by Prince Bernhard, son-in-law of the beloved Queen Wilhelmina, the *Stoottroepen* were military units comprised of former members of the Dutch Resistance. The Dutchmen did not look much like real soldiers—some reportedly even wore wooden shoes— but they had been resisting the Germans long before the Americans' arrival, and their resolve to contribute to their country's liberation greatly impressed those 29ers who were helping to fulfill that goal.

There was something about the Dutch that American soldiers found alluring. Gerhardt's boss, Maj. Gen. Charles Corlett of the XIX Corps, remarked that the initial contacts between Americans and the locals were "deeply pleasing," leading him to conclude that the Dutch "are more like Americans than any other Europeans." Corlett's aide, Capt. George Forsythe, commented that the Limburgers were "very wonderful people," and the Dutch border towns just behind the front, with which the 29ers would become entirely familiar over the next five months, became a "kind of second home" for GIs. Another of Corlett's officers commented, "The hospitality and kindness to the American soldier could not have been equaled. [The Dutch] had their problems, intensified by shortages of food and clothing, of limitations on their activities, by increased danger from shelling and bombing, but they never let us forget their gratitude for what the men of the American Army were doing to give them back their freedom."

The Dutch revealed their deep admiration to their liberators at a moving ceremony in Maastricht on October 15, 1944, during which throngs of natives repeatedly called for "three cheers for the U.S. Army"—in English. Corlett recalled that a local communist pamphlet published in the immediate aftermath of liberation falsely accused Maastricht's *burgemeester* (mayor), Willem Kessenich, "of collaboration with the Germans and practically everything except murder." Surprisingly, those accusations delighted Kessenich, who remained mayor until 1967. "Holland is again a democracy," he declared. "For four long years, such a paper would have been impossible. The God-given right of free speech has returned."

The 29th Division's former combat partners from Normandy, the 2nd Armored and 30th Infantry Divisions, beat the 29th to Holland by more than two weeks, but the 29ers would ultimately have much more enduring contacts with the Dutch people because those two divisions would eventually pull out and move south to join the fighting in the Ardennes during the Battle of the Bulge. It did not take the 29ers long to learn the Dutch had an insatiable curiosity about the strangers in their midst. Cooper of the 110th Field Artillery remembered that the 29th's appearance

> attracted scores of Dutch citizens. Children and adults seemed genuinely hospitable and showed intense interest in everything the Americans did. Bent on seeing the kitchen trucks, on peering through [artillery observation] periscopes and field glasses, or on examining guns, jeeps, radios, and telephones, numerous small boys persistently snuck into our positions. The battalion was their first "circus" in many years, and their admiration was equaled only by their curiosity. Oddly enough, when the guards tried to chase them away, the youngsters seemed unable to comprehend a word of English. Only when they wished to ask questions could the boys understand and make themselves understood.

A member of the Dutch *Stoottroepen* in Valkenburg's old quarter.

In a pastoral corner of farmland about four miles south of Valkenburg, the men of the 175th Infantry and its direct-support 105-millimeter how-itzer outfit, the 224th Field Artillery Battalion, pitched their tents on a sce-nic plateau just north of the main Maastricht-Aachen road for a stay no one thought would last very long. An impressive ridge south of the Maas-tricht road known as the Gulperberg, marking the northern fringe of the hilly country of south Limburg, dominated the campground. All agreed that the scenery was spectacular, and fortunately, the war had hardly touched it. Autumn was in the air, and morning and evening temperatures had become downright chilly.

The cannoneers of the 224th occupied a section of farmland near the village of Margraten. They could not know that six weeks later, the Ninth U.S. Army would acquire a few dozen acres southwest of town to set up what was intended to be a temporary military cemetery for the burial of American war dead. After the war, the American Battle Monuments Com-mission would establish the site as a permanent cemetery containing the remains of 8,302 U.S. Army personnel. Three members of the 224th Field Artillery Battalion—Capt. Robert Yeuell, Sgt. John Leger, and T/4 Joseph Culpepper—now lie in the same fields where, for just a day or two at the end of September 1944, they spent a blissful break out of range of enemy guns before moving back to the front.

The 29th Infantry Division had last faced enemy bullets on the day of the German surrender at Brest. It seemed as if an age had passed since that memorable day, a sentiment that was perhaps accentuated by the 550 miles the 29ers had traveled in that interval. Remarkably, only twelve days had elapsed since the surrender—a period the U.S. Army considered more than sufficient for the 29ers to recover from their broken spirits.

By September 30, the time had come for the 29ers to face enemy bul-lets again.

3. VOLKSGRENADIER

The German army that had struggled to turn back the Allied invasion of Normandy and then contain its opponents in their slender beachhead was no more. Those worn-out survivors lucky enough to have escaped the Allied onslaught had trudged back to Germany to await reorganization and orders to return to the front to help prolong a fight most of them now knew was useless. The totality of their defeat was heightened when, in mid-October 1944, they would learn of the death of Field Marshal Erwin

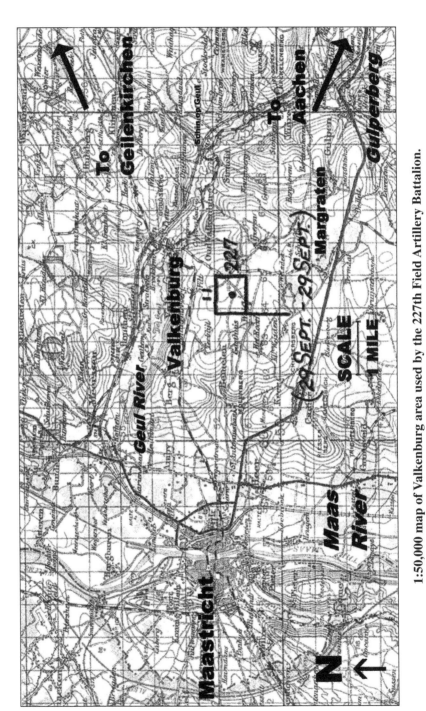

1:50,000 map of Valkenburg area used by the 227th Field Artillery Battalion.

Rommel, the man who had led them for the first six weeks of the Normandy fighting and whose name in the past had symbolized to friend and foe alike the might of German arms. The Desert Fox had supposedly succumbed to the wounds he had suffered in Normandy in July, but those in the highest reaches of the German Army knew the nefarious truth: Rommel had consumed a cyanide capsule at the instigation of two of Hitler's henchmen to save his family from Gestapo retaliation over his supposed involvement in the July 20, 1944, plot to assassinate the Führer.

Hitler's insistence to his generals that they must stop the Allies on Germany's western frontier necessitated the prompt shipment of vast numbers of reinforcements to the front. Those new troops had to materialize regardless of the dearth of fresh German manpower, now thoroughly drained after more than five years of unremitting conflict. Just as important, at least in Hitler's mind, was the fanaticism those reinforcements would bring to the front, for in the aftermath of the July 20 plot, when the tepid loyalty of many senior officers to the Nazi regime was exposed, the Führer's inner circle reasoned that drastic steps must be taken to eradicate symptoms of defeatism at all levels of command and to enhance German soldiers' incentive to fight.

If the loyalty to Hitler of untold numbers of old-school officers was suspect, dedicated Nazi officials had to take an active role in raising and training new divisions, as galling as that prospect would be to many Germans. The result was the *Volksgrenadier* (People's Grenadier) division, nineteen of which were organized in the immediate aftermath of the July 20 assassination attempt, with many more to come. The *Volksgrenadier* concept embodied the Nazi philosophy that if Germans wished to forestall catastrophe, an already broadly militarized nation must mobilize its manpower to an even greater extent and inculcate in its fighting men a fervor to defend the homeland to the last. As Hitler declared, the Nazis must "adapt the whole of public life to the requirements of total warfare in every respect."

To carry out that ambitious aim, Hitler greatly widened the powers of Germany's minister of the interior, Heinrich Himmler, by adding to his responsibilities the command of the *Ersatzheer* (Replacement Army). This put a fanatical SS man in charge of all matters related to army conscription and training, including the establishment of the *Volksgrenadier* divisions. A German Army officer, Gen. Friedrich Fromm, soon to be executed for his alleged role in the July 20 plot, had formerly held those responsibilities. The significance of the move was clear: each *Volks-grenadier* division, although a component of the German Army, would be raised, trained, and indoctrinated in part with SS values, and when it reached the front, all its soldiers, from the commanding general down to the lowest private, had to adhere to Hitler's guiding principle that death in defense of the Fatherland was preferable to surrender. "I believe that the war we are now waging is what I call the people's holy war, and that the only army that can win this war must be the National Socialists' People's Army," Himmler declared. "It must be clear to everyone that this army must be imbued with a National Socialist worldview."

Hitler's selection of Himmler, a man with little practical military experience, to one of the German Army's most important jobs surely disgusted conservative military men, but in the current climate, overt protest was out of the question, and even furtive whispers among like-minded men about the Nazis' folly entailed grave risk. No one was safe now, as Rommel's demise had established, as long as Himmler's men controlled the training of the German Army.

In the late summer and fall of 1944, as each *Volksgrenadier* division completed its hasty and inadequate preparation of no more than six weeks, Hitler dispatched it to the Western Front, whether it was ready for combat or not. In a period of less than two months, the Führer made twenty *Volks-grenadier* divisions available to Rundstedt, a much-needed reinforcement pipeline that helped the elderly field marshal hold back the onrushing Anglo-American armies at Germany's frontier. As the surprised 29ers were about to discover, although the new *Volksgrenadier* divisions were rumored to be second-rate units comprised of unimpressive physical specimens, the spirit they brought to the fight was apparently little different from the highly motivated paratroopers the 29th Division had battled in Normandy and Brittany.

That the Americans recognized their opponents' extraordinary resiliency was revealed by the U.S. War Department's wartime manual TM-E 30-451, *Handbook on German Military Forces*, which stated:

> The cause of this toughness, even in defeat, is not generally appreciated. It goes much deeper than the quality of weapons, the excellence of training and leadership, the soundness of tactical and strategic doctrine, or the efficiency of control at all echelons. It is to be found in the military tradition which is so deeply

ingrained in the whole character of the German nation and which alone makes possible the interplay of these various factors of strength to their full effectiveness. . . . Thus, even the old and sick perform, to a certain point, with the courage of despair.

To that despair could also be added delusion, as Frederick Graham, a *New York Times* reporter with the Ninth Army, noted in his description of a German prisoner: "One 21-year-old lieutenant of infantry we talked to said in a matter-of-fact manner that he believed Germany eventually would win because the German soldier was better than the American he had met and because Germany had a new secret weapon. He admitted he had not the faintest idea what the secret new weapon was, but with smiling patience, as if sorry for the questioner's ignorance, he added that he was sure that it would turn the tide of the war. If I have ever seen a sincere man, it was he."

Hitler's immediate need was for hordes of well-armed foot soldiers, men who would shoulder the German Army's innovative new assault rifle, the Sturmgewehr 44, and take their place in the front lines and sacrifice their lives if necessary to stop their opponents from setting foot in Germany. They came from civilian life, men and boys who at an earlier point in the war would have been considered too old or too young for infantry service. They came from the Luftwaffe, from the Kriegsmarine, and from wounded and shell-shocked veterans of units that had been destroyed by the enemies of the Reich. If the number of available men in a division's subordinate units did not meet manpower strengths dictated by tables of organization, teams reminiscent of the Royal Navy's infamous eighteenth-century press gangs roamed the local area to squeeze out as many fresh recruits as possible.

Every detail about a *Volksgrenadier* division suggested that a U.S. Army infantry division would greatly outclass it. At full strength, a *Volksgrenadier* division had only 70 percent of the 29th Division's manpower. It was also inferior to the 29th in terms of artillery firepower, modern communication equipment, rear-echelon support, and, above all, mobility. The 29th Division, with its abundant supply of trucks and jeeps, was the perfect representation of a progressive mid-twentieth-century mechanized army. In contrast, a *Volksgrenadier* division, with an organizational table calling for more than 3,000 horses, seemed a symbol of a bygone age. Only a supremely confident German general could imagine how such a scrawny and outdated military unit could hold its ground against the U.S. Army's renowned firepower.

When the 29ers first got a close-up look at some of their *Volksgrenadier* opponents who had been taken prisoner, it was difficult to conceive how such unsoldierlike troops would fight so fiercely against such great odds. "For the most part [the enemy] consisted of troops who, in spite of short periods of service, had profited by their limited training," a 29th Division report indicated. "They were largely men who had previously been considered either too old or too young for combat service or who had occupied civilian positions of such a nature as to defer them from military service."

Virtually all 29ers would soon learn that the *Volksgrenadier*s, with all their military flaws, were highly resolved to fight.

THREE

Schierwaldenrath

1. PATROLLING AND THAT KIND OF BUSINESS

It had been known for centuries as the city of Charlemagne, but for a few weeks in the fall of 1944, it was the city of Hitler.

German generals on the Western Front had recently felt the effects of the Führer's dogged fixation that Aachen, Germany's westernmost city and the ancient capital of the Holy Roman Empire—celebrated by the Nazis as the First Reich—must never fall to the Americans. One of Hitler's stern Führer directives had recently specified that "German cities and villages are now included in the combat zone. This fact must make us fight with fanatical determination and put up stiff resistance with every able-bodied man. Each and every pillbox, every village and city block, must be a fortress against which the enemy will smash himself to bits. . . . In every locality in Germany where there is fighting, all able-bodied men, regardless of age, are at the disposal of the local military commander to reinforce the defensive forces."

The German commander in the Aachen sector, Gen. Friedrich Koechling, recalled that "the Führer directive was worded particularly starkly. It made it clear that those commanders in whose sectors a pillbox was lost to the enemy would be personally held responsible for such loss." Koechling later characterized that order as "incomprehensible," but his opinion was irrelevant, for at that desperate stage of the war, any German general who failed to adhere blindly to Hitler's edicts faced a bleak future—if he had any future at all.

If ever there was a case of the proverbial irresistible force versus the immoveable object, it was at Aachen, for the Americans were just as resolved to capture that city of 165,000 residents as the Germans were to hold it. The intensity of the struggle had been established weeks before the 29th Division's arrival when several U.S. Army divisions had endeavored to avoid a frontal assault by enveloping the city, forcing its garrison to wilt like a plant deprived of sunlight and moisture. It had nearly worked, but when the 29th arrived on the scene in late September, the Germans' Aachen defenses had certainly not wilted, even though the Americans had the city nearly surrounded. Indeed, a 29th Division liaison officer with the XIX Corps reported to Gerhardt: "German SS troops in Aachen in civilian clothes have signed a pledge to fight to the last man."

If the Allies wished to carry on an irresistible offensive for more than a few days, they would have to solve the severe logistical difficulties that had surfaced following their electrifying blitzkrieg across France. Until the Belgian port of Antwerp was operative, it was difficult to believe they could attack anything at all, not to mention keeping more than a million soldiers clothed, fed, and equipped as winter loomed. Eisenhower's solution was to maintain the initiative by sharply prioritizing his efforts, limiting Allied fall offensives to just one or two that offered at least a small possibility of success.

Ike revealed his principal priority in a September 13 cable to his chief subordinates: "The maneuver plan is to push hard over the Rhine on our northern flank." Two weeks later, he denoted that the opening phase of that plan was to "thrust, so far as current resources permit, towards Cologne and Bonn," a design he later ordered Bradley to take up as his "first mission." A hasty glance at a map indicated that if those two German cities were Eisenhower's immediate objective, Aachen stood squarely in the way. Could the Americans bypass it?

Whether one thought of Aachen as an indispensable military objective or a city with purely symbolic value depended on one's position in the Allied military hierarchy. Gerhardt's boss, Corlett, leaned to the latter interpretation, an argument voiced by his aide, Captain Forsythe, who later suggested somewhat irreverently that orders to seize Aachen immediately originated in the highest reaches of the Anglo-American command, which strove to establish to the Soviets that the western Allies were capable of capturing a major German city. So far, however, the Americans had failed to capture the city for the obvious reason that they were attacking the Germans where they were strongest. Taking Aachen would clearly cost dearly in men and resources—would that cost be offset by any substantive strategic benefits?

Everything the 29th Division would endeavor to do over the next month would be intimately related to the struggle for Aachen. Three times since D-Day, the 29th had battled successfully, at terrible cost, to gain control of essential German-controlled cities: St. Lô, Vire, and Brest. But this time, there would be a crucial difference. In the past, the 29ers had bulled their way directly into those ruined cities by sheer force; at Aachen, they would play a supporting role, diverting the enemy's attention from the exertions made by other American divisions to seize the city. Working outside the limelight would be a welcome change, although all 29ers had long since abandoned hope that they would ever serve on what staff officers euphemistically referred to as a "quiet sector."

The most positive change in the 29th Division's fortunes from Gerhardt's perspective was that his outfit would be shifting from Maj. Gen. Troy Middleton's VIII Corps, with which it had fought at Brest, to Corlett's XIX Corps. Gerhardt's one-month relationship with Middleton had been frosty. In contrast, the 29th had served for more than two months under Corlett in Normandy, and the bond between the two generals was palpable. Indeed, Corlett recalled his "delight that Charlie Gerhardt with his fine 29th Division was on his way to me."

On September 22, while the 29th Division prepared to move from Brest to Holland, the commander of the U.S. First Army, Lt. Gen. Courtney Hodges, had held a conference at his Verviers, Belgium, command post, attended by his three corps commanders: Corlett, Maj. Gen. Joseph Collins of the VII Corps, and Maj. Gen. Leonard Gerow of the V Corps. For two hours, the generals hammered out the most effective strategy to fulfill Eisenhower's goal of advancing to the Rhine before winter. All agreed that the major effort must be in the north, where Corlett and Collins would concentrate on penetrating the Germans' West Wall fortifications, taking Aachen, and finally pushing eastward to Cologne and Bonn. A witness to the conference remarked, "One of the results [of the meeting] was that the attack of XIX Corps had been postponed until such time as the 29th Division arrives in the line. Neither General Collins nor

Maj. Gen. Charles Corlett.

General Corlett have the slightest doubt as to their ability to smash through provided gas and ammunition are at hand in more plentiful quantities than before." Corlett, therefore, was in a hurry to move the 29th Division to the front since he could not "smash through" as Hodges wished until its arrival.

At fifty-five, Corlett, a member of the West Point class of 1913, was thought to be somewhat advanced in age for an active combat commander; indeed, his weather-beaten face made him appear much older. His impressive achievements in the Pacific, which included command of the Alaskan Department and the seizure of Kwajalein in a brilliant amphibious assault, as well as his unbroken record of success in Normandy, made Corlett's age irrelevant to Ike and Bradley. According to Corlett, "Ike told me he was not looking for genius or brilliance—just good common sense. [Eisenhower said], 'Pete, I want you to go down to XIX Corps and create a family feeling in that organization.'" This Corlett did effectively, despite a short fuse, and he later confessed that he "loved every man and officer" in the XIX Corps. One ominous factor was that Corlett's abrasiveness rubbed Hodges the wrong way. Presently, the relationship between the two generals soured, and as a consequence, Corlett's military career was in grave danger of being snuffed out by Hodges. In that event, Gerhardt's status, too, would be fragile.

The evening the bulk of the 29th Division arrived in Holland, September 29, Hodges convened another conference at Verviers with his three corps commanders, but this time, the meeting carried extra weight because of two special attendees, Eisenhower and Bradley. According to Eisenhower's aide, the upbeat Ike wished "to inform all commanders of the role they and their troops are playing at present in major strategy. Their role is largely static until we have achieved satisfactory build-up of supplies." As an aside, Ike, ever the friend of the fighting soldier, remarked somewhat acidly that he was going "to chase the SOS [Services of Supply] out of Paris and make it a well-ordered rest center for combat troops," which a witness said "tickled everybody."

As related by his aide, Bradley agreed with Eisenhower's strategy: "Our mission now is largely a static one, concerned with probing attacks and bettering our position." Since Gerhardt's 29th Division was about to enter the line, the assembled generals decided that one of those probing attacks could be initiated by Corlett's XIX Corps in two days, on October 1, north of Aachen. The object was to punch through a tough section of the West Wall and encircle the city by joining up with Collins's VII Corps at Würselen, a town with which the 29th Division would soon become entirely familiar.

If the 29ers were about to be dragged into another violent vortex of combat, Gerhardt needed to describe to his men what the top brass expected of them over the next few weeks. At 9 A.M. on September 29, at the new division command post in an orchard just outside the Dutch village of Oorsbeek, he called a meeting of all 29th Division regimental and battalion commanders, along with their operations officers. Their immediate object was to relieve the 2nd Armored Division in the front lines in order to free that celebrated tank outfit, known as "Hell on Wheels," to exploit the expected breakthrough of the West Wall by the 30th Division in early October. Once the 29th was deployed to the front, it was to "prepare to exert pressure on the Siegfried Line [West Wall] in support of the main attack by the 30th Division." In short, the 29th Division was to carry out a diversion, which Gerhardt defined to his audience as "patrolling and that kind of business."

As the 29th Division was about to learn, "that kind of business" would be much more complicated than Gerhardt implied. The next day, the general traveled to XIX Corps headquarters at Heerlen to lunch with his old friend Corlett and discuss how he intended to carry out his mission. On the drive over in *Vixen Tor*, an incensed Gerhardt noticed two 29th Division jeeps on the roads with their canvas rain hoods deployed. It was drizzling—autumn rain in Limburg seemed to be the norm—but any use of rain hoods by 29th Division vehicles was strictly forbidden, and not a single 29er could ever have the temerity to claim ignorance of that order. Soon one or more terrified soldiers would find themselves standing at attention in front of Gerhardt, listening to a torrent of words that could vary, depending on his mood, from a firm lecture to a ferocious tongue-lashing.

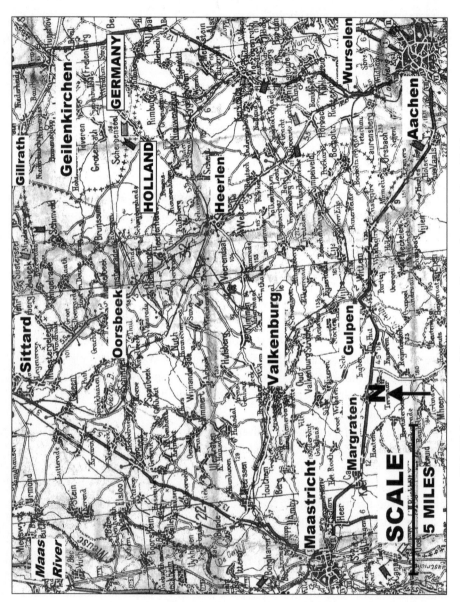

29th Division Area of Operations, September–October 1944.

The relief of a unit in close proximity to the enemy was one of the trickiest of military maneuvers, as specified in field manuals:

> [A] relief is preceded by a detailed reconnaissance of the sector and routes by officers of the relieving regiment. All commanders down to and including platoon leaders should visit the position prior to executing the relief. Commanders must familiarize themselves with the dispositions and defensive arrangements of the outgoing units and with the known hostile dispositions. . . . Guides from the outgoing regiment meet each platoon and conduct it to its position.

The Germans were known for their uncanny ability to detect and promptly exploit a relief to the fullest, and if it were not carried out with the utmost stealth and skill, the startling reception initiated by the Germans would be memorable.

On September 29, Gerhardt initiated the relief by sending forward reconnaissance parties and liaison groups to examine the ground occupied by the 2nd Armored Division and, immediately on its left (west), the 113th Cavalry Group. Those 29ers, first among thousands of comrades who would soon follow, drove northward from Valkenburg by jeep, passing through the verdant Dutch farmland and old-world villages with names like Amstenrade, Klooster, and Grootdoenrade. Those were undeniably friendly places, but an entirely different world lay ahead: Germany. No broad river or majestic mountain range delineating the border here, just a simple barbed-wire fence, beyond which stretched flat farmland to the horizon. The citizens on the far side of that fence were the enemy, and as signs on the fence clearly indicated, the Germans did not want people to cross it: *Achtung! Zivilischer Verkehr Streng Verboten!*—Warning! Civilian Traffic Strictly Prohibited!

Something meaningful had to be done to mark that momentous occasion, and Battery B, 110th Field Artillery Battalion, under the command of Capt. Charles Cole, came up with a way to do it. At 5:41 P.M. on September 29, the Number 2 section chief, Sgt. Roy Mossi, pulled the lanyard on his 105-millimeter howitzer, triggering a resounding boom that sent the first of what eventually would be thousands of 29th Division shells arching over the enemy's home turf to do their deadly work.

A 105mm howitzer gun crew of the 110th Field Artillery Battalion.

The 29th Division had been struggling toward this goal since February 1941. Now it was a part of history.

2. INDIAN FIGHTING

The division soldiers held varying opinions on how their outfit could most effectively "exert pressure on the Siegfried Line" while the 30th Division made the main breakthrough north of Aachen, but Gerhardt's opinion was the only one that mattered. Something about the word "diversion" rubbed the offensive-minded Gerhardt the wrong way. The 29th's role in the upcoming campaign clearly was be secondary, but the confident general believed his troops could simultaneously divert the enemy's attention and still accomplish decisive terrain gains, the first of which was the immediate capture of Geilenkirchen, a vital hub in the enemy's West Wall.

None of Gerhardt's chief subordinates had any idea what the general expected of them in the days ahead, even as the 29th Division's situation began to crystallize on September 30 when the 115th Infantry moved up to the front to relieve the 2nd Armored Division just across the

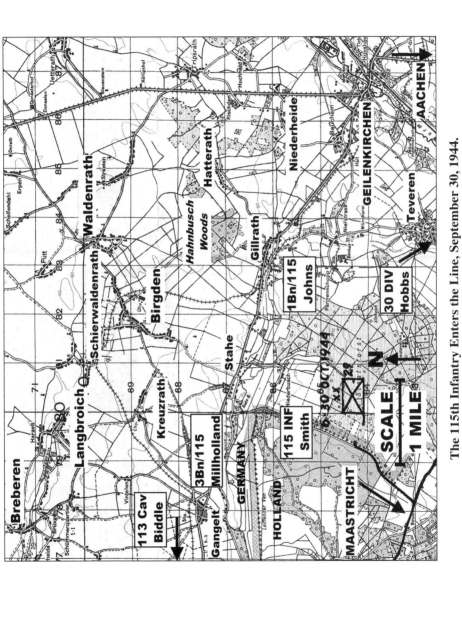

The 115th Infantry Enters the Line, September 30, 1944.

Dutch-German border near Geilenkirchen. The relief represented a moment of supreme vulnerability, but it was executed in textbook style: quietly, quickly, and after dark. Most important, the Germans failed to notice. Only two of the 29th's nine infantry battalions—about 1,400 men—were now deployed in the front lines, occupying an extraordinarily lengthy L-shaped front of more than six miles. The 115th's 3rd Battalion took up the long stem of the L between the villages of Gangelt and Gillrath, facing north; the 1st Battalion held the base of the L on the right between Gillrath and Teveren, facing east, little more than a mile from Geilenkirchen.

The task at first did not appear much of a challenge. The Germans were nowhere in sight, and intelligence reports offered no evidence that they were prepared to hold their ground to the last man on the 29th Division's new front. At dawn on October 1, the duty officer in Gerhardt's war room tent optimistically reported to the XIX Corps: "Want to let you know that everything was very quiet down here last night. The 115th sent some combat patrols out in front of the 3rd Battalion. They got about 300 yards and they didn't have any enemy contact. That was on the left. The 1st Battalion, 115th, which was on the right, sent out some patrols in front, and they had no enemy contact." Could the Germans have pulled out? If so, the 29ers could be on the Rhine in a matter of days. Such an accomplishment would put the division in the headlines on the home front, for sure. True, Corlett had mandated that the 29th's role be strictly secondary, but here was an opportunity for the division to exploit the Germans' apparent feebleness.

The 115th Infantry's commander, Lt. Col. Louis G. Smith, who had carried out the 29th Division's surrender negotiations with the Germans at Brest only two weeks earlier, did not profess that kind of optimism. Known by his prewar comrades in the Baltimore Gas and Electric Company and the Maryland National Guard as "L. G.," the portly Smith was described by a 29er as "a very smart individual, but not a domineering type of commander." On the morning of October 1, Gerhardt castigated him: "Your patrol activities [last night] amounted to nothing. Get your foot in there and get up against that line! I don't want a lot of stuff about the woods full of Germans!" An hour later, Gerhardt phoned Corlett and declared, "We are going to begin to push these Germans around! We are inside Germany quite a way, and we are going to push them right back into the Rhine!" That demonstration of bravado apparently made no impression on Corlett, who did nothing to restrain his impulsive subordinate.

Lt. Col. "L. G." Smith, commander of the 115th Infantry.

Smith failed to counter Gerhardt's unfettered confidence. The general pointedly asked Smith, "I don't think there are many [Germans]—are there?" Smith responded meekly, "No, sir; I don't believe so," although at that point Smith had little idea of the enemy's strength. The next morning, after Smith had pushed his patrols deeper into Germany, Gerhardt observed, "I understand you occupied fourteen unoccupied places last night." As delicately as he could, Smith pointed out, "Well, sir, some of them weren't unoccupied."

Compared to what the 29ers had endured in Normandy and Brittany, their first few days in Germany should have been easy. They were anything but. That alarming situation developed with the abruptness of a train wreck, for everything Gerhardt desired his division to do, he set out to do in remarkable haste, with a bullheaded determination to press an offensive even though his men were not ready and the enemy's intentions were unclear.

The neighboring 30th Division's set-piece assault on the West Wall, scheduled for the morning of October 1, would begin after the Ninth Air

Force saturated German lines with bombs for two hours. The 29th therefore had less than twenty-four hours to familiarize itself with its new surroundings before supporting that offensive with a diversionary attack. The 29ers' muscles still ached from days in cramped forty-and-eights and trucks; unit commanders had no idea where the Germans had prepared their strongpoints, if any; communications networks were still being set up; quartermasters had yet to convey sufficient supplies to the front; and most important, only two-thirds of a single infantry regiment, dispersed over a six-mile front, had been inserted into the line. How could such a meager force achieve decisive results?

The 29th Division clearly needed more time. Daybreak on October 1 brought no sunlight, just a dreary, consuming overcast and steady drizzle. Such weather was hardly suitable for a concentrated aerial assault, but so far, the top brass had provided no word to Gerhardt that the 30th Division's attack would be delayed until the onset of more suitable conditions. The 29th had to go ahead. The 29ers peered through the ethereal morning mists for their first good look at the landscape, and what they saw jolted them. The twelve-mile journey north from Valkenburg into Germany had evidently brought them beyond the Limburg hills to a wholly different kind of topography, which, according to Cooper, "was unlike any which the [division] had seen in Europe. Highly reminiscent of the Carolina and Virginia coastal plain, it consisted of level, sandy loam fields, pinewoods, and occasional sandy ridges. Only a mile or two apart, compact brick villages, in which most of the farmers lived, dotted the landscape, and the enemy fully utilized these centers as strongpoints."

Joe Ewing described the land as "giant parade grounds, [extending] for miles in seemingly unending flatness . . . [with] patches of dark pine woods, all sandy and dismal, uprooted trees, dead cattle and horses, and great holes in the walls of red brick houses. About the streets of the towns, sheep and pigs and goats wandered forlornly, and in the fields, abandoned cows mooed plaintively for someone to milk them." This type of terrain would take time to get used to and would require a different way of waging war than the methods of Normandy and Brittany. The first and most obvious trait about the landscape the 29ers picked up was that no one could survive in daylight in the open pastureland. It consisted mostly of low crops, such as beets, turnips, and cabbage, and almost every foot of the fields was observable by the unseen enemy, lying in wait in sturdy brick farm buildings topped with the rust-colored ceramic roofs so characteristic of the Rhineland. The 29ers would need a few days to grasp that the Germans resolved to hold the ground by discounting conventional linear defense in favor of self-contained strongpoints in the compact villages, scattered over the countryside like squares on a checkerboard.

The villages typically were situated so close to one another that the open ground could be covered by deadly crossfires. "The only possible cover was inside the towns," Cooper noted. "The open ground beyond the towns gave the troops the feeling that they were ducks sitting on a pool table, waiting to be shot." The classic U.S. Army response to such a tactical dilemma, overwhelming firepower, was almost impossible to achieve because no high ground existed that could provide artillerymen with good observation. Even worse, the 29th Division, like every other outfit on the Western Front, suffered from a severe shortage of artillery ammunition.

The only way for the 29ers to traverse that ground and force the Germans out of their defenses was to attack at night. Regrettably, the XIX Corps was in such a rush to commit the 29th in support of the 30th Division's imminent offensive that for a moment on the morning of October 1, it seemed as if the 29ers might have to get moving in daylight. But at 8:40 A.M., the XIX Corps' G-3, Col. Gustavus West, phoned the 29th's war room with the welcome news that the overcast weather would cause "a washout today."

The 29th Division would get a breather, but only until sunset. Its rightmost outfit, the 115th's 1st Battalion, would move first as soon as

The "unending flatness" of the Rhineland.

darkness set in. The essential object of its commander, Lt. Col. Glover Johns, was to avoid a frontal assault on the heavily fortified city of Geilenkirchen and instead envelop it from the north by seizing the villages of Hatterath and Niederheid.

The thirty-two-year-old Johns was unique among the division's infantry battalion commanders. First, his U.S. Army branch lapel pins were the crossed sabers of the cavalry, not the infantry's crossed rifles. A much more amazing detail, however, was his staying power: he had continuously held command of the 1st Battalion since June 14, just eight days after D-Day. No other infantry battalion commander in the 29th could come close to matching that longevity—an amazing record given the high toll of battlefield leaders from death, wounds, or Gerhardt's temper.

By this stage of the war, Johns's luck and military abilities impressed all 29ers, some of whom also perceived in him a hefty ego. Most of Johns's peers, however, did not know of the September 1941 incident that helped launch his career in the 29th. Only three years before, Johns had been a mere lieutenant in Corpus Christi's Troop I, 124th Cavalry, a component of the Texas National Guard's 56th Cavalry Brigade under an obscure brigadier named Charles H. Gerhardt. During the Louisiana Maneuvers, the 56th had acted as the main mounted scouting force for the "Blue" army led by Lt. Gen. Walter Krueger, and as Johns later related, his platoon "had the dubious pleasure of capturing 'Georgie' Patton [commander of the 2nd Armored Division in the "Red" army] in his command post, some thirty miles behind the front." That kind of dashing leadership delighted Gerhardt, and once he placed Johns in command of the 115th Infantry's 1st Battalion in June 1944, he decided to leave him there in the hope that even more aggressive behavior of that kind would emerge. Johns therefore knew his commanding general better than his brother officers, and the salient detail he grasped, one that many others discounted, was that "no junior officer ever said 'no' to General Gerhardt." Although Johns admired the general, some of his innermost feelings about Gerhardt, entirely repressed during the conflict, emerged after the war when he characterized Gerhardt as "a gutty, pushy, arrogant little bastard . . . with a Napoleonic complex."

Johns was born for soldiering. A Corpus Christi native, he graduated from the Virginia Military Institute in 1931 at nineteen years of age, too young by two years to be granted a Reserve commission as a second lieutenant, but old enough to enlist as a private in his local Texas National

Guard cavalry outfit. Johns eventually rose to first sergeant of that troop and later gained a cavalry commission. But as the U.S. Army swelled in the aftermath of Pearl Harbor, the astonished Johns found himself in 1943 sitting behind a desk in a dead-end job as military attaché to Costa Rica, while many of his Texas National Guard comrades were about to enter combat at Salerno. He rejected the next post to which the U.S. Army directed him, an offer he recalled as a "plush diplomatic assignment" in Mexico City, and instead moved to Fort Leavenworth for "a get-rich-quick course at the Command and General Staff School." That schooling, plus a bit of "fast talking," earned him a promotion to major, a transfer to England, and a slot as a liaison officer in the 29th Division. His old boss, Gerhardt, now preparing his division for its critical role in the D-Day invasion, welcomed him but promptly expressed his theory that his liaison officers should prepare themselves as substitutes for infantry battalion commanders, whose attrition rate in Normandy was expected to be high. When the commander of the 115th Infantry's 1st Battalion, Lt. Col. Richard Blatt, suffered a mortal wound late on June 6, Gerhardt gave Johns the job little more than a week later.

By the time the 29th Division moved into Germany that fall, Johns had commanded the 1st Battalion for nearly four months. He understood that what Gerhardt expected of him on the evening of October 1 at Hatterath and Niederheid would certainly be tough, but as Johns knew from his Texas National Guard days, one did not say "no" to the general. Johns's principal dilemma was that he knew next to nothing about the enemy. In contrast, his neighbor, the 30th Division, had been provided with intelligence that one XIX Corps report noted "was as complete and accurate as that furnished for the invasion landing on Omaha Beach." An hour before sunset, Johns dispatched scouts toward his objectives in an attempt to learn details that corps-level intelligence should already have provided, but Colonel Smith told Gerhardt that they "couldn't get through." The 115th's operations officer, Maj. William Bruning, stated the obvious when he reported to the war room: "It is bare ground and hard to get across. We are going to shove them out under cover of darkness and see how it works."

They "shoved out" at about 1 A.M. on October 2 from the town of Gillrath, advancing in near-total silence through the ominous pastureland, dimly lit by a full moon and occasionally illuminated more brightly by the eerie light of an enemy flare. Company C on the left, under the command of 1st Lt. Warren Hecker, headed toward Hatterath; Company A on the right, led by Capt. Mack Hays, pushed on to Niederheid. Happily, no enemy fire yet, but presently the 115th Infantry's imperfect intelligence caused Johns's men to walk straight into a minefield that had been recently emplaced by their comrades in the 2nd Armored Division. No one was hurt, but it could have been a disaster.

No Germans yet. Company C moved into Hatterath on both sides of an old farm path without firing a shot. It had been easy enough so far, but the 29ers could not help harboring a sensation that the enemy knew exactly what was going on. They were right. "The Germans made it evident, very quickly, that they did not like the idea of Hatterath remaining in American hands," Johns observed. "Late in the morning, they started across the fields from the Hahnbusch [woods]. They came in force—and they came as if they meant to stay." The situation was perilous because Johns was on his own with no backup, and, as he noted,

> The town of Hatterath lay in one of those exasperating pockets of poor radio transmission, and although battalion operators at Gillrath [Johns's command post] could actually see the spot where Company C's radios were known to be, it was only rarely that a message could get through. We laid 110 and 130 [telephone] wire and repaired it constantly, but the direct fire of the enemy's 88s in the daytime and frequent artillery and mortars [the next] night made the job risky, and frequently delayed it for hours.

Consequently, Johns had to survive with little help from his direct-support artillery battalion, Cooper's 110th Field Artillery.

Meanwhile, Hays failed to push Company A into Niederheid because, much to his astonishment, the woods adjacent to that village contained a substantial body of the enemy. He wisely shifted his men a mile to the north to help Hecker's Company C at Hatterath, a move that appreciably increased Hecker's chance of holding it. The Germans suddenly emerged out of Hahnbusch woods in such large numbers from several directions at once, however, that Johns feared "the Krauts were going to do a job on the boys." Their mad charge toward Hatterath displayed a lack of finesse that the 29ers had never before seen in their opponents. One could hardly categorize such a practice as cutting-edge military tactics, but since the Americans were so outnumbered, the Germans seemed as if they could overwhelm the defenders by sheer weight of numbers. The 29ers opened fire with abandon, striving to make every shot count because, once their ammunition ran out, replenishment would be impossible in daylight. The 29th Division had officially reentered the conflict.

The Germans suffered grievously from the GIs' fire, but they kept coming. The only available American weapons with heavier hitting power than M1s and BARs were a couple of air-cooled .30-caliber machine guns and light 60-millimeter mortars, but the soldier in charge of those weapons, Company C's 2nd Lt. Clyde Hull, displayed an expertise in their use that contributed mightily to the enemy's ultimate trouncing. The twenty-nine-year-old Hull had joined the Maryland National Guard as a private in 1940 at Frederick, and as an enlisted man, he had already gained a Bronze Star for valor at St. Lô and a Silver Star at Brest, after which he had been rewarded with one of the U.S. Army's greatest marks of respect: a battlefield commission as a lieutenant. To that impressive array of honors, Hull was about to add one more, the Distinguished Service Cross, just one step below a Medal of Honor. Hull would be one of only forty 29ers to gain that exalted decoration in World War II.

From a series of observation posts with a decent view of Hahnbusch woods, Hull used a sound-powered telephone to direct the fire of his three 60-millimeter mortars with remarkable precision. Johns recalled:

> By this time the Germans were making good headway across the fields. Hull suddenly saw a single German appear within a few yards of him. 'Keep those 60s going!' he shouted over the phone as he simultaneously shot the German. [Hull was armed with a Thompson submachine gun.] Five more Germans followed the first, and their fire caught him. He went down and played dead. They went past him, but he swung his Thompson on them and killed all five. When the attack was over, the field was strewn with dead and wounded Germans, mostly with 60-millimeter mortar fragments in their hides. Medics carried Hull off.

Johns himself was in Gillrath, a mile behind the action, but he might as well have been in Paris for all the good he could do as a result of signal troubles and lack of artillery support. His men in Hatterath were nearly surrounded, but after hours of close-range fighting, the Germans finally backed off, establishing a precedent the Americans should have noticed: in that kind of wide-open terrain, defending a village in daylight was much easier than attacking it. Over the next few weeks, it would be the Germans who defended their villages, while the 29ers did most of the attacking.

If Corlett needed a diversion on October 2, Johns had certainly given it to him. Two of the 1st Battalion's rifle companies at Hatterath were in a fix, however, far out in front of the main line, sandwiched between a forest on one side and a village on the other, both held strongly by the enemy. If the Germans managed to mount another counterattack the following day, October 3, Johns's men could be annihilated. In the meantime, ammunition had to be brought up, and as Johns noted, "For thirty-six hours, the only means of getting it into Hatterath was on [five] tanks." Johns failed to mention that those tanks, a platoon of Company A, 747th Tank Battalion, led by a lieutenant named Claver, could not even move without the cover provided by a smokescreen supplied by the 110th Field Artillery.

Gerhardt would not allow the Germans to reseize the initiative. The general had grandiose plans of carrying out more than a diversion on October 3, a resolution that was accentuated when, at 7:40 A.M., Corlett phoned from XIX Corps headquarters with instructions to "put pressure on Geilenkirchen" in the same locale where Johns's battalion had run into difficulties the previous day. Gerhardt phoned Smith at the 115th's command post and demanded with biting sarcasm: "What became of those fourteen battalions of Germans that were going to jump on you last night? . . . Put pressure on [Geilenkirchen]!"

If Smith was to exert pressure, even Gerhardt had to admit that his frontline troops badly needed reinforcements. On the afternoon of October 2, the general had ordered the 115th's 2nd Battalion, led by one of Gerhardt's favorites, Maj. Tony Miller, to pull out of its reserve position and seize the Hahnbusch woods, where the Germans had massed to attack Johns's men in nearby Hatterath. But the 2nd Battalion had no chance of crossing that deadly open ground adjacent to the woods in daylight, and Miller wisely decided to wait until nightfall to attack.

The Germans had always disparaged the Americans' habitual practice of shutting down major operations after sunset, but this time, Miller's 29ers carried out a difficult nighttime attack expertly. They made it over the open fields into the woods with hardly a shot fired in response, but according to *Baltimore Sun* reporter Holbrook Bradley, "The pine trees were so close together it was almost impossible to move any distance

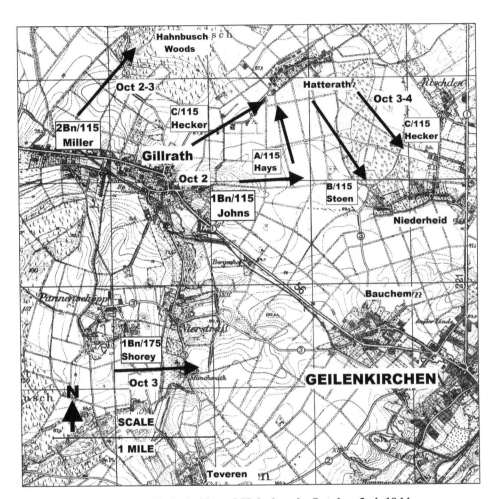

Hahnbusch
Woods

Oct 2-3

Hatterath

Oct 3-4

2Bn/115
Miller

C/115
Hecker

C/115
Hecker

Gillrath

A/115
Hays

Oct 2

B/115
Stoen

1Bn/115
Johns

Niederheid

Bauchem

1Bn/175
Shorey

GEILENKIRCHEN

Oct 3

N

SCALE

1 MILE

Teveren

Hatterath, Niederheid, and Hahnbusch, October 2–4, 1944.

ahead without breaking through underbrush. . . . [It was] reminiscent of jungle fighting." For the moment, in the claustrophobic and gloomy woods, the GIs faced more difficulty from unseen enemy barbed wire and "Bouncing Betty" mines than they did from machine-gun and rifle fire, but those nuisances did not prevent Miller's men from completing their task. When daylight on October 3 revealed the type of terrain the men had seized during darkness, Bradley noted with amazement: "One lieutenant found he had established a .30-caliber machine gun only five yards from a German emplacement" that fortunately had been abandoned. As the 2nd Battalion prepared to spend its first full day in Germany, Miller produced a bottle of Scotch from his haversack that he had been saving for just this occasion to share with his staff. He did not realize his outfit would remain in those deadly woods for almost three weeks.

All three of Smith's battalions were now in line, but Gerhardt further reinforced them on the rainy and chilly morning of October 3 by sending over the 1st Battalion, 175th Infantry, commanded by Maj. Miles Shorey. Shorey's men moved to the extreme right of Smith's line, directly opposite Geilenkirchen, thereby freeing Johns to concentrate his entire battalion in Hatterath with orders to secure it and capture nearby Niederheid. At 5:30 P.M. on October 3, Johns sent Companies A and C, supported by Claver's platoon of five Sherman tanks, across the bare fields between the two villages, and the result was a near-disaster. According to the official regimental history, "The enemy sensed the attack and laid down an intense barrage of 120-millimeter mortar and heavy artillery fire that caught the companies as they were moving across an exposed area. Some 35 were wounded and several others killed [mostly from Company A]. So severe was the shelling that the proposed attack had to be cancelled, and the companies withdrew to Hatterath." The Americans obviously had a great deal to learn about fighting in that sort of terrain.

Meanwhile, Miller's 2nd Battalion spent October 3 securing Hahnbusch woods, a mission that would ultimately reduce the enemy pressure on Johns's men in Hatterath by a considerable factor. It was a perplexing job, since the 29ers had bypassed dozens of enemy troops in the woods the previous night. According to Bradley,

> A German machine gun our troops had overlooked wounded three Yanks before the position could be blown sky high by a couple of rounds from heavy [81-millimeter] mortars. . . . Small units, usu-

ally squads or sections, fanned out ahead of the company [Company G, led by 1st Lt. Robert Rideout] to clear the way. The men crawled a few yards, then stopped to listen, at the same time attempting to keep in as close contact as possible with other units to the left and right of them.

Despite Rideout's report to Miller that he was "having difficulty maintaining control and direction due to the undergrowth," by late afternoon the 2nd Battalion was in full control of Hahnbusch, a task that had cost eight casualties, including two killed.

Miller expected the Germans would come back, and he was right. The following day, October 4, the enemy let loose at dusk with an intense artillery barrage against the position occupied by Company F at the far edge of the woods. It was so accurate that the 2nd Battalion journal recorded fifteen casualties in a thirty-minute period. German infantrymen dashed into the woods moments after the barrage lifted, but as the journal observed dryly, they were "beaten off by Company F," which took twenty-one enemy prisoners. The overriding lesson Miller learned from this affair was that his men must dig in as deeply as possible to avoid casualties from German artillery. The 29ers would heed that lesson, and after a few days, Miller's front featured plenty of the zigzag trenches not unlike those the doughboys used in the last war.

By now, every member of the 115th suspected that Gerhardt was trying to do too much with too little. The enemy's bloody repulse of Johns's October 3 attack on Niederheid should have provided clear evidence that the Germans were holding that town in force, and therefore, by pinning substantive German troops on his front, Gerhardt's directive from Corlett to divert the enemy's attention from Aachen by putting pressure on Geilenkirchen had been fulfilled. Any attempt to accomplish more with the limited forces on hand would court trouble. But Gerhardt's orders to Johns were clear: Niederheid must be taken at once.

As usual, darkness was the attackers' ally, and Johns's men were able to traverse the open fields toward their objective without drawing the Germans' attention. At 1:30 A.M. on October 4, the wary and by now exhausted 29ers pushed forward in the gloom, trusting the compass-reading ability of their NCOs to point them in the right direction. The temperature remained unpleasantly cold, so for the first time, many 29ers donned woolen GI overcoats. Company B, led by 1st Lt. Julian Stoen, and

Company C, under Hecker, led the way, accompanied by Claver's five tanks, while the battered Company A under Hays stayed behind in Hatterath.

An immense patch of woods lay between the attackers and Niederheid that the 29ers had to pass through if they were to reach their objective. Whether Johns's men would meet opposition in those woods was anyone's guess. Progress was promising at first. According to Johns, "The two companies banged their way into the woods, grabbed off a few prisoners, broke up some annoying machine guns, and separated for their respective objectives": Company B toward Niederheid, Company C to the northern part of the woods.

When the sun rose and the 29ers took in their surroundings in the hazy morning light, however, they immediately knew they were in trouble. They did not have nearly enough men to hold both town and woods, and they were far out in front of any sources of help. As both outfits pushed toward their goals, a large body of Germans suddenly materialized on the outskirts of Niederheid. Even veteran 29ers had never before seen so many enemy soldiers in one place, and their intent was plain: "They came out of the woods in the east, in a long, thin line," one Company C machine gunner recalled just a few days later. "My sergeant said 'wait,' so I held my finger on the trigger and checked my sights. Then he said, 'Let 'em have it!' Christ, there were over a hundred of 'em and not a goddamned one of them got in the woods."

Despite that effort, the 29ers were in deep trouble. Stoen's Company B and Hecker's Company C had separated in the woods and completely lost touch with each other, yielding a gaping hole between them. Although American machine guns had broken up the German attack from Niederheid, large groups of the enemy had infiltrated into the woods from other directions. Their leaders knew the forest well, whereas the 29ers did not, and when prowling German scouts reported back on how widely the Americans were divided, the enemy set out to surround and annihilate each American company in turn.

The 115th's official history described the subsequent battle as "vicious, close-in fighting, resembling at times Indian warfare." Lurking Germans suddenly filled the woods around Company C, and they would have been imperceptible had they not occasionally opened fire with ripping blasts from their assault rifles. The 29ers returned fire, but it was like shooting at specters. A cascade of German bullets whistled through the damp woods, nipping leaves and twigs from the trees inches from the Americans' heads. "The Germans kept coming despite great losses and cut Company C in two," Johns reported. "The company CP [command post] was cut off, and the rifle platoons on the north edge of the woods were taken from the rear. Lt. [Joseph] Blau and Lt. Hecker were both slightly wounded in the attack. An 88 fuse, complete, was taken from Hecker's back."

The Niederheid attack was shaping up as a fiasco. That it did not end that way was due to the decisive effort of Lieutenant Stoen to salvage the situation. Stoen was on his way to Niederheid with Company B when a furious fusillade broke out behind him in the shadowy woods. Obviously, Company C was in trouble. Acting on his own initiative, Stoen abruptly abandoned the move toward Niederheid and turned his men around. "The Krauts didn't even know we were in the woods," Stoen wrote. "When my boys came through the brush and saw those bastards [Germans] milling around, putting on Company C's overcoats [taken from American prisoners] . . . they went wild. I didn't have any control in that damn forest anyway, but I didn't need any. The boys took the Krauts to a cleaning and in nothing flat had Company C 'uncaptured.'" Lieutenant Claver of the 747th Tank Battalion later reported that seventy-three Germans emerged from the woods with hands over their heads as American prisoners.

Stoen had initiated a remarkable reversal of fortune, which would shortly gain him a Silver Star. He had saved the day for Johns, but still, the 1st Battalion had failed to achieve Gerhardt's goal of capturing Niederheid. In fact, no 29th Division unit ever would. By nightfall of October 4, Johns's 29ers were back where they had started in Hatterath. Johns had to admit it had been "a rough day," so much so that the 1st Battalion's casualty count of approximately fifty represented its costliest day of fighting since Normandy.

Johns did have an impressive haul of German prisoners, which would surely help to fill in the 29th Division's poor intelligence picture. As he later noted somewhat insensitively, "As war goes, it was not a bad trade."

3. DECISIVE ACTION

Johns's prisoners trudged under close guard back to the regimental headquarters, hands behind their heads, to begin a new phase of their lives whose outcome they could only guess. The sullen arrogance and brazen stares of some made their predicament more difficult, as it prompted angry 29ers to demonstrate their hatred for everything the Nazis had done to bring the world to its current plight. The countenances of most German captives, however, were fixed with deep anxiety, coupled with the usual trauma triggered by close-range combat and a near-death event on the battlefield. It hardly seemed natural to express compassion to a hated enemy, but a few kind-hearted 29ers took pity on the most wretched of the prisoners by wordlessly proffering a cigarette and a light from a Zippo.

The captives' new lives would begin to stabilize when they came before their first interrogators. As any good 29th Division intelligence officer knew, the best time to extract vital information from German prisoners was as soon after their seizure as possible, when fear loosened tongues and the lingering shock of battle triggered stupefaction. One method some crafty 29ers had learned to accentuate the Germans' mortification was to remove the enemy prisoners' belts, for the doughboys had learned that waist measurements of German Army trousers often did not match the wearer's waist size. Minus a belt and his weapon, therefore, a German soldier could be transformed from a fearsome warrior focused on killing Americans into a comical figure out of a Chaplin movie, focused only on keeping his pants from falling down.

This first batch of German prisoners would provide the earliest hints to Gerhardt's G-2 about what kind of war the 29th Division would face in this new theater. The division's uncanny knack of drawing the German Army's most formidable units as opponents, from Omaha Beach to St. Lô to Brest, was a pattern that the law of averages dictated must eventually change; indeed, the initial POWs brought in for interrogation suggested that the change had finally occurred. No twenty-year-old Aryan *Fallschirmjäger* this time, with their distinctive camouflage smocks and paratrooper helmets. Instead, a much less impressive lot of tense enemy captives plodded in front of their interrogators. At first glance, it seemed as if many of the enemy troops could not even have passed a U.S. Army physical for conscription into military service. Further, an astonishing number claimed they were not even German. A typical report, noted down in the 115th Infantry's S-2 journal at 4:15 A.M. on October 3, observed: "Two prisoners taken from 1st Company, 167th Infantry [Training Battalion]. Both POWs are Poles. The company is two-thirds Polish." Some cynical 29ers, in fact, would soon come to believe that Poles populated half the German Army.

Invariably, an American interrogator's first action was to unceremoniously snatch from an enemy prisoner's pocket his *Soldbuch*, the small olive-green paybook featuring a Nazi swastika topped by an eagle on the cover. Soldiers experienced in this sort of work knew exactly what to look for in the book and where to find it. The *Soldbuch* had twenty-four pages, but for the moment only one, page 4, was of significance to the captors, and to reach it, they had to flip past the captive's identifying photograph on the inside cover and through myriad personal details on the first three pages, including name, rank, birthplace, height, weight, religion—even shoe size. Section C on the fourth page, labeled *Feldtruppenteil—Kompanie*, which translated to "Field Unit" (usually battalion and regiment) and "Company," featured the details the Americans needed to know. Given the Germans' renowned military efficiency, their opponents were amazed at how easy it was to obtain key information from a simple glance.

Careful examination of a multitude of *Soldbücher*—the 29th Division would capture 524 Germans during October—painted an encouraging intelligence picture. Gerhardt's men apparently faced some second-string enemy troops, primarily the 176th Infantry Division and the 183rd *Volksgrenadier* Division, neither of which could match the intensity and firepower of the *Fallschirmjäger* the 29ers had battled at Brest. On paper, the 176th seemed entirely mediocre, comprised of a jumble of miscellaneous units hastily thrown together and committed to the front to help stop the Allied juggernaut before it reached the Rhine. The German Army had categorized the unit as a "replacement and training division," a title the Americans assumed would hardly fill 176th recruits with confidence. Included in the units rustled up to form the 176th were the 22nd Luftwaffe Regiment, several "training" battalions, a "home guard" battalion, and supposedly even a battalion-size unit comprised of men with severe hearing problems. With only 7,000 men on its rolls, the 176th was half the size of the 29th Division.

A cursory glance at the "Polish" prisoners from the other enemy unit on the 29th Division's front, the 183rd *Volksgrenadier* Division, led the Americans to the erroneous conclusion that it was no better than the pitiable 176th. U.S. Army intelligence officers did not yet know what to make of the *Volksgrenadier* divisions that were starting to appear at the front, other than the obvious detail that they had been raised and trained hastily. Whether *Volksgrenadier* personnel could hold their ground against a modern opponent, no one yet knew; events would soon establish beyond doubt that they could.

The U.S. Army's wartime handbook on German military forces accurately noted that "the significance of the *Volksgrenadier* division lies in its decrease of personnel [10,000 rather than the 12,350 in a standard 1944 German infantry division] and increase of small automatic weapons." A *Volksgrenadier* division included only six infantry battalions, in contrast to a U.S. Army infantry division's nine; the German formation carried only thirty-six artillery pieces of 105-millimeter size or greater, as opposed to the American division's sixty-six. The Americans could not help considering the *Volksgrenadier* division a comparatively puny organization, especially in light of the reputedly second-rate pool of recruits from which it was built. That notion, however, changed completely the first time the U.S. Army engaged these "people's grenadiers" in battle.

One quality that made the *Volksgrenadier* division truly revolutionary was its striking firepower at company level and below. In manpower, a *Volksgrenadier* infantry company was little more than half the size of a U.S. Army rifle company, but its capability to churn out bullets at close range was noticeably greater than its American counterpart. Of the 119 grenadiers in a German company, 73 were armed with automatic weapons—nine machine guns and sixty-four MP40 machine pistols or new Sturmgewehr 44 assault rifles. In contrast, the American rifle company of 200 men possessed only eleven automatic weapons, nine of which were automatic rifles. Accordingly, when American and German squads came into close contact, an astute listener could quickly identify the source of the gunfire: the haphazard *pop-pop-pop* of M1s, interspersed with the sluggish *rat-tat-tat* of machine guns and BARs, dominated American fire, whereas the prevalent clamor emanating from German grenadiers came mostly from short bursts of automatic fire, either the distinctive tearing *rrrrrip* of their copious machine guns or the somewhat less hurried fire of their machine pistols and Sturmgewehr 44 assault rifles.

Two out of the three nine-man squads comprising a *Volksgrenadier* infantry platoon were armed entirely with the Sturmgewehr 44, although shortages of that weapon sometimes led to squads being equipped with MP40 machine pistols instead. The innovative Sturmgewehr 44 was a firearm ahead of its time, effectively combining the traits of a submachine gun and a rifle. All infantrymen were vitally concerned with their weapons' portability, and the Sturmgewehr 44 received high marks on that score. At around eleven pounds, it weighed about the same as an M1 rifle and was eight pounds lighter than a BAR. More important, its thirty-round banana-clip magazine held ten more bullets than a BAR and twenty-two more than an M1. True, its effective range of about 300 meters was less than an M1 and much less than a BAR, but World War II infantrymen had already learned that most skirmishes erupted at ranges of much less than 300 meters, so the Sturmgewehr 44's limited range was not a serious drawback. In the rare cases in which long-range fire was needed, a *Volksgrenadier* company's nine MG42 machine guns were more than sufficient.

A late-war U.S. Army intelligence bulletin derisively categorized the Sturmgewehr 44 as "mediocre" and added, "Because it is largely constructed of cheap stampings, it dents easily and therefore is subject to jamming. Although provision is made for both full automatic and semi-automatic fire, the piece is incapable of sustained firing and official German directives have ordered troops to use it only as a semi-automatic weapon. In emergencies, however, soldiers are permitted full automatic fire in two- to three-round bursts." The Americans concluded somewhat disingenuously that the Sturmgewehr 44 was "a bulky, unhandy weapon . . . [whose] design appears to be dictated by production rather than military considerations." Nevertheless, the assault rifle concept, as established by the Sturmgewehr 44, would fundamentally alter the way armies fought in the postwar world, a change that first emerged in the late 1940s when the Soviets adopted Mikhail Kalashnikov's enduring AK-47.

The 29th Division's first battle against a *Volksgrenadier* unit in the opening days of October had demonstrated yet again the Germans' expertise at defensive warfare, a proficiency that was surely heightened by the enemy's resolve to defend the Fatherland. Although Rhineland terrain was noticeably more open than the claustrophobic hedgerows of Normandy and Brittany, the 29ers still had to exert great effort in ground and air reconnaissance to pinpoint precisely where the enemy intended to fight. The Americans, who had never gotten used to the enemy's near-invisibility in the *bocage*, now noted that the Germans had organized their defensive front based on the checkerboard pattern of the Rhineland's farming and mining villages, apparently practicing to perfection the tactics laid down in their *Truppenführung* (Troop Leadership) manual, whose cardinal directive for defense stated, "The main battle area must be organized in depth."

German soldiers also learned from the manual that "a well-constructed battle area normally consists of a chain of mutually supporting positions with obstacles, trenches, and individual firing positions. . . . The plan of defense should be difficult to identify from the ground or from the air. Adjacent positions must be able to provide mutual support." According to *Truppenführung*, "The optimal situation for the defender is when the enemy is forced into a frontal attack." The 29th had been forced to do exactly that in its initial October effort to fulfill Gerhardt's wish to "push the Germans around." As usual, whenever the 29th Division had achieved a limited tactical success, the Germans invariably pushed right back, and no matter how positive the 29ers were that the enemy would counterattack, they always had trouble holding their gains.

Rumors abounded in the American camp that the Nazis had reached the bottom of their manpower barrel and, as a result, *Volksgrenadier* divisions would be populated by unimpressive physical specimens. That notion was true to a large extent, but what the 29ers failed to grasp was that those men would be no pushovers: the indoctrination provided by the German Army to its recruits, based on years of practical war-fighting experience, emphasized individual initiative, and even more important, the officers and NCOs who led those recruits into battle were encouraged to "think and act independently [and to] make calculated, decisive, and daring use of every situation." One of the most studied paragraphs of the *Truppenführung* manual declared: "The first criterion in war remains decisive action. Everyone, from the highest commander down to the youngest soldier, must constantly be aware that inaction and neglect incriminate him more severely than any error in the choice of means." As any 29er would soon admit, that kind of teaching was effective and generally yielded tough soldiers—even if their pathetic appearance at times triggered ridicule among the Americans.

Apparently, the United States and Germany prepared their young men for war by entirely different methods. Just a few weeks before the 29th Division entered the line in Germany, Gerhardt had ordered his staff to conduct a survey among the thousands of enemy prisoners his division had captured at Brest. The surprising results revealed that German infantrymen did not think highly of their opponents. Although enemy soldiers universally agreed that American artillery was impressive, they commonly believed that the U.S. Army was overly dependent on heavy firepower. "Americans are very cautious in attack, and I believe they would favor sacrificing materiel to men," asserted one prisoner. Another expressed a similar opinion more forcefully: "Americans are not aggressive enough, and Germans could get the best of them if they did not have such artillery and mortar support." Declared another: "Americans are bad soldiers. They walk in the open, make a lot of noise, and are not watchful. I led some patrols of platoon strength through enemy lines for several hundred yards and each time withdrew without being noticed."

Uncle Charlie was sure to make a note of that.

4. CAPTAIN SCHMITT

The three days from October 2 to October 4, 1944, may have been a shocking introduction to combat in Germany for Johns's 1st Battalion, 115th Infantry, but for the outfit on his immediate left, Lt. Col. Randy Millholland's 3rd Battalion, they would be infinitely worse. Johns had learned the hard way in the Hahnbusch woods that the enemy was far from dead. Millholland was now on the verge of learning it in a much more devastating way and triggering a controversy over the next few weeks that would abruptly swirl all the way up the chain of command to the headquarters of the U.S. First Army.

Millholland carefully synchronized his attack with Johns's, opening at 1 A.M. on October 2. While Johns's 1st Battalion set out from Gillrath to Hatterath, Millholland's 3rd Battalion, on Johns's left, jumped off from an east-west road cutting through Stahe toward two farming villages, Kreuzrath and Birgden. There was nothing of military significance in those two towns, other than the obvious detail that the enemy occupied them, but Millholland was about to learn that the Germans' fighting prowess had apparently increased now that they were defending their home turf.

Millholland utilized the standard U.S. Army assault technique of "two up, one back" with his three rifle companies. On his left, Company K, under Capt. Waldo Schmitt, pushed out cautiously toward Kreuzrath across a series of flat farm fields that were not as cloaked in darkness as the 29ers would have liked thanks to a full moon and the enemy's frequent flares, several of which, according to a witness, "lit the countryside for miles around." Holbrook Bradley described the night sky as "clear and cold, dotted with thousands of stars." Meanwhile, on Schmitt's right, 1st Lt. Alvin Ungerleider's Company I set out on a parallel course toward Birgden. Millholland held back Company L, under Capt. Earl Tweed, as a reserve, to be committed as needed.

Fortunately, the enemy did not fire a shot in response. For a few hours, a relieved Millholland thought his night attack had caught the enemy by surprise. By the time the sun peeked over the eastern horizon, Schmitt's men were already in Kreuzrath, while Ungerleider's were securing the southern fringe of Birgden. Dawn's early light, however, revealed startling developments that crushed the 29ers' confidence. Kreuzrath lay like an island in a sea of featureless pastures, and when Schmitt swept his binoculars northward across a 180-degree arc toward the German lines, he could plainly perceive enemy activity everywhere. Schmitt, whose combat experience dated to Omaha Beach, knew the Germans well enough to grasp that he had to be ready for anything.

Meanwhile, Ungerleider's men were getting their first look at Birgden, and their principal conclusion was that this was no ordinary German town. Like other nearby communities, it was essentially a one-street village, but in Birgden's case, that street stretched on for more than 2,000 yards, broken only in the town center by a triangular village green with a sturdy church at its apex. Company I pushed steadily up the main street, checking house by house for the presence of the enemy, but once Ungerleider got a sense of Birgden's size, he radioed back to Millholland with some concern: "Colonel, this town is too damn big for us!"

Ungerleider's words signaled the beginning of a crisis for Millholland that would not abate for two days. The 3rd Battalion's intelligence officer had just completed an interrogation of a few German prisoners, and he reported to Millholland the apparently reliable, but entirely unwelcome news that an enemy battalion of about 600 men occupied the 3rd Battalion's front, two of whose companies were deployed in the northern part of Birgden. If true, that report indicated that Ungerleider's task was about to become appreciably more challenging.

Millholland's worries intensified at 10 A.M. when Ninth Air Force medium bombers on a bombing run aimed at the enemy's West Wall defenses north of Aachen came roaring in at under 10,000 feet and accidentally dropped their loads—fifty-seven bombs, according to one witness—in and around the 3rd Battalion's command post at Stahe. For the 29ers, it was a nasty taste of what their opponents had experienced so regularly at the hands of Allied airmen. Three of Millholland's staff were wounded, and several German refugees in nearby camps, including two children, were gravely injured. Furthermore, the errant bombs disrupted Millholland's ability to communicate with Schmitt and Ungerleider.

It was an inauspicious time for communication problems, for those two company commanders needed all the help they could get. In the dark at Birgden, Company I had somehow bypassed some scattered German outposts south of town, and sometime after dawn, one of Ungerleider's squad leaders, Sgt. Harold Pietz, had the astonishing experience of watching some shadowy figures approaching Birgden from the same direction most of the 29ers had come just an hour earlier. When Pietz shouted out a challenge, an enemy soldier, obviously just as surprised as Pietz by the encounter, answered him in German.

Lt. Col. Randolph Millholland, commander of the 3rd Battalion, 115th Infantry.

That incident promptly triggered a deadly and cacophonous fight, swirling back and forth across Birgden without pause for the rest of the day. It was so chaotic that Millholland could do little to help except for taking the wise step of committing Tweed's Company L to aid Ungerleider. For an hour or so, the Americans' fortunes appeared dismal. As the regimental history noted, "German machine guns opened up with full force and blanketed the town with lead." In the confusion, Company I split into two distinct groups: one under Ungerleider in Birgden itself and another that pulled back to the start line at Stahe under the mistaken impression that someone had ordered a retreat.

Meanwhile, Schmitt's 29ers in Kreuzrath observed the nearby fighting with consternation. So far, the Germans had concentrated not on Kreuzrath, but on Birgden. As Schmitt could readily see, however, they could turn on him at any moment. In the language of the ordinary fighting man, Kreuzrath was a lousy place to fight a war, far too isolated in enemy territory and in full view of the Germans, who were obviously preparing to drive the Americans back all across the 3rd Battalion's front. Schmitt managed to get a radio message to Millholland, but his tone was bleak. Even worse, for the moment, Millholland could do little more than to order five M5 Stuart light tanks from the 747th Tank Battalion's Company D, under the command of 1st Lt. Chester Klingerman, to bring ammunition and supplies to Kreuzrath and remain there to help hold the town.

At 10:30 A.M. on October 2, a message from the 115th Infantry's command post arrived at the 29th Division's war room, and when Gerhardt read it, he became irate. "Company K reports they are just about surrounded by Germans," the journal noted. "We are getting a lot of artillery from woods to the east. Company I got two [German] POWs, who report that they had [earlier] captured fifteen of our men." Next to that journal entry, Gerhardt took a pen and angrily made a one-word notation in bold handwriting: "Disgraceful!" Half an hour later, Gerhardt phoned the 115th's command post and roared: "I don't want any more reports like that in here again! You'd think that we'd never been in combat before! You make sure that Colonel Smith gets that. Push that thing on forward!" Old-timers who knew the general's moods suspected that somebody's head would soon roll; it was just a question of whose head.

By the afternoon of October 2, Birgden had two owners: the Americans in the south, the Germans in the north. The triangular village green separated them, but at Gerhardt's insistence, the 29ers were about to cross that tiny piece of no-man's-land and try to push the Germans out by sheer force. There was no subtlety to it: Tweed's Company L would attack past the green toward a railroad cutting through the northeastern segment of Birgden; Ungerleider's Company I would follow a road that forked off the main street at the church, striving to drive the enemy out of town to the northwest toward a neighboring village named Schierwaldenrath.

The 115th Infantry had carried out house-to-house fighting in the past, notably at St. Lô in Normandy, but in that July 1944 battle, the enemy had been fleeing and did not contest control of the city with much resolve. At Birgden, however, the Germans more than matched their opponents in numbers and obviously held orders to fight for every house. The type of close-in fighting that ensued was enough to unnerve even the toughest veterans—invisible German snipers opened up on unsuspecting 29ers from upper-story windows; roving machine-gun teams fired MG42 bursts from alleyways and then disappeared; enemy infantrymen flung potato masher grenades, which flew end-over-end with a whoosh to land with a metallic clatter around the 29ers's feet, followed by a one- or two-second delay before they exploded, usually with grim results. The Germans came from everywhere at once, and for a few agonizing minutes, it seemed as if every 29er in Birgden would be killed or captured. A 2:56 P.M. war room journal entry captured the strain of the moment: "Companies I and L getting considerable trouble. Getting hit by Jerry from both sides and front. Fighting is house-to-house."

A few 29ers led by 1st Lt. Dwight Gentry of Company I had taken refuge in one of those houses, actually a large work-shed adjoining a home on the west side of town, backing up against an orchard. Gentry described one of the soldiers fighting from inside the shed, T/Sgt. Olin Murphy from Michigan, as the best fighting soldier he had ever seen, who "probably has killed as many or more Germans than any man in the 29th Division." He was about to kill several more. "[The Germans] came in first from the orchard, an outright assault—screaming the way frenetic Germans can scream," wrote Cpl. Jean Lowenthal in an October 14 edition of *29 Let's Go* after interviewing both Gentry and Murphy. "Within the course of fifteen minutes, the cool red head [Murphy], shooting it out man for man, killed three of the oncomers. Two of them he dropped within a range of fifty yards; the other, who was coming from around a haystack 200 yards away, he nailed through the head. Murphy had them lying in the orchard like apples." Later, another Company I officer said of Murphy: "He's so good that you overlook his outstanding traits. Things other men get decorated for are generally routine with Murphy."

As darkness set in, the enemy finally backed off, but Gerhardt remained dissatisfied because the Germans still controlled Birgden's northern half. The general, whose mood had worsened by the minute, called off the effort at 7:06 P.M. with noticeable irritation. "Get on your initial objectives [Birgden, Kreuzrath, and Schierwaldenrath] first thing in the morning," he barked to Smith, who replied misleadingly, "We have everything in pretty good shape." Everything was definitely not in good shape.

That night, several tanks from the 747th Tank Battalion's Company A, led by 1st Lt. Homer Wilkes, brought food and ammunition over the perilous no-man's-land to help Ungerleider and Tweed in Birgden. As Wilkes later reported, "The tanks were then kept at the front for outpost duty and to repel counterattacks." Members of the 747th were well acquainted with

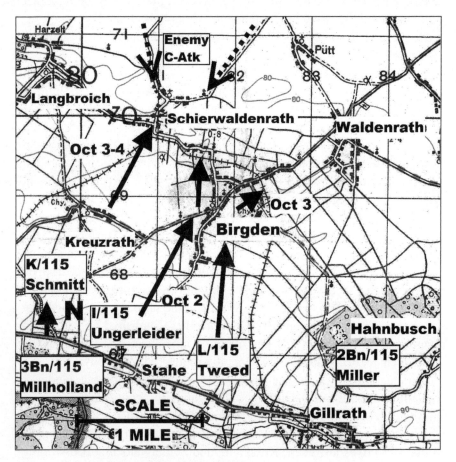

Birgden and Schierwaldenrath, October 2–4, 1944.

the 29ers from the Normandy campaign, but the kind of mission to which Gerhardt had now committed them left them with an ominous feeling that proper tank tactics were something the 29th Division did not understand. "The terrain was flat as a table," Wilkes observed. "Therefore it was unfavorable tank country [and] no defilade positions could be found."

Early the next morning, October 3, Gerhardt's volatile temper exploded when he discovered that the 115th Infantry was not ready to press ahead. Major Bruning phoned division headquarters to explain why Birgden and Schierwaldenrath were still not in American hands, bluntly pointing out some of the difficulties his regiment was currently facing. First among those problems was that the 115th's knowledge of the enemy was poor. Gerhardt was not the type of leader to seek dialogue among staff officers regarding his intentions, and at 9:54 A.M., he contacted Smith and growled, "This fellow Bruning needs a little sharpening up! He's beginning to question things and argue about it. The attitude in this division is 'get it done' regardless of the handicaps!"

Twenty-five minutes later, the bellicose Gerhardt concluded that Smith was failing to exhibit the necessary confidence and resolve to "get it done," traits the general considered paramount in a military leader. "You are the commander," Gerhardt snarled. "So quit calling up here asking if you can do so and so!" To emphasize his displeasure, Gerhardt phoned the 115th Infantry's command post at 11:57 A.M., this time reaching Smith's executive, Lt. Col. Harold Perkins. "Get on that objective and get on it quick!" the general roared.

Several times in the recent past, that sort of unrelenting coercion by Gerhardt had brought the 29th Division stunning success. The current situation was vastly different, however. Orders were orders, but no experienced staff officer could imagine how the unexceptional farming villages Gerhardt had ordered Smith's 115th Infantry to capture could offer any meaningful benefits to Corlett in the struggle to capture Aachen. Birgden, Kreuzrath, and Schierwaldenrath were not located on dominating terrain, nor were they strategically situated at the nexus of a vital road network. Furthermore, they could hardly be categorized as important stepping stones to a more critical objective, since nothing but miles of flat pastureland and more anonymous Rhineland farming settlements lay ahead. Above all, Corlett had directed the 29th Division to "put pressure on Geilenkirchen." The mission Gerhardt was demanding of Millholland did not contribute to that goal.

Those 29ers who grasped the reality of their new surroundings were beginning to understand that the only significance of Millholland's objectives was that the enemy occupied them. Here was war in its most brutally simplistic form: the 29th Division must kill Germans wherever it could find them; beyond that, Gerhardt had no plan. Veteran 29ers were entirely familiar with that sort of futile warfare, but this time, the effort to carry it out so hastily, with limited resources and little thought given to execution, triggered profound reservations among those men who had to obey the general's wishes. If the 115th had to effect a diversion, so be it; the men would loyally fulfill that task, as they always had, even though more planning time was required. But the 29ers had good reason to believe that a diversion would be limited to more subtle means of fooling the enemy. Instead, Gerhardt forced the 115th to fight a battle of attrition against entrenched Germans, whose numbers the Americans could only guess. If that was a diversion, it was a kind of warfare the 29ers wanted nothing to do with. But the general had forcefully declared his intent, and as Maj. Lucien Laborde, a 115th staff officer, remarked: "General Gerhardt was definitely not the kind of commander to whom one expressed objections. No one ever dared to question his judgment."

The first step in this disagreeable situation was to secure Birgden. Ungerleider's and Tweed's considerably shrunken companies, down to only about 250 men combined, would need time to achieve that end, as close-in street fighting against a stubborn enemy was among the roughest of military operations. Bitter fighting raged in Birgden all morning and afternoon on October 3, and much to Gerhardt's dismay, it was 5 P.M. before Millholland could report that the town was in American hands.

In all probability, the Germans would be back, as they had retreated less than 500 yards away to a cluster of small homes, soon known to the Americans as the "Island," situated halfway between Birgden and Schierwaldenrath. To forestall the enemy's expected "enthusiasm"—as Gerhardt euphemistically referred to any form of German offensive action—Millholland had firm orders to strike first by sending Captain Schmitt's Company K across the open fields north of Kreuzrath to seize Schierwaldenrath.

A calamity of epic proportions was about to unfold. It was sparked by a general's obsession to carry out an attack most 29ers on the scene thought was a terrible idea. Nevertheless, soldiers used to following superiors' orders without question executed it dutifully and resourcefully, but the results were so spectacularly futile that Company K would shortly cease to exist.

It all began at 1 P.M. on October 3 when the Company K field phone abruptly buzzed at Schmitt's command post, situated in a dilapidated German dugout behind a wrecked Kreuzrath farmhouse. Schmitt's operator answered and heard the voice of "Lagoon Blue-3," the 3rd Battalion's operations officer, Capt. Dana Tawes, asking urgently for his boss, Millholland, who had moved up to the front to inspect Company K's positions at Kreuzrath. When Millholland came to the phone, he learned to his astonishment from Tawes that Gerhardt had ordered Smith to seize Schierwaldenrath, and orders were clear "to get Company K going" toward that objective immediately.

Millholland discussed the prospect with Schmitt, and both agreed that no option existed except for the obvious one: a direct assault across the open pastures separating Kreuzrath from Schierwaldenrath. Millholland later noted that from the start he viewed such a maneuver as "a very risky undertaking." He resolved to take steps to stop it and hurried back to Smith's 115th command post, a place that contrasted sharply with the meager foxholes at the front. "Covered with heavy logs and sand bags, it seemed one of the most well-protected sites we have seen," reporter Bradley wrote. Here Millholland thrashed out the matter with Smith for more than an hour and "advised against further advance of the company." Two weeks later, Millholland recalled Smith's uncompromising attitude: "The regimental CO agreed that the situation was unhealthy, but said that the advance was ordered by division and that Company K must advance at once and would take the town of Schierwaldenrath." Evidently, one of Smith's core traits, as described by a loyal subordinate, had surfaced: "Colonel Smith followed orders directly and did not question them. He did what he was told to do."

No way around it now: orders had flowed down inexorably from the top, and Millholland had to obey them. Company K would advance to Schierwaldenrath, under conditions reminiscent of the senseless 1854 "Charge of the Light Brigade" in the Crimean War. Even if, as Lord Tennyson wrote in his celebrated verse depicting that military disaster, "someone had blundered," Schmitt's men had no choice but to carry on with the same devotion to duty exhibited by the British light cavalry at Balaclava ninety years ago: "Theirs not to make reply; theirs not to reason why; theirs but to do and die."

A crestfallen Millholland returned to his command post at Stahe at 2:45 P.M. and phoned Schmitt with the bad news. Millholland observed: "It was agreed that the attack would be made in semi-darkness and that mortar and heavy weapons would not fire until the attack was discovered by the enemy. Artillery was alerted to fire on-call missions." Schmitt had only about eighty-five men available for the attack, hardly a quantity that could accomplish decisive results, but Millholland helped him out as much as he could by providing a platoon of four .30-caliber machine guns from Company M as well as the five light tanks from Company D, 747th Tank Battalion, under Klingerman.

It was not nearly enough. When Schmitt convened an officer's call at 3 P.M. to plan the attack, the 3rd Platoon's leader, 1st Lt. Samuel Hodges, nephew of the First Army's commander, Lt. Gen. Courtney Hodges, recalled: "We all bitched about it." Also present was Company K's senior NCO, 1st Sgt. Clyde Bowers, who observed, "The company officers expressed doubt that they could make the attack OK, pointing out that the town was 2,000 yards [actually 1,600 yards] beyond our present position." An experienced 29th Division officer noted, "Schierwaldenrath was surrounded by flat and bare terrain by at least 800 yards around. It was ideal terrain for the defender's machine guns." Only a windmill, standing like a lone sentry about 250 yards south of town near a railroad track, broke the monotonous cabbage and turnip fields between Schmitt and his objective. As Bowers remembered, the meeting closed when "Captain Schmitt admitted it would be rough, but said that he thought they could make it."

The twenty-eight-year-old Waldo Schmitt was a highly experienced soldier who had spent his entire ten-year military career in the same regiment in which he currently served, the 115th Infantry. In 1934, at the age of seventeen, he had graduated from an organization he loved, the Boy Scouts, to enlist as a private in the 115th (known then as the 1st Maryland, a component of the Maryland National Guard). Schmitt climbed in stature over the next several years to become a highly respected NCO in Service Company, which carried out its weekly drills at the Silver Spring Armory in the Maryland suburbs of Washington, D.C. During the 29th Division's annual two-week summer camp, Schmitt routinely instructed new guardsmen in the use and care of the M1917 Enfield bolt-action rifle. In civilian life, Schmitt commuted downtown for a job at the Library of Congress.

Sgt. (later Capt.) Waldo Schmitt in 1940.

Shortly before the February 3, 1941, mobilization of the 29th Division, Schmitt, along with about 100 other Maryland National Guard enlisted men, entered an officer candidate course in the Lord Baltimore Hotel. After an improvised program lasting only thirteen days, he was commissioned as a second lieutenant and transferred to Company E, an ordinary rifle company. On D-Day, now commander of that same company, he had landed on Omaha Beach at 11 A.M. and promptly led his outfit up the heavily mined bluffs beyond the beach, an act that would earn him one of the first of hundreds of Silver Stars awarded to members of the 115th Infantry in World War II. But his initial combat experience was abruptly terminated when three German machine-gun bullets pierced his abdomen and thighs during Company E's afternoon attack against St. Laurent-sur-Mer, one of the last enemy bastions still holding out on the coast. A Company E soldier who observed him in a seated position leaning against a fence post noted: "He had the pallor of a man in shock who had not long to live. . . . [Only] the availability of plasma saved his life." According to that same soldier, "Several months later he returned to the regiment, still limping from his wounds, when, perhaps if he had tried, he could have avoided being sent back."

Upon his return, Smith assigned Schmitt to the command of Company K. Before the Schierwaldenrath attack, several Company E members who had served under Schmitt at Omaha Beach demonstrated their esteem for him by visiting his command post to reminisce about D-Day and the training period in England. One of them, PFC Wayne Cheatham, remembered, "We all thought of Captain Schmitt as tops." Another, PFC William Wilch, declared: "I want to go on record that Captain Schmitt and the platoon leaders whom I served with were the bravest, most honest, caring, capable, and humble men I ever met or even heard about. They were the best, an example of the flower of our generation. I feel lucky that we had such fine officers to lead us." The high regard with which infantrymen regarded Schmitt continued when he joined Company K, as PFC William Cottrill revealed: "Without question, he was a man for all men, respected by everyone in Company K." A fellow officer described Schmitt as "about six feet tall, in excellent physical condition, with a charm about him—an air that he was a commander."

Had it not been for Adolf Hitler, Waldo Schmitt's military career would have been limited to Monday night drills at the Silver Spring Armory and two weeks of annual training at Camp Ritchie. He only had to look to his father for inspiration. Dr. Waldo Lasalle Schmitt was one of the most celebrated zoologists in the United States and a familiar figure on the Washington, D.C., social scene, a man whose affiliation with the United States National Museum, an arm of the Smithsonian Institution, dated to 1910, and who had accompanied President Roosevelt on a voyage to the Galapagos Islands in 1938 on the cruiser USS *Houston*. Schmitt's scientific knowledge greatly impressed Roosevelt, and the president remarked with his legendary wit in an August 27, 1938, speech at Hyde Park: "Doctor Schmitt was such a success that we decided to change the Smithsonian to the 'Schmitt-sonian.'" Roosevelt also asked Schmitt during that voyage if there was any particular "thing or animal" he hoped to find. "Oh, yes,

Mr. President," Schmitt replied. "I am writing a monograph; I have been on it two years, and the one thing I am searching for in these waters of Mexico and the islands of the Pacific—I want to find a burrowing shrimp." Roosevelt responded: "Why leave Washington, Dr. Schmitt? Washington is overrun with them. I know that after five years!" Eventually, Schmitt found his shrimp on the island of Socorro, about 350 miles off the west coast of Mexico. The shrimp soon came to be known informally as the "ghost shrimp"; the president christened it the "Schmitty Shrimp."

For the younger Schmitt, achieving the status of his extraordinary father would have been difficult, but he never had the chance to try. The war intervened, and instead of following an academic pursuit, Capt. Waldo Schmitt now faced the much more perilous duty of studying how to accomplish Gerhardt's impossible mission at Schierwaldenrath while keeping as many of his men alive as possible. The best way to do the job was to move as quickly as possible, with Klingerman's tanks out in front and infantrymen spread out behind in a dispersed and ragged skirmish line. A narrow dirt path cutting through the cabbage fields connected Kreuzrath and Schierwaldenrath, and Company K would advance along that axis toward its objective. The 3rd Platoon, under Hodges, characterized by Millholland as "a damned good platoon leader," would move on the right, followed by the company command group under Schmitt, still limping from his D-Day wounds. The 1st Platoon, led by 2nd Lt. John Sullivan, and the 2nd Platoon, under 2nd Lt. John Vicek, would press ahead on the left. When Schmitt's apprehensive and silent men moved out at about 4:30 P.M. in the fading light, many of them must have wondered whether the luck that had kept them alive through the maelstrom of Normandy and Brittany was finally about to run out.

It was. Within a few hours, almost all would be dead, wounded, or prisoners of the Germans, including Schmitt. The attack actually began well. According to First Sergeant Bowers, "Everything worked smoothly; it was right out of the book." "The book," however, failed to specify how an attack against a position occupied by a much stronger enemy could succeed. When the leading 29ers passed the foreboding windmill and reached the railroad track just short of Schierwaldenrath, all hell broke loose. "The Germans had been asleep until that time," Bowers remembered. "Then they woke up."

According to a 747th Tank Battalion report, Klingerman, who had just told Schmitt that he "did not think it advisable to use tanks in the attack," moved his M5 light tanks out first and they "traveled in front of the infantry all the way." The tanks made it into Schierwaldenrath first, although one M5 commanded by Sgt. John Russell toppled into a ditch and had to be abandoned. Schmitt's 29ers followed—too slowly, according to Klingerman—and cloaked by the elongated evening shadows, they scrambled up the main street, through narrow alleyways, into backyards, searching for suitable positions from which to defend the town against the enemy's inevitable counterattack.

With so few men under his command, Schmitt would find it an impossible challenge. The town was small, consisting only of about fifty brick buildings, but the layout of its streets, like the letter "H" turned on its side, would greatly accentuate Schmitt's problem. By about 5:30 P.M., Company K and Klingerman's tanks had managed to occupy the southern fringe of town, but their task became increasingly difficult as they strove to secure Schierwaldenrath's northern half by moving up the short north-south connector street, at the head of which lay the village church. "Enemy fire split the company as it fought into town," Bowers observed. "[Hodges's] platoon, followed by Captain Schmitt, found less opposition on the right. They moved ahead and lost physical contact with the 1st and 2nd Platoons on the left." According to Hodges, "My platoon ended up in a house near the center of town. The Germans had left so fast there was hot food on the table."

The momentum of the American assault enabled the 29ers to grab some unwary Germans as prisoners, who were promptly escorted to the rear, but their interrogation by one of Millholland's intelligence officers revealed disturbing news, punctually forwarded to division headquarters: "A POW reports that there are 500 Germans in [Schierwaldenrath]," the officer declared. Gerhardt's response to that sort of unsubstantiated rumor could be expected, and the officer prepared for that by concluding: "Take it for what it's worth." As those who were fighting in Schierwaldenrath would soon discern, that intelligence was actually worth a great deal because it was true. Had Millholland held the authority to act on that information, he would have immediately pulled Schmitt out. But only one person had the power to change fate: Charles Hunter Gerhardt, Jr.

Night came, and with it Schmitt's sense of isolation in lonely Schierwaldenrath intensified by the minute. Company K's hand-held SCR-536 radios did not work well within the town—no surprise there—and consequently, Schmitt could not even figure out the location of his own platoons, let alone predict whether any help would eventually arrive from Millholland. According to a report based on interviews with three survivors prepared a week later by a U.S. Army historian, T/Sgt. David Garth, "Captain Schmitt decided to dig in and hold for the hours of darkness. He postponed the 'cleaning out' of the village until the next morning." Two runners from Vicek's platoon, Sgt. Frank Sturinola and Pvt. Gus Dodas, made it back to Kreuzrath, where Bowers and a communications team had remained in the Company K command post, to report that "they had reached their assigned objectives and were dug in." Schmitt himself, along with a few radio operators and runners, moved into the same house occupied by Hodges and a portion of his platoon.

All night long, Company K members huddled in basements to avoid the enemy's continuous artillery barrage, which appreciably worsened just before dawn, a clear hint that German troops would soon be swarming through the town. One detail was certain: if Schmitt was to hang on, he would need substantive assistance by first light, and if radios could not carry his urgent message to Millholland, then humans would have to do. As related by Garth's report, one member of a Company M machine-gun team got back to Kreuzrath leading two walking wounded and contacted Millholland by phone back at 3rd Battalion headquarters in Stahe: "He described the situation in the town and said they would need help."

In Kreuzrath, Bowers strove frantically to communicate with Schmitt. "At about 2100 hours, PFC Jay McCahn, a company radio operator, suggested that Bowers borrow an SCR-300 radio from the regimental anti-tank company to see if they could find out what the score was," Garth wrote. "At about 2130 McCahn and Bowers tuned in on the frequency on which Company K was netted to battalion. They heard Schmitt's radio operator [PFC Lindsay] Roland, calling the 3rd Battalion CP, but he evidently was getting no response." Bowers broke in and asked to speak to Schmitt. "[Schmitt] asked Bowers to relay his transmissions to the battalion CP. . . . [Later], at about 2200 hours, Schmitt requested artillery support. Lieutenant [Warren] Finke, forward observer for the 115th's Cannon Company, took over from McCahn to adjust the artillery fire as called for by the company commander. These fire missions were continually relayed through the rear CP as the night went on. Targets for these fires were described [by Schmitt] as 'self-propelled guns and enemy mortar positions.' Throughout the night Bowers personally maintained the radio watch with [Schmitt], relaying calls for artillery fire to the battalion CP."

The supporting artillery fire was reassuring, but it could not solve Schmitt's dilemma. At dawn on October 4, that dilemma was about to intensify, for under cover of darkness, the Germans had moved up a 250-man task force, accompanied by four *Sturmgeschütz III* self-propelled assault guns, and were preparing a direct assault on Schierwaldenrath from several directions simultaneously. Early-morning conditions, described by one member of the 747th Tank Battalion as "so foggy that no one could see anything," greatly facilitated the enemy's actions. The Germans announced their presence to the startled 29ers by the squeal of the treads on their *Sturmgeschütz III*s, ear-splitting bursts from MP40 machine pistols, and the whooshes of close-range discharges of their deadly *Panzerfaust* antitank launchers.

Before the Americans could react, the enemy was swarming through the streets of Schierwaldenrath, shouting wildly, firing weapons with abandon, and hurling grenades through windows. Klingerman's tanks could do nothing to stop the onslaught, as the 75s of the *Sturmgeschütz III*s greatly outclassed their puny 37-millimeter main guns. Only three American tanks remained in town since, during the night, Klingerman had used his tank to tow Sergeant Russell's Stuart out of the ditch in which it had tumbled and both vehicles had returned to Kreuzrath. The enemy's relentless assault immediately dispatched one American tank, commanded by a Sergeant Nolan, with a 75-millimeter antitank round or a *Panzerfaust* warhead, which penetrated the Stuart's slim armor and set the vehicle on fire, badly burning some of its occupants and forcing them to race for the protection of a building. Within the next thirty minutes, the remaining two tanks, commanded by Sergeants Cooney and Milanski, were also methodically hunted down and destroyed, again driving the survivors into nearby buildings.

Just before the German attack, Sgt. Walter Carbaugh of Company K's weapons platoon had set up a .30-caliber air-cooled machine gun in the backyard of a house on the west side of town, aiming it across the vast open fields over which he thought the enemy might approach. He was right, but as Carbaugh and his four-man crew peered through the patchy mist hanging over those fields at first light, the 29ers abruptly realized it was almost too late. According to Garth's report, "Carbaugh saw a German tank swing around the western margin of a patch of woods. It was accompanied by about ten enemy riflemen and came directly at his position. He fired four boxes of ammunition at the tank and its complement of troops, but that failed to stop the armor. With no anti-tank grenades or bazookas available, Carbaugh withdrew his squad to the shelter of a nearby cellar and watched as the tank advanced on his position and crushed his machine gun beneath its tracks." Carbaugh and his four comrades were among the lucky few to escape Schierwaldenrath and eventually make it back to Kreuzrath, although one of them, Sgt. Raymond Whobrey, was badly wounded.

On the opposite side of town, in the house occupied by Lieutenant Hodges and part of his 3rd Platoon, Schmitt contacted Bowers in Kreuzrath by radio and bluntly informed him that his situation was desperate. "We're receiving lots of small-arms fire and self-propelled guns are coming into our positions," Schmitt bellowed in an obvious state of high tension. Bowers could plainly hear bullets and shells through the earpiece, which forced Schmitt to shout. When Schmitt reported, "I must take cover from this fire," an apprehensive Bowers suspected the end was near. Schmitt descended into the basement along with several other men. Still, according to the company communications sergeant back in Kreuzrath, Sgt. Vincent Persicco, "The captain was on the radio almost all the time. . . . He finally called for artillery [eventually directly on his own position]—as much as he could get—and he told them to keep it coming until he said stop."

Hodges and a small band of his platoon held the second story of that same house and recalled, "Germans were everywhere." The enemy's *Sturmgeschütz* assault guns rumbled noisily down the street, stopping now and then to open fire with a tremendous blast from their long-barreled 75s, aimed directly and at almost pointblank range at any house they suspected harbored Americans. Now that all the American light tanks were destroyed, the only way a 29er could knock out a *Sturmgeschütz* was by using a bazooka, but as usual, those weapons were in short supply. An American tank crewman who had escaped his burning Stuart and fled into the house observed a Company K lieutenant order one of his men to grab a bazooka and fire out a window at one of the enemy's assault guns, but the GI declined, professing ignorance of that weapon. "Upon hearing this, the lieutenant became very angry," the tanker recalled. "Taking the weapon from the soldier, the officer went after the [assault gun] himself. But upon attempting to fire, he discovered the bazooka was inoperable."

Private Cottrill remembered, "Several times the Germans attempted to penetrate into the houses, but were repulsed. Word was passed down to move back if possible, but it was too late. Three in our house made a run for it and were cut down." Around 6:30 A.M., the gunfire and explosions in Schierwaldenrath had become so intense that Bowers, in nearby Kreuzrath, knew Schmitt could not escape.

Klingerman promptly mounted his Stuart and directed Sergeant Russell's tank to follow him at top speed from Kreuzrath to Schierwaldenrath across the now-familiar cabbage fields, bathed in a vaporous ground fog that gradually dissipated in the intensifying dawn light. Unhappily, it was far too late for the tanks to do any good. As a 747th Tank Battalion report noted, "About one hundred yards inside the town, Klingerman's tank was hit and set afire. Russell saw Klingerman and his three other crew members leave the tank and go into the building housing the Company K command post. . . . A few minutes later Russell's tank was hit three times by enemy anti-tank fire, and he was forced to abandon the tank, with his crew, one of whom was wounded. Russell took shelter in a building about fifty yards from the CP [command post], but was unable to reach the CP because of heavy small-arms fire and occasional artillery fire."

The reason for Millholland's objection to Gerhardt's Schierwaldenrath directive had now become abundantly clear: no reinforcements were within reach to rescue Schmitt. At the 3rd Battalion command post in Stahe, an anxious Millholland had learned of the crisis when a message came in from Kreuzrath at 7 A.M. stating, "Company K getting repeated counterattacks with tanks and infantry—men in bad shape." An hour later, a call came in announcing, "Company K is completely surrounded and all their communications have been completely cut off. The twenty-five remaining men are still holding the line and awaiting help." Two weeks later, Millholland's lingering frustration was still discernible when he wrote in a report of the Schierwaldenrath affair: "The regimental CO [Smith] was kept advised of the situation by phone. He said that the company must hold its ground and that there was no help available." That was not the kind of answer Millholland wanted to hear, but as a 115th staff officer pointed out, "Had Colonel Smith chosen to disobey or circumvent General Gerhardt's orders, he would have been in deep trouble"—and that was not a risk Smith was willing to take.

By 8 A.M., the end was near. Schmitt and twenty-five survivors were trapped inside two or three houses on the east side of Schierwaldenrath, running low on ammunition and under constant small-arms and 75-millimeter cannon fire. Hodges noted, "The Germans were so close, I remember shooting down at them from the second floor and hitting a man in the back of his neck. When we hit someone, you could see him fall. I would fire out of the window, then drop back." Others dropped grenades out the windows but could not linger long enough to observe the results.

Meanwhile, from the basement, Schmitt contacted Millholland through Bowers's radio and pleaded: "Will I get more men and tanks? What are your instructions?" A despondent Millholland replied, "No—none available. I cannot order a withdrawal. But you are on the ground, and I am not, and you will have to use your better judgment." A few minutes later, another radio call from Schmitt was answered by Captain Tawes, Millholland's operations officer, who had once led the 3rd Battalion in Normandy because of the high attrition rate among officers. In this, the last conversation between Schmitt and his comrades back in American lines, Tawes repeated Millholland's line of reasoning and urged Schmitt to take matters into his own hands, orders be damned, implying that a withdrawal from Schierwaldenrath was the only rational option left. But as Tawes later lamented, "He didn't do it; it was probably because he was too good a soldier to go against instructions."

It was already too late, for the Germans had finally closed in. The survivors of Hodges's platoon retreated into the same basement occupied by Schmitt, the last ten men of Company K to hold out in a fight that by now evoked Custer's Last Stand. The 29ers peered out the basement's street-level windows, striving to figure out if they had any means of escape. They did not. Cottrill observed, "Hearing a tank roll up outside the house, we believed our support had broken through. I looked out a window into the flash-suppressor of a German Tiger tank [actually a *Sturmgeschütz*] only a few feet away, larger than a wash tub. . . . Being the last house on the block, I guess we were the final remnants of Company K to be taken. I remember we got into quite an argument as to who would wave the white flag."

Hodges's account corroborated Cottrill's: "A tank poked its nose through one of those glass windows into the room we were in. If it had fired that thing, we would have been splattered over the wall—everybody—and you never saw so much white [cloth] come out. I don't know where it came from, but it did. 'Americans—surrender!' There wasn't anything else to do."

Back at the company command post in Kreuzrath, Persicco remembered the end: "[Schmitt] kept talking to us, and then there was an ominous silence. We tried and tried to contact him again, but we had heard from him the last time. Counting the mortar section that was left behind, my men, and the few who managed to escape, there were nineteen men left in Company K."

The reinforcements Schmitt needed, expected, and deserved never materialized—for the obvious but entirely regrettable reason that none were available. From the beginning, Millholland and Smith knew they could offer no support to Schmitt in Schierwaldenrath because all their troops were already in the line. Gerhardt, too, provided no backup, although several 29th Division infantry units were in reserve within striking distance. As Hodges recalled, "Captain Schmitt and I were talking about it. . . . Other units were supposed to move up on our flanks to protect us. We were also supposed to have air support. We didn't have any of it."

If Millholland had a copy of the U.S. Army's leadership bible, *Field Manual 100-5*, known simply as *Operations*, he would have wondered how Gerhardt could have violated one of the cardinal principles of American offensive tactics: "After the attack is launched, the reserve and the fires of supporting arms are the principal means available to the commander for shaping the course of action and for enforcing a favorable decision. The primary mission of the reserve is to enter the action offensively at the proper place and moment to clinch the victory. . . . Choosing the proper time at which the reserve should be used is often the commander's most difficult and most important decision."

But no reserve materialized. At 7:42 A.M. on October 4, almost precisely the moment when Schmitt and Hodges were making their last stand, Gerhardt phoned Smith and growled: "Going to get anywhere today? [You] ought to get somewhere!" Less than an hour later, a liaison officer at Millholland's command post, a Lieutenant Huffman, radioed back to division headquarters: "They're having some trouble up there [in Schierwaldenrath]. The enemy is pretty much in force. . . . They are now surrounded and being pushed back all the time. They have artillery coming at them from right and left. Some heavy artillery coming from the north." Next to this entry in the war room journal, an angry Gerhardt penciled in one word: "Exaggerated!" As events that day unfolded, it was entirely evident that Huffman's report was in fact truthful.

Even more regrettable was the division commander's failure to adhere to the wishes of his boss, Corlett, who phoned Gerhardt at 10:16 A.M., just as most of Company K's survivors were being marched away as prisoners, and declared with no possibility of misinterpretation: "Don't stick your necks out up there now!" Later that day, with a firmness stiffened by the unfortunate events at Schierwaldenrath, Corlett added: "I would like to be careful not to bring on a big fight on your front." Unhappily, Gerhardt had already brought on a "big fight," and the 29th Division had lost.

According to unwritten U.S. Army values, a disaster of such magnitude could not pass without an official explanation, especially when one of the victims was the army commander's nephew and another was the son of an eminent scientist and acquaintance of the president. Someone had to shoulder the blame, rightly or wrongly, and at best, he could expect a reprimand and, at worst, relief from command with orders to head home to the States, reputation in tatters. The U.S. Army may have had a few generals in its long history who were willing to accept full responsibility for a military disaster, but Gerhardt was not one of them. The fires in Schierwaldenrath still smoldered in the aftermath of Company K's annihilation when the general began to seek out subordinates to hold accountable for the calamity, and perhaps unsurprisingly, that search did not turn inward to delve into his own role in bringing it about. Such an attitude derived from Gerhardt's unshakable self-confidence, so strong that the possibility of failure was unimaginable.

If someone other than himself was to be accountable for the fiasco, Gerhardt knew from the start that it had to be Smith. From the general's perspective, the 115th's unfortunate commander was an obvious choice, for Smith was not the type of subordinate to whom Gerhardt could ever display respect. The two men were opposites. Smith looked more like a bank teller than a warrior; a subordinate described him as "humble and somewhat meek." Another depicted him as "very unmilitary in character, but a good soldier," and a third noted that he was "a nice man, as pleasant as could be, but he clearly had an inferiority complex"—an attitude in all probability shaped by Gerhardt's caustic view of field-grade officers with National Guard origins, citizen-soldiers whose experience at military science was for years limited to only one night per week and two weeks each summer. Gerhardt, the charismatic West Point graduate and dashing cavalryman who passionately believed that aggressive and impulsive soldiers gained more military success than bookish ones, could not allow himself to consider that Smith, a brilliant electrical and mechanical engineer trained at Johns Hopkins University, could effectively lead men in battle.

At 7:20 A.M. on October 5, Gerhardt phoned the 115th's command post and announced brusquely to Smith: "Colonel [Edward] McDaniel [29th Division chief of staff] is coming down to take over. You are to come up here as acting chief of staff." Later, Gerhardt also relieved Smith's operations officer, Major Bruning. Presently, Gerhardt contacted his boss, Corlett, to attest to Smith's failings: "The 115th had a bad day yesterday," Gerhardt began. "It lost about two-thirds of a company. They had this battle for a town and then reared back and then the [German] Home Guard came in and took over. I relieved Smith this morning. . . . Smith was up for promotion [to full colonel], but he obviously can't do it, so we wanted to block it." Somewhat sarcastically, Gerhardt concluded: "He is a good executive officer." Corlett certainly realized Gerhardt's account was disingenuous, for the Germans in Schierwaldenrath were not from a "Home Guard" unit, but from a battle group drawn from the 351st Regiment of the 183rd *Volksgrenadier* Division—hardly the equivalent of a parachute or panzer unit, but still an integral element of the German Army, whose members, as all dogfaces could attest, could never be underestimated.

Significantly, Gerhardt did not offer any specific evidence of Smith's wrongdoings, nor did he suggest anything Smith could have done to avoid defeat. That Smith had no viable alternatives on October 4 other than to disobey Gerhardt's orders was a detail Corlett probably never learned because his understanding of the battle derived only from Gerhardt. The other side of the story would have established beyond doubt that Millholland's battalion was far too dispersed to carry out an effective attack. It occupied a frontage of over 4,000 yards whereas *FM 100-5* advised that a battalion preparing to launch a major attack occupy between 500 and 1,000 yards. Furthermore, Smith lacked reserves to exploit success, his fire support was entirely inadequate, and his troops had not been in line long enough to know the enemy's strength. As *FM 100-5* declared, "Military intelligence is an essential factor in the estimate of the situation and in the conduct of operations." Smith had carried out Gerhardt's directive in an unwinnable situation, with no voice of dissent, and had lost his job because of it. Eventually, Smith's loyal subordinates would defend his honor. One asserted bluntly that Smith took the punishment quietly because "he did not wish to have blame directed toward Millholland."

Those few 29ers who grasped the truth about Schierwaldenrath whispered among themselves that National Guard officers such as Smith would never get a fair chance from West Pointers like Gerhardt and Corlett, and plenty of evidence from the recent past corroborated that theory. Yet anyone who understood Gerhardt could hardly be surprised by Smith's relief, for the general had always been much more demanding of field-grade officers like Smith than he had been of ordinary fighting men. In the four months since D-Day, McDaniel was the 115th's fifth commanding officer.

In the aftermath of Schierwaldenrath, Gerhardt did cast a much farther-reaching net of blame for the disaster than anyone had witnessed before. This time, to the profound shock of many 115th members, he strove to indict soldiers far more junior than Smith for their supposed misjudgments. That almost all of those soldiers were by then dead or prisoners of the Germans—and therefore could not provide their side of the story—was immaterial. All that mattered to the general was that a handful of Schierwaldenrath survivors had provided evidence that many Company K members had taken refuge in buildings during the battle. Those accounts triggered a volcanic eruption from Gerhardt, who concluded that Schmitt had violated one of the 29th Division's cardinal tenets by setting up his command post inside a building and allowing his men to fight defensively from within houses. Gerhardt passionately maintained that such practices, which "should be avoided at all costs," greatly lessened the 29th Division's indomitable offensive spirit and yielded initiative to the enemy. Countless times in the past, 29ers had ignored Gerhardt's imperative as a matter of survival, but the general chose to ignore this. Now Schmitt had undeniably been caught in violation of that rule, and Gerhardt would certainly not ignore it.

Early on October 5, Gerhardt bellowed to a subordinate: "There was no reason for losing that company! Whatever you do, keep out of any buildings. That's very important!" Later, to another minion, the general declared, "Anyone who wants to get in trouble with the Krauts, let him get into a building and get jumped on. The point is to get out in the open, dig in, and use the weapons. There was an outfit in the 115th that was massacred for doing that!" Gerhardt's dissatisfaction with Schmitt was so strong that he noted in his October 1944 summary of 29th Division operations that Schierwaldenrath was "an example of very bad security, choice of position, and leadership. Exactly the same principles of failure were apparent at Alta Villa," a September 1943 defeat suffered by the 36th Division near Salerno, witnessed by Gerhardt as an observer.

Over the next few weeks, many members of the 115th seethed when they observed Gerhardt's unforgiving attitude toward Schmitt displayed in briefings at which the general derisively urged 29ers "not to do a 'Schmitt' and get caught by the enemy inside buildings." Gerhardt went even further, greatly overstating his case by claiming, "They were in a house eating and just surrendered. . . . It is just criminal!"

Gerhardt did not inquire among the fighting men what they thought of his philosophy, for he knew they would be incredulous. Maj. Lucien Laborde, an esteemed staff officer who respected Smith, Millholland, and Schmitt highly, later observed caustically: "General Gerhardt made a fool of himself at Schierwaldenrath." An enlisted man from Schmitt's company also scornfully rejected Gerhardt's analysis: "The headquarters boys were critical of Captain Schmitt's action. . . . However, from my observation of him as a leader during training and on Omaha Beach, I consider him one of many unsung heroes."

Maj. Lucien Laborde of the 115th Infantry and later 29th Division headquarters.

Gerhardt's rules might have seemed sensible when viewed from the comparative calm of the 29th Division's war room, but frontline 29ers had more practical matters on their minds than to pay heed to practices that made no sense when in close contact with the enemy. In the past, in the chaos of battle, the 29ers had routinely ignored the general's steadfast rules, and they had done so again at Schierwaldenrath. When examined from Schmitt's perspective, one can hardly conceive how his men could have behaved otherwise. For Gerhardt to accuse Schmitt of culpability for the fiasco raises the obvious issue of the general's evasion of his own responsibility. Only one man had ordered the attack, and that was Gerhardt. With limited manpower and no backup, that order specified that Schmitt seize an enemy-occupied town, knowing nothing about its defenses or the size of its garrison. Furthermore, he was forced to hold on with no support against an overwhelming enemy counterattack. The disaster had more to do with an astonishing imprudence, triggered by gross overconfidence and faulty intelligence, than it did with alleged violation of 29th Division rules by a mere company commander. Gerhardt's intractable attitude sealed Company K's fate the moment it launched the attack.

The Germans were again in control of Schierwaldenrath, which became evident as dozens of disheveled and shell-shocked 29ers emerged from basements with their hands over their heads, hoping they would still be living an hour later after the jittery, fuming Germans disarmed them. Even greater danger came from friendly fire, as PFC Cottrill noted: "As they marched us through town in the middle of the street, our own artillery was laying in a continuous overhead barrage, spraying us with shrapnel." A German captain named Eggert tried to get some useful information out of the Americans while they were still dazed, and one of his reports noted that "a small [American] sergeant was in one group and appeared to be very talkative." Hodges, however, recalled that most 29ers said little to their opponents: "The ten of us [in one building], including Captain Schmitt, our tank commander [Klingerman], and myself were lined up in the street and searched. [We gave] name, rank, and serial number." Cottrill observed that "a German soldier took my graduation ring, saying he needed it for a filling in his tooth—poor guy."

The 29th Division had just suffered its most devastating defeat of World War II. The triumphal enemy promptly marched its prisoners out of town. "We were aligned in single file, with Germans on each side," recalled Hodges, who occupied a spot in the forlorn procession just behind

Schmitt. The Germans had only just begun to escort the 29ers down the road when an American artillery barrage abruptly descended on the column with uncanny accuracy. Schmitt was immediately hit. "There was pandemonium," Hodges observed. "The captain was on the ground, screaming and cussing; others, including Germans, were hit and scrambling for cover. . . . I tried to help the captain: he had two slits in his chest and no blood. I rolled him over. There was a big gap in his back; the shrapnel had gone through his body and come out his back. He was still alive. We found some boards and carried him to a German aid station along with several others."

The Germans moved Schmitt and other wounded 29ers by ambulance to a military hospital at Wassenberg, a nine-mile journey. As for the unwounded, the enemy separated officers and enlisted men and dispatched them by truck and train to prisoner of war camps as distant as Poland. During those journeys, many would experience the terror of Allied bombing raids on German railroad yards while locked inside boxcars. Cottrill recalled that as German guards steered the Americans off the train to march to a prison camp, "Many of us were abused by civilians, and in particular by a German sergeant, in response to an air raid."

On the afternoon of October 4, German medical personnel brought Schmitt into a Wassenberg hospital ward, where he was tenderly cared for by a German Red Cross nurse, Elizabeth Frachterna. She later noted that Schmitt's wound, apparently through one of his lungs, was grave, and he had already lost much blood. For hours, he clung to life and even managed to converse in short whispers with a fellow Company K member lying on an adjacent gurney, Pvt. Wilbur Dinning. Presently, German nurses arrived to move Dinning to another room so doctors could treat his wounds. As the nurses wheeled Dinning out, Schmitt whispered: "I will be gone when you get back."

He was. As an American officer noted in a June 1945 interview with Dinning, "When he returned from the operating room, he saw what appeared to be Captain Schmitt's body covered by a sheet, and the Germans told him he was dead." Nurse Frachterna, who was standing by Schmitt's cot as he died, reported that the cause of death was "internal bleeding." Waldo Ernest Schmitt, dedicated 1932 Eagle Scout from Takoma Park, Maryland; trustworthy Library of Congress employee; admired Maryland National Guard soldier; and decorated veteran of Omaha Beach, was dead.

No U.S. Army general in World War II could endure for long in a combat command if he allowed the traumatic impact of battle to seep into his psyche. In the heat of combat, leaders rarely had the luxury of reasoned decision-making and often had to implement impulsive judgments that could, especially against opponents as skilled as the Germans, lead to dozens, if not hundreds, of casualties within a few hours. Reflecting on those judgments, especially those that went awry, could in due course trigger hesitation. As Stonewall Jackson remarked so famously, effective military leadership depended on "never taking counsel of your fears." Only a general with a steely self-confidence could carry on knowing how each decision influenced men's lives, for that sort of leader recognized his ultimate goal was to win battles, and eventually wars, by continuously maintaining the initiative and maintaining a positive attitude at all times.

Every man in the 29th Division understood that Gerhardt was that kind of leader and generally accepted, and sometimes even admired, his demanding style as an integral contributor to the 29th's impressive combat record so far in World War II. One of his battalion commanders noted, "I think I acquired some characteristics of boldness from Gerhardt's teachings. Positiveness and non-equivocation are extremely important attributes of a good leader."

If, as Generals Marshall and Eisenhower so often insisted, the fastest way for the GIs to return home was to pummel the enemy to extinction with a ferocious application of American military power, then in theory Gerhardt's aggressive approach to warfare should have contributed to that goal. As *FM 100-5* noted in its chapter on military leadership, "[Commanders] must be resolute and self-reliant in their decisions, energetic and insistent in execution, and unperturbed by the fluctuations of combat. . . . *A bold and determined leader will carry his troops with him no matter how difficult the enterprise* [italics in original]." Apparently, no U.S. Army division commander in the European theater could satisfy those requirements better than Charles Gerhardt.

The U.S. Army's top brass in Europe, including Eisenhower and many of his subordinates, seemed to agree with that notion. They viewed Gerhardt as a hard-hitting general, one who had molded a first-class division out of a National Guard organization whose proficiency many professional soldiers had doubted since its 1941 call-up. To his boss Marshall, Eisenhower had once even categorized Gerhardt as "highly acceptable to me." Everything Ike and Bradley had demanded of the 29th Division had been accomplished. Still, some of Gerhardt's superiors harbored serious doubts about his competence, particularly since the close of the siege of Brest, after which Gerhardt had unwisely opened a divisional house of prostitution and then promptly departed on furlough for England, an act he later discovered was strictly prohibited by General Bradley. The fact that no one could locate Gerhardt for six days added to Bradley's displeasure.

And then there were the casualties, which in the 29th Division amounted to over 15,000 men in only four months of combat. Bradley's administrative staff at 12th Army Group concluded that that figure exceeded any U.S. Army division's losses in the European theater since D-Day. True, the 29th Division had the misfortune of always finding itself in the middle of remarkably intense combat, but some senior U.S. Army officers were beginning to wonder whether its commanding general's leadership style had contributed to his division's astonishing casualty rate. Such an assertion was harsh, and considered by many as unfair, but Bradley apparently believed it, for after the war, he professed acerbically: "[Gerhardt's] enthusiasm sometimes exceeded his judgment as a soldier." It seemed that the U.S. Army, which encouraged enthusiasm among its top leaders, did not want enthusiasm to go too far.

Since its arrival in Holland less than a week prior to Schierwalden-rath, the 29th Division had come under the control of a new army commander, Lt. Gen. Courtney Hodges of the U.S. First Army. Gerhardt knew little of Hodges's personality and leadership traits since, for most of its combat career, the 29th had served under army commanders like Bradley, Simpson, and even the fearsome Patton. Just a few days after his division entered the front lines, however, Gerhardt was about to learn something about his new army commander under decidedly ominous circumstances. Normally, an army leader had only occasional contact with mere division commanders, since command protocol demanded that he issue orders through corps, which in turn would pass them down to division. But in the aftermath of Schierwaldenrath, the fifty-seven-year-old Hodges, a West Point dropout who had thereupon enlisted in the Army as a private in 1906, had an abiding interest in Gerhardt and the 29th Division because his nephew, Sam, had been missing since the battle, and for two weeks, the 29th Division had sent no word concerning Sam's fate.

An annoyed Hodges demanded from the 29th Division staff everything it knew about Sam, and on October 19, he dispatched his junior aide, Capt. Francis Smith, to the 29th's war room to "obtain the complete story on the general's nephew." Gerhardt sent Smith with an escort to the 115th's new commander, Colonel McDaniel, who in turn forwarded him to the 3rd Battalion to meet with Millholland. "Colonel Millholland said that Sam had gone into battle as a 'platoon leader, and a damn good one,' that he had done a magnificent job with the company, and possessed tremendous guts," Smith noted to General Hodges in a report of his visit.

As for the Schierwaldenrath incident, Millholland informed Smith that none of the five officers who had participated in the assault, including the tanker Klingerman, had returned to American lines.

Lt. Gen. Courtney Hodges, commanding general of the U.S. First Army.

But Millholland added the vital detail that a German soldier captured three days later "had seen five American officer prisoners [on October 4]. One officer was described as stocky, five feet, ten inches tall, and wearing a leather jacket. Lieutenant Hodges was known to possess a leather jacket."

Smith's report concluded: "The general consensus of opinion in [115th Infantry] headquarters, where I talked with Colonel McDaniel and Lieutenant Snyder [3rd Battalion intelligence officer], a close friend of Lieutenant Hodges . . . was that there is a reasonable hope that Hodges was among those captured, though they have no exact information." As for his boss's annoyance with the 29th Division for failing to provide a timely report on Sam, Smith noted, "There is no exact reason given for the delay in this information reaching the army commander." In all likelihood, that statement greatly lessened General Hodges's appraisal of Gerhardt.

That appraisal was lowered even more when Hodges perused a written report of the Schierwaldenrath affair prepared by Millholland. Something must be amiss within the 29th Division, for Millholland's very first paragraph categorized the assault as "a very risky undertaking" and went so far as to state that he had advised Colonel Smith "against further advance of the company." Such an experienced soldier as Hodges understood that battalion commanders commonly labeled orders from above as "risky," but Schierwaldenrath went far beyond the ordinary qualms of battle. The ultimate result of the attack had established beyond doubt that it had been extraordinarily risky, so much so that virtually an entire U.S. Army rifle company and an attached tank platoon had been destroyed. Most important, Millholland's report was firmly at odds with Gerhardt's highly implausible suggestion to his superiors that Schmitt and his men had acted irresponsibly by violating 29th Division procedures and practicing incompetent tactics. Indeed, Millholland's implication was clear that Schmitt and his men had acted bravely and done the best they could under hopeless conditions.

Any doubts harbored by Hodges about Gerhardt's judgment would vanish within the week because Bradley was about to remove the 29th from Hodges's chain of command and attach it instead to U.S. Ninth Army. A fiasco like Schierwaldenrath, however, could not be purged from the consciousness of the U.S. Army's top brass. To be sure, Gerhardt's aggressive style could be impressive, and those types of generals were rare enough that Bradley could not cavalierly dispose of them in the aftermath of a single blunder, but as the sacrosanct words of the Army's *Operations* manual noted: "A good commander avoids subjecting his troops to useless hardships; [and] he guards against dissipating their combat strength in inconsequential actions or harassing them through faulty staff management." At Schierwaldenrath, Gerhardt had apparently allowed his aggressiveness to overrule his better judgment, and a calamity had ensued. Would it happen again?

After the war, impelled by the profound shock of his son's fate, Dr. Waldo Lasalle Schmitt, one of the Smithsonian Institution's senior scientists, would use his impeccable research skills to embark on a quest to learn how the Schierwaldenrath battle had unfolded. That fixation consumed years, triggering many thorough interviews with 29ers who had served with his son and resulting in the accumulation of dozens of files, packed with official 29th Division reports and letters from his son's comrades. According to Sam Hodges, with whom Schmitt first met in Atlanta in June 1945, Doctor Schmitt had heard nothing from the U.S. Army concerning his son except that he was missing in action. Only on the last day of that month did Schmitt finally receive a letter from the adjutant general of the U.S. Army informing him "with sorrow" that his son was dead, but American graves registration personnel had so far not managed to locate Captain Schmitt's grave. In a plaintive letter to Hodges, Doctor Schmitt asserted, "I will return to Europe and try to find his remains."

For a scientist of such matchless rationality as Schmitt, what emerged from his Schierwaldenrath investigation was galling, as in retrospect his conclusion concerning Company K's October 3 attack confirmed what every 29er already knew: Capt. Waldo Ernest Schmitt had died in the line of duty, attempting to fulfill an impossible operation of little practical military value that never should have been initiated. This was not the first time in 29th Division history a parent had lost a son in an irrational military adventure, and it certainly would not be the last, but the elder Schmitt could not let it go. He believed the responsibility for Schierwaldenrath could only be ascribed to one man, but his opinion of Gerhardt would remain unspoken. Schmitt's only passion was to honor the memory of his son by defying Gerhardt's scorn for Company K and proving beyond doubt that the company's simple dedication to duty reflected great credit on the fighting men of the 29th Division. Not a single 29er other than Gerhardt would contradict that.

Schmitt may have learned with certainty that his son was dead, but for five agonizing years, the Army failed to locate his son's remains. Postwar evidence provided by a priest at a Catholic church in Wassenberg established beyond doubt that the Germans buried Captain Schmitt on October 6, 1944, at the nearby church cemetery, in grave 28. He had been the first American interred in that cemetery; over the next six weeks, seven other Americans, reportedly mostly aviators, were laid to rest near Schmitt in tightly clustered plots marked with crosses in a forlorn cemetery corner against a high stone wall. On April 25, 1946, a U.S. Army graves registration team traveled to Wassenberg, and with the help of the cemetery caretaker, Franz Gansweid, disinterred the remains of seven Americans and transferred them to the U.S. military cemetery at Neuville-en-Condroz, Belgium.

Despite the German priest's records that the Germans had buried eight American servicemen in the Wassenberg cemetery, only seven remains were disinterred. Later, evidence established the identification of only five of those seven, but no solid proof would emerge that either of the two unknowns was Schmitt. Two years later, in May 1948, an American investigator named Gerard Croize journeyed to Wassenberg to unravel the mystery, but his report provided no answers:

> I learned from the cemetery caretaker that the graves were not numbered at all, while the deceased were buried according to their approximate date of death. The former burial sites of the U.S. deceased were pointed out to me . . . [but] the location of Grave 28 could only be approximately established. . . . [Captain Schmitt] died on October 4, 1944, and was buried on October 6. This grave was found between one that was laid out on October 7 containing a Serb [Ivan Sivanov] and one that was laid out on October 5 containing a German [Walter Schubert]. The spot between these two graves is believed to be the former burial site of Captain Waldo Schmitt, and was found to be excavated and empty.

Croize concluded that if Schmitt's body could not be located, it might have been accidentally removed in March 1947 by a British Army team that had disinterred three British soldiers from Wassenberg for reburial at the Commonwealth Reichswald Forest War Cemetery, one of whose identity was in question. On June 17, 1948, an American team traveled to that cemetery to examine the body that Croize supposed could be Schmitt; ultimately, dental records proved that it was not.

The mystery was finally unraveled by chance in late April 1950, when Gansweid was disinterring the body of the Serb, Ivan Sivanov, from his resting place near the stone wall of the Wassenberg cemetery. The Germans had supposedly buried Schmitt next to Sivanov, but a surprised Gansweid discovered two wooden caskets in the same grave, one on top of the other. One body was Sivanov; the other, confirmed beyond doubt by a U.S. Army dog tag, was Capt. Waldo Ernest Schmitt. The U.S. Army coroner's report noted: "Remains in skeletal form; teeth intact in skull; ID tag found with remains; remnants of two O.D. [olive drab] shirts, two woolen undershirts, one trousers, one field jacket, one set of captain's bars."

On July 14, 1950, a U.S. Army officer traveled to Doctor Schmitt's office at the Smithsonian and "informed him of the positive identification of his son." The same day, Schmitt received an official letter from Capt. J. F. Vogl:

The remains have been casketed and are being held in above-ground storage pending disposition instructions from the next of kin, either for return to the United States or for permanent burial in an overseas cemetery. . . . In order that this office may take immediate action toward the final disposition of the remains of your son, it is urged that you complete the enclosed form, "Request for Disposition of Remains," and mail it to this office, without delay. May I extend my sincere sympathy in your great loss.

Doctor Schmitt filled out the form, specifying his wish for the Army to return his son's body to the United States. His instructions stipulated that "the remains are to be delivered to the Lee Funeral Home [on Massachusetts Avenue in Washington, D.C.], which will do the cremating of remains." The U.S. government promised to pay Schmitt $75 to cover the cost of cremation.

Sometime in early October 1950, Captain Schmitt's casket was shipped by rail from the Neuville-en-Condroz military cemetery to the port of Bremerhaven, where it was placed onboard the Victory ship *Lt. James E. Robinson.* Waldo Schmitt would finally return to the United States on November 2, 1950, when the *Robinson* docked at the Brooklyn Navy Yard in New York City. The casket was picked up by a U.S. Army escort, transported to the Jersey City railroad station on Tuesday, November 14, and placed aboard the Baltimore and Ohio Railroad's Train Number 27, the legendary "Royal Blue," southbound for Washington, D.C., the city where Schmitt had spent most of his life prior to overseas shipment with the 29th Division in 1942. The escort held orders that, at the wish of Doctor Schmitt, it "will not contact next of kin and will be dismissed when remains are signed for by the funeral director." Furthermore, those orders stipulated: "Delete name [of Doctor Schmitt] from all publicity and news releases."

At 1:30 P.M., Train 27 chugged to a stop next to a platform in Washington's Union Station. Passengers clutched their coats and suitcases and shuffled toward the coaches' exit doors. When they reached the platform they hurried toward the terminal, too focused on their business to notice some soldiers shifting a casket from a baggage car onto a wheeled metal cart, and a somber man in a black suit from the Lee Funeral Home waiting patiently on the platform for the soldiers to do their duty. Their duty would be complete when they shifted the casket into a waiting hearse.

Capt. Waldo Schmitt of the 29th Infantry Division had finally come home.

5. RED HORSE CAVALRY

General Gerhardt and all 29ers, for that matter, were not used to defeat. They had marched into Germany on the first day of October 1944, brimming with confidence that the enemy was on the run and the war's end near. Within a few days, the German Army, now defending its home turf, had crushed that illusion with dramatic force.

A single military setback was one thing, but when one examines the perilous military situation into which the 29th Division innocently pressed forward as it rejoined the battle after Brest, Gerhardt's unchecked self-assurance, broadcast to his subordinates with exhortations to "to get it done" regardless of difficulties, could easily have triggered disasters even worse than Schierwaldenrath. When the division crossed the Dutch-German border on September 30 and took over its new sector, it became responsible overnight for a front of such extended length—more than sixteen miles—that even two divisions would have been hard-pressed to defend it adequately. Remarkably, the general initially deployed less than one quarter of his available infantry strength into that long line, spread so thinly that had the Germans been in better shape, they could have broken through the American front with ease.

Under conditions of that kind, major American offensive action should have been out of the question; anyone who had graduated from the U.S. Army's Command and General Staff School at Fort Leavenworth, Kansas, as Gerhardt had in 1933, should have grasped that line of reasoning intuitively. As bluntly stated in the Army's *Operations* manual, a book Gerhardt had to know intimately in order achieve general officer rank, "Concentration of superior forces . . . at the decisive place and time, and their employment in a decisive direction, creates the conditions essential to victory. . . . Main attacks are characterized by narrow zones of action, strong support of artillery, tanks, and other supporting weapons, effective support of combat aviation, and deep echelonment of reserves."

Gerhardt professed the value of his military education when he wrote of his two-year period at Fort Leavenworth from 1931 to 1933: "The Command and General Staff School is the turning point in a man's military education, for here he associates with future commanders and really learns the essentials of troop leadership, logistics, tactics, and techniques." Why, then, did Gerhardt diverge so dramatically from those "essentials" stipulated in Army textbooks and insist in early October 1944 that the 29th Division undertake offensive action across its sixteen-mile front, with inadequate manpower, resources, and support? The evident answer to that question is that Gerhardt had yet to grasp what his fellow generals in the 2nd Armored and 30th Infantry Divisions had already learned: the demise of the German Army on the Western Front had been greatly exaggerated.

At 6 P.M. on September 30, Corlett assigned his XIX Corps reconnaissance unit, the 113th Cavalry Group, to Gerhardt to guard the left of the 29th Division's oversized front. Nicknamed the "Red Horse Cavalry," the 113th was an Iowa National Guard outfit called into federal service by President Roosevelt in January 1941, just a few days before the 29th Division received the same one-year call-up order. Since its initial entry into combat in Normandy in July 1944 under the command of forty-three-year-old Col. William Biddle, the 113th Cavalry, an all-mechanized unit of 1,500 men and 450 vehicles, had attained elite status in the view of its appreciative corps and army commanders. In a four-day span from September 5 to 8, Biddle's men had executed a remarkable 128-mile dash across Belgium in the wake of the routed enemy, far out in advance of the rest of the rest of the army, a drive that one GI recalled as "slightly nuts . . . when you're ducking 88s and being kissed by *beaucoup* beautiful girls at the same time; when the cafés open up, give away all their wine, and you dance in the streets while a burp-gun is still rattling away within a block. That's a funny kind of war." The Ninth Army's

Col. William Biddle, commander of the 113th Cavalry Group.

commander, Gen. William Simpson, recalled that the 113th Cavalry "demonstrated beyond question that it was a highly disciplined and well-trained unit."

The 113th's assignment to the 29th Division would trigger one of the toughest challenges in Biddle's career. From the low ground of the Maas River on the 29th's left flank to the link-up point with the 115th Infantry at Gangelt, Biddle had to cover a ten-mile sector, described by Simpson as "a staggering distance for a unit of that size." Furthermore, Biddle's intelligence officers possessed virtually no information on the enemy.

Everything about Gerhardt's and Biddle's backgrounds led to the conclusion that they would get along famously. Both were graduates of the U.S. Military Academy, as were their fathers. Both men had joined the close-knit cavalry branch upon graduation, spending much of the interwar period practicing old-fashioned soldiering when the horse was still an integral element of the U.S. Army and polo was the cavalry officer's sport of choice. The high command thought highly of Gerhardt and Biddle, and as the Army swelled in size in 1941, both officers were selected for positions of lofty responsibility. That year, Gerhardt jumped two ranks from lieutenant colonel to brigadier general and, only one year later, would gain a second star and take command of the 91st Infantry Division in Oregon. A protégé of one of the Army's most esteemed interwar soldiers, Gen. Frank McCoy, Biddle was shipped to London as a military attaché in June 1941 and would later serve as a senior liaison officer in the November 1942 invasion of North Africa. Soon thereafter, he returned to the States to take command of the 113th Cavalry.

Had a war not been in progress, the relationship between Gerhardt and Biddle would have been close, anchored by their mutual affection for horse soldiers and a deep devotion to military service. But leadership of major combat units in an active war theater was hardly an endeavor that cultivated camaraderie. Attaining success at that command level, as Gerhardt and Biddle both appreciated, required a hard shell and an ability to exert command with absolute authority and occasional ruthlessness.

Every 29er understood that Gerhardt wielded power that way, but Biddle was an outsider, not used to the 29th Division's unique commanding general. Further, Biddle was wholly accustomed to exercising his own judgment and initiative in combat since the 113th Cavalry Group, as prescribed by official Army doctrine, generally conducted semi-independent operations, sometimes at considerable distance from supporting infantry divisions. Indeed, the 113th Cavalry was analogous to a mini-division, and its high-spirited officers and men felt most at ease when Biddle was in full control of their fate. Although Colonel Biddle did not hold general officer status—and Gerhardt was his senior by two ranks—the 113th's subservience to Gerhardt could not have been particularly intimidating to Biddle because he typically dealt directly with more exalted commanders, such as Corlett at corps level or even Hodges and Simpson at army level. That Biddle and his men were admired by leaders more senior than Gerhardt was established by Simpson, who observed after the war: "I was greatly honored to have commanded such a great combat unit."

At the recently concluded siege of Brest, two subordinates similar to Biddle had fallen under Gerhardt's control, and the arrangement had not been smooth. The commanders of the renowned 2nd and 5th Ranger Battalions, Lt. Col. James Rudder and Maj. Richard Sullivan—both highly decorated veterans of the D-Day landings—practiced the kind of independent leadership the Army expected of Rangers, and the results had so far been impressive. That command style did not impress Gerhardt because Rudder and Sullivan did not strike the general as team players, a characterization the two Rangers would have admitted was true because both were used to working autonomously and could be prickly when their beloved troops were placed under generals who did not grasp the Rangers' unique capabilities. Gerhardt, who never forgave poor teamwork, once angrily referred to Sullivan as a "spoiled boy" and even threatened to relieve Rudder for insubordination. In the fall campaign in Germany, Biddle and his cavalrymen were about to learn something about Gerhardt which those Rangers already knew.

The relationship got off to a rocky start on the morning of October 1, just a few hours after Biddle learned of his attachment to the 29th Division, when Gerhardt phoned the 113th Cavalry's command post and declared with his usual bravado, "Colonel [Leroy] Watson [the 29th's assistant commander] is coming over this morning to your headquarters. . . . We are going to get somewhere, so get yourself in a frame of mind. We're going to get up to that Siegfried Line—and quick!"

If Biddle had any uncertainty concerning how Gerhardt's vague directive would apply to his unit, that uncertainty evaporated at 9:30 that morning upon Watson's arrival: "[Watson] soon made it clear that the 29th Division considered the 113th Cavalry Group too 'defensive-minded'. . . . In reply [I] explained that my group had been disposed on a ten-mile front

with a defensive mission, and to that extent could be considered 'defensive-minded.'" To Biddle's astonishment, Watson announced that the 29th
was about to launch an offensive, one in which the 113th Cavalry would
be expected to play a major role. The cavalrymen must "go places" on
October 2 by rupturing the enemy's line, formed behind a small stream
known as Saeffeler Creek, and advancing a considerable distance across
the open terrain beyond.

The appalled Biddle did not hesitate to state his opinion of the proposed operation: "In view of the enemy's defensive strength and the fact
that the Germans held the commanding ground and hence had superior
observation, [I] did not recommend this operation unless at least one battalion of infantry were attached," he wrote in an October 1944 report.
"Recommendations" from subordinates annoyed Gerhardt, and he brushed
aside Biddle's concerns. "We are not going to give you enough infantry to
spread along your line, but if you run into something you can't handle,
we'll throw a battalion in," the general declared early on the morning of
October 1.

Biddle could have pointed out with some justification that U.S. Army
doctrine did not advocate using cavalry in the kind of frontal assault con-
templated by Gerhardt. "Mechanized cavalry units are organized,
equipped, and trained to perform reconnaissance missions employing
infiltration tactics, fire, and maneuver," the *Operations* manual noted.
"They engage in combat only to the extent necessary to accomplish the
assigned mission." But Biddle was enough of a realist to admit that actual
combat had differed appreciably from "the book" since D-Day, and now
that Allied armies were stretched thin on the Western Front, virtually
every field-grade and general officer had to undertake tasks that would
have seemed implausible in training. As loyal soldiers, they had to carry
out those tasks to the best of their abilities. Still, what Gerhardt had
directed Biddle to do was analogous to sending a lightweight against a
heavyweight in a prizefight.

Gerhardt was courting trouble: Biddle's cavalrymen would pay a high
price if the enemy resisted with greater force than expected. In a postwar
analysis of cavalry operations, Biddle observed

> [Cavalry] suffered due to a lack of an effective primary weapon in
> the armored car [the M8 Greyhound, armed with an outmoded 37-
> millimeter gun], inadequate rifle strength, and inadequate caliber

An M8 Greyhound armored car of a U.S. Army cavalry unit in action in 1944.

of the assault gun [the M8 motor carriage, armed with a short-bar-reled 75-millimeter howitzer]. . . . Suitability for limited rather than prolonged missions was demonstrated due to relative light-ness in equipment. . . . Personnel shortage was noticeable, partic-ularly with regard to men available for dismounted combat.

Like any commander of a first-rate military unit, Biddle was confident that his men would carry out their duties regardless of the odds. In that same postwar report, Biddle recalled the cavalry's extraordinary "esprit de corps. . . . The traditional heritage of the cavalry arm characterized the operations of mechanized cavalry units and made possible the perform-ance of many missions of great difficulty."

Whether the mission Gerhardt demanded of Biddle would be merely difficult or actually impossible was anybody's guess. Certainly, no field manual would have recommended an assault against a prepared enemy position by a unit of only 1,500 men, simultaneously tasked to cover a frontage of more than ten miles. Even a conventional infantry regiment like Smith's 115th—more than twice the size of the 113th, much more heavily armed, and backed up by a direct-support artillery battalion— would be hard-pressed to carry out Biddle's mission.

The 113th Cavalry Group consisted of only two main fighting units, the 113th and 125th Cavalry Reconnaissance Squadrons, each of which was highly mobile, but about 20 percent smaller than a standard 871-man infantry battalion. A squadron contained three 139-man cavalry troops, analogous to infantry companies, but again much smaller. Biddle's job was made even more difficult because one of those six troops (Troop B, 125th Cavalry) had been detached to provide headquarters security, known derisively as a "Palace Guard," at General Hodges's First Army command post in Verviers, Belgium. To compensate Biddle for that transfer, Corlett assigned him two tank companies from the 744th Tank Battalion, but those units could hardly substitute for cavalrymen who were expertly trained to fight the enemy on foot. Moreover, the 744th was one of the Army's rare light tank battalions, equipped not with Sherman tanks but M5 Stuarts whose 37-millimeter guns and thin armor plates were thoroughly behind the times. Employing them in a frontal attack against the enemy's much more state-of-the-art weapons could be suicidal. Corlett also dispensed to Biddle the 747th Tank Battalion's Company C, commanded by Capt. Frederick Chappell, a unit equipped with seventeen much more survivable Shermans.

Normally, U.S. Army cavalry units lacked organic artillery, but Gerhardt rectified that deficiency by loaning Biddle the 111th Field Artillery Battalion and its twelve 105-millimeter howitzers, currently available because the unit to which the 111th was normally attached, the 116th Infantry, was in reserve. Biddle was also given a vague promise of air support, an enormous benefit if it actually showed up, but as the 30th Division was simultaneously making the XIX Corps's main effort near Aachen, the 113th Cavalry would clearly not be high on the pilots' priority list.

The XIX Corps's effort would begin at 9 A.M. on October 2, so Biddle had to work quickly to prepare his men for the assault: draw up orders, brief subordinate commanders, shift units to proper jump-off positions, and coordinate with a supporting artillery battalion Biddle had never worked with before. If the 113th Cavalry stood any chance at all, Biddle would have no choice but to strip most of his front of troops to achieve a concentration opposite that short stretch of Saeffeler Creek where Gerhardt demanded a breakthrough.

Had the Germans realized the degree to which Biddle had thereupon weakened his left flank, they could have walked through that sector of the 113th's line without firing a shot. To defend that area, all in Dutch territory, Biddle took a calculated gamble by deploying only two dozen cavalrymen, armed with jeep-mounted machine guns, to cover a five-mile front between the Maas River and the Dutch-German border. Their job would be to maintain contact with the 1st Belgian Brigade on the far side of the Maas while patrolling their lengthy front in jeeps. Meanwhile, some attached engineers from Company B, 121st Engineer Combat Battalion, would prepare the many bridges in that vicinity for demolition in case the enemy demonstrated an inclination to attack.

Such a trivial force could act as nothing more than a tripwire, but it was a risk Biddle had to accept because, as he stated in his monthly report, "The terrain did not favor offensive operations." He was entirey correct. That low-lying locale, bounded on the west by the sluggish Maas, was crisscrossed with man-made waterways, notably the famous Juliana Canal, and several small streams. One of those watercourses, known to the locals as the Vloed Beek, had been canalized by Dutch engineers and was bordered by steep dikes that were impassable to vehicles except at bridges.

Despite Gerhardt's recent avowal that he would not support Biddle with any 29th Division infantry, the general relented on the afternoon of October 1 and ordered the 175th Infantry's 3rd Battalion, led by Lt. Col. William Blandford, to move up to the front and take over Biddle's right flank, a sector of more than three miles, tying in with Smith's 115th Infantry at Gangelt. The entry of Blandford's unit into the line, completed after nightfall on October 1, freed several of Biddle's scattered units and allowed him to concentrate more effectively for the upcoming assault.

Biddle's attack just might work if it could catch the enemy by surprise. But if the Germans outnumbered the cavalrymen and could launch their counterattack faster than Biddle could bring up reinforcements, even surprise would not guarantee success. Biddle resolved to make his attack against a two-mile segment of Saeffeler Creek, just inside the Dutch-German border. The task of cracking the enemy's line on the creek's north bank was assigned to the 113th Cavalry Squadron under the command of twenty-nine-year-old Allen Hulse, a 1938 U.S. Military Academy graduate. Hulse's troopers would carry out that attack on foot, like ordinary infantry, a role to which generations of U.S. Army cavalrymen were thoroughly accustomed and which in 1944 was still characterized by its traditional label, "dismounted combat."

Hulse's men would not find Saeffeler Creek much of a barrier, as a soldier could in most places traverse that modest stream in one leap without getting wet. Hulse's real challenge would come later, when the cavalrymen set out to seize two diminutive farm hamlets on the stream's far side: Isenbruch and Havert. Those places were certainly occupied by Germans. Whether they were merely outposts or the enemy's main line of resistance was anybody's guess. Hulse would soon find out.

Saeffeler Creek may not have been an obstacle to men on foot, but it certainly was an impediment to vehicles. If Biddle wished to commit to the upcoming battle the 113th Cavalry's profusion of armored cars, as well as his attached Stuart and Sherman tanks, Hulse's men had to seize bridges or, in the event the Germans had demolished them, build their own. Biddle therefore assigned to Hulse two XIX Corps engineer companies—Company B, 82nd Engineer Combat Battalion, and Company B, 234th Engineer Combat Battalion. Biddle planned to move his vehicles over the creek as soon after H-Hour as possible to assist Hulse's dismounted troopers in their difficult task. As Gerhardt pointed out to Biddle by telephone just prior to the attack, "The whole thing hinges on you getting across [those] bridges."

Gerhardt's optimism was unbounded. Just an hour before Biddle's 8 A.M. attack on October 2, the general spoke by phone to Corlett at XIX Corps headquarters. "I think [the enemy line] will break today," Corlett declared. Gerhardt promptly responded: "We are going to break it!"

Biddle was not so sure. Just a few minutes after his men jumped off, he suspected that the 113th Cavalry Group was not going to "break" anything except perhaps the spirits of its own fighting men. Every move Hulse's men and vehicles made in that featureless landscape could be observed by the enemy, and as Biddle later noted, "The advance met stiff opposition immediately" in the form of unforeseen minefields and cleverly camouflaged enemy resistance nests, inflicting losses in American men and vehicles that mounted by the minute. This was no mere line of enemy outposts; the Germans were obviously present in force, determined to hold every foot of ground of their native soil, and Biddle could do little to ameliorate the rapidly deteriorating situation into which his unit had been swept by Gerhardt's firm attack order.

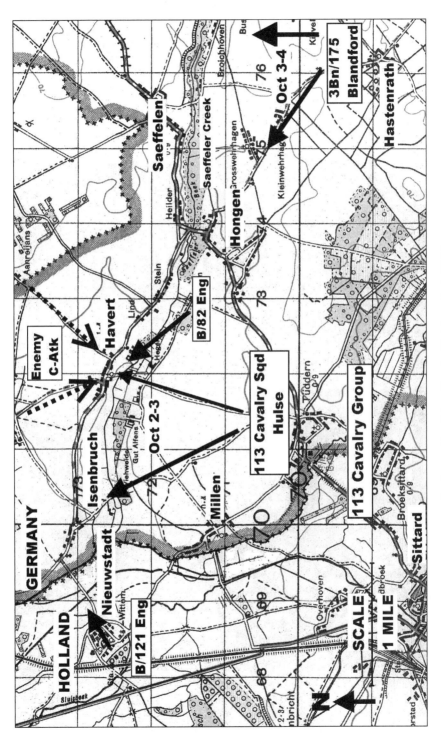

Action at Saeffeler Creek, October 2–4, 1944.

Biddle managed the battle from a forward command post in the village of Millen, less than a mile south of Saeffeler Creek. There, it would be easy for him to stay in close touch with his frontline troops—and difficult for Gerhardt to stay in touch with him. At 10:15, the 113th Cavalry's executive officer, Lt. Col. Jeff Hollis, contacted Gerhardt from the 113th's main headquarters at St. Josef's College in Sittard, Holland, and informed him that the attack had run into heavy opposition. Gerhardt offered not reinforcements, but criticism: "I understand the stream is only eighteen inches deep! You get across it! I am not going to have you stalled there!"

But stalled they were. The bleak pasturelands bordering Saeffeler Creek were covered by a deadly crossfire of German machine guns, and if the Americans wished to move across that lethal ground and attain their objectives on the stream's far side, they would need much more than just a few hundred dismounted cavalrymen. Had Biddle possessed armored vehicles as formidable as the enemy's fearsome Tigers or Panthers, he might have succeeded, but his puny armored cars and light tanks were easy targets for the Germans' proficient antitank gunners. Biddle succeeded in pushing several tanks over a minuscule bridge near Isenbruch, but as they fanned out on the north bank, Biddle later noted that the enemy's work was made much easier by the tankers' "terrain difficulties, particularly in the form of low, soft ground and small canals." Even worse, the Germans had strewn mines profusely over that ground, and those sinister weapons soon took a heavy toll of Biddle's vehicles.

The American tankers exhibited astonishing gallantry in a hopeless cause. Two members of the 113th Cavalry Squadron's Troop F, an outfit equipped with eighteen undersized M5 Stuart tanks, were posthumously awarded the Silver Star for bravery in the futile morning attack on Isenbruch. Staff Sgt. Paul Smith, one of the rare Iowa guardsmen remaining with the 113th since its 1941 mobilization, commanded an M5 that was immobilized by a German mine, an event necessitating an immediate departure from the tank if the crew hoped to survive. Smith later returned to the vehicle alone in an attempt to get it moving, but the nearby burst of an enemy artillery shell killed him. Biddle awarded the other Silver Star to PFC Martin Romanik, a Pennsylvanian, whose M5 was knocked out by an enemy antitank gun at the forefront of the American advance.

The failure of the Isenbruch assault could not entirely be blamed on the Germans, for the performance of American equipment was substandard. In fact, equipment breakdowns in the 747th Tank Battalion's Company C, temporarily attached to the 113th Cavalry, so disturbed Biddle that late on October 2 he contacted the 747th's commander, Lt. Col. Stuart Fries, to recommend the relief of its company commander, Captain Chappell. Company C's Shermans were the most powerful weapons available to Biddle, and without them, he would have little hope of success. The company was supposed to have seventeen Shermans, but it showed up with only fifteen, four of which were promptly withdrawn due to malfunctions in their 75-millimeter guns' recoil mechanisms, thereby preventing gunners from ejecting spent shell casings from the breeches. With some alarm, Witte also reported to Fries: "They are short of ammo."

Colonel Watson, whom Gerhardt had dispatched to keep an eye on Biddle, reported a much more disturbing story to the war room at 7:15 P.M.: "The captain reported to me himself [that] he only had five tanks whose guns could shoot." An angry Biddle maintained that such an appalling state of readiness was "less than satisfactory," but according to Fries, those glitches were "beyond [Chappell's] control," and Fries therefore argued against relieving his subordinate. Fries would soon defend that view in a report: "The continuous use of tanks, day and night, for many days is not efficacious inasmuch as cumulative minor mechanical failures will put many tanks out of action for days, which preventative maintenance could catch if time were allowed." Fries also displayed compassion because he knew Chappell had been traumatized at 3:15 P.M. when Company C's executive officer, 1st Lt. Kenneth Wilcox, was killed by enemy fire while standing next to Chappell near Isenbruch.

To Gerhardt, however, Fries's contention that his tanks were overused was utterly unacceptable and smacked of sloppy attention to details. When the general learned of Chappell's malfunctioning tanks at Isenbruch, he growled to Fries: "I received a report that your captain up with the cavalry yesterday quit. Bring him in—and I want to talk to you!" (In the end, Gerhardt did not relieve Chappell.)

Gerhardt's irritation with Biddle, too, was manifest. At 7:15 P.M. on October 2, when the general learned from Watson that Biddle's attached engineers had failed to complete a critical bridge over Saeffeler Creek just south of Havert, he became enraged. According to Watson's report, "[The engineers] are taking quite a shellacking down there. They lost two six-by-six [trucks] trying to put [the bridge] in. . . . They've had quite a number of casualties. When these engineers try to put in the bridge, they got shot up by small-arms fire. There's still a fight going on all along that creek." Biddle explained to Gerhardt that "the stream runs pretty close to the town; we are across the stream, but the town is held by the enemy." That detail did nothing to ease the general's ugly mood. In the 29th Division's war room journal, next to the transcript of Watson's report on Biddle's failed effort to complete the bridge, Gerhardt later penned in scathing commentary: "Read manual on river crossings. Principles employed here are very amateurish."

That evening, Biddle returned to the 113th's command post and promptly engaged in a frosty conversation with Gerhardt, during which Biddle admitted he had failed to achieve his objectives for the obvious reason that the enemy line "was pretty heavily held." The general retorted: "Are you going to get somewhere tomorrow? We want to get somewhere now! Get across there and get up on the initial objective. . . . Give it all you've got!"

But before Biddle could follow Gerhardt's advice, it was the Germans who gave it all they had. At 11:30 P.M., just as Company B of the 82nd Engineer Battalion was about to complete the bridge over Saeffeler Creek near Havert, the enemy launched a major counterattack that caught Hulse's 113th Cavalry Squadron by surprise. A cavalry officer named Reynolds phoned the 29th Division's war room and reported that the attack was "very well coordinated, with about 200 to 250 men supported by machine guns, bazookas, and at least one self-propelled gun. They had a bonfire of some kind that lit up the whole place, and of course they could see our positions. Our people were forced back across the creek by about 300 to 350 yards." Biddle was fortunate that Gerhardt was asleep when that message arrived, but when the general read a transcript of it later that morning, he expressed his skepticism in a single word, penciled in the margin: "Doubtful."

As for the vital bridge, Reynolds reported, "It was just about completed when the [enemy] attack was launched. When [the engineers] fell back, they ripped up as much of it as they could." A few hours later, an irritated Gerhardt spoke with Biddle's second-in-command, Lt. Col. Jeff Hollis, and said, "I understand the Krauts pushed you around a little bit last night." Those who knew Gerhardt understood that when Krauts "pushed around" 29ers, there had to be an immediate American response. The general issued orders to Hollis to that effect in the form of a question, as though he were a stern parent lecturing a naughty child: "You are going to work on that bridge that they took away from you last night?" Hollis had no choice but to respond with a meek "Yes, sir."

Without reinforcements, which Gerhardt would so far not provide, Biddle would have acute difficulty accomplishing on October 3 what he had failed to accomplish on October 2. Nevertheless, he had to try. The villages of Isenbruch and Havert, on the far side of Saeffeler Creek, hardly seemed worth such a major effort, but the Germans' firm resolve to defend them established beyond doubt that they considered those two places critical in Hitler's scheme to defend the Fatherland. More to the point, if Biddle did not hold Isenbruch and Havert by nightfall, the general would surely view the 113th Cavalry's performance as second-rate, a judgment Biddle wished to avoid at all costs.

At 6:30 A.M. on October 3, the cavalrymen set out to retake the ground the Germans had seized during the night. If they could drive the enemy back over Saeffeler Creek, they could resume the bridging operation and then move armored vehicles over the stream to aid the foot troops in a direct attack against Havert. But nothing went right from the start. As Biddle reported in a post-battle report,

[The attack] proceeded slowly, against heavy fire. By 0715, forward elements had almost returned to the stream, but smallarms and some 20-millimeter fire [from antiaircraft guns used in a ground role] were being received. . . . The CO, 113th Cavalry Squadron [Hulse], arrived on the scene and personally launched an advance, which succeeded in reaching the stream, by which time however, [the enemy] resumed a heavy and effective fire. Accordingly, the squadron found it impossible to cross the stream and reestablish the bridgehead.

At Isenbruch, Biddle's troopers fared no better. Even the slightest movement of men or vehicles over the open ground south and east of that village drew a torrent of ripping machine-gun bursts, inflicting fifteen American casualties in minutes. Biddle visited the front lines that afternoon in an effort to get the assault moving again, but even he had to confess that without additional help, pressing the attack further would be suicidal. When Biddle reported that view to the 29th Division's war room, Gerhardt would certainly not be pleased.

Biddle did manage to get some outside help in the form of four P-47 Thunderbolt fighter-bombers, armed with 500-pound bombs, which roared in shortly after 11 A.M. with orders to drop their loads on Havert. At noon, however, an air-ground observer reported to the war room that "visibility was too bad" and therefore the P-47s would not bomb Havert for fear of accidentally hitting American troops, located just a few hundred yards south of that village. Instead, the pilots dropped their bombs in and around the village of Schalbruch, a mile to the north, which the Americans suspected harbored an enemy command post, but that air strike had no immediate impact on Hulse's attempt to take Havert.

Biddle was normally the type of commander who led from the front and left the management of the 113th's rear-area headquarters to his executive, Hollis. Under 29th Division control, Biddle would not be free to roam the front lines at will and inspire his men, which he noted in the 113th's report covering the October 3 action: "At [Gerhardt's] direction, [I] had returned to my CP several times during the day in order to make telephonic reports." Ordinarily, Gerhardt did not tolerate pessimism on his subordinates' part, but when he asked Biddle on the afternoon of October 3, "How're you doing?" there was something in the tone of Biddle's response—"Not very good. . . . I've been thinking, and I can't see what to do"—that led the general to conclude that Biddle was expressing realism, not pessimism. When Biddle asked, "I wonder if we could get some infantry?" Gerhardt turned him down, but a persistent Biddle had the temerity to add, "Another thing that would help would be quite a push on my right." It was hardly typical within the 29th Division for a subordinate to make suggestions of that kind, but a weary and somewhat sarcastic Gerhardt sighed, "Yes. It would."

Gerhardt had actually already initiated the "push" Biddle had requested with Lt. Col. William Blandford's 3rd Battalion, 175th Infantry, which at Gerhardt's order had moved into the sector on the 113th Cavalry's right on the night of October 1. But Blandford faced the same dilemma as Biddle: too few troops (about 600) and too much front (3.5 miles). Covering such a long line would have been tough for a much larger force, and even Gerhardt would later have to admit to Corlett that "[Blandford] is stretched awful thin"—so thin, in fact, that initially Colonel William Purnell, the 175th Infantry's commander, and his operations officer, Capt. Henry Reed, naturally assumed that when Blandford's outfit was shoved into the line, it would be expected to undertake nothing beyond Gerhardt's standard requirement for "aggressive patrolling."

To Reed's and Purnell's astonishment, Gerhardt promptly demanded that Blandford's 3rd Battalion push ahead on October 2 with the object of rupturing the enemy's line behind Saeffeler Creek. To accomplish that challenging mission, Blandford would have to do what Biddle had just done—concentrate his meager manpower on a narrow front for the assault and cover the rest of his sector with nothing more than a thin outpost line. Blandford would take most of the day to effect such a concentration, which was minimal at best, and by the evening of October 2, the most he could do to satisfy Gerhardt's insatiable desire for progress was to send out strong patrols toward the creek with orders to report back on the most promising axis of attack the next day. For the first time since the 3rd Battalion had fought its way into the streets of Brest two weeks before, Blandford's 29ers were about to reenter combat.

Patrols alone could not satisfy the general. On the morning of October 3, Gerhardt phoned Purnell and, in his matchless style, demanded, "How far are you across the stream?"

The surprised Purnell responded, "We're not across yet."

"We have been fooling around for two days on this thing!" the general snarled.

Col. William Purnell, commander of the 175th Infantry.

Purnell, a Harvard-educated lawyer, knew how to articulate his case, however. With an audacity Gerhardt was not used to, he declared, "We're strung out over a wide place. I think it will take a battalion attack [at Blandford's focal point] to get across."

That triggered an angry and somewhat irrational retort from Gerhardt: "You should not be strung out! You are going to get across and on that objective today—and with what you have! You will not get the 2nd Battalion [currently in division reserve]."

Still, Purnell did not back off, pointing out with complete justification that "this started as a patrol mission" and therefore he would need more time to prepare and strengthen the assault. This served only to inflame Gerhardt even more: "I don't care what story you tell me! You and your S-3 [Reed] had better get it straight!"

The general's propensity to hurry was greatly accentuated by the unexpectedly hard fighting that Purnell's neighbors—Smith's 115th Infantry on the right, Biddle's 113th Cavalry on the left—had experienced on October 2. Gerhardt surmised that Purnell's October 3 effort would find a weak spot in the enemy's line or at least would draw enemy attention away from Smith and Biddle, thereby leading to a breakthrough somewhere along the front. As Gerhardt noted to Purnell, "This cavalry on the left is stuck, and they are not going to get anyplace until you get across. So get in there!" If Purnell did indeed "get in there," however, the 29th Division would be sucked even more deeply into a battle that was originally conceived by Corlett as merely putting pressure on Geilenkirchen in support of the 30th Division's main effort to crack the West Wall near Aachen. Gerhardt's method, now characterized by diffused attacks across a front of eleven miles, was unfortunately not the type of diversion Corlett had in mind.

The intense eruptions of gunfire Blandford could hear beyond his flanks, where the 115th Infantry and 113th Cavalry were undertaking their futile efforts to fulfill Gerhardt's orders, provided unmistakable evidence that his job would be tough. Impelled by Gerhardt's intensity, Blandford began his attack at 4 P.M. on October 3 as the sun dipped close to the western horizon. By now, the Germans had taught the 29ers the lesson that what began well did not always end well, for the enemy's sly propensity for drawing the 29ers into a vulnerable position and then slamming them with a vicious counterattack was yet again about to be revealed. That counterattack would hit Blandford's men with all the explosiveness of a lightning bolt.

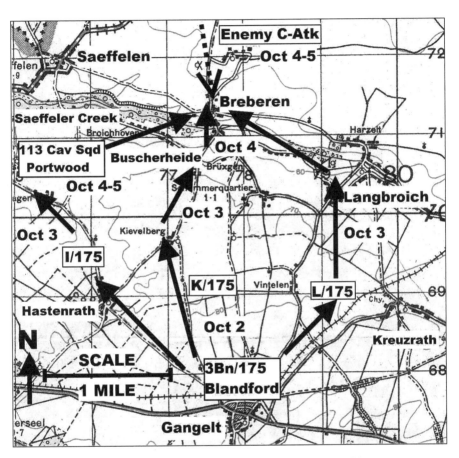

3rd Battalion, 175th Infantry, October 2–5, 1944.

Blandford's goal was to gain Gerhardt's requisite foothold over Saeffeler Creek by using three companies—K, L, and M—to seize a small bridge on the southern periphery of a village known as Breberen, but before that could be accomplished, they would have to push German outposts out of two neighboring settlements south of the creek, Buscherheide and Langbroich. Meanwhile, Company I would hold the rest of the 3rd Battalion's extended front, a mission that under normal circumstances should have been assigned to a battalion.

Blandford made good progress. By dusk, Company K controlled Buscherheide, and Company L occupied Langbroich. But as Purnell reported ominously to Gerhardt at 7:07 P.M., the "enemy was displaying a little enthusiasm," and the outlook for the next day, October 4, was troubling.

At 7:56 A.M. on the fourth, Corlett phoned Gerhardt and declared, "I would like to be careful not to bring on a big fight on your front. . . . [Blandford] has a pretty good defense set up, so why not just hold until we get a little more strength?" Had that statement been phrased in the form of an order rather than a question, it would have saved Blandford from a severe defeat and high casualties, but Gerhardt chose to ignore the question, ordering Purnell to keep the 3rd Battalion moving toward Breberen, despite a further warning from Corlett an hour later: "Don't stick your necks out up there now!"

By 11 A.M., Company K had advanced across the little Saeffeler Creek bridge and captured Breberen, to be joined a few hours later by most of Company L. As Blandford related, "Having then a bridgehead over the creek, we were preparing to strengthen it when word came from division that we were to turn over the town to the 113th Cavalry Group and revert the 3rd Battalion to division reserve. Relief was set for some time after dark." Blandford's unit, in the line for only three days, had somehow managed to accomplish what Gerhardt had demanded—so far.

As for Biddle's futile effort on the left, Gerhardt revealed to Corlett: "The cavalry is about wound up." In fact, as Corlett had recently been hinting to Gerhardt, the enemy's unexpectedly fierce resistance along Saeffeler Creek indicated that it was about time the 29th Division "wound up" its offensive as well. On the morning of October 4, Biddle reported to the 29th Division's war room to consult with Gerhardt face-to-face. In Biddle's October report, he noted: "[Gerhardt] explained that the offensive to the north had not been successful and that the division would cease its effort in that direction and regroup. . . . In the meantime, the division was to defend."

Biddle could have concluded that meeting by declaring to his new boss, "I told you so," for the 113th Cavalry's two-day offensive, undertaken at Gerhardt's order but against Biddle's advice, had inflicted little harm upon the enemy, gained virtually no ground, and resulted in nearly sixty American casualties and the loss of over thirty vehicles. It was telling that many of the lost vehicles were M8 Greyhound armored cars, which a U.S. Army field manual on cavalry operations had clearly specified were "not designed for offensive combat." Such an ineffectual and costly frontal assault, according to Biddle, was not the way generals were supposed to employ U.S. Army cavalry. His frustration with Gerhardt emerged in his October report, which at one point noted caustically that the order to withdraw one stalled cavalry troop from an exposed position near Isenbruch "was received with enthusiasm and obeyed with dispatch."

Gerhardt, critical as always, noted to Corlett that Biddle's heavy loss in vehicles represented "unskillful use of the materiel" and promptly ordered his chief of staff, Col. Edward McDaniel, to visit the 113th's command post and demand an explanation for that loss. Biddle's report observed that McDaniel's investigation "revealed that those losses had been unavoidable under the conditions."

Biddle had at last been relieved of the burden of carrying on this unproductive offensive, but he still had to fulfill the mission of relieving Blandford's battalion at Breberen on October 4, which could become extremely tricky because the relief had to be performed at night while the 29ers were still in close proximity to the enemy. An operation of that kind was one the Germans would invariably attempt to exploit, and in early evening, shortly before Biddle's cavalrymen's scheduled arrival, they did exactly that. The Germans appeared, as they always did, with an abruptness and ferocity that never failed to surprise and unnerve their opponents, pounding into Breberen in the twilight from three sides at once, about 200 strong, led by a formidable Mark V Panther tank. Blandford recalled the subsequent action as "a confused fight in the dark . . . during which one of our men claimed to have hit the German tank three times with a bazooka round at pointblank range without damaging it as it stood in a village street."

At 10:24 P.M., Purnell contacted Gerhardt and elevated his classification of the enemy's effort from "enthusiastic" to "highly enthusiastic."

From his command post in Hastenrath, nearly two miles distant from Breberen, Blandford could do little to control the chaos threatening to swal-
low up both Companies K and L. For more than an hour, the battle was
desperate. The 29ers failed to destroy or immobilize the Panther, which
churned with impunity down Breberen's main street, hammering American resistance nests with 75-millimeter cannon fire. Meanwhile, the
aggressive German infantry followed in the wake of their indestructible
war machine and snatched up dozens of dazed American prisoners, overwhelmed by the enemy's sudden onslaught.

The only factor that prevented a repeat of the Schierwaldenrath fiasco
was the timely appearance of two platoons of the 113th Cavalry Squadron
under the command of a captain by the name of Portwood, who, fortunately for Blandford, was on his way to the front at Biddle's behest to
direct the nighttime insertion of his troops into Breberen to replace the
embattled 29ers. The cavalrymen had come to the rescue, but would they
themselves need rescuing by dawn? According to the 113th's action
report, "The arrival of [Portwood's] force definitely checked the enemy
and after some delay permitted the infantry, which had suffered considerable losses and had been driven to the southern part of the town, to commence an orderly evacuation."

But Portwood's men fared no better against the enemy's lone Panther
than the 29ers, and for a while, it seemed as if that tank alone could drive
straight through Breberen, impervious to American fire, and roll all the
way to the 29th Division's war room, shooting up everything in its path.
Portwood's force included five light tanks from the 744th Tank Battalion,
armed with such puny 37-millimeter guns that only a reckless tanker
would dare challenge a Panther in a face-to-face duel. "[The Panther] was
well protected by infantry, and it maneuvered between buildings so that
only its front was exposed," Biddle recalled. "Accordingly, although
numerous hits were made on it with bazookas and 37-millimeter guns, no
damage was inflicted. On the contrary, it made slow but steady progress
toward the southern edge of town, and the position of the [American]
bridgehead force became more and more critical."

So critical, in fact, that Biddle was forced to yield Breberen to the
enemy completely by granting Portwood permission to withdraw his men
across the Saeffeler Creek bridge, their only remaining escape route. "The
enemy holds the town," Captain Reynolds radioed the 29th's war room at
3:36 A.M. on October 5. "Our people are south of the bridge, and the

bridge area is sort of no-man's land. . . . Tank destroyers [from Company C, 821st Tank Destroyer Battalion] are dug in, but they can't work them up any closer. . . . [Portwood's force] is to continue to delay and maintain contact and if necessary fall back to the high ground."

The enemy had inflicted yet another stinging defeat on the 29th Division. When company clerks filed their morning reports over the next few days, Blandford's 3rd Battalion, 175th Infantry, had 125 fewer men on its rolls than when it entered the line on October 1—a number that included an astonishing 61 men missing, 45 in Company L alone, most of whom were assumed captured during the chaotic nighttime fighting in Breberen. Aside from killing or wounding an unknown number of Germans—in all probability, far fewer than the Americans lost—Blandford's men had gained nothing and, in fact, by October 5 were back where they had started four days earlier.

So much for Gerhardt's boast that the 29th Division was going to push the Germans right back to the Rhine.

6. SERGEANT HUMPHREY

If World War II was "a sergeant's war," as so many astute U.S. Army generals insisted, then Sgt. Edward Chidley Humphrey, known by his comrades simply as "Ned," was one of the main reasons why the 29th Division's Company B, 121st Engineer Combat Battalion, was such an exceptional unit. Humphrey had just gained his second Silver Star for valor, a record which no 29er had surpassed in the fourteen weeks since D-Day and which was particularly impressive given Gerhardt's stingy attitude regarding combat decorations. That Humphrey was an engineer, not an infantryman, rendered that accomplishment still more notable.

Humphrey's latest exploit had taken place on September 16, 1944, when he and two sappers brazenly snuck into a tunnel leading under the walls of German-held Fort Montbarey, just outside Brest. That strongpoint had been holding out for days against the 29th, but after Humphrey's party had secured the tunnel, engineers hastily carried forward nearly a ton of explosives, which, when detonated, stunned the German garrison and promptly led to its surrender.

Sergeant Humphrey was about as different from the average 29th Division NCO as it was possible to be. For starters, he was thirty-five, much older than a typical sergeant in the division. True, Gerhardt's rear-echelon outfits were populated by dozens of grizzled master sergeants that age or older, but Humphrey, a mere buck sergeant only recently promoted to that rank, was a member of an organization that regularly experienced the worst of frontline combat. Generally, only much younger men partook in that type of ruthless pursuit, and among that set, Humphrey stood out as a wonder. Had Humphrey been an uninspired soldier, his younger comrades might not have taken much notice of his advanced age, but he was an achiever, a fighter possessed with not only extraordinary bravery, but also a rare impulse to get things done regardless of risk. Those traits could change the course of a battle; they could also bring about one's death in an instant. So far, Humphrey had been lucky and had indeed changed the course of battles in Gerhardt's favor.

The 29th's rolls featured scores of men who could claim countries other than the United States as birthplaces. Most of those had been born in Eastern Europe and emigrated from their wrecked countries in the social upheaval following World War I. Ned Humphrey, however, was one of the rare 29ers who could claim England as his homeland. A native of Shropshire, a county bordering Wales that was one of the most bucolic locales in England, Humphrey was reared for the life of a rural English gentleman. Not many enlisted men in the division had experienced the world of foxhunting and dog breeding; as a young man, Ned had become entirely familiar with those pursuits.

His father, William Humphrey, was an accomplished dog breeder and managed a kennel with more than a thousand gun dogs, mostly setters and spaniels, sold to hunters for retrieving prey. Described as a "doyen of field sports in the British Isles," the elder Humphrey was also known for his expertise in falconry, in which he "demonstrated his skill before kings and heads of state both in Europe and America. . . . Among those who saw his demonstrations were the Emperor of Germany, Wilhelm; the King of Spain; the Czar of Russia; and President Franklin D. Roosevelt in America."

William Humphrey was so skilled at what he did that in 1922, a wealthy New York banker, Erastus Tefft, brought him and two of his sons, including Ned, across the Atlantic and hired them to manage Tefft's Star Ridge Hunt in Brewster, New York. The forty-four-year-old Tefft, a graduate of Yale and a member of the Governing Committee of the New York Stock Exchange since 1902, took fox hunting seriously. He spent lavishly on his hobby, and as part of the agreement with the Humphreys, William purchased a pack of Welsh foxhounds and conveyed them to Brewster to see how they would do against local foxes in terrain far different than they were used to. Ultimately, they did famously, thanks in part to the teenage Ned, who took on the role of Star Ridge Hunt's "whipper-in," the member of the hunt who cared for the hounds and watched over their movements, whip in hand, during the chase. As a relative later noted, Ned "was at one with a dog."

For the three Humphrey men, such a perfect match between profession and passion was highly agreeable. Foxhunts in Putnam County, New York, were not much different from those in Shropshire, and Tefft, a beneficiary of the economic boom of the Roaring Twenties, seemed to have a limitless supply of money. But the Humphreys' lives revolved around much more than dogs, falcons, and horses. Brewster was just an eighty-minute train ride to New York City, where the Humphreys would have no difficulties discovering new social circles in which to mingle. The entrepreneurial possibilities were great, as one Humphrey relative later noted: "What did these three Humphreys bring to America? Well, everything. Horses, Welsh foxhounds, falcons, gun dogs, tractors, hand-knitted stockings, English-tailored suits and shirts, books, paintings, prints, and antiques en masse—if you wanted something from England, they knew

Ned Humphrey's British passport photo, 1928.

where to go. It was without doubt a huge operation." William Humphrey, sometimes accompanied by Ned, made the trans-Atlantic journey back to England several times per year in support of that venture.

But then came Black Tuesday, October 29, 1929, and suddenly, people like Erastus Tefft had neither money nor clout. The Star Ridge Hunt was no more, and the disconsolate Humphrey clan was forced to carry out the task of shooting Tefft's horses to feed the dogs. Ultimately, when money ran out, the dogs, too, had to be destroyed. The completion of that horrifying chore meant that the Humphreys would no longer have jobs, and all three decided to part ways and find fresh outlets for their talents. William Humphrey returned to England, but his two sons decided to start their lives afresh in the United States.

Ned's new life took root 2,200 miles westward, in Salt Lake City, Utah, a place whose geology, weather, and social framework could hardly be more different from Shropshire. There would be no fox hunting in the tight canyons and desolate mud flats surrounding Salt Lake City, but something about that part of the world took hold of Ned Humphrey and did not let go. In February 1937, he married a local girl, a Mormon named Amy Clark, and within the next three years, the couple became parents of two children, Georgina and William. But on November 3, 1940, when half a world away London was digging out from another devastating German air raid and Americans were two days away from choosing between Franklin Roosevelt and Wendell Willkie for president, Ned Humphrey's family was ripped apart by tragedy. That day, Amy, her parents, her two infant children, and her younger brother piled into an automobile to visit relatives in Brigham City, fifty miles north of Salt Lake City. During a snowstorm, a terrible accident occurred, and Amy, just twenty-three years old, was killed, as were both of her parents. The two children survived, although Georgina suffered a severe arm injury.

Thirty-one-year-old Ned Humphrey had abruptly become a widower, responsible for the upbringing of Georgina, just two years old, and William, still four months shy of his first birthday. Amy's sister Thelma, a remarkably compassionate woman who had three children of her own, would intervene to help Ned put grief out of his mind by assuming most of the responsibility for nurturing the two Humphrey children. Ned would therefore be freed to focus on making a living as a builder and strive to restore some normality to his life.

No one residing in the United States in 1941, however, would find life normal. Congress had recently enacted the Selective Service and Training Act, casting more than a million American males into uniform—in peace-time. Peace would not endure for long; by the close of the year, the United States was an active partner with Great Britain, Ned's homeland, in the war against the Axis powers. For the local Salt Lake County Selective Service board to call Ned into uniform seemed inconceivable: he was thirty-two years old, a widower with two children, and still a British citizen. But on March 22, 1943, Local Board Number 15 mailed to Edward Chidley Humphrey an order from the President of the United States to "report for induction." Ned read the well-known words:

> Greeting: Having submitted yourself to a local board composed of your neighbors for the purpose of determining your availability for training and service in the land or naval forces of the United States, you are hereby notified that you have now been selected for training and service therein. . . . This local board will furnish transportation to an induction station. You will there be examined, and, if accepted for training and service, you will then be inducted into the land or naval forces.

Soon, in a letter to his sister Winnifred in England, Ned enclosed a photo of himself and wrote on the back: "This is my last picture in civilian clothes, April [1943] last, in Salt Lake City." From now on, Ned's clothes would be provided by the U.S. Army.

The harsh life of a U.S. Army enlisted man hardly seemed a good fit for a man of Ned's background, but Private Humphrey adapted splendidly to military life. The Army eventually assigned him to the Corps of Engineers, an appropriate posting given Ned's acumen and skill in construction. His training complete, Ned now wondered where he would be deployed. Would it be to the Pacific theater? Or perhaps the Mediterranean, where the Italian campaign was currently in full swing? More likely, it would be to the land of Ned's youth, England, where Americans were gathering in massive numbers for the invasion of France, rumored to be scheduled for 1944.

It would be England, specifically the 16th Replacement Depot, whose members were informed that they would eventually be deployed to the front to fill the ranks of American units depleted by the initial burst of fighting in Normandy. Humphrey, still a mere buck private—the lowest rank in the U.S. Army—promptly began to learn the engineer skills he would need for survival in combat against a resolute enemy, including the use of bangalore torpedoes, wire cutters, mine detectors, and demolition charges. Even with the replacements' protracted training, however, Humphrey occasionally received a forty-eight hour pass. While most of his comrades invariably headed to London by train, Private Humphrey would borrow a car and drive to his father's home, The Stiperstones, near Snailbeach, Shropshire. Some indulgences that had been in short supply for British civilians due to wartime rationing—chocolate, cigarettes, jam, canned fruit—were issued by the U.S. Army to its soldiers in profusion, so much so that Humphrey would gather items saved in his footlocker, as well as treats donated by a generous supply sergeant, throw them into his borrowed vehicle, and head for home. He would share those treats only among his family. As one relative later noted about Ned's homecoming, "The Stiperstones is a very small community. . . . Nothing moves without everybody knowing. Uncle Ned would telephone when he was five miles away, someone would open the garage door. Uncle Ned would come up the valley, do a 'hand-brake' turn straight in, the door closing behind. The car would be unloaded with all the goodies he had brought with him."

On June 19, 1944, Humphrey crossed the Channel and joined Company B of the 121st Engineer Combat Battalion, the 29th Division's highly efficient sapper outfit. That company had suffered grievous losses on Omaha Beach, including fifty-four men taken prisoner, when the Germans launched a fierce counterattack against the slender beachhead on the morning of June 7. The unit had to be rebuilt almost from scratch, but with the infusion of more than eighty replacements like Private Humphrey, Company B quickly rejoined the fight. For the next month, Humphrey was in combat almost continuously, supporting the 116th Infantry in its exceptionally difficult passage through the Norman *bocage*.

On July 11, the day the 29th commenced a concerted offensive toward St. Lô, Humphrey gained his first Silver Star. According to the citation, Humphrey

> took over his squad in the absence of his squad leader and through his leadership and courage not only successfully completed the mission of the squad, but also aided other squads with their mission. The attack was made in the face of heavy enemy artillery,

mortar, and rifle fire. When the infantry fell back for reorganization, Private Humphrey ran up to three tanks, which had become bogged down, and through his encouragement and drive, made them move forward again. Private Humphrey personally placed the charges and blew the gaps for these tanks to advance.

As most Allied divisions raced toward Germany in the aftermath of the Normandy breakout, the 29th Division set off in exactly the opposite direction, into Brittany, to seize the port of Brest. It was there, on September 16 at Fort Montbarey, that Ned Humphrey, now a sergeant and squad leader, would gain his second Silver Star.

On October 1, just days after arriving in Holland, Gerhardt attached Company B, now commanded by Capt. Sidney Smith, to Biddle's 113th Cavalry Group, and by the next morning, Sergeant Humphrey and his fellow sappers were back in the front lines again. It did not take the 29ers long to realize that this part of the front, the extreme left flank of the division's sixteen-mile sector, a sodden and bleak piece of Dutch terrain neither side cared much about, was an unhealthy place. For the engineers, it was also remarkably lonely, as the nearest 29th Division unit was somewhere to the southeast, seven miles away. Company B had been used to waging war backed by the assembled might of the 116th Infantry, the organization to which it was normally attached. Now the men of the 116th were nowhere in sight. Instead, the only GIs Humphrey detected when he initially reported to his post in the village of Nieuwstadt on October 2 were a meager number of troopers from the 125th Cavalry Squadron, who were too busy patrolling their lengthy front in jeeps to chat. In the past, Humphrey had gained decorations for valor by boldly carrying out offensive operations. This time, his orders specified a strictly defensive mission. Those orders directed Humphrey to prepare the bridges traversing the small waterways east of Nieuwstadt for demolition in the event the Germans tried to attack through the village.

But on October 2 the situation changed dramatically. That morning, a reluctant Biddle carried out Gerhardt's order for an offensive by throwing his 113th Cavalry Squadron into its rash attack across the Dutch-German border. Humphrey's alert 29ers in Nieuwstadt could hear the cacophony generated by that attack since one of the 113th's objectives, Isenbruch, was situated just a mile to their east on the German side of the border. Whether Smith's Company B would be ordered to support Biddle's effort by advancing against Isenbruch from the west while the cavalry attacked from the opposite direction, no one knew. Nor on the following morning, October 3, did anyone bother to inform the engineers in Nieuwstadt of Biddle's difficulties. The haziness of the situation was exemplified by a blunt 9:30 A.M. entry in the 121st Engineer Battalion's journal: "3rd Platoon [of Company B] subject to 113th, who know nothing."

In early afternoon of October 3, Humphrey gathered the other seven men of his squad and headed straight east out of Nieuwstadt, directly toward the German border, somewhere behind which lay the enemy's front line—no one knew exactly where. The 121st's October 1944 action report specified Humphrey's task as "mine clearance," which presumably would be carried out on the Nieuwstadt–Isenbruch road, a narrow track 1,000 yards in length, lined with decorative poplars in the fashion of countless other Limburg and Rhineland thoroughfares. The 29ers were used to that kind of mission since they had systematically trained for it and carried it out successfully several times in actual combat, using knives and mine detectors as their tools of choice. All would agree that it was a hazardous occupation, for the cunning Germans habitually disguised their lethal mines masterfully and never arranged them the same way twice. An occasional booby trap made the clearance work still more perilous.

What Sergeant Humphrey's squad was not used to was performing its job in the absence of hefty infantry support; nor was it accustomed to operating with such imperfect knowledge of the enemy. From their lowly standing within the division's hierarchy, the engineers could not have known that Gerhardt expected the cavalrymen in that locale to "get somewhere . . . quick," despite the doubts bluntly expressed by Biddle that his men could indeed get anywhere. The obvious purpose of Humphrey's mission to clear the Nieuwstadt–Isenbruch road of German mines was to prepare for an offensive movement of infantry or vehicles via that route. That was a wholly sensible contemplation since the enemy in Isenbruch had stopped Biddle's troopers in their tracks for two days, and an attack astride the Nieuwstadt road could envelop that strongpoint and drive the Germans out, as Gerhardt demanded. But if Biddle lacked the manpower to attack from Nieuwstadt, a likely scenario given that Biddle's 1,500 men were stretched over ten miles, Humphrey's assigned task made little sense since there would apparently be no infantry or vehicles to pass through the mines the engineers were supposed to clear.

Nevertheless, the mission had to proceed. Humphrey and his seven followers were about to undertake a task far more dangerous than they could have imagined, one that had no immediate purpose and no direct support. The predictable result was tragedy, the kind of snafu that was repeatedly afflicting the unfortunate 29th Division during the first days of October 1944. Humphrey and his band moved out from Nieuwstadt, progressing 500 yards eastward as far as a modest bridge traversing the Vloed Beek canal. The 29ers warily crossed over, apparently under the assumption that their primary concern would be German mines, not German soldiers. What little Humphrey knew of the enemy's whereabouts hinted that the main German line would be situated another 500 yards ahead, behind another narrow waterway, Rodebach Creek, delineating the Dutch-German border. The 29ers did not realize that the Germans considered the Vloed Beek canal, not the Rodebach, their forward defensive line. They would learn the truth soon, and indeed, the Allies would not muster sufficient manpower to budge the Germans from the line of Vloed Beek canal until January 17, 1945, three and a half months later.

Instead of advancing into no-man's-land, Humphrey's squad was walking unsuspectingly straight into enemy lines. Somewhere in the saturated fields and woods between the canal and Rodebach Creek lay camouflaged German outposts, from which stealthy patrols intermittently set out to gain intelligence of their opponents. When, at about 3 P.M. on October 3, one of those patrols caught Humphrey's party on the canal's west bank by surprise, the 29ers did not stand a chance.

The only reference to the ensuing struggle in 29th Division records was a vague 4 P.M. entry in the 121st Engineer Battalion's journal: "Captain Smith reports five [actually four] enlisted men cut off in vicinity of [Vloed Beek] canal at 692729 [a map coordinate]. Two enlisted men are reported wounded, one evacuated. Sergeant Humphrey of detail cut off." What happened next to Humphrey's group, no one knew. By the next morning, none of the four 29ers had returned to Nieuwstadt. A glum Company B first sergeant therefore had no choice but to enter their names as "missing in action" on his morning report.

He would have been much glummer had he known that two of the four were already dead and that one of them was the redoubtable Ned Humphrey. That disheartening detail, however, did not surface for more than four months, and throughout that interval, Humphrey's Company B

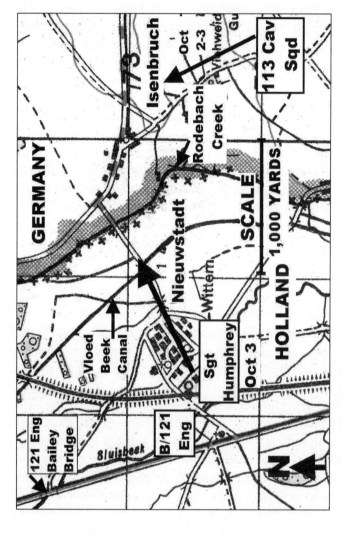

Sgt. Edward Humphrey, Company B, 121st Engineers, October 3, 1944.

comrades convinced themselves the four men were still alive in a German prisoner of war camp.

Back in Shropshire, Humphrey's father, William, would shortly learn of his son's "missing" status. On January 26, 1945, he wrote a letter to Ned's Company B platoon leader, Lt. Warren Doehler, asking for details of the action in which his son had disappeared. Doehler replied on February 12:

> I shall, to the best of my ability, try to give you all the information you request. Sergeant Humphrey was more than just one of my squad leaders; he was a well-liked man who I should like to call a personal friend. Your son was leading a mine clearance party, and by some freak chance they got behind German lines and were cut off. Four of the men made it back through the lines [two of whom were wounded, Pvt. Minor Cooke and PFC John O'Brien; O'Brien later died]. But your son and three others [Cpl. James Bain, PFC Emilio Cardiel, and Pvt. Ignatz Man-fredi] never returned. Knowing Sergeant Humphrey as a soldier, my personal belief is that he was captured by the enemy. If he had been alone I would say he fought till death, but having three men with him, and knowing his feeling for men under him, I firmly believe all were captured. This feeling is also shared by men who made it back. They said all four were safely in a fox-hole when they left. . . . I might add that Sergeant Humphrey was the bravest and most gallant squad leader I've ever had in my command. There was no mission too tough for your son. You have a right to be mighty proud of him, whatever the final find-ings may be. . . . Let us all hope this mess will soon be over and save further distress and sadness.

But there would be much greater sadness because by the time William Humphrey received Doehler's letter, he already had another piece of cor-respondence in his possession, this one a more official letter from the Adjutant General's Office at the War Department in Washington, D.C., informing him that his son was dead. According to that letter, "Evidence considered to establish the fact of death was received by the Secretary of War from the German government through the International Red Cross." The passage of information of that sort between warring states was so slow that eleven weeks had elapsed since the Germans' November 14 notification to the Red Cross of Humphrey's death.

The Germans buried Humphrey and Private First Class Cardiel north of Isenbruch, in a pastoral field alongside the Dutch-German border, but the Allies did not overrun that part of Germany and locate Humphrey's grave until January 1945. On March 17, U.S. Army graves registration personnel reburied Humphrey and Cardiel side by side at the U.S. Military Cemetery at Margraten, only a mile from the 121st Engineers' first bivouac in Holland when the 29th Division had arrived from Brest in late September 1944. (The other two members of Humphrey's squad listed as missing on October 3, Corporal Bain and Private Manfredi, had both been taken prisoner and survived the war. At thirty-eight, Bain was even older than Humphrey and, like his squad leader, had been born in Britain.)

William Humphrey, himself a veteran of both the Boer War and World War I, now had to partake in the morbid process undertaken by the United States government after World War II to offer the remains of American servicemen back to their grieving families. The War Department's postwar policy stipulated that a deceased soldier's next of kin must choose between two options: either consent to that soldier's permanent burial in an overseas U.S. military cemetery under the compassionate care of the American Battle Monuments Commission or direct the soldier's remains to be sent back home at government expense, including a seventy-five dollar allowance for private funeral expenses, for reburial in a private or national cemetery.

On November 28, 1947, the U.S. government submitted that choice in a letter to the Salt Lake City home of Ned Humphrey's son, who had been christened William after his English grandfather. Nearly a year transpired before the War Department figured out from the American Red Cross that the deceased soldier's son was only seven years old, and since Ned Humphrey's wife had died in the tragic 1940 car accident, the person who must make the decision regarding Ned's remains was his father, currently residing at The Stiperstones in Shropshire, England.

On June 7, 1949, almost exactly five years after the Omaha Beach invasion in which Ned Humphrey's unit had participated, William Humphrey received an Air Mail Special Delivery letter from America that read:

> The Department of the Army will comply with the wishes of the next of kin in accomplishing the Program for the Return of World War II Dead. You will understand, I am sure, that the magnitude of this worldwide program requires close adherence to predeter-

mined schedules. This program is rapidly approaching completion. The remains of your son have been disinterred [on July 22, 1948], casketed, and are currently resting in above-ground storage [at Margraten] pending disposition instructions from you for return to the United States or for final overseas burial. It is vitally necessary, therefore, that your decision be recorded with us by the return of the completed Disposition Form.

On June 10, Humphrey replied: "It is the wish of my late son's two orphaned children, Georgina C. Humphrey and William C. Humphrey, who are living with their aunt, Mrs. Thelma White in Salt Lake City, Utah, that their father be buried beside their mother in the cemetery at Salt Lake City [actually in Murray, just south of Salt Lake City]." The Department of the Army responded: "Mrs. White has been advised of your wishes and will be notified when the remains are enroute to the United States. Ample time will be given for her to complete all funeral and other arrangements desired."

On July 26, 1949 in Antwerp, Belgium, Ned Humphrey's remains were hoisted aboard USAT [U.S. Army Transport Service] *Carroll Victory*, a Victory ship that had already conveyed thousands of deceased American servicemen from Europe back home. In Humphrey's case, it was a protracted journey of thousands of miles, but finally, in early September 1949, Ned's body arrived in San Francisco, California.

William and Georgina Humphrey at their father's funeral, September 24, 1949, in Murray, Utah.

On September 23 at 7:45 P.M., the Western Pacific Railroad's Train Number 2, originating in Oakland, pulled into Salt Lake City's train depot. An escort of smartly dressed U.S. Army soldiers emerged from a baggage car bearing Sgt. Edward Chidley Humphrey's coffin, draped with the Stars and Stripes, and carried it into a hearse provided by Jenkins Mortuary of nearby Murray City. The next day, Saturday, September 24, at 2 P.M., Humphrey was laid to rest in Murray City Cemetery next to his wife, Amy, in a service conducted by a bishop of the Mormon church. In a poignant photograph from the funeral, Humphrey's two children, William, age nine, and Georgina, eleven, stand solemnly at the gravesite as William clutches the folded American flag that had covered his father's casket.

Ned Humphrey, one of the most remarkable soldiers in the history of the 29th Infantry Division, was again with his family.

FOUR

Nothing Will Be Held Back

1. AS QUICKLY AS HUMANLY POSSIBLE

If General Gerhardt could not shove the Germans back to the Rhine, then someone else would have to do it.

Was the demise of Nazi Germany imminent, as so many Allied soldiers had lately presumed? Clearly, the number of believers was dwindling by a considerable factor every day, as the top brass absorbed the hard lessons recently learned by the 29th Division and so many other outfits on Germany's western frontier. It was not just the enemy's renewed vigor that contributed to fading optimism; it was also the Allies' monumental supply problems, the deteriorating weather, the elongated front line, and inter-Allied command quarrels.

One key American general who still believed arrived in France on October 6, 1944, for a one-week inspection. Gen. George C. Marshall, U.S. Army Chief of Staff, was the creator of the American army that Eisenhower and Bradley were now wielding with such devastating effect, and he craved to witness its efficiency firsthand. But his main interest was Germany's downfall, which he hoped would occur speedily so that Ike's men could return home for redeployment against Japan.

"I went through five armies, eight army corps, sixteen divisions [including the 29th Division], and also saw the commanders and staffs of eight other divisions," Marshall recalled. This tour should have provided ample opportunity for hardened American battle commanders on the Western Front to offer the U.S. Army's top soldier a realistic depiction of the German Army's remarkable capacity to endure. Whatever accounts those commanders provided Marshall, however, did not have much impact on him, for when he returned to Washington, his unbounded confidence that the European war could soon be brought to a victorious end seemed to have increased rather than diminished. In a top-secret brief on October 23, 1944, Marshall wrote:

> The Combined Chiefs of Staff direct that [Eisenhower] conduct operations with the objective of completing the defeat of Germany by January 1. Nothing will be held back. This course of action will require such measures as the commitment of reserves, the continuous employment of divisions, the minimum essential development of lines of communications, the employment of hitherto secret weapons, and employing strategic air in all-out tactical operations wherever and whenever the advance of the ground troops can be thus facilitated. . . . We will give maximum support for this all-out effort. Insofar as is humanly possible, all requirements will be met. Nothing will be withheld which is available and can be of assistance now.

Not everyone agreed with Marshall's vision for ending the war; in fact, the closer one got to the front, the more unrealistic Marshall's confidence seemed. In London, the British Army's top soldier, Field Marshal Sir Alan Brooke, mockingly recalled in his October 26 diary entry "the wonderful telegram from Marshall, in which he seems to consider that if we really set our heart on it, and bank on it happening, irrespective of what happens in the future should we fail to do so, we ought to be able to finish the war before the end of the year!"

Bradley, whose meteoric rise in the U.S. Army's hierarchy was largely because of Marshall's esteem for him, observed: "I was very optimistic up until the first week or so of September . . . [but] if they were going to quit, it seemed to me they would have quit before they started building up [along the West Wall]. . . . When General Marshall came over in October, I had gotten over my optimism and was quite surprised, to say the least, at his feeling that Germany might quit before Christmas." He later added: "We would be lucky to reach the Rhine by Christmas."

Another Marshall protégé, Eisenhower, grasped the strategic and logistical difficulties on the Western Front as well as anyone, but he still clung to the faint hope that a supreme Allied effort just might trigger Nazi Germany's collapse before the onset of winter. Even if the great and concerted endeavor articulated by Marshall was a fantasy, Ike still had to do something, and despite the Allies' swelling logistical difficulties and the Germans' evident resolve to defend their homeland fanatically, he wrote to Bradley on October 8, 1944: "Plans of both [Bradley's 12th and Montgomery's 21st] Army Groups must retain as first mission the gaining of the line of the Rhine north of Bonn as quickly as humanly possible."

To help accomplish that challenging mission, Eisenhower had bestowed a relatively generous amount of materiel to Corlett's XIX Corps, of which the 29th Division was an integral part. Events on Corlett's front during the first week of October, however, had sharply clarified which of those accomplishments were "humanly possible" and which were not. The XIX Corps's 30th Division had succeeded in its initial task of cracking the enemy's formidable West Wall and had made considerable progress toward its immediate goal of encircling Aachen, but Corlett's much more meaningful objective of pushing all the way to the Rhine opposite Düsseldorf seemed more unfeasible by the day—a lesson the 29th Division had learned in seventy-two hours of brutal and futile combat against a rejuvenated enemy. As the eminent historian Russell Weigley later noted, "In the battle for Aachen, the final spasmodic effort of the once-overwhelming Allied onslaught of July and August clutched at a local victory, and then died."

The 29th Division's role in that local victory had admittedly been trivial—and some caustic observers might have added that it had been executed ineptly. When the 30th Division breached the West Wall near Aachen on October 2, the neighboring 29th had endeavored to distract enemy attention with piecemeal attacks. The U.S. Army's official history of the campaign went so far as to note that the 29th Division's diversion "fooled the German division commanders for several hours," but if so, those enemy generals were sufficiently astute observers of American military doctrine to easily distinguish the difference between Gerhardt's fragmentary attacks and the 30th Division's full-fledged assault. The Germans knew the truth. Nevertheless, the 29ers continued to carry out that ineffectual method of warfare for three days, costing the division and its attached units more than 500 casualties, gaining virtually no ground, and inflicting little hurt upon the enemy. If Gerhardt learned one overriding lesson from that lamentable episode, it was that his German counterparts were paying sharp heed to Hitler's directive to defend every foot of the Fatherland.

The 30th Division had ably demonstrated that given strong concentration of assault forces on a narrow front, overwhelming artillery and air support, strategic surprise, and plenty of reserves to reinforce success, the Germans' defenses could indeed be shattered. By the time Gerhardt called off his diversionary operation early on October 5, the 30th Division had broken through the West Wall about ten miles north of Aachen at Übach, pushed deep into enemy territory, and repulsed the enemy's inevitable counterattacks. The 30th Division's victory provided Corlett with a rare opportunity for a decisive breakout. When that breakout occurred, as Corlett expected it soon would, Gerhardt yearned for his 29th Division to play a major role.

On the evening of October 4, Corlett hinted that Gerhardt's wish would soon come true, advising that the 29th should avoid "getting into any brawls" and prepare to attack Geilenkirchen in conjunction with Maj. Gen. Ernest Harmon's 2nd Armored Division, which Corlett had recently thrown into the West Wall breach with orders to exploit the breakthrough. If Corlett could effectively coordinate Gerhardt's and Harmon's operations, the Germans would face a devastating one-two punch: a frontal attack on Geilenkirchen by the 29th, while the 2nd Armored moved up from the south to surround it. If the scheme worked, that sector of the front could break wide open, and the Americans could be on their way to the Rhine, just as Gerhardt had earlier bragged. The 29th Division had suffered many setbacks in the past few days, but they would be forgotten in an instant if it could seize Geilenkirchen in one bold stroke.

If the division were to participate in that imminent battle, Gerhardt needed to make some immediate changes, adjustments not only to the division's physical deployment, but also to the 29ers' attitudes. The division's contribution to the campaign had so far been limited to piecemeal attacks against inconsequential German villages, but an abrupt shift of gears, defined by a set-piece assault on a heavily fortified town like Geilenkirchen, a key West Wall redoubt, would be infinitely more challenging. Gerhardt had to rebalance his combat power, repositioning as many troops and as much artillery as possible to his right flank, where the 29th Division's lines lay within sight of Geilenkirchen's rooftops and church spires, little more than a mile away. The fundamental element of that rebalancing would force the war room staff to reorient the 29th's axis of attack from north to east, a taxing shift because the division still held responsibility for a sixteen-mile L-shaped front, the overwhelming portion of which faced north. At the village of Gillrath, within easy sight of Geilenkirchen, that line made a sharp turn ninety degrees to the south for two miles, and it was from that comparatively compact sector that the 29th Division's upcoming attack would be launched.

Unforeseen shifts of that kind were always tricky for staff officers, especially in the middle of combat, and when on the afternoon of October 4 Gerhardt announced to his astonished subordinates "to be set to go at 12:01 A.M. on October 6," those difficulties would be strikingly accentuated by the obvious need for haste. Was the ferocious and interminable combat of Normandy and Brittany about to begin again? If so, the general needed his men to know that however difficult their first four days of combat in Germany had been, the upcoming frontal assault on the West Wall could be even tougher. At a conference on October 4, Gerhardt announced:

> Our long extended front didn't jell. I have authority from the corps commander to take a crack at the Siegfried Line provided we don't get into a battle that uses too much artillery. . . . Initially we didn't put enough pressure on the big town [Geilenkirchen]; corps wants it. The 113th Cavalry takes over in its old zone. The 175th Infantry moves over [to the right]. It already has the 1st Battalion in [the line opposite Geilenkirchen]. . . . This combat is entirely different than anything we have had before. It is small unit stuff. To me it seems like a waste of time fighting through each building of a town. Instead of that, go around it and throw WP [white-phosphorus shells] on it. With these long fields of fire, it is bad news to cross them in the daytime. Do it at night. Troop leadership is the key to the whole business, and if an order doesn't allow two hours of daylight reconnaissance for platoon leaders, somebody has missed the trick. . . . Engineer means will be vital to the [assault]. Each battalion ought to have a spot to go through the wall, and it will be on a broad front. If we get to the Rhine before we fold up for the winter, we will be lucky.

The 29ers indeed got very lucky, not because they made it to the Rhine, but because at the last moment Corlett cancelled the Geilenkirchen attack. For the 29ers, there would be neither breakthrough nor breakout—at least for a while. That unexpected development was decidedly good news to the fighting men who would have withstood the worst of the offensive, but Gerhardt, Corlett, and Harmon probably would have preferred the chance to play their roles in a great victory and thereby gain laurels for themselves and their commands. Until the Allied high command cleared up the supply mess behind the front, which worsened by the day, they would not get the chance. Rumors from the Communication Zone hinted that both ammunition and gasoline were in such short supply, and the ability to transport existing stocks so limited, that Allied commanders had to reduce operations only to those considered essential.

Apparently, what the 29th Division was about to do was not considered essential. Disregarding the advice of his own corps commanders, Corlett and Collins, the First Army's commander, Gen. Courtney Hodges, elected to focus his effort entirely on the capture of Aachen, the ancient city of such symbolic importance to Hitler that he refused to yield it to his opponents, even though by October 7 the Americans had nearly encircled it. But if, as Collins contended, "Aachen had little military significance to either the Americans or Germans now that XIX Corps, as well as our VII Corps, could bypass it on the way to the Rhine," why not let the city's enemy garrison waste away while the Americans proceeded eastward to more important objectives?

Hodges's directive could not be avoided, however, which directly reflected Bradley's conviction that, because of the supply crisis, "the best we could hope for . . . would be a mid-November offensive." A somewhat disillusioned Corlett, already in Hodges's doghouse due to the XIX Corps's prolific use of its scarce artillery ammunition in the October 2 assault on the West Wall, therefore had to halt all major offensive action in his sector except for those missions directly related to the encirclement and eventual subjugation of Aachen. Corlett visited the 29th Division's command post at noon on October 6, and as noted in the war room journal, "[He] released us from our [new] mission . . . and directed that we continue our present mission of defending the corps left flank, continuing to probe toward the Siegfried Line in the right of our zone." In a phone conversation with Gerhardt a few hours later, Corlett clarified his new strategy: "I told Harmon to button up his northern push [at Geilenkirchen] and to hold where he is. I would like to have you hook up pretty closely with him there. Also do a little patrolling out toward Geilenkirchen. We don't need Geilenkirchen: we can go around it or bypass it. We have to loosen up Aachen."

For Gerhardt, it was a stunning disappointment. If Corlett was to focus his attention on Aachen, Gerhardt could do little to help that effort beyond what he had already done so unsuccessfully. No reasonable soldier could harbor any further hope that the 29th Division could sidetrack the Germans from the XIX Corps's real objective, and given the division's elongated front and lack of reserves, Gerhardt would find it no easier than before to concentrate a formidable force on a narrow front to strive for a decisive breakthrough. Even worse, with artillery ammunition in such short supply, offensive action would have to be severely curtailed, and Gerhardt's artillerymen would practically have to cease the practice of harassing fire, which they had performed so expertly in happier days.

In short, if Gerhardt sought glory for the 29th Division, he would not find it in this remote corner of Germany.

2. RED RAIDERS

There had to be something Gerhardt could do. The U.S. Army's standard practice of badgering the Germans by means of "aggressive patrolling," carried out wherever and whenever possible, would not be enough. Gerhardt yearned to teach the Germans the essential lesson that they were holding the line opposite the U.S. Army's vaunted 29th Infantry Division and therefore the Americans would always hold the initiative. But even Gerhardt had to admit that over the past several days, the enemy had effectively countered his every move and inflicted a stinging defeat upon his division. (The general, always averse to acknowledging enemy skill, would prefer to define the setback as a "disappointment.") The mounting frustrations of the first four days of October obviously still rankled Gerhardt. No matter: if Gerhardt had to reestablish American battlefield supremacy with limited resources and no backing from corps or army, he came up with the perfect way to do it.

Ordinarily, generals gauged progress on the battlefield by the pitiless ratio of ground gained versus casualties suffered. In the titanic struggles in Normandy and Brittany, the 29ers had understood that daily terrain gains, if any, were measured in yards, not in miles, and the ratio of those gains to the number of dead and wounded 29ers often yielded the shocking realization that a unit would cease to exist before its ultimate objective was attained, barring an infusion of considerable numbers of replacements.

According to Gerhardt's novel scheme, however, terrain gains—more specifically, *permanent* terrain gains—were not the point. Rather, the objective was simply to punish the enemy, physically and spiritually, and to establish the reality that as long as the 29th Infantry Division was in the line, the Germans could not let down their guard for a second.

It was a strategy of vindictiveness and retaliation, pure and simple; it would be applied as brutally as possible—as often as possible. By now, Gerhardt and every 29er had relearned basic German tactics. The enemy typically employed minimal troops to maintain a thin defensive line, held reserves behind the front, and counterattacked with those reserves as swiftly and violently as possible at any American penetration of the line. But according to Gerhardt's new theory, if he had no intention of permanently holding ground, 29th Division units could penetrate the enemy's meager front line at will, inflict as much damage as possible, and then retire to American lines before the Germans' inevitable response, leaving the enemy a calling card that the U.S. Army's Blue and Gray Division had paid a visit—and would return.

Such maneuvers, carried out with surprise and speed, were more accurately defined as "raids" rather than "attacks," and had Gerhardt ordered them in the 29th Division's first few days in the line in Germany, the Schierwaldenrath and Breberen disasters could have been avoided. But that sort of second-guessing only wasted time. To Gerhardt, the only matter of importance now was to avenge past failures by giving the Germans a lesson in the American way of warfare, 29th Division–style.

If Gerhardt's intention was not to gain ground and the enemy held the front only with scattered outposts, what more could be accomplished other than killing and capturing a handful of Germans? The point, according to the general, was for the 29th to display contempt for everything German—soldiers, buildings, forests, even farm animals—and to do it in such a ruthless way that the Germans, on their own soil, would get a taste of the brutality they had inflicted on the rest of Europe over the past five years. The general provided a simple set of instructions for his new stratagem: "Massacre every Kraut in the place and level it!" Had the division still been fighting in Normandy, Brittany, or even nearby Holland, such a ploy would hardly have been feasible, for the impact on the local French or Dutch citizenry, all supposedly friends of America, would have been immeasurably harsh. But this was Germany—Hitler's Nazi Germany— and Gerhardt held not the slightest remorse about "massacres" and wanton destruction.

Currently, the German town of highest significance to Gerhardt was Schierwaldenrath, the nondescript farming village where the 115th Infantry's Company K had recently been annihilated. U.S. Army air photographs revealed that Schierwaldenrath contained forty-two buildings, and the general hoped that when the 29th Division entered the town, forty-one of them would be gone—every single edifice except the village church. That accomplishment would surely teach the Germans a lesson.

On October 5, Gerhardt selected one of his favorite commanders, Lt. Col. Glover Johns of the 115th Infantry's 1st Battalion, whom he knew had the skill and drive to carry out the task with all its associated brutality. As the 29th Division's most senior infantry battalion commander, Johns grasped his commanding general's psyche well enough to know exactly what Gerhardt wanted him to do. If he were to level Schierwaldenrath, Johns recalled, "I requested the works in supporting fires: an air strike, a company of tanks, two platoons of tank destroyers, and a company of 4.2-inch mortars, and a twenty-minute artillery preparation on the objective." Perhaps Johns did not know the general as well as he thought he did, for those kinds of requests for help irked Gerhardt. "A properly trained battalion can do any damn thing in the world," the general had once proclaimed. "The leader has got to have some skill, some imagination, some knowledge. With these things, there are no limits to its success." When on the evening of October 5 Gerhardt read in the war room journal of Johns's lengthy request for support, he noted caustically, "What do they get? [Only] engineers for demolitions!"

Johns reflected upon the impending task and drew an ominous conclusion, noting what the unfortunate Captain Schmitt of Company K had already observed a few days in the past: "The terrain in front of Kreuzrath is flat and bare, offering no cover whatsoever between the villages and the objective." Tactical predicaments of that kind could be addressed given time and a trained staff. Schmitt had had neither, but Johns had both—one full day, in fact, to prepare for the challenge, set for the morning of October 7. Counting Johns, the battalion staff employed nine men to design the scheme, all experienced soldiers familiar with tactical planning. These included Johns's executive officer, Maj. Malcolm Weller, as well as his S-3 (operations) officer and an assistant; an S-2 (intelligence) officer; an artillery liaison officer from the 110th Field Artillery Battalion; and three senior noncommissioned officers, including the battalion sergeant major.

"[On October 6] company commanders were acquainted with the out-line of the plan and sent to reconnoiter the area in front of the village of Kreuzrath and the town of Birgden," Johns wrote. "Observation from the church tower in Birgden afforded a perfect view of the entire area over which the engagement would be fought, excepting [Schierwaldenrath] itself." Johns even managed to adhere to some of the inviolable princi-ples of the staff officers' bible, *Field Manual 101-5: Staff and Combat Orders.* Johns wrote: "The plan was carefully considered from all angles by the entire staff, and when no further suggestions could be made, the company commanders were called in for the issuance of the formal order. . . . This was an excellent example of the rare opportunity for a battalion CO to issue a full five-paragraph field order." Every U.S. Army officer had learned how to write such an order, the paragraphs of which were to cover information, mission, execution, administration, and command. Of these, the most crucial was the second, mission, "which consists of a statement of *what, when, how,* and *where* the force as a whole is to oper-ate." War by the book, however, had not helped much in the past. Would it work this time?

The benefit of time also yielded ample intelligence on the Germans, gained in part from aerial photos and nighttime patrols undertaken on October 5, which pinpointed enemy resistance nests by provoking their fire. By the time Johns was ready to initiate the raid, he possessed a much greater sense of the Germans' capabilities than had Schmitt. Not many 29ers had returned to American lines after Schmitt's attack, but Johns had the good fortune of coming across one in Birgden, 1st Lt. James Kolson, a machine-gun platoon leader from Company M, whose "information con-cerning the nature of the buildings and the general layout of the town was invaluable," according to Johns. Furthermore, "[Kolson's] detailed account of the enemy counterattack also provided extremely useful details that could be woven into the plan of attack, defense, and withdrawal."

The key word was "withdrawal." Whereas the unfortunate Schmitt had held orders to seize and hold Schierwaldenrath and had been denied permission to leave when matters deteriorated, Johns expected to get into and out of the village within five hours, an interval considered sufficient for the engineers to complete their demolitions. With approximately 300 men—three times as many as Schmitt had—Johns's 1st Battalion would commence its move across the deadly open ground between Kreuzrath and Schierwaldenrath at 4 A.M., about an hour before first light. In contrast,

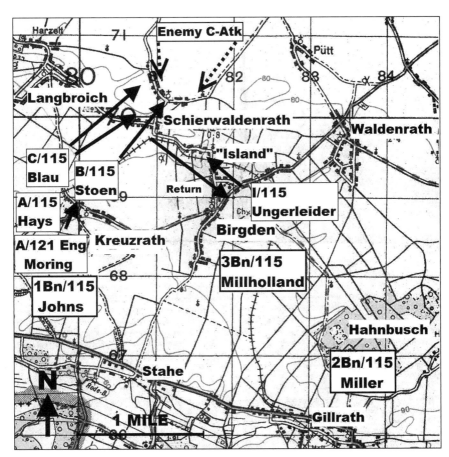

Raid on Schierwaldenrath, 1st Battalion, 115th Infantry, October 7, 1944.

Schmitt had been given no choice but to begin his move an hour before sunset, providing the enemy an opportunity to organize a counterattack during the night. Johns's men would just be settling into their defensive perimeter around Schierwaldenrath when the sun rose, and if they were lucky and the typical ground fog burned off quickly, they would be able to observe the enemy's preparations for its usual counterattack.

A preliminary artillery barrage might warn the enemy something was afoot, so Johns decided to skip it. Orders specified that the 1st Battalion, currently in reserve in Gillrath, would move out for the front a few minutes after midnight on October 7, allowing four hours for the 2.5 mile journey to the jump-off point at Kreuzrath. Right on time at 4 A.M., Company C, led by 1st Lt. Joseph Blau, and Company B, commanded by Johns's favorite, 1st Lt. Julian Stoen, advanced into the foreboding fields toward Schierwaldenrath. "Every man knew what he was going into and what his specific job was to be," Johns wrote. "He knew what to expect and what to do about it. Bazooka teams and antitank grenadiers were groomed for the role they would doubtless play, and their positions picked in advance on the map. Each was given a specific mission and told to carry it out at all costs."

Company A, under Capt. Mack Hays, would follow in the wake of the first two companies, and sappers from Company A, 121st Engineers, commanded by Capt. Leland Moring, would bring up the rear. This was no ordinary attack. Platoon leaders designated several burly riflemen to carry heavy coils of barbed wire so that a hasty defensive perimeter could be set up around the village. Every soldier, from captains to privates, stuffed their pockets with extra grenades, including many of the thermite variety, which burned upon detonation for several seconds at exceptionally high temperatures and would be useful in setting houses afire. Bayonets, which most infantrymen had never before used in battle, were to be affixed to rifles. Above all, the men held strict orders not to use any firearms until the Germans opened fire. The point of Johns's mission was to obliterate Schierwaldenrath, and that work would be carried out by the engineers, each of whom would carry two satchel charges, both filled with twenty pounds of C2 plastic explosive. Moring's men were experts at demolitions, and they intended to apply that skill to every house in Schierwaldenrath by placing four C2 satchel charges in each edifice, one in each corner.

The plan could fall apart in a second if German pickets, who reportedly occupied a windmill in no-man's-land about 1,000 yards in front of the American lines, detected the Americans' assault and opened fire, thereby rousing Schierwaldenrath's garrison. Fortunately for Johns, however, the windmill was either unoccupied or its occupants were not alert. "Minute after minute ticked slowly away," Johns recalled. "When and from what sector would the firing start? Why didn't the outpost in the windmill open up? Will the [attackers] bump into a patrol? Are Jerry's listening posts asleep? What the hell?"

It took the Germans almost thirty minutes to realize their opponents were up to something big. By that time, Johns's men were already in Schierwaldenrath carrying out the tasks they had reviewed in their heads a dozen times. The 29ers carefully followed Johns's instructions to avoid Schierwaldenrath's main street, every foot of which was covered, according to intelligence reports, by a deadly German 20-millimeter antiaircraft gun sited near the church. Instead, as Johns noted, they "advanced across the back yards and orchards." Johns's plan was working almost perfectly, and the village's defenders, clearly caught by surprise by the rapidity of the Americans' assault, were quickly overwhelmed. That evening, reporter Lou Azrael wrote:

> The Germans never really got going. Many of them, who had apparently been sleeping in the basements of houses, did not come out into the open. . . . Sergeant Alton Shaff [one of the 29th Division's most decorated soldiers, a forty-year-old who had been Company A's first sergeant since 1927] of Frederick, Maryland, led a squad which wiped out two groups of Germans who refused to surrender. Lieutenant Joseph Blau of New York City flung a hand grenade into a basement where twenty Germans were concealed. All were killed or wounded. In another basement he destroyed a German battalion command post, killing a major and taking a lieutenant prisoner.

From his battalion headquarters in Kreuzrath, darkness prevented Johns from observing the fighting, but the sounds of battle were a different matter. Those sounds proved conclusively that the 29ers were doing well. "It was the right kind of fire," Johns noted. "The deep thump of an M-1 pointing away from the listener, and the *chunk-chunk-chunk* of our BAR. Very few Jerry shots, and finally only one or two sharp bursts from his machine guns. Then a fire started on the left front [in Company C's sector]. Another in the center. A thermite grenade could be seen burning fiercely inside a building: you could see it shining out a window, but it burned out without catching the building."

One member of Company A, Cpl. James Burkert, noted something odd about Schierwaldenrath's houses: "Most of the windows were out, and any glass in the place was broken. All the houses smelled the same. Evidently, [German] women must have bought perfume by the gallon. Perfume bottles would get broken from the explosions, and every house smelled to high heaven. It would actually soak into your clothes. You could taste it until you went out of the house."

One indicator of success was the steady flow into American lines of German prisoners, ninety-nine of whom were brought in by the end of the raid, many half-dressed. One member of Company C, Pvt. Anthony Gass, was returning to Kreuzrath after suffering a wound when he stumbled into twenty-two terrified Germans in a trench, all of whom meekly complied with his harsh command to accompany him back to American lines. Those Germans who gave themselves up were the lucky ones. Some enemy troops hiding out in Schierwaldenrath cellars who braved a few American grenades and resisted subsequent calls for surrender ended up buried alive when Moring's engineers remorselessly blew up the buildings in which the Germans had taken refuge.

That series of nearly continuous explosions began shortly after first light, when, as Johns observed from nearby Kreuzrath, "Huge mushrooms of flame, smoke, and debris began to blossom all over town, calling cards from the 115th Infantry courtesy of Company A, 121st Engineers." If the engineers were truly to level Schierwaldenrath, as Gerhardt had directed, every building in town save the church would have been destroyed, but Moring's men were forced to depart after having blown up only about 80 percent of the town. The unfortunate town of Schierwaldenrath was therefore not, according to strict definition, "leveled." However, if it was any solace to Gerhardt, the 115th Infantry's new commander, Col. Edward McDaniel, reported to the war room that morning: "No single house was left intact."

So far so good, but Johns needed no reminder that several times in the recent past, American soldiers had found it easy to get into German villages, but infinitely harder to get out. Schierwaldenrath would be different, Johns reasoned, because the 1st Battalion would enter and exit so quickly that the enemy's counterattack would plow into the village only to find the elusive Americans gone. But at about 7:30 A.M., the nature of the battle changed profoundly when the Germans sent up two red flares north of town. The Americans correctly assumed they were signals for the enemy's expected counterattack. There might still be time for the GIs to withdraw before that happened, but a snag arose when Johns received a call from the 115th's command post, ordering the 1st Battalion to postpone its withdrawal so that several 747th Tank Battalion tankers could come forward to recover two M5 Stuart tanks they had abandoned in Schierwaldenrath on October 4. Such an order represented a major, and nonsensical, change of plan. In the midst of battle, however, how many orders emanating from a command post far behind the front ever made sense?

What happened next proved why the Germans were such formidable opponents. Even veteran 29ers who fully understood their tactical proficiency had to admit that the speed of the Germans' reaction to the Schierwaldenrath raid and the intensity of their ensuing counterattack were amazing. Amid an intense artillery and mortar barrage, the enemy came swarming toward Schierwaldenrath with hordes of infantry and, according to Johns, more than a dozen tanks, some of which the 29ers swore were the type of German panzer they feared most: the Mark VI Tiger, a sixty-ton behemoth armed with a dreaded 88-millimeter main gun. (The presence of Tigers in Schierwaldenrath has never been substantiated. Throughout World War II, 29ers commonly referred to any large German tank as a "Tiger" even though such tanks were extraordinarily rare. One veteran tanker in the 2nd Armored Division who regularly fought alongside the 29th Division observed, "Tiger tanks were very common in the newspapers. I saw two.") The enemy tanks on Johns's front were most likely Mark V Panthers, from the same outfit that had successfully attacked the 175th Infantry in Breberen on the night of October 4. However, a German Army organization equipped with Tigers, *schwere Panzer Abteilung 506* (506th Heavy Tank Battalion), was indeed operating near Aachen at the time, and a few of its tanks could conceivably have been detached to Schierwaldenrath.

Carrying out a successful withdrawal while engaged in close-range combat was among the trickiest of military maneuvers. The security of all depended on carefully coordinated movements controlled by an overall commander who remained in close touch with the situation every minute, but those movements could swiftly turn chaotic if the enemy pressed home a vigorous assault, triggering inevitable pandemonium as key officers and NCOs became casualties, telephone wires were cut, crucial messages went undelivered, escape routes were cut off, and panicked soldiers abandoned positions without orders, leaving others in the lurch. Indeed, for a few nerve-wracking minutes, it seemed to Johns as if all those adverse events might come true. Apparently, the enemy stood on the verge of inflicting upon his battalion the same terrible setback that had befallen Schmitt's Company K.

The barbed wire the GIs had hastily deployed on the northern periphery of Schierwaldenrath did nothing to impede German tanks. The only weapons that could stop them were bazookas and rifle grenades, both of which required an operator with a steely nerve since their effectiveness depended on opening fire in close proximity to the enemy. Even then, the chance of penetrating the thick frontal armor of heavy German tanks was minimal. Nevertheless, several plucky 29ers tried. As related by Johns, "A grenadier in Company C [supposedly Sgt. Elmer Michaelis] disabled one [tank] by standing up straight behind a hedge and firing his last grenade into one of the huge tracks at seventy-five yards, after seeing two previous shots explode on the turret without stopping it. . . . Another bazooka man had not been so fortunate. He stood up to slug it out with a tank, got three hits on it, but was permanently KO'd by a white phosphorus shell."

Now was as good a time as any to kick off the carefully planned withdrawal, which could only begin when Johns himself transmitted by radio the prearranged code phrase "Maneuver Q." However, instead of receiving that signal, incredulous officers and senior NCOs learned from Johns that regiment had ordered that they would have to hang on for a little longer while 747th Tank Battalion crews recovered the disabled Stuart tanks. According to a U.S. Army historical officer who interviewed witnesses a few days later, a Company B NCO replied, "But, sir, [we] can't. There are six Tiger tanks out there shooting like hell!" Johns replied: "God damn it, that's an order! Hold 'em!"

The unequal fight between lightly armed 29ers and heavy German tanks continued for a short while, but Lieutenant Blau, Company C's commander, radioed Johns and bluntly articulated the urgency of the situation. "Sir, this is Charlie 6 [Blau's radio call name]. No more officers in Baker Company; all my officers have been hit, and so have I. I'm sorry, sir, but we've done about all we can. We've got to execute 'Maneuver Q.'" The historical officer's report noted Johns's reply: "OK. Pull out, according to plan; and don't leave any prisoners or casualties behind."

Although Johns confessed that the withdrawal was "somewhat disorganized"—which was confirmed by company clerks when they prepared their morning reports after the raid and discovered sixteen missing 29ers—the American exit from Schierwaldenrath was a cleverly executed maneuver that signified a rare accomplishment for the 29th Division in World War II: it completely fooled the enemy. Had the Germans understood their opponents' true intent from the start, they probably would not have attempted to smash into Schierwaldenrath with a frontal assault and would have adopted the far more sensible strategy of cutting off the Americans' line of retreat. When the Germans finally grasped the Americans' purpose, it was too late to do anything about it, and even then they misjudged their opponents' course of action because they expected Johns's men to retreat to Kreuzrath, whence they had come. Instead, Maneuver Q's object was to withdraw not back to Kreuzrath, but to the nearby village of Birgden, just two thirds of a mile to the southeast of Schierwaldenrath.

The moment Johns initiated Maneuver Q, he shifted his 1st Battalion command post by jeep from Kreuzrath to Birgden, and when he arrived, he did not have to wait long for the first groups of his battalion to arrive, all of which had just pulled out of Schierwaldenrath in a direction the Germans did not expect. The engineers came in first, overflowing with amazing stories of blowing enemy troops in the upper floors of houses into the air upon the detonation of their C2 explosives. (An engineer officer, 1st Lt. John Huff of Virginia, would later be awarded his second Silver Star since D-Day for "coolly organizing parties for the evacuation of the wounded . . . under intense enemy mortar, machine gun, and sniper fire.") Companies B and C trudged in next, not nearly as enthusiastic as the engineers, their disheveled riflemen fresh from toe-to-toe battles with German tanks. The rearguard, Company A, arrived last, having held back the enemy surge long enough for everyone else to evacuate the town. Its commander, Captain Hays, gained the Silver Star for "remaining in the town until all his casualties had been moved from the area and all prisoners had been evacuated. Only after the prearranged withdrawal had been executed did Captain Hays leave the town."

The Americans never could have fooled the Germans so well at Schierwaldenrath if the 115th's 3rd Battalion, currently holding Birgden under the command of Lt. Col. Randolph Millholland, had simultaneously fulfilled a vital mission. A cluster of farmhouses, nicknamed the "Island" by the 29ers and supposedly occupied by the enemy, lay halfway between Birgden and Schierwaldenrath. If Johns's men attempted to retreat to Birgden through the Island and Germans occupied its buildings, the 29ers would be massacred. Millholland assigned the unenviable task of clearing the Island to Company I, under the command of 1st Lt. Alvin Ungerleider. It promised to be murderous work, but when Company I jumped off at 4:05 A.M., just minutes after Johns's raid began, its astonished members crept up to the farm buildings in the pre-dawn darkness and discovered that the Germans were nowhere in sight. The worst Company I had to endure while occupying the Island was a comparatively modest enemy artillery barrage at about 5:30 A.M. When the barrage subsided, Millholland ordered up several litter bearers in case of an influx of wounded 29ers from Johns's outfit in Schierwaldenrath. It was a wise precaution. In a few hours, those litter bearers would be the busiest men in the 115th Infantry.

McDaniel had instructed Johns to search for information in Schierwaldenrath related to Company K's recent demise, by means of either physical evidence or interrogation of enemy prisoners. As McDaniel later related to Gerhardt, "There were none of our [Company K] dead in the streets. . . . Just a rumor by a [German] prisoner to the effect that he had heard that some [American] officers and about sixty enlisted men had been evacuated [as prisoners] through [German lines]." Gerhardt concluded: "That sounds likely."

As the 1st Battalion retreated into Birgden, the curious Johns inquired of his men's experience. "'A little rough, but OK,' was the inevitable reply, usually accompanied by a wry grin and a remark about how Jerry would remember this day," Johns wrote. As he later observed in his official report on Schierwaldenrath, "Jerry slipped—and we caught him. . . . In fact, he was so confused that he called for [artillery barrages] in the wrong places, and they fell harmlessly behind and to the right of [our troops]."

The Americans would remember that day, too—not only because they had avenged the loss of Schmitt's Company K and had given the Germans a good drubbing, but also because they had paid a high price to do it. In addition to the sixteen missing 29ers, some of whom turned up over the next few days, five men of Johns's battalion had died and forty-eight had been wounded, including six officers, among them Blau and Stoen. Additionally, one engineer had been killed, one wounded, and three missing. (The wounded engineer Sgt. Donald Young, from Ohio, would later gain a

Silver Star for "refusing to leave his men until after the successful completion of the mission.") As about 325 29ers had gone into Schierwaldenrath on the morning of October 7, those casualties—all suffered in a period of little more than four hours—nearly amounted to a 25 percent loss rate. Casualty figures that high could swiftly cripple a unit and send its morale plummeting, although Johns observed his losses "were not more than could be expected in such an action." He lamented, "Had the battalion withdrawn thirty minutes sooner, it would have accomplished [success] with negligible loss." As for the tanks for which Johns had delayed his withdrawal, they were never recovered.

Johns had settled an old score with the hated enemy, and his men had established beyond doubt that they were skilled soldiers. "This operation proved conclusively the value of a raid in battalion strength," Johns wrote. "It completely destroyed the equivalent of a full company of the enemy. . . . Thorough planning, detailed reconnaissance, well-trained, well-led, and above all aggressive troops can assure a successful assault on dug-in enemy troops. . . . Surprise is, as always, the biggest supporting weapon an attacking force can have." But Johns also had to confess that the vigilant enemy had ultimately snatched the initiative from the Americans just hours after he had initiated the raid. Johns was loath to admit it, but in an October 10 report to Gerhardt, he concluded, "Four hours is the absolute maximum that a small force can expect to hold a large area against an aggressive enemy."

The outcome of Johns's raid pleased Gerhardt. "Now there's something that worked out swell," the general declared. "This is what can be done when we do this thing right." Surprisingly, however, the tenor of Johns's October 10 report exasperated Gerhardt, who did not think 29ers should credit the enemy with an aptitude for "aggressive" behavior. The general promptly telephoned McDaniel and exclaimed, "Johns needs a rest because he is losing his perspective. . . . Who have you got to take over that outfit if he went away for a while?" Caught by surprise, McDaniel replied, "I'd have to think it over." (Ultimately, Johns was not relieved.)

In keeping with the general's philosophy that successful U.S. Army units could always be defined by superlative morale, Gerhardt affirmed that the Schierwaldenrath raid was particularly satisfying because it restored the 29th Division's spirit, which had taken a beating in its first week in the line in Germany. Johns capitalized on his accomplishment and tried to regain a little favor from his boss by assigning his outfit a new nickname, one befitting its radio call-sign in the 115th Infantry's signal network as the "Red" battalion.

No longer would the 1st Battalion, 115th Infantry, be known as "The Clay Pigeons of St. Lô." It was now "The Red Raiders."

3. ARE YOU WITH ME?

Leveling entire enemy villages was just one method of notifying Nazi Germany that its calamitous fate in World War II was sealed. Even as Johns's "Red Raiders" were flattening Schierwaldenrath, the 175th Infantry's Company A was employing an entirely different method of harassment. That scheme took shape on the morning of October 6 when the 175th's commander, Col. William Purnell, mulled over ideas concerning Gerhardt's directive to "go into one of these towns and just take the whole thing apart." The problem was that no suitable German-held towns existed on the 175th's front that Purnell could "take apart."

With the exception of the 3rd Battalion's unfortunate foray into Breberen on October 4—a period when Gerhardt still desired to occupy German villages, not destroy them—Purnell's 175th Infantry had fortunately avoided enemy "enthusiasm" in its first week in the line. As of the morning of October 6, the battered 3rd Battalion rested behind the front while the 1st and 2nd Battalions held the far-right of the 29th Division's line, facing east directly toward the key city of Geilenkirchen, a little over one mile distant and still held resolutely by the enemy. The front was comparatively quiet for the moment, and both battalions had settled into mucky trenches and dugouts and so far had not seen much fighting. On October 6, however, when Gerhardt pronounced his new raiding strategy, their luck was about to change. As the 175th's monthly report for October 1944 noted: "Activity was [now] confined to strong raids on enemy positions with the purpose of capturing prisoners, harassing the enemy, and improving our defensive positions."

That those positions needed much improvement was obvious. Even a military novice could perceive from a single glance at the 29th Division's war room map that Purnell's 1st Battalion, commanded by Maj. Miles Shorey, was in a fix, occupying an awkward position northwest of Geilenkirchen that the wily Germans were sure to exploit. Shorey's battalion had just occupied the village of Hatterath, seized by Johns's 1st Battalion, 115th Infantry, on October 2. The enemy occupied strong defenses

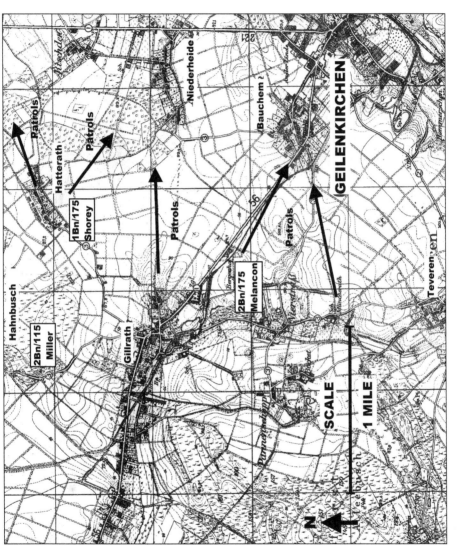

175th Infantry Patrols, October 6–9, 1944.

in a semicircle around Hatterath, some of which were situated in thick woods within range of a rifle shot. "This woods had been a source of trouble for our troops for several days," reporter Lou Azrael wrote. "The Germans had fortifications there from which they were pouring mortar fire and sniping constantly." If the enemy managed to mass sufficient troops in the woods, unobserved by the 29ers, they could snatch Hatterath from their opponents anytime they wanted.

To block that unfortunate scenario, Purnell's operations officer, Capt. Henry Reed, radioed the war room at 9:13 A.M. on October 6, calling for an air strike on the woods with "some oil bombs put on it to burn the thing out." (Reed was apparently referring to U.S. Army Air Force jellied gasoline bombs, an incendiary explosive later known as "napalm.") Purnell did not have much faith in that method. That afternoon, he telephoned the war room and declared, "We are going in at 2300 with Company A [commanded by 1st Lt. Michael Dunn of Ellwood City, Pennsylvania] to clear out those woods. . . . What we want to do is burn the woods down." An enthusiastic Gerhardt replied: "That's the stuff!"

As related by the 175th's action report of the affair, "The plan was to set the enemy-held woods afire and thus clear out fields of observation. . . . [Company A members] carried white phosphorus grenades and improvised gasoline bombs. The gasoline bomb consisted of a five-gallon can of gasoline and crude oil. Around the can were three turns of a primer cord [a flexible cord filled with a small amount of explosives] and a twenty-second fuse, with a fuse igniter."

Unlike Johns, who moved into Schierwaldenrath without a preparatory artillery barrage, Shorey called upon the 175th's direct support 105-millimeter howitzer unit, the 224th Field Artillery Battalion, to soften up the Germans' defenses in the woods and force the occupants to keep their heads down. As Azrael reported, it worked: "Before the Germans got out of shelters into which the artillery barrage had driven them, the infantrymen were upon them with rifle fire, and the woods were blazing . . . [and] burning many [Germans] to death." Back at the 175th's command post, Reed noted in a 1:25 A.M. message to the war room on October 7: "The woods are burning beautifully."

Not quite. Azrael, who did not participate in the raid, would have been more faithful to the facts had he stated that the raid literally fizzled out. Just thirty minutes after Reed's buoyant message, Purnell observed more soberly, "We exploded the gas cans, they went off beautifully: but the woods were too wet to burn." Those contradictory messages, one coming immediately after the other in the war room journal, angered the exacting Gerhardt, who expressed his annoyance by penning a bold question mark next to the transcript of each message when he sat down that night for his habitual reading of the journal. On the positive side, Company A managed to get in and out of the woods with only a single man wounded, Pvt. Cicero Phillips, while snatching twelve German prisoners who promptly provided valuable intelligence on the enemy's Geilenkirchen defenses. Those results pleased the general enough to cause him to blurt to Purnell: "Good going!"

Purnell could have saved his men a great deal of work, however, had he thought of asking the locals their opinion of setting the Hatterath woods on fire. Given the steady October rains in this corner of the world, local residents would have scoffed at the strange ideas of their would-be conquerors. The Americans would soon learn that during the rainy season, the devil himself could not ignite those woods with the fires of hell.

The 29ers were just beginning to perceive that the division's arrival in Germany had triggered a fundamental change in the way the division carried out its business. During the 29th's extended training periods in the States and England, the men had focused primarily on tactical exercises in daylight for the logical reason that the U.S. Army's legendary firepower could be applied effectively against the enemy only if artillery forward observers or fighter-bomber pilots could actually see their targets. Such methods were invariably practiced during the Normandy and Brittany campaigns, during which the 29th Division carried out most of it offensive activities when the sun was up. At dusk, Gerhardt would usually bring operations to a predictable conclusion with his standard directive to regimental commanders: "Shut down for the night." The Germans, in contrast, had learned by necessity to undertake important military operations in darkness, thereby avoiding their opponents' firepower. They practiced nighttime maneuvers expertly, as the jittery 29ers could attest.

Ordinarily, the Germans held the initiative at night. But in their first week in the line in Germany in October 1944, the 29ers strove to rectify that lamentable state of affairs by taking a crash course in night fighting. To be sure, the 29ers regularly conducted nocturnal patrols and even occasionally undertook nighttime attacks, most notably the 116th Infantry's highly successful September 5 assault that had captured the German bastion at La Trinité, just west of Brest, during the recent fighting in Brittany.

That type of assault was rare—and usually unsuccessful. That the 29ers would swiftly have to learn to conduct it more routinely, and with greater proficiency, was obvious to all, for on the flat and featureless German landscape near Geilenkirchen, any American infantry or armor unit the enemy could perceive in daylight would promptly be decimated by machine guns, mortars, and deadly 88s. Even worse, the 29th Division's secondary mission in XIX Corps's Aachen offensive suggested that tactical air support in the foreseeable future would be minimal and artillery ammunition would be severely restricted. In short, lacking its standard firepower, the 29th Division's chances of overcoming the tenacious Germans on their home turf would be no better than the Yankees' chances of winning the pennant without DiMaggio.

In October's opening week, the 29ers had so far performed night operations adequately, some might even say skillfully, save for the debacles at Schierwaldenrath and Breberen, but those veteran warriors who had fought the enemy since D-Day knew that the German troops defending Aachen, although still formidable fighting men, were hardly the equals of the elite paratroopers who had made the 29ers' lives hell at St. Lô and Brest. The 29ers needed time to sharpen their skills and get a feel for enemy intentions and capabilities, as the 175th's initial patrols west of Geilenkirchen revealed. One Company E group, which Purnell referred to as a "combat patrol" because it consisted of a thirty-man platoon rather than just a handful of men, silently slipped out of its frontline trench after dark on October 7 with the object of blowing up a large German pillbox near Bauchem, an important hinge of the West Wall. As a 175th staff officer reported to the war room: "[The platoon's] leading squad was fired on by two machine guns from each flank and was pinned down. The platoon leader attempted to flank to the left with his two remaining squads. Owing to the [German] flares and being pinned down by machine gun fire, the platoon was disorganized and withdrew to the west with no casualties." The German pillbox remained intact; the 29ers would save the unused satchel charges for another time.

Simultaneously, a 1st Battalion patrol tried to sneak after sunset into the same Hatterath woods that Company A had failed to ignite the previous evening. According to the 175th's report, "[The patrol] reached the edge of the woods, was fired on, had one casualty, pulled back and tried to flank it from the north side, and was fired on by about ten riflemen. It had a lot of difficulty trying to keep control on account of the fog."

The 29ers were finding out that the key to nighttime operations was indeed "keeping control" while remaining silent. If soldiers could barely see their leader or even the men directly ahead of them in column and could not speak above a whisper, how could they reach their objective in the patches of thick woods near Geilenkirchen? One 29er recalled the chilly October nights in Germany:

> Darkness was absolute in the forests. A Company G [115th Infantry] patrol hacked off a length of telephone wire and passed it along to each man in the patrol so that every man might have contact with others in the group, even though the pitch darkness made it impossible for any man to see his neighbor. Another device to aid patrols in returning to their point of departure without wandering aimlessly in the woods for several hours was the firing of a clip of tracer ammo from a BAR straight into the air from the site of a company or platoon CP.

If the GIs could see the tracers, however, so could the Germans, and if the 29ers did not shift that CP to a new location soon, the enemy was sure to hit it with an uncannily accurate mortar barrage. Moreover, if the Germans fired their standard red flares over a 29th Division patrol and pinpointed it in open ground, a single well-placed enemy machine gun could inflict heavy casualties in seconds.

On the morning of October 9, Gerhardt issued an edict that must have triggered astonishment and joy in those who heard of it. For a unit that held only a secondary role in the Aachen offensive, the 29th Division had been suffering an inordinate number of casualties—so many, in fact, that Gerhardt realized with alarm that his already depleted rifle companies could shrink to the size of platoons if replacements did not rejuvenate them soon. Unhappily, the general learned that the XIX Corps's replacements would flow mostly into the 2nd Armored and 30th Infantry Divisions, which had been shouldering the burden of the Aachen fight for more than a week. "I'm going to stress this casualty business because replacements are running low," Gerhardt announced to his regimental commanders. "I'm going to make it disagreeable for a while for all concerned: we are not going to lose any more men or any crew weapons." Later, at a staff meeting, the general emphasized his point: "You commanders are going to have to answer to me in the future to justify your casualties!" Incredulous listeners must have wondered if the general had turned a new leaf. No matter: for once, Gerhardt had issued a directive his field-grade officers would have no trouble adhering to—and all 29ers would agree was long overdue.

A total avoidance of casualties was impossible as long as the 29th Division occupied a frontline position within close range of the Germans, especially when, somewhat inconsistently, Gerhardt still insisted on "aggressive patrolling" at all times. At least there would be no debacles in the near future like Schierwaldenrath and Breberen if the general held to his word.

He did. Starting on October 10, the day the 29th Division began adhering to Gerhardt's new philosophy, the 115th and 175th Infantry Regiments suffered a total of 369 casualties in the remaining twenty-two days of October, including forty-one killed in action. One could hardly consider that figure "light," but compared to what had transpired before, it was. At least half a dozen times in Normandy and Brittany, the 29th had lost far more than 369 men in a single day. Indeed, the division's casualty count for October 4 and 5, 1944, the two tragic days of Schierwaldenrath and Breberen, during which the 29th had conducted a "diversion," had exceeded that figure.

Had Gerhardt eliminated the adjective "aggressive" from his patrolling requirement, those casualties would have been fewer, but he had almost never ordered anything so far in World War II that was not overtly aggressive. On the 175th's front near Geilenkirchen, the prerequisite for aggression indicated that Purnell's 29ers had not only to pinpoint enemy positions, but also destroy them. That was an impossibly tough requirement, as S/Sgt. Malo Flaten and S/Sgt. Glenn Zanto of Company E learned on one nighttime patrol. German grenades wounded both Flaten and Zanto as they slipped under strands of barbed wire, but they pressed on toward a pillbox that was illuminated by the Germans' own flares. They got to within grenade range, but the enemy's resistance was so fierce that they could go no farther and eventually had to pull back. "I guess it was the German final protective line that held us up," Flaten remarked a few days later. "But we had gone in, stirred 'em around, done plenty of shooting. We didn't complete the mission, but the regimental commander [Purnell] said, in a way, we'd done the job since we had discovered the enemy's main line of defense, detected the kind of weapons he is employing, and a thing or two about his trench system."

Early on October 9, one of Purnell's patrols employed aggressiveness to good effect and destroyed one of the Germans' menacing West Wall bunkers near Bauchem. Several of those impressive concrete structures were clustered on the fringe of the village, linked by an elaborate trench system, and if Gerhardt must someday take Geilenkirchen, the 29ers would have to learn how to destroy them. The bunkers' walls, at least five feet thick, appeared virtually indestructible, but the 29ers carried sufficient explosives to reduce at least one to a pile of rubble, a performance that a proud Purnell described to Gerhardt as "a good show."

That afternoon, Purnell learned his boss's sudden desire to avoid casualties was entirely genuine. "I have been thinking about sending two 2-man groups into Bauchem to stay for the night and get us some info on mortar positions and for possible future info for an attack on that town," Purnell told Gerhardt. "I hate to risk them and was wondering [if I should]?" The general responded, "I don't think it's worth it to risk them," to which an astonished and secretly delighted Purnell promptly replied, "All right, sir," before Gerhardt changed his mind.

On October 13, a member of the 175th Infantry's 3rd Battalion Headquarters Company, T/Sgt. Joseph Farinholt, gained his third Silver Star for valor, a remarkable accomplishment that no 29er—and few members of the entire U.S. Army for that matter—had achieved in World War II. With the simple declaration, "C'mon guys, we've got a job to do," Farinholt led a small group of 29ers into a field in the midst of a fierce German artillery barrage to rescue several seriously wounded members of Company L who had been caught bunched in the open. According to his Silver Star citation, "Farinholt administered first-aid treatment and personally evacuated four casualties to a place of safety." Although only twenty-two years old, Farinholt, nicknamed "Lightning Joe" because of his boxing prowess, had six years of military experience, having joined the Maryland National Guard at Baltimore's Fifth Regiment Armory in

T/Sgt. Joe Farinholt of the 175th Infantry. "Lightning Joe" would gain four Silver Stars in less than five months.

1938 at age fifteen. The unit in which Farinholt enlisted, Company B, 5th Maryland Infantry, was then commanded by Capt. William Purnell. In late November 1944, Farinholt would take his achievement one step farther by gaining a fourth Silver Star.

While Purnell's 175th Infantry was prodding unremittingly against the West Wall defenses of Geilenkirchen, the new commander of the 115th Infantry, Col. Edward McDaniel, held orders from Gerhardt to probe northward over the familiar and deadly ground around Schierwaldenrath and Birgden. The 29ers must have wondered what the point was. Infantrymen already knew that ground intimately and had a good sense of the Germans' scheme of defense. Most important, Corlett had heard enough reports of failure already and had no intention of wasting more men. Nevertheless, as the 29th Division's former chief of staff, McDaniel knew Gerhardt's mercurial ways and took it for granted that the 115th could not sit still as long as it was in the line.

The exhausted members of one of McDaniel's outfits, Lt. Col. Tony Miller's 2nd Battalion, must have felt as if they were the 29th Infantry Division's forgotten men. Miller, who had carried out surrender negotiations with the German commander of Fortress Brest just three weeks before, had moved his battalion into the Hahnbusch woods on the afternoon of October 2, and it remained there for almost three weeks, eventually transforming that forest into a warren of trenches and dugouts worthy of the Great War. Meanwhile, Gerhardt had rotated so many other infantry battalions in and out of the front on either side of Miller that he found it difficult to keep his neighbors straight. It was not an easy assignment. The Germans were close—at some points just a few hundred yards away—and in those stagnant conditions, the antagonists had ample opportunities to give each other fits by means of raids, barrages, and sniping. Indeed, in fourteen of the battalion's nineteen straight days in the line, at least one of its members was killed or went missing in action. The total number of its casualties throughout that period was a staggering 121, not counting many men who had succumbed to a malady new to the 29th Division known as "trenchfoot." (The cause, as noted by the 29th Division's chief surgeon, Lt. Col. Edmund Beacham, was trenches that "often had a foot of water in them.") The wily enemy kept Miller's weary and sodden men in a perpetual state of vigilance, a situation that would in all probability increase combat exhaustion cases within the 2nd Battalion by a considerable factor.

An example of the type of stress endured by the members of the 2nd Battalion occurred in a rare daytime patrol conducted by 1st Lt. Warren McNulty's Company F from Hahnbusch on October 9. That ten-man team went out at 12:15 P.M. looking for trouble on a task defined euphemistically by the battalion journal as "securing information and prisoners of war." Trouble was encountered less than a minute after emerging stealthily from the tree line, as the journal reported: "The patrol got about seventy-five yards out and drew rifle, machine gun, mortar, and SP [self-propelled artillery] fire, not only on themselves but on battalion positions. Four rounds of heavy stuff fell near the CP from the vicinity of Waldenrath. . . . Company F reported one casualty from artillery." At sunset, the unfortunate Company F "reported two more casualties when long-range artillery scored a direct hit on an emplacement."

The pinpoint accuracy of the Germans' artillery fire infuriated Miller, who ached for retribution. Revenge would come in time. The best Miller could do for the moment was to direct his troops to put more muscle behind their GI shovels. Just five minutes after the direct hit on the Company F trench, Miller sent out an explicit order: "Company commanders are to spend tomorrow [October 10] in strengthening and improving emplacements to cut down on casualties while companies are on the defensive."

If Miller's retaliation were to be effective, the 29ers had to hit back at the enemy much harder than the enemy was hitting them. Miller could not achieve that aim without holding decent observation of German lines, for only then could he call in artillery fire and air strikes. In the flat terrain surrounding Hahnbusch, dominant observation of the Germans was not easily attainable, but 1st Lt. Charles Fitch, the officer responsible for Company H's six 81-millimeter mortars, resolved to try. At 1 P.M., Fitch grabbed a pair of binoculars and cautiously moved out toward a slight rise of ground on his front, bringing along a radio operator, Pvt. Andrew Gula, to transmit messages back to the mortar positions when he spotted a suitable target. It was a rash act, for as Fitch searched for enemy targets, the Germans watched his every move. Twenty minutes later, a few enemy mortar rounds exploded right on target, killing both Fitch and his radio operator.

To Miller, the deaths of Fitch and Gula were the last straw. Something would have to be done, and soon, to obstruct the Germans' ability to drop shells with impunity exactly where they wanted. By now, Miller was

entirely familiar with the surrounding landscape, and he knew his difficulty stemmed from an immense granite obelisk standing between the villages of Waldenrath and Straeten, about a mile north of Hahnbusch
woods. A clerk in the 2nd Battalion's Headquarters Company, PFC Art
Plaut, described the structure as "an old tower whose original purpose had
been obscured with time. Perhaps it had been a water storage tower, perhaps a watchtower, remnant of an earlier day. No matter what it had been,
it was currently being used as an observation post by the enemy. . . .
Movement during daylight hours had to be virtually eliminated, so menacing was the enemy fire."

The 29ers had endeavored to bring the tower down, but nothing had
worked: "The artillery and tank destroyers tried to knock over this mam-
moth Hun observation post and just skinned the bark off it," wrote Cpl.
Jean Lowenthal, the editor of the division's daily newsletter, *29 Let's Go*.
"The heavies [155-millimeter guns] took a smack at it and chipped a little
deeper. The Air Corps nicked it too. Nobody could make the blasted thing
tumble over—nothing would cave it in. It was too big."

Just how big? One 29er asserted that it possessed a square base 60 feet
on each side and stood 175 feet high. A base that size would have made its
footprint bigger than the world's tallest obelisk, the Washington Monu-
ment. Regardless of its actual dimensions—other accounts contended that
it stood no more than 125 feet—the only detail concerning Miller was its
obvious solidity. According to Lowenthal, "Every inch of its massive
walls was constructed of solid concrete blocks, three to four feet thick."

As any good infantryman understood—and Miller was an exceptional infantryman—the only way to eliminate the loathsome tower
would be to send in a team of infantry and engineers at night and blow it
up. At first, that task seemed suicidal since the 29ers would have to
advance in darkness over a mile of wide-open terrain, under the enemy's
ubiquitous flares, to reach a site the Germans valued highly and would
surely defend forcefully. More to the point: if 500-pound U.S. Army Air
Force bombs could not bring down the tower, could engineers carry out
the job with explosives?

Miller resolved that it had to be done, but any plan to do it would have
to deal with so many perplexing difficulties that it seemed as if another
Schierwaldenrath was in the works. The daunting job fell to the members
of Company G, led by 1st Lt. Robert Rideout, along with five men from
Company A, 121st Engineers, each of whom hauled forty pounds of TNT.

At three minutes after 8 P.M. on Friday, October 13, Rideout's group, totaling about ninety men, moved out into the open ground between Hahnbusch and the tower, creeping steadily forward without a sound through
the sodden cabbage fields. On missions of this kind, the wary 29ers had
learned the value of patience, since forward progress at such a deliberate
pace was unavoidably slow, and it could take nearly three hours to traverse only a mile. Once or twice, tension mounted as the Germans fired a
flare, forcing the men to hug the cabbage fields and remain motionless for
minutes at a time, but two hours into the mission, Rideout reported "good
progress [and] no opposition."

Good news would turn bad at 11 P.M., as the Germans' barrage of hiss-
ing, multicolored flares suddenly swelled considerably. As they floated
slowly to earth, the prone 29ers, striving to remain invisible and motionless among the low cabbage leaves, were bathed in a surreal, dancing light
that abruptly turned night into day. The flares themselves were harmless.
Much more critical was whether they would presently be followed by
whizzing bullets and bursting shells, a terrifying contemplation that led
every man to wonder if he would ever make it back to his lines in one
piece. If he did, he suspected that he would shortly become a prime candidate for the acute disorder labeled "combat exhaustion."

The Germans had caught Rideout's men in the open. The moment of
discovery had occurred when a vigilant German sentry guarding the tower
heard something suspicious out in the gloomy pastureland—probably
29ers trying to pass through barbed wire—and shouted out an alarm. A
German-speaking 29er had replied in the sentry's language, but apparently
not convincingly enough. Within seconds, the sentry sounded a blaring
horn, and everything was chaos. More flares and, soon thereafter, a deluge
of machine-gun bullets and mortar rounds. The terrified 29ers quickly
grasped that if they wished to live, now was the time to depart. Company G
men started filtering back to Hahnbusch, glad to be alive, providing tales
of confusion and fear to anyone who cared to listen—what Gerhardt used
to define derisively as "disaster reports." The men related that at least four
of their number had stood up, dropped their weapons, raised their hands in
the air, and surrendered. At twenty minutes before midnight, almost four
hours into the raid, a frustrated Rideout reported to Miller by radio:
"Impossible to accomplish mission—am coming in."

With more than a quarter of Rideout's men still missing hours after
the raid, Miller and his alarmed staff understandably were edgy, knowing

full well that if Gerhardt had been present, his explosive temper would surely have burst. At 12:12 A.M. on October 14, the 2nd Battalion journal noted: "G Company 'Big Boy' [Rideout] back, reported by phone to [battalion] CP. . . . Men waited for orders, which weren't forthcoming, and when a few men started going for rear, the rest followed. Control lost; men returned in disorganization."

Happily, the raid's outcome was not nearly as bad as Miller had initially thought. Tracer rounds fired straight up into the air in Hahnbusch guided lost 29ers back to their lines, and by dawn, only three men were still missing, all apparently taken prisoner. (Only one was a Company G member, PFC Edward Hollenbeck; the other two, Pvts. Joseph McGough and William Harlow, were engineers.) None of the raiders had been killed, and only two wounded.

According to the Gerhardt school of soldiering, if at first you don't succeed . . . Miller had to try again. The sooner the better, and this time, the attempt would be much more subtle. At 2:15 P.M. on October 14, just a few hours after all of Rideout's men had finally been accounted for, a 2nd Battalion journal entry noted: "Regimental order for battalion to send ten-man patrol [later increased to fifteen] with five engineers to demolish water tower tonight." Every man would be a volunteer, led by two daring NCOs, S/Sgt. Gale Carroll of Company G, a Texan, and S/Sgt. Eugene Mowery of Company A, 121st Engineers, from Ohio.

The Germans had conclusively established their inclination to protect the tower the previous night, so could an even smaller American team do any better? With luck, the enemy would think it unlikely their opponents would be so audacious as to try again so soon. No sane 29er, however, could ever assume the Germans would not be alert; therefore, the key to success would be stealth, timing, and control, as Miller carefully explained when he detailed the mission to Carroll, Mowery, and the eighteen other participants at the 2nd Battalion command post just before 9 P.M. on October 14. Miller, whom a fellow 29er observed was "famous for his fighting talks," concluded: "You've an hour to go before you move out. This tower has been the cause of many of your buddies getting killed or wounded. It looks right down our throats. It's gotta come down. Are you with me, men?" According to a witness, "The answer came, twenty full voices: 'Yes!'"

With faces blackened and bayonets affixed to rifles, the 29ers slipped out of the woods and into the muddy fields at 10 P.M. The patrol's best

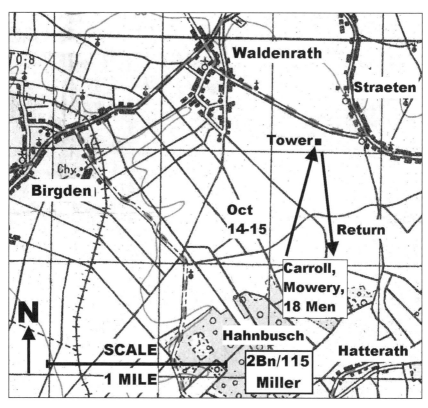

Sergeant Carroll's October 14–15 Raid at Waldenrath.

defense in the featureless terrain would be darkness, but that advantage could vanish in an instant with a well-timed enemy flare. Each man carried several hand grenades, but orders specified that M1 rifles had to be unloaded to encourage stealth and avoid accidental shooting of fellow patrol members. To maintain the control that had been lacking in Rideout's earlier raid, prior to jump-off Carroll cut a lengthy piece of telephone wire and wrapped it around the wrist of every member of his team. As a witness related, "Sergeant Carroll, at the point of the V-formation, controlled the group by pulling on the wire." Even in the dark, Carroll knew where he was going since he had been over much of the ground between Hahnbusch and the tower several times, as recently as before dawn that morning on a personal reconnaissance.

This time, if a German sentry challenged the patrol, Carroll made sure his men would lie still in the fields and offer no response. If the sentry persisted, the 29ers would reply with grenades, not words. "The men bent low as they crossed the field to avoid silhouetting themselves and becoming targets," Plaut wrote. "Passing into a cabbage patch without incident, the patrol suddenly hit the ground and froze when the Germans sent up an illuminating flare. Not far from where they lay, the men could hear [German] voices and sounds of movement. Apparently the enemy saw nothing to disturb him, for after the one flare died down, the patrol was able to move forward again." The battalion journal corroborated that detail at 11 P.M. by noting, "Companies report all OK."

So far, so good . . . and the only thing the unsuspecting Germans accomplished by firing a few more flares over the next twenty minutes was to illuminate their own tower and guide Carroll's stealthy patrol directly toward it. The intrepid sergeant zigzagged his team through a gap in the surrounding wire, into a warren of enemy trenches and dugouts (fortunately unoccupied), past craters blasted by countless American artillery shells whose failure to bring down the robust tower had triggered the current mission. There it was, straight ahead. Carroll knew he had to seize the moment: "We headed straight for the tower. I saw what I thought was a machine gun emplacement and went up to investigate. I brought my men up when I found it wasn't manned. No talking; I tugged the wire, and they came along. . . . We were at the tower." By a stroke of luck, the Germans had apparently failed to deploy sentries, or they were lax in their duties.

Led by Mowery, the engineers instantly went to work, shedding their forty pounds of explosives and placing them at regular intervals around the tower's base. Meanwhile, Carroll directed his riflemen to establish a defensive cordon in case the unwary enemy woke up and responded with a sudden counterattack. But the 29ers did not linger for long, since the engineers were experts at their jobs. As Carroll related, "It took them about thirty seconds." When all was ready, Carroll signaled for a hasty departure, and the moment Mowery ignited the fuses, set for a considerable delay, Carroll noted: "We took off like big-ass birds."

Shortly after midnight on Sunday, October 15, the event Miller and all members of the 2nd Battalion had been waiting for finally occurred. When the explosion's reverberating blast reached American lines in Hahnbusch, every 29er knew exactly what it meant. Sergeant Carroll had done it. Had it not been for strict rules requiring silence in frontline foxholes, the entire battalion would have erupted in cheers. That elation was displayed in a 12:51 A.M. journal entry whose author reflected the significance of the achievement by typing strictly in capital letters: "PATROL ACCOMPLISHED MISSION. WATER TOWER BLOWN UP."

The patrol made haste to get away and had traveled a short distance toward American lines when the detonation took place, but at that point, its return became infinitely more hazardous since the startled Germans, now fully alert, realized what their opponents were doing. "The group had gone about 200 yards more and were stumbling through another cabbage patch when someone called out something in German from a position to the front," a witness observed. "Sergeant Carroll fired at that 'someone' with his M-1 and then, as if by signal, the enemy opened up with rifles, burp guns, machine guns, and grenades. Our men returned the fire with automatic weapons and grenades, but were forced to remain close to the ground as Germans on one flank fired several illuminating flares." Within a few minutes, the enemy added a mortar barrage, described by another witness as "intense," but fortunately for the 29ers, the Germans' accuracy was deficient, and the salvos landed harmlessly in adjacent fields.

As the flares faded out, the men, by now somewhat scattered, pushed on. "We wriggled and crawled on our bellies like a bunch of snakes heading for home," Carroll remembered. "Before we got completely past that nest of bastards, I thought we had silenced them for good." As the 29ers neared Hahnbusch, they dared to rise up and dash for American lines, but more flares forced them down again while "bullets cut vicious paths a few feet over the cabbage plants." Carroll remarked, "One of our men, a runner who had volunteered to come along, ran into a Jerry out in a beet patch on the way, and he broke his carbine stock over the bastard's head. Whap!"

Around 1 A.M., members of the patrol slowly started trickling back into American lines. When Carroll later called roll back at Company G's command post, he discovered that out of his original complement of twenty, one man was missing, who was believed to have been wounded during the hectic withdrawal and was in all probability now in the Germans' hands. Three others were wounded but were now safe in an American dugout. Impressed onlookers, including the delighted battalion commander, Tony Miller, offered the proud raiders plaudits for their stunning triumph, and eventually, Carroll, along with Mowery, would receive the Silver Star for heroism. Mowery's award would be an Oak Leaf Cluster to an earlier Silver Star he had gained in Normandy five days after D-Day.

Even so, a fussy Gerhardt had a point to make with the 115th Infantry. At 8:40 that morning, he phoned McDaniel and grumbled, "I am reading the report of our fellow who went with your Company G on the raid. He mentions each man had face blackened, grenades, bayonet fixed—but no ammo." McDaniel responded, "We went out with unloaded rifles so they wouldn't shoot each other." An angry Gerhardt declared: "Don't ever do that again! Training should take care of that. A fellow who issues that order should lead the patrol!"

Col. Edward McDaniel, commander of the 115th Infantry.

Gerhardt's criticism could not dampen the appreciation for Carroll's accomplishment held by all 29ers occupying foxholes and trenches in and around Hahnbusch woods, a sentiment derived from the "immediate decrease in the amount of mortar and artillery falling on the front-line elements." Even better, Miller's battalion rounded up some German prisoners during nighttime patrols over the next few days, and interrogation revealed some interesting information. "Two POWs captured by White [2nd] Battalion are from 3rd Platoon, 1st Company, 351st *Volksgrenadier* Regiment [183rd *Volksgrenadier* Division]," the 115th's S-2 journal noted. "Both are Poles who are not too intelligent. They knew that four men were atop the tower prior to its being blown down. . . . It scared everybody in the area." That report reinvigorated the disheartened 115th Infantry and, to some extent, helped offset the Schierwaldenrath disaster.

If, as Gerhardt asserted, the current state of affairs was "entirely different than anything we have had before," the 29th Division had to conjure new ways to make the Germans' lives hell. The general cherished several methods of doing so. One of the most important was to revitalize the art of sniping. As an irritated Gerhardt would soon learn, however, that goal could not be achieved for some time because hardly anyone remained in the division who was a trained sniper. Plenty of 29ers were expert marksmen, and U.S. Army tables of organization and equipment specified that one man per rifle platoon had to be armed with a bolt-action M1903-A4 Springfield rifle, with attached telescopic sight, and trained as a sniper, but the 29th's introduction to combat in Normandy swiftly established that war-by-the-book differed significantly from reality. The division's sniping skills evaporated a few weeks after D-Day as most of those GIs trained as snipers became casualties. Of those who survived, almost all hastily discarded their Springfields in favor of semi-automatic M1 Garands because, in the close combat characteristic of the Norman bocage, using the much slower bolt-action rifle could be fatal. Furthermore, the verdant environment of the hedgerows effectively shielded the Germans, who showed themselves only rarely.

Combat in Brittany in August and September had been little different, although, during a two-week period in the line north of Brest during which the front lines hardly shifted, the 115th Infantry managed to harass the Germans with aggressive sniping. Nevertheless, Gerhardt's expectation that every 29th Division unit could revive its sniping skills while on line in Germany was swiftly established as unrealistic. Late on October 9, a war room duty officer phoned the 175th Infantry at Gerhardt's order to inquire about the regiment's snipers. The 175th's operations officer, Capt. Henry Reed, remarked: "Our 1st Battalion has four; 2nd Battalion has two. The general report was that they were active during the day, firing on individuals, but we have no report of effect. We have only seven [Springfield] rifles, four of which are serviceable. I would like to suggest that due to the fact that the 'sniper' has always been considered very low, we change the name to something else. I think that would help a lot in getting the men more interested in this."

Next to the transcript of Reed's answer in the journal, Gerhardt scribbled a single word in bold handwriting: "LOUSY!" A few hours later, the general, in one of his explosive moods, phoned Purnell. "I wish you would take your Captain Reed and shake the living hell out of him!" Gerhardt snarled. "What I am reading now in the journal has to do with my request for info on snipers. In it he says you have only seven rifles—and you're supposed to have twenty-six [actually twenty-seven]. Only four of them are serviceable. That is a bad reflection on you. Any officer who would write that and leave his commander out on a limb, I wouldn't have him! I would run him so far, we wouldn't hear from him again! And where does he get the idea that the sniper isn't important? I'd say he is the most important man we have!" The humbled Purnell knew his response had to be limited to "Yes, sir."

Even the supposedly proficient 115th Infantry came under criticism. When a 1st Battalion report indicated that it possessed neither sniper rifles nor men trained in their use, Gerhardt phoned McDaniel and bellowed, "This business of sharpshooters is lousy! If you haven't got riflemen, as this says, it's no wonder you can't win any battles. Do something about it quick!"

The general had a point. If the 29th Division's role in the XIX Corps's Aachen offensive was secondary, it could contribute little to the main goal except to harass the enemy. In all previous conflicts involving rifled weapons, sniping had been established as one of the most effective means of harassment in positional warfare, and as Gerhardt routinely pointed out, the flat and open terrain in the division's sector was perfect for that kind of combat. The opposing lines of outposts were typically separated by only a few hundred yards, usually with unobstructed lines of sight between them—an easy shot for a trained 29er armed with a sniper rifle, assuming the Germans would be careless enough to reveal themselves in daylight.

But a disappointed Gerhardt had learned that not many of his 29ers were familiar with sniping skills, a state of affairs he resolved to rectify with all possible speed by instituting crash courses. At the general's insistence, McDaniel set up a 115th Infantry sniper school in an abandoned building near Gangelt, only recently used by the Germans for training non-commissioned officers. The commander of the regimental headquarters company, Capt. Frank Bergstein, organized the school, whose course of instruction lasted about one week. Bergstein's instructors taught the basics of the M1903-A4 Springfield, a nine-pound rifle with a five-round magazine that was still in manufacture in American arsenals during World War II, including thousands produced by Smith-Corona, the legendary typewriter manufacturer. Despite plenty of practice shooting, one attendee, Pvt. Ray Moon, remembered the lessons as "haphazard" since the teachers did not know much more than the students.

As any 29th Division rifleman who took up Gerhardt's challenge would appreciate, on-the-job training turned out to be the best means of learning sniper skills. Doing the job right depended on shrewdness and patience. If the sniper wished to live, he had to practice extraordinary prudence, for the moment he fired a shot, the enemy would be determined to retaliate, and any sniper taken alive by the Germans would not live for long. The sniper's primary secret to success was to find a suitable firing position separated from a potential enemy target by 600 yards or less, the maximum effective range of a Springfield '03 equipped with a sniper scope. That position had to offer cover and a reasonably secure means of entry and exit. Adept use of camouflage, too, would allow a sniper to remain hidden while patiently waiting for a target that might not present itself for hours, if ever.

One detail on which all agreed was that sniping was more challenging and perilous than it looked. Moon learned that fact the hard way on a mission he undertook in late October near Schierwaldenrath. Armed with a Springfield '03, a pair of binoculars, and little else, Moon stealthily took position before dawn in the upper floor of an abandoned farm building on the edge of no-man's-land. Like any good 29er, he knew German troops were rarely careless, but once in a while, they slipped up. Moon waited some time for that moment, and his patience was rewarded when he caught an enemy soldier who had unwisely shown himself while answering a call of nature—"with his pants down," as Moon recalled. Moon let fly with a single shot, which he thought found its mark, but what he

noticed over the next minute caused any satisfaction over his accomplishment to evaporate. Three German soldiers, little more than 100 yards
away, were swiftly working their way toward the building he occupied,
and the alarmed Moon knew for certain what they meant to do. Perhaps
they had detected his location from a muzzle flash or a plume of smoke—
no matter how they knew, they were coming fast with deadly intent. There
was no question of staying put and fighting, for a bolt-action Springfield
was entirely inadequate against those odds. Moon had an escape route,
which he took with an alacrity that probably saved his life.

Next time, he would sling an M1 carbine over his shoulder—just
in case.

FIVE

Würselen

1. AN OVERSUPPLY OF FIGHTING

As General Gerhardt had so accurately observed, the 29th Infantry Division's experience in early October 1944 was entirely different from anything it had undergone before. In the battle for Aachen, other units had gained laurels while the 29th tied down the Germans on an inconsequential front to which the top brass gave virtually no thought. Actually, all 29ers except Gerhardt found that new situation agreeable, for they had learned from past battles that the struggle for vital objectives, such as St. Lô, Vire, and Brest, certainly put the division in the headlines at home, but those headlines were accompanied by casualty lists of almost unimaginable length. The enemy's obvious resolve to retain Aachen, a treasured part of the Fatherland that Hitler had ordered his troops to hold to the last man, implied that the fight for the city could be worse than anything the 29ers had endured in Normandy or Brittany. If American newspapers would soon display headlines blaring the imminent fall of Aachen, they would feature not the 29th, but the 1st and 30th Infantry Divisions, along with the 2nd Armored Division. Let those other outfits have their days in the sun—the 29ers already had plenty, and far too many of their comrades lay buried deep in the soil of France as a result.

The first two weeks of October 1944 proved conclusively that anonymity did not yield tranquility. The 29ers may have occupied a "quiet" sector beyond the public's sphere of attention, near no essential objectives, but unhappily, their new surroundings were only slightly less perilous than the places where they had previously fought so intensely. The 29th Division and its attached units suffered more than 800 casualties in early October, nearly a quarter of whom were taken prisoner. The division had never before lost prisoners to the enemy in such substantive numbers, a detail that predictably infuriated Gerhardt. Even worse, the Germans had inflicted several stinging defeats on the 29th, while American terrain gains were few and entirely meaningless. It was difficult for Gerhardt to admit, but his unbounded optimism of late September, which had featured a boast that his division would push the Germans back into the Rhine, had been utterly crushed. It had not even managed to come close to capturing Geilenkirchen, the only objective on Gerhardt's front that held any value at all to his boss, Gen. Charles Corlett of the XIX Corps.

Those 29ers who worked in close proximity to Gerhardt and understood his volatile disposition whispered among each other that the general's current mood was particularly foul. Gerhardt had unleashed his legendary temper with increasing frequency and escalating intensity in daily episodes that caused the supposed offenders to cringe, hoping their careers in the 29th Division would not soon come to an ignominious end. Stunned witnesses to those outbursts could only avert their eyes and pray they would not be next. In one typical explosion, Gerhardt phoned Capt. Edward Jones, commander of the 29th Cavalry Reconnaissance Troop, on October 16. Normally, Jones was one of the general's favorites, a fellow cavalryman with a forceful personality and an aggressive leadership style that had brought high praise from Gerhardt in the past. But the general had recently noticed some unsoldierly behavior among Jones's men, including a failure to adhere to proper saluting procedures, and he snarled to his staff that the cavalrymen's disciplinary standards were "trash." "This is the last time I am going to talk to you about this!" Gerhardt bellowed to Jones. "The next time, I'm going to relieve you. Your outfit is not up to division standards. For two days, you have reported no training schedule. You'd better have one for today! You people should be the best in the 29th Division, and if you can, you'll make up your mind to do it!"

The general's surly mood was understandable. The 29th Division's unbroken string of success had ended. The spotlight would shine on other divisions during the protracted battle for Aachen, and even Corlett had paid little attention to the 29th. Even worse, he had offered Gerhardt little in terms of critical supplies. The most notable items Gerhardt needed, but would not receive, were artillery ammunition and air support, the lack of which paralyzed any notion of a grand offensive. Gerhardt even had to carry out his objectionable mission lacking one third of his infantry strength since Corlett had insisted upon detaching the 116th Infantry from the division and assigning it as the XIX Corps reserve, a coveted status every member of the regiment innocently hoped would be tranquil. Alas, that status turned out to be anything but. As the 116th's intelligence officer, Capt. Robert Walker, wryly noted about Aachen, "There was an oversupply of fighting available."

In its reserve role, the 116th's future would be determined not by Gerhardt, but by Corlett. The 116th Infantry, the renowned Virginia regiment that in the not-too-distant past had been Gerhardt's favorite and most skilled combat outfit, had successfully stormed Omaha Beach in the opening hours of the D-Day invasion, but in doing so had lost more than 1,000 of its 3,200 men in an eighteen-hour period. The 116th was positively not the same regiment on October 1, 1944, that it had been when it gained the coveted Distinguished Unit Citation on June 6, but it was still an integral element of the 29th Division, and Gerhardt could accomplish little without it.

Unhappily for the general, for much of the month of October, he would have to learn to live without it, a situation that may have initially pleased the 116th Infantry's commander, a forty-four-year-old former World War I enlisted man named Col. Philip Dwyer, but which would eventually draw the regiment into the worst of the widening battle for Aachen. When that brutal mêlée mercifully ended in late October, in retrospect Dwyer would probably have preferred to remain under Gerhardt's tutelage. As difficult as the general's leadership style could be, it would surely have been preferable to what the 116th experienced at Aachen. Attached to both the 30th Infantry and 2nd Armored Divisions, the top brass committed a cardinal sin in Gerhardt's eyes by splitting up the 116th Infantry and committing separate components to bewildering and deadly battles all across the Aachen front under the command of unfamiliar generals whose concern for the welfare of the 116th did not match the

Col. Philip Dwyer, commander of the 116th Infantry.

degree to which they nurtured their own units.

In his monthly "Battle Lessons and Conclusions" report for October 1944, Gerhardt pondered that state of affairs and bluntly condemned it: "It was demonstrated through the actions of the 116th Infantry that troops operate best under their own command and when not committed piecemeal. Experience of this division shows that troops already committed [for lengthy periods] have very little offensive value, and that a rotation policy is of necessity the answer to continuity in action." That report's last sentence may have seemed to some a meager excuse for the division's failure to accomplish any substantive goals in October, but Gerhardt's point was entirely valid. Had Corlett not detached the 116th Infantry from the 29th, three additional battalions of infantry would have been at Gerhardt's disposal, and he would have been able to deploy riflemen along his extended front in greater density and rotate them in and out of the front lines more frequently. Consequently, the outcome of the division's October efforts in all likelihood would have been more noteworthy, and disasters such as Schierwaldenrath and Breberen might have been avoided for the obvious reason that Gerhardt would have committed far greater resources to the fight. Gerhardt's questionable generalship in those tragic affairs raised doubts about his judgment, but no one could deny that the 29th Division had joined the battle in western Germany in October 1944 lacking a major component of its combat power.

At 7:45 P.M. on September 30, 1944, just two days after the 116th Infantry's troop trains had arrived in Holland after their long journey across France from Brittany, Corlett attached the 1st Battalion, commanded by Maj. Tom Dallas, to the 30th Division and shoved it into a

four-mile section of the front line between the villages of Horbach and
Orsbach, just a few miles northwest of Aachen. For the members of Dallas's outfit, moving back into the struggle with no real chance to enjoy the
pleasures of Holland was unfortunate; much worse was the forced separation from their 116th Infantry comrades and the distinctive and familiar
environment of the 29th Division. Never before in the division's combat
history had a major combat unit been separated from Gerhardt's war room
by such a considerable distance—nearly thirty miles.

For four days, the 1st Battalion alone would hold a section of the line
that should have been held by three battalions, but happily, the Germans, distracted by American offensive moves in other sectors, remained passive.
Later, Dallas's men would receive help holding the line from the 2nd Battalion and the XIX Corps's 247th Engineer Combat Battalion. From their frontline foxholes in the new sector, just inside Germany, the 29ers could clearly
perceive the renowned West Wall, the enemy's extensive line of defenses on
Germany's western frontier. The line was particularly strong in this location
because Hitler had recently ordered it upgraded to bolster his hold on
Aachen. The Germans had designed the West Wall's bunkers and pillboxes
to blend in with the terrain, but they meant one element of their defenses,
known as "dragon's teeth," to be in plain sight. Dallas's men had no trouble
spotting those pyramidal concrete structures, devised as tank obstacles,
because hundreds of them were arrayed beyond the 1st Battalion's front line
in a narrow band that stretched for miles across the undulating landscape,
appearing from a distance like a line of lifeless white sentinels guarding the
gates of Germany. Ominously, the last time 116th Infantry veterans had seen
anything like those obstacles was on Omaha Beach.

Dallas's 29ers would obviously have a tough time punching through
that sector of the West Wall, but fortunately, their new boss, Maj. Gen.
Leland Hobbs, informed them they would never have to. Hobbs, the
highly respected commander of the 30th Division and classmate of
Dwight Eisenhower in the West Point class of 1915, demanded little of
Dallas's men except to hold the 30th's far-right flank securely at the point
where it linked up with the 1st Division to the south. For men who were
used to Gerhardt's uncompromising requirement for belligerent behavior
toward the enemy, even in a quiet sector, Hobbs's attitude surely was a
relief. As the battalion's October 1944 report noted, "Orders [were] simply to hold the line and to do no active patrolling, nor demonstrate any
aggressive action."

That was indeed welcome news, but the members of the battalion grasped there was no such thing as a completely quiet sector when fighting the Germans. On the night of October 8, T/Sgt. Leo Nash, a Company A platoon sergeant and one of Dallas's finest soldiers, went out with three men on a routine check of the 2nd Platoon's outposts. Nash, a native of Freeport, Illinois, had participated in the first wave of the D-Day invasion and had the appalling experience of watching dozens of comrades die at his side on the sands of Omaha Beach only minutes into the landing. By October 1944, Nash was one of only a few Company A members remaining with the outfit who had survived the Omaha Beach landing. Another survivor, PFC John Barnes, remembered Nash as "the greatest infantry soldier I had the privilege to know in my eleven months of combat in World War II."

Everything was satisfactory at the outpost line, but when Nash's team started back to their foxholes, someone stepped on a mine, severely wounding Nash. His men carried him back to an aid station, but if he were to live, he needed intensive care. The medics tied Nash to a litter and fastened it to a jeep for the journey to a rear-area hospital. "Word spread within the company," Barnes recalled. "One by one we came down to the crossroad. . . . He was barely conscious. We knew he would not make it. Silently, we passed him as if in review, touching him with a quiet farewell." Nash was evacuated to England and hung on for about a week before he succumbed to his wounds. Later, Nash's grandmother, who "raised him like one of my own boys," remembered the condolence letter she had received from a 116th Infantry chaplain, stating that Sergeant Nash "will always be remembered for his courage and bravery."

For the men of the 116th Infantry, working for a commanding general other than Gerhardt would be peculiar. But if Hobbs desired neither active patrolling nor demonstrations of aggressive action, the 29ers would certainly obey with pleasure and offer no dissent. Such orders caused the men to wonder: what kind of outfit was this 30th Division?

As the 29ers would soon learn, it was a first-rate unit at least equal to the 29th Division in every respect. On October 2, about ten miles north of Aachen, two of the 30th's infantry regiments, the 117th and 119th, had commenced an infinitely more challenging task than any 29th Division outfit would face that month, a setpiece frontal assault against a well-defended sector of the Germans' vaunted West Wall, cunningly situated behind the barrier of the thirty-foot-wide, swift-flowing Würm River and featuring dozens of apparently indestructible concrete bunkers and other formidable defenses. It seemed like an impossible mission, but it worked. Two days later, the 30th Division was surging through a broad breach it had made in the West Wall, and Hobbs would soon report to his boss Corlett: "We have a hole in this thing big enough to drive two divisions through. I entertain no doubts that this line is cracked wide open." Hobbs thereupon set out to guide the 30th south toward the 1st Division, about nine miles away, an interval the top brass now defined as the "Aachen Gap," and if the two divisions could link up, Aachen would be encircled and its capture inevitable. By October 8, after the 30th had traversed much of the distance toward the planned junction point, the village of Würselen, a proud Hobbs once again signaled to Corlett: "The job is finished as far as this division is concerned."

Not quite. As the U.S. Army's chief historian of the Aachen campaign, Charles MacDonald, observed, "In the nine days that followed, the three-mile distance remaining [between the 30th and 1st Divisions] before the job actually was completed was to become a route bathed in blood and frustration." So much frustration, in fact, that Hobbs would need considerable help to finish a task he thought he had already accomplished and a frazzled Corlett would lose his job.

For a few blissful days, it seemed as if the 116th Infantry would miss it all. While the 1st Battalion had kept a passive watch over the enemy on the 30th Division's right flank—a task all members agreed was not too bad—the 2nd and 3rd Battalions had trained for nearly a week behind the front, their normal repertoire of rifle marksmanship and squad tactics augmented by extensive practice with demolition charges and bangalore torpedoes in case Hobbs would need their help to destroy the Germans' numerous West Wall bunkers.

The commander of the 2nd Battalion, Maj. Charles Cawthon, recalled one curious incident that ocurred during training at an ad hoc rifle range behind the front:

A platoon firing demonstration remains in mind by reason of three or four horses, probably made stray by the war, suddenly appearing at full gallop along a ridge directly in the line of machine gun and rifle fire. There was an involuntary murmur of dismay among the viewers, watching from a hillside behind the firing line, as the horses, in line astern and tails and manes flying—a beautiful and pathetic sight—appeared to gallop through the interlocking lines of tracer bullets. The firing halted momentarily and then resumed as the horses disappeared over the ridge, so far as I know unhurt.

The 30th Division's expertise in destroying enemy pillboxes, revealed so fiercely to the enemy on October 2 and 3, had led to the happy conclusion that Hobbs would not need the 116th's help. The encirclement of Aachen appeared imminent; assuming the Germans could do little to prevent it, Dwyer's men reasoned that their exalted status as "corps reserve" could last for a long time.

The first crack in the 29ers' contented lives occurred on October 4, not because of German "enthusiasm," but because of the 30th Division's stunning success. Hobbs was indeed correct when he boasted that the crack his men had made in the enemy lines was big enough to thrust "two divisions through," for that is precisely what Corlett intended to do when he committed a major part of Maj. Gen. Ernest Harmon's 2nd Armored Division to the battle in the 30th's wake at Übach on the afternoon of October 3. Harmon's division held orders to ram through the Germans' last-ditch defensive lines and transform a mere breakthrough into a decisive breakout in the first stage of what Eisenhower confidently hoped would be a drive all the way to the Rhine. "The Germans put up ferocious resistance both from their stationary defenses and from a substantial force of tanks," Harmon recalled. "Elimination of the pillboxes was slow and dangerous work. Some we disposed of by firing tank shells or 155-millimeter rifled artillery through their gun slits. Others, held by particularly determined defenders, fought on until tank-dozers heaped up earth around their doors and buried the occupants alive."

No breakout had happened yet, but one of Harmon's powerful tank-infantry combat commands led by Brig. Gen. John Collier—nicknamed "Pee Wee" because of his diminutive stature—held orders to achieve that goal by pouring through the gap in the West Wall on October 5. Harmon promptly concluded, however, that Collier could fulfill his mission only with help from the 116th Infantry, a necessity arising not from the Germans' capacity to resist but because the 2nd Armored Division was such an atypical U.S. Army organization. In fact, among the ninety divisions raised by the Army for overseas service in World War II, only one other division—the 3rd Armored—was configured identically to Harmon's renowned "Hell on Wheels" outfit. Both divisions adhered to an obsolete table of organization and equipment dating to 1942, a time when American proponents of armored doctrine assertively professed the theory that U.S. Army tanks, mass-produced and led by daring combat leaders like Patton, would be the dominant pieces of military hardware in World War II. Only two years later, all major world armies, including Germany's, had modified that theory based on conclusive combat lessons proving that tanks could accomplish little on a modern battlefield without substantive bodies of supporting ground troops. In short, because of dramatic improvements in anti-tank weaponry, even the most vigorous proponents of blitzkrieg had to admit that tanks could no longer win the war on their own.

The brainy head of U.S. Army Ground Forces, Lt. Gen. Lesley McNair, once blurted that the 1942 armored division was "so fat there is no place to begin," and he had a point. In Harmon's 2nd Armored Division, the ratio of tank to infantry battalions was two to one, whereas in every other U.S. Army armored division in 1944 (save the 3rd), the ratio was one to one. The German Army, the originator of blitzkrieg, had adopted a ratio still heavier in infantry once its panzer generals absorbed the lessons of early World War II combat. In late 1943, when thirteen U.S. Army armored divisions were drastically reorganized into much leaner outfits based on those same lessons, the 2nd and 3rd had already been deployed to England and were preparing for the momentous cross-Channel invasion of Normandy. The top brass considered both divisions so far along in training that they excluded them from the restructuring. Accordingly, the 2nd and 3rd entered Normandy with their 1942 organization intact, and they would never transform to the more up-to-date tank-infantry arrangement preferred by most armor officers.

Harmon must have considered it somewhat paradoxical that the only way to address the 2nd Armored Division's "fat" was to swell it to even greater size by borrowing infantry from nearby divisions. On the evening of October 4, as Harmon prepared to do what all armored commanders dreamed of—thrusting boldly through the front lines and dashing madly beyond—he knew Pee Wee Collier's combat command had to be reinforced by a substantive body of ground troops, and he therefore requested from Corlett a battalion from the 116th Infantry, currently in corps reserve. Corlett granted that request, and soon the 116th's 3rd Battalion, commanded by Lt. Col. William Puntenney, was on its way to the 2nd Armored Division for hasty on-the-job training in tank-infantry cooperation.

In an era in which meteoric promotions within the U.S. Army were the norm, Puntenney had experienced a particularly notable military career. Three months after the 29th Division's February 1941 mobilization, Puntenney was still a college student at the University of Arizona and a cadet in that school's ROTC program. Commissioned as a second lieutenant in May 1941, the Army sent Puntenney on his first assignment to Fort Bliss, Texas, to join the 7th Cavalry, the renowned regiment of Custer and the Little Bighorn, still operating as a mounted unit. Over the next several months, he would get to know an intimidating brigadier general named Charles H. Gerhardt, a fellow cavalryman whom Puntenney later remembered as his "nemesis." Observed Puntenney: "All I wanted to do was stay out of his way."

It was not to be. An amazed Puntenney soon ascertained that the general had a fondness for him, and when the 91st Infantry Division was raised at Camp White, Oregon, in mid-1942 with Gerhardt as its commander, the general selected Puntenney as his aide-de-camp. It was the beginning of a tempestuous father-son relationship that would endure for three years. Puntenney, still the general's aide, accompanied Gerhardt when the general shifted to England in July 1943 to take command of the 29th Division. Gerhardt eventually assigned him a role any cavalryman would covet, command of the 29th's Cavalry Reconnaissance Troop. Puntenney led the troop ashore in Normandy shortly after D-Day, but his tour of combat duty with that dashing outfit lasted little more than a month. On July 13, 1944, determined to do everything necessary to bring about the swift capture of St. Lô, Gerhardt had replaced the top two officers in the 116th Infantry's 3rd Battalion, assigning Maj. Thomas Howie as commander and Puntenney as his executive. Four days later, Howie died in Puntenney's arms, the victim of a German mortar shell, and Howie entered newspaper headlines as "The Major of St. Lô." The battalion was now Puntenney's, a daunting job for a young captain who had never before commanded at that level and indeed had only graduated from college three years before. Three months later, by now bumped up two ranks to lieutenant colonel, Puntenney still held that same command, and more important, he still held the respect of his demanding commanding general.

Puntenney's men learned that working with a large and experienced tank organization like the 2nd Armored Division offered several advantages. Above all, the 29ers avoided much wear on their legs by adopting the armored infantryman's practice of hitching a ride on the topside of the Shermans' huge steel hulls. Moreover, 3rd Battalion men had never seen tanks in such profusion, for when armor had supported the 116th in the past, the Shermans had generally appeared only in trifling driblets. But now, as Collier's powerful combat command prepared to cross the Wurm and advance toward the sound of the guns, Puntenney's impressed 29ers saw more than one hundred Shermans, two entire tank battalions from the 66th Armor—greater than the number of tanks in a German panzer division. How could the Germans stop such a juggernaut?

If Harmon was to achieve his coveted breakout, Collier's force first had to smash through the Germans' defensive line, and to do that, it would have to overcome several strongpoints in the checkerboard farm villages scattered across the typically flat Rhineland landscape. Collier formed two all-mechanized tank-infantry task forces, each comprised of an entire tank battalion of more than fifty tanks, an infantry company, and smaller reconnaissance, engineer, tank destroyer, and self-propelled artillery units. The Americans had learned armored warfare well: not a single soldier would have to walk to the battlefield, and the vast firepower at Collier's disposal, including on-call Ninth Air Force fighter-bombers, would surely convince the Germans that their opponents had surpassed their mastery of blitzkrieg.

Pee Wee Collier's force, including Puntenney's 116th Infantry passengers riding on the tanks, moved out from Rimburg on the Wurm's west bank on the afternoon of October 5, with the immediate object of crossing one of the flimsy bridges thrown across the river by American engineers over the past seventy-two hours. As the 29ers would soon learn, moving a roadbound column of such immense length was both tricky and dangerous, since the perceptive Germans knew that when the Americans reached the bottleneck at the Wurm bridge, they would be highly vulnerable to artillery fire. Tankers subject to a German artillery barrage would find the experience troublesome, but usually not fatal, since the Shermans' steel hulls protected the occupants from high-explosive shell fragments. For infantrymen jumbled on top of a tank, however, that same barrage would be an infinitely more terrorizing event. Puntenney's action report related, "As the columns crossed the bridge over the Wurm River, they encountered intense artillery and mortar fire, ranging from 50-millimeter to 150-millimeter," and under that kind of fire, no one needed to issue an order to the 29ers to dismount from the tanks immediately and take the sensible action of moving on foot a few hundred yards upstream to a safer crossing point. Somewhere on the far side of the river, no longer under German artillery fire, the 29ers remounted the tanks, and the column proceeded eastward. Perhaps working directly with tanks was not such a desirable experience after all.

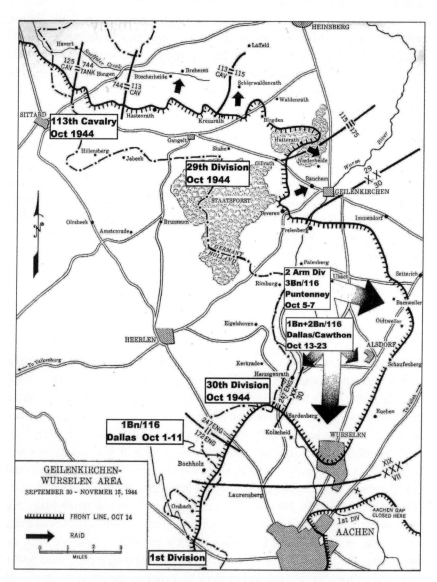

The 116th Infantry at Aachen, October 1–23, 1944.

The column pressed on, past several massive slag heaps and abandoned coal mines that were common to this industrial region of Germany. As an expressive clerk in Company K logged on his daily morning report, "We are now fighting in the country that for thirty years has given the world a hot foot." At key road junctions, gesticulating military policemen guided the tanks along the proper path, but for the moment, darkness prevented Collier's command from coming into direct grips with the Germans. The next morning, October 6, the advance resumed, and the vehicles plunged eastward along a typical Rhineland country road, bordered on both sides by seemingly endless lines of decorative trees. In peacetime, the bucolic surroundings would have been striking, but now, as *Baltimore Sun* reporter Bradley observed, the environment was anything but serene: "Along the road, trees were either broken off just above the ground or had most of their limbs torn off. . . . In the field off to the left were two German self-propelled 75s and a Mark IV tank [casualties of an October 4 German counterattack against the 30th Division], all burned out." The Americans would inevitably bump into formidable enemy resistance momentarily, so Collier had to deploy his command from its unwieldy road column into formations better suited for battle. In due course, as his two task forces reached their designated jump-off points, they diverged from the main road and struck out toward their immediate objectives, the farming villages of Oidtweiler and Baesweiler. The fighting over the next few days would determine whether the enemy line centered on those two hamlets would collapse, leaving Collier's mobile force free to exploit through the breach. If the Germans held, the combat would surely descend into yet another indecisive and costly battle of attrition.

The 3rd Battalion's Company L, led by Capt. Maurice McGrath, joined the northern column, composed mainly of the 2nd Battalion, 66th Armor, and headed for Baesweiler. Company I, commanded by 1st Lt. James Myers, moved with the 1st Battalion, 66th Armor, in the southern force, and pressed forward toward Oidtweiler. Company M, a heavy-weapons outfit, attached four water-cooled Browning machine guns and their crews to each column. For the moment, Puntenney held 1st Lt. Elmer Reagor's Company K in reserve. Puntenney's battalion, which had last been in combat on September 18 in the streets of Brest, was about to meet the foe again.

The German defenders had neither the skill nor the weaponry of the paratroopers whom the 116th had battled at Brest, but they were obviously

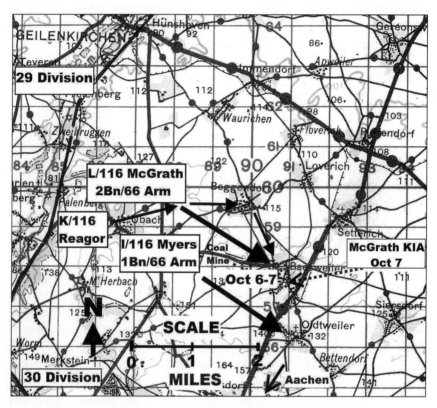

29 Division

L/116 McGrath
2Bn/66 Arm

K/116
Reagor

I/116 Myers
1Bn/66 Arm

Coal
Mine

Oct 6-7

McGrath KIA
Oct 7

N

SCALE

0   1   2

MILES

Aachen

30 Division

Puntenney's 3rd Battalion, 116th Infantry, October 6–7, 1944.

not ready to admit defeat as some GIs had hoped. A 3rd Battalion action report summarized the Germans' attitude by describing their fire, both small-arms and artillery, as "withering." The weather on October 6 was uncommonly bright, with little overcast, thereby allowing Ninth Air Force fighter-bombers to batter German strongpoints repeatedly from the air. Even so, neither McGrath's nor Myers' column came close to reaching its objective, and both would have to wait for daylight on October 7 to try again.

During the October 6 fighting, one of McGrath's medics, T/4 Arlie Sneed from Texas, gained a Silver Star for rendering vital aid to several wounded 29ers. As related by Sneed's citation, "T/4 Sneed, amid the continuous shelling, rushed to the assistance of the wounded and administered first aid treatment. Unable to evacuate the seriously wounded, he made his way to a nearby unit and secured an armored vehicle for their evacuation. T/4 Sneed's timely and heroic actions undoubtedly resulted in saving the lives of these wounded men."

The breakthrough Harmon sought hardly appeared imminent. Nevertheless, the Americans were in good position to resume their attack on October 7, especially because of Collier's prudent decision to seize the village of Beggendorf, about a mile northwest of Baesweiler, with an armored column reinforced by Puntenney's reserve outfit, Reagor's Company K. If the Americans could seize Beggendorf, Collier could attack Baesweiler on October 7 from three sides. A Company K platoon leader, 1st Lt. Ben Snipas, recalled the entry into Beggendorf on the afternoon of October 6:

To reach the town, we traveled all the way through a field of beets. Just short of town, the tanks stopped at an orchard. I called for members of the 3rd Platoon to join me in the orchard. It contained dozens of foxholes, which appeared to have been recently occupied. . . . We quickly moved through the orchard and into the first two houses, which we checked for German soldiers and also checked what appeared to be the main street of town. No [Germans] were visible. . . . Looking down the road a few hundred yards, I spotted a German Tiger tank, planted in the middle of the road and probably spoiling for action. . . . I notified a tank commander [from the 66th Armor] that we saw a Tiger about 200 yards down the street in a stationary position. [He] requested a tank destroyer be sent, since it was equipped with a 90-millimeter [actually 76mm] cannon. . . . I was concerned about a possible artillery barrage, so we walked back briskly through the orchard toward the line of houses where we had left our platoon.

In a few seconds, the enemy artillery fire Snipas had worried about materialized, hitting the orchard with uncanny accuracy. Snipas and his radio operator were severely wounded and promptly evacuated by jeep. That barrage signaled that the Germans in Beggendorf had finally woken up and were making a stand at the far end of town, but the 29ers and tankers managed to evict the last enemy defenders by nightfall—in part because of the actions of another Texan, PFC Pedro Mesa, a Company K BAR gunner who maintained such heavy covering fire on German strongpoints that his comrades quickly overcame them by close assault, killing or capturing twenty-one Germans. Six weeks later, Mesa would be awarded a Silver Star for his actions at Beggendorf. Company K also took a large batch of prisoners, including, as the company clerk noted, "five civilians who probably had fought well in the last war."

The events of the following day, October 7, would establish why combat could transform even enthusiastic idealists into cynics, and by nightfall, Puntenney's frustrated infantrymen must have wondered whether their generals had learned anything at prewar Command and General Staff School classes. The main purpose of Pee Wee Collier's attack had evaporated on the afternoon of October 6 when Corlett contacted his three division commanders to inform them of imminent changes in the XIX Corps' operations. The U.S. First Army's commander, Courtney Hodges, had insisted that the lingering Allied supply crisis on the Western Front would permit him to provide Corlett with sufficient materiel to support only a single major attack, which had to focus entirely on the encirclement of Aachen. Consequently, a 2nd Armored Division blitzkrieg toward the Rhine, the first tentative steps of which Collier had taken on October 6, was now out of the question. With luck, a breakthrough might occur in a few weeks. For now, Corlett directed Harmon and Collier to take up good defensive positions and dig in. Meanwhile, Hobbs's 30th Division would make the main effort by striking due south toward Würselen, closing the Aachen Gap.

Nevertheless, Harmon and Collier felt that a continuation of their attack to the east on October 7 was justified by the need to secure the favorable defensive line they would apparently have to hold for the foreseeable future. The 2nd Armored Division, along with Puntenney's battalion, therefore had to press forward for at least one more day. That pronouncement triggered a severe struggle for control of Baesweiler and Oidtweiler, two villages Corlett did not need if his primary mission was to encircle Aachen. Although the October 7 battle ended in the Americans' favor, they paid a toll of casualties defined by a 3rd Battalion report as "very heavy."

The death of one of Puntenney's men at Baesweiler was particularly hard for the battalion to bear. Captain Maurice (pronounced "Morris") McGrath, commander of Company L, was a twenty-six-year-old Philadelphia native who had matured in his three-year Army career into one of the 116th's most respected officers. McGrath had joined the 26th "Yankee" Division in August 1941 while still enrolled at Temple University Law School. After gaining a commission as a second lieutenant in August 1942, he was reassigned to the 29th Division's 116th Infantry and, the following month, accompanied the regiment on its deployment to Britain aboard the ocean liner *Queen Mary*.

McGrath was at first consigned to a rifle company as a platoon leader, but a knee injury during one of the 29th's grueling twenty-five-mile hikes in Dartmoor triggered a transfer to Service Company, a unit that was not expected to fight in the front lines. "He didn't like this transfer and tried several times to get back to a line company," one of his fellow officers remembered. "Colonel Canham [the 116th's commander] refused him and told him to carry on with the new job. So he took hold and dug in and learned to like it. . . . He made a wonderful job of it, and the Colonel looked on Mac just like a son."

Capt. Maurice McGrath, commander of Company L, 116th Infantry. He was killed in action at Baesweiler, October 7, 1944.

On D-Day, McGrath and his shaken comrades from Service Company learned the hard lesson that on Omaha Beach, even rear-echelon troops were in danger every second. Several weeks later, McGrath provided a two-page account of his June 6 activities on Omaha Beach to a U.S. Army historian, Lt. Col. S. L. A. Marshall. Upon reading McGrath's words, Marshall scribbled a note at the bottom of the affidavit: "It seems to me that this captain's whole course of action on this day is unusually enterprising."

In Normandy, McGrath suffered two wounds, one of which was in the abdomen and severe enough to keep him out of action for more than a month in England. While he was away, the regiment awarded him a Bronze Star for meritorious service. Now commanding the 116th Infantry's Company L, he returned to the 116th in late August for the attack on Brest. In the 29th Division's opening assault on that great port city, he gained a Silver Star for gallantry.

One brother officer who had attended Officer Candidate School with McGrath and had served with him ever since described him just a few weeks after his death as "the most daring man I have ever met," adding that the enlisted men "hold in their hearts an attitude toward him that all officers look for from their men." He could be hard, as one subordinate noted when he recalled how a V-Mail letter he had written to his wife was censored by McGrath: "Captain McGrath proceeded to bawl me out something awful for what he thought I was trying to tell my wife about where I was located. The funny thing about that deal was I didn't even have the slightest idea where I was except that we were in France—and that was no secret to anyone."

Christianity provided McGrath much-needed solace throughout his military career. He participated in 116th Infantry religious services whenever possible, although the last service he attended before his death was actually not a military service at all, but a Catholic mass held in an alley behind a ruined French church near Brest. One of McGrath's best friends in the 116th, 1st Lt. Donald Anderson, remembered that he and McGrath "were fully armed and sat on our helmets" during mass. American artillery fire and bombs had destroyed the nearby church, and Anderson remarked that "as we walked into the alley, we were appalled when we realized [the French] were reading a list of their dead, many of whom we had accidentally killed. . . . One of those killed was the local priest."

In a postwar letter to McGrath's brother, Anderson spoke for all members of the 116th when he noted: "Combat was mainly a numbness; bone-weary tiredness, a curiosity, and stark moments of utter terror." The impact of that kind of life on McGrath was profound. A few weeks after D-Day, he released his deep emotions—and expressed his faith in God—by composing a poem entitled "Confusion":

My brain is wracked, my spirit bent
I don't know where to turn
My scheme of life is all upset, rent,
Warped, distorted, left to burn,
Upon the shores of life's angry ocean.

Tossed into this new world reign
Of Terror, loneliness and greed that is blind
I wander aimlessly seeking in vain
Something to grasp, to hold; to find
A haven, a refuge free from commotion.

Oh confusion! A world upturned
From the civilized to the jungle land
You sent me searching far and I returned
With God—who has given me a guiding hand
In whom I found solace, comfort and devotion.

Company L's October 7 attack on Baesweiler was a venture that promised from the start to be tough and costly because of the wide-open terrain the 29ers and their accompanying tanks from the 66th Armor had to cross in broad daylight, as well as the presence of four formidable German pillboxes between the Americans' jump-off point and their final objective. Interrogation of prisoners also revealed the troubling detail that the Germans had sown mines across all approach routes to town. Reporter Bradley witnessed the opening of the attack and described it to his Baltimore readers: "The guns of an American battery opened up with a roar. . . . Overhead there was the high-pitched whistle of outgoing shells and the angry *carrump* as high explosive shells landed among the enemy positions. The ground where the battle is taking place is so flat that we could see the columns of dirt rise where the shells hit."

Screeching high-velocity shells from Collier's tanks and tank destroyers blasted the German defenders out of the four pillboxes west of Baesweiler. Now McGrath's Company L dashed over the stumpy sugar beet crops toward the town's outlying houses, bypassing a massive 200-foot coal slag pile sitting incongruously in a field like an ancient pyramid in the Egyptian desert. Nearby was the abandoned Karl-Alexander mine, until recently one of Nazi Germany's most productive sites for the excavation and production of coal.

On the far side of the slagheap, in the western periphery of Baesweiler, a few dozen German infantrymen manning a trench hastily dug by locals prepared to stem the American tide just as Hitler had ordered them to do, to the last bullet if necessary. The Germans' opening fusillade forced the 29ers to drop to the ground, but McGrath sensibly refrained from making a frontal attack on that strong position. Instead, he patiently waited for troops and tanks to come to his aid from Beggendorf, effectively outflanking the enemy's formidable position from the north. A couple of German armored vehicles suddenly appeared in Baesweiler, but they could make no headway against the concentrated fire of Collier's tank destroyers. As Bradley remarked dryly, "There was no further trouble from these."

Eventually, the German defenders hastily abandoned their trenches and yielded Baesweiler to their opponents, failing in their effort, at least this time, to fulfill Hitler's commandment. The Americans, not known for their tactical subtlety, had outmaneuvered the Germans.

McGrath gathered up those Company L members he could find and directed them into Baesweiler immediately. Bradley later noted, "It seemed better off than other towns we have seen here in Germany. The streets were littered with broken branches of trees, and a few houses showed signs of heavy shelling, but generally there was less destruction than had been expected." The Germans, however, were about to increase Baesweiler's level of devastation by bombarding the town and its new owners unmercifully for the next several hours. Shortly after nightfall, Luftwaffe aircraft would join that effort, one of the first times in the war that German pilots dropped bombs on their own homeland.

McGrath advanced into Baesweiler with his men, but he would have little time to savor the accomplishment. Any officer who had been with the 29th Division since Omaha Beach understood that the longevity of rifle company commanders could be remarkably short, and McGrath's tenure as Company L commander, seven weeks in duration, was by now longer than the norm. According to a friend in his former unit, Service Company, "[McGrath] gave me a letter and asked me to mail it in case anything happened. I insisted to him that he stop talking such nonsense, but he declared that he had a feeling and only hoped and prayed if and when [he was killed] that it would be in Germany." In a lonely corner of Baesweiler, in which a subordinate remembered that McGrath "was the only one in the street," that premonition was about to come true.

An abrupt and highly accurate surge of German mortar shells caught McGrath in the open, and one of them exploded within a few feet, felling him with a serious chest wound. Whether or not Gerhardt's standing order to avoid buildings influenced McGrath's behavior can never be known. The first 29er to reach McGrath, S/Sgt. Fred Rutkowski, strove to save him, and the captain was still living when stretcher bearers arrived to evacuate him to the 3rd Battalion aid station with all possible speed, but later that day, Capt. Maurice McGrath died of his wounds. The 29th Division had lost another remarkable soldier.

One mile to the south of Baesweiler, 1st Lt. James Myers' Company I held the job of securing the 2nd Armored Division's south flank by seizing Oidtweiler. That mission was accomplished by sunset on October 7, although Myers's success cost Company I dearly. As a liaison officer later reported to Gerhardt, Company I was "badly in need of reorganization . . . with thirty men unaccounted for." The company morning report for that day indicated that twenty-seven of those thirty men were wounded— seven "seriously"—while three were listed as "non-battle casualties." Remarkably, Company I suffered no deaths on October 7.

For Puntenney's 3rd Battalion, the battle was over: Harmon may not have achieved his coveted breakthrough and subsequent dash to the Rhine, but at least he had secured the defensive position that the 2nd Armored Division would hold with little alteration for the next seven weeks. For the first three of those weeks, the 3rd Battalion would remain continuously in the line under Harmon's command, ensuring that German "enthusiasm" did not interfere with Corlett's main object at Aachen. Three days of battle had sharply depleted the battalion's ranks. On October 9, Harmon spoke with Gerhardt, his classmate from the West Point class of 1917, and declared that Puntenney's men "are pretty tired." An alarmed Gerhardt rejoined, "Don't you encourage them to say they're tired! We don't go in for that kind of business!"

If tiredness was not acceptable in the division, Puntenney's 29ers were fortunate that for the rest of their period in the line under Harmon, the Germans did not test them. The immediate front would remain surprisingly quiet; the antagonists now focused entirely on Aachen. The battle line was quiet enough on October 26 for Company K's 2nd Lt. Carl "Chubby" Proffitt, first baseman on the undefeated Plymouth Yankees 116th Infantry baseball team in 1943 and holder of the Distinguished Service Cross for heroics in Normandy, to take a few of his platoon members on a hunting expedition. According to the company morning report, they "nailed a German steer on the run, and T/4 [Chow] Owyang, oriental chef from the west coast now serving as a runner and rifleman, prepared a fine steak festival for the men. Ever Forward!"

Finally, on October 29, Harmon returned Puntenney's battalion to Gerhardt and the 29th Division. Tired or not, there's no place like home.

2. TREAT THEM LIKE THE BEST

The 116th Infantry was about to be sucked into a battle that veterans would define as the regiment's toughest fight of World War II. For a unit that had landed at H-Hour on Omaha Beach, that statement was telling. Senior U.S. Army leaders controlling the 116th Infantry's fate utterly failed to foresee the enemy's firm resolution to retain the regiment's objective, Würselen, a drab and nondescript Aachen suburb German commanders had defined as the decisive point in their efforts to retain this part of their homeland.

The American high command radiated confidence at first: Hobbs's 30th Division needed only to advance a few miles southward to Würselen and a little farther beyond to close the Aachen Gap, and the city's fate would be sealed. The 30th had shattered the Germans' notorious West Wall just a few days in the past, and compared to that arduous job, the present task should be easy. At First Army headquarters, General Hodges's aide, Maj. William Sylvan, noted in his diary on October 8: "It is hoped that the circle closing in Aachen will be completed by tomorrow." According to the 30th Division's 1946 official history, closing the Aachen Gap "appeared to be a relatively easy task. . . . To move the 4,000 yards to the division boundary [at Würselen] appeared at worst a two-day job."

Unfortunately, Hodges's fixation on capturing Aachen with all possible speed caused him to order Hobbs to attack the Germans frontally at the place and time they most expected. The enemy, just as resolved to hold Aachen as their opponents were to capture it, had recently rushed the 8,000 men of the fresh 246th *Volksgrenadier* Division to the city. Furthermore, the German high command, typically stingy when it came to responding to frontline commanders' continual calls for help, ordered considerable reinforcements to the scene, including the entire 116th Panzer Division, many smaller armored formations, and plentiful corps- and army-level artillery units. The Americans' unsubtle tactics, as well as the Germans' unexpected manpower and artillery strength, would cause hundreds of casualties in the 116th Infantry over the next several days and would prevent the regiment from ever fulfilling its assigned mission.

For five days, Dwyer's 116th Infantry, minus Puntenney's battalion (still with the 2nd Armored Division), stood on the sidelines, observing the progress of the 30th Division's attack toward Würselen. Reserve status was much more desirable than being a component of a major frontal attack on a dug-in enemy, but duty anywhere near the front was always hazardous, a detail that emerged with startling suddenness at 12:15 P.M. on October 7, when a jeep from the 2nd Battalion's communications section, occupied by five 29ers transporting coils of telephone wire, detonated an unseen German mine. The explosion killed four occupants and seriously wounded a fifth. The battalion's commander, Maj. Charles Cawthon, noted: "I considered our small crew of signalmen as good as any in the army. . . . To lose such soldiers on a dreary dirt road to a casual exclamation of high explosive was a personal blow." (The four dead 29ers were Cpl. Wimburne Phinney, Pvt. Hairston Cumberland, Pvt. Earl Potter, and Pvt. Marcus Segan.)

By October 9, the 30th Division's rightmost regiment, the 119th Infantry, had actually pushed ahead almost all the way into Würselen as a result of successful penetrations of the German line in two consecutive days of hard combat. The enemy reacted to the American success with its standard counterthrust, one that was particularly violent because it contained plenty of those weapons American infantrymen feared most: tanks. For several days, the 119th's spearhead was almost cut off, but Hobbs was so strained in striving to stand his ground in the face of the enemy surge, and his division so depleted by ten days of unremitting combat, that he knew a junction with the 1st Division somewhere beyond Würselen would still be a long way off. At midday on October 12, Hobbs reported to Corlett with some concern: "We are being attacked all along our front: being

pecked at in some places; strong in others; and building up in others."
Corlett displayed little sympathy, blurting to Hobbs later that day: "General Hodges tells me we have got to close the gap some way."

After the war, Corlett recalled:

> During this period I was subjected to terrific pressure. I have a
> record of the telephone conversations of the period between General Hodges and myself and between members of his staff and my
> staff. The continual refrain was, 'When are you going to close the
> gap?' In each instance I explained that we were closing the gap,
> but we faced close-in pillbox and village street fighting. . . . Upon
> my suggestion that VII Corps [under Maj. Gen. J. Lawton Collins,
> the command to which the 1st Division belonged] help a bit, or
> that fighting at some other point along the front might relieve
> some of the pressure on us, Hodges became very angry.

Hobbs clearly needed help. At 12:15 P.M. on October 12, Corlett
issued orders attaching the 116th Infantry's 1st and 2nd Battalions to the
30th Division. The rest period had ended. As noted in the 116th's October
action report, the regiment was "entrusted with the mission of closing the
gap between the 30th Division and the 1st Division." Corlett and Hobbs
discussed various plans to maneuver around Würselen, but they abandoned them all, as 30th Division historian Robert Hewitt wrote, because
either they "involved too many unknowns" or "they felt they were short
on troops." To the dismay of Dwyer's two battalion commanders, Tom
Dallas of the 1st and Charles Cawthon of the 2nd, the 116th's assault had
to be made on an extraordinarily narrow front, across a belt of flat, open
ground directly against a jumble of buildings on Würselen's northern
periphery, occupied by a fully entrenched and resolute band of Germans
who had firmly held their position against the 30th's surge for days. At
least Dallas and Cawthon would be solidly supported by Sherman tanks of
Companies B and G, 66th Armor, loaned to Hobbs for the attack by Harmon's 2nd Armored Division.

The 116th had to launch a frontal attack—always a rough proposition—but Corlett saw no alternative. When intelligence reports indicated
the alarming news that German prisoners had been captured not only from
the 116th Panzer Division, but also the renowned 1st SS Panzer Division,
known as *Leibstandarte Adolf Hitler* (Adolf Hitler's Bodyguard), Corlett

realized that one of those momentous historical moments, when a proverbial irresistible force met an immovable object, was about to occur. On October 12, Corlett spoke with Hobbs and declared, "If the 116th Panzer and [*Leibstandarte*] *Adolf Hitler* are in there, this is one of the decisive battles of the war."

In a June 20, 1947, letter to 29th Division historian Joe Ewing, Hewitt wrote: "The reason for the Würselen attack went something like this: It is a frontal attack and therefore may be costly. But if we put on the pressure and take losses, we can have a speedy linkup. The Würselen attack had the shortest distance to cover [compared to other plans]. It was hoped, too, that after the first German defenses were overpowered by brute force, the rest of the advance would be easier. It didn't work that way." In his 1946 30th Division history, Hewitt observed more bluntly: "The action called, in high degree, for willingness to take losses in gaining ground—one of the most difficult things to communicate along the chain of command." Had the 29ers grasped what was expected of them, many of them surely would have felt like sacrificial lambs. Mercifully, the top brass's deliberations were beyond their sphere of awareness, even for battalion commanders Dallas and Cawthon and regimental commander Dwyer.

The 116th Infantry would have to carry out the attack working with unfamiliar leaders, in unfamiliar territory, and even lacking its direct-support 105-millimeter howitzer unit, the 111th Field Artillery Battalion. The regimental intelligence officer, Capt. Robert Walker, recalled, "It would be our first experience with a different division headquarters. Vaguely, I didn't like it, but we tried to consider it a distinction to be assigned to a very important task. We resolved to do our best, and if possible impress the 30th Division with our rolling thunder!"

The objective, Würselen, lay just beyond the 116th Infantry's new sector of the front, which the regiment stealthily took over from a battalion of the 119th Infantry just after dark on October 12. The new surroundings were centered on the mining village of Bardenberg, whose derelict condition was entirely familiar to every 116th combat veteran. "The roads were littered with glass, dirt, and rubble from blasted buildings," Holbrook Bradley wrote. "Telephone and power lines were broken and drooped from fallen pole to fallen pole. . . . Buildings on both sides of the street were scarred and pitted with shell holes, and pockmarked by machine gun fire. A few houses still had roofs intact and an occasional window unbroken."

Jump-off would be at 9 A.M. on the thirteenth, with Dallas's 1st Battalion on the left and Cawthon's 2nd Battalion on the right. Phase lines, carefully delineated by staff officers between Bardenberg and Würselen on 1:25,000-scale maps, would gauge both outfits' progress. Each phase line was assigned a code name based on a woman's name: Ann, Bertha, Catherine, Daisy, Edna. The news that Hodges craved to hear within the next forty-eight hours was that the 116th had reached line Edna; in that event, the 29ers would be shaking hands with GIs from their landing partner on Omaha Beach, the 1st Infantry Division—and Aachen would be surrounded.

PFC John Barnes of Company A observed: "It was Friday the 13th of October. A black day for us." That day, the regiment and its accompanying tanks made it to line Ann and a little beyond, but the gain of about 1,000 yards was by far the most lengthy daily advance it would achieve for the next ten days. The junction point with the 1st Division just beyond Würselen was still some 2,800 yards away—more than a mile and a half—and the Germans sent a clear message: in the battle for Aachen, Würselen would mark the line from which they would not retreat. If the Americans were determined to take the town, they must be prepared for a battle of colossal intensity. The 116th's monthly action report corroborated that the Germans were dead serious in their resolve. It defined enemy resistance as "extremely heavy—in the form of SP [self-propelled guns], dug-in tanks, mortars, and small-arms fire." As Captain Walker noted, "It was evident that Hitler's troops had orders to stand and die."

For a short while, the fury of the Americans' opening attack on October 13 suggested they might make a quick breakthrough. Preceded by several impressive air strikes by screeching P-47 Thunderbolts and a thunderous artillery preparation, the 29ers and their supporting tanks dashed into the flat landscape between Bardenberg and Würselen with such confidence and ferocity that it seemed as if nothing could stop them. As Cawthon related, "The [2nd] Battalion had much experience and was as rested as an outfit can expect to be in war."

Cawthon was extraordinarily fortunate to work closely with one of the 2nd Armored Division's most exceptional soldiers, Capt. James Burt, the commander of the 66th Armor's Company B. The twenty-seven-year-old Burt was a 1939 graduate of Vermont's Norwich University, a notable source of U.S. Army cavalry officers. Two years later, he joined the 2nd Armored Division, then under the command of a blustery major general

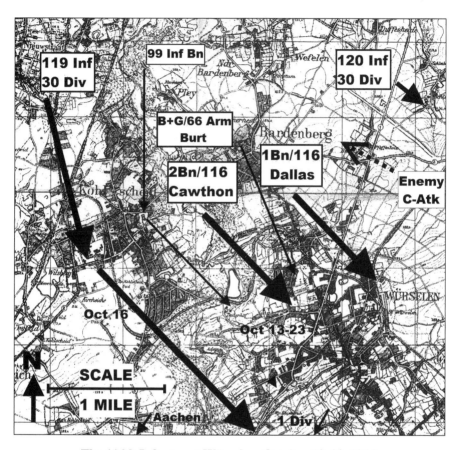

The 116th Infantry at Würselen, October 13–23, 1944.

named George Patton. Burt would remain with the "Hell on Wheels" outfit until war's end. He participated in both the North African and Sicilian
campaigns and came ashore in Normandy on Omaha Beach just a few
days after D-Day. That kind of lengthy combat experience taught Burt
that the seizure of Würselen would require the closest cooperation
between infantry, tanks, artillery, and fighter-bombers. That his men readily provided a major part of that cooperation to the appreciative 29ers
was recognized by Cawthon, who observed that "the tankers were
aggressive and used all their firepower." One anonymous member of
Cawthon's battalion also saluted the proficiency of Burt's tankers in the
attack's opening phase: "We had encountered difficulty in taking a small
group of buildings. The enemy was dug in in front of the town, and there
was an open stretch of about seventy-five yards to cross before reaching
them. We arranged with a supporting tank to lay down machine gun fire.
By relaying hand signals, this fire was maintained until we had almost
reached the objective. . . . The objective was taken without a shot being
fired by the enemy."

Cawthon and his men had never seen such effective use of tanks. Burt
was all over the battlefield, both on foot and in his personal vehicle, helping to propel the assault forward. A U.S. Army citation for valor later
recorded:

> When infantrymen ran into murderous small-arms and mortar fire,
> Captain Burt dismounted from his tank about 200 yards to the rear
> and moved forward on foot beyond the infantry positions where,
> as the enemy concentrated a tremendous volume of fire upon him,
> he calmly motioned his tanks into good firing positions. As our
> attack gained momentum, he climbed aboard his tank and directed
> the action from the rear deck exposed to hostile volleys [from a
> German 20-millimeter anti-aircraft gun], which finally wounded
> him painfully on the face and neck. He maintained his dangerous
> post despite pointblank self-propelled gunfire until friendly
> artillery knocked out those enemy weapons and then proceeded to
> the advanced infantry scouts' positions to deploy his tanks for the
> defense of the gains that had been made.

"There was no hospitalization for this wound," Burt recalled. "An aid
man with tweezers pulled most of the small fragments from my face. . . .

At least one came out a month later when shaving." Fragments remained in Burt's face for the rest of his life.

Apparently, the fresh 29ers and Burt's tankers would provide the impetus Corlett so desperately needed to close the Aachen Gap. "Going in right behind the artillery preparation, infantry and armor made it across the open stretch and into the built-up area [of Würselen] at the first bound," Cawthon wrote. "Here, the going became rougher." The primary reason it became so rough was that the German commander had been profusely supplied with artillery, and he knew exactly where to apply it. Since the 116th's attack route between Bardenberg and Würselen was so narrow and predictable, the 29ers were highly vulnerable to the enemy's barrage, which made their crusty first sergeants' standard warning to avoid bunching up especially important. In the 30th Division's official history, Hewitt described the fire as "bitterly heavy, succeeding in neutralizing many approaches to the network of enemy positions." Walker substantiated that claim when he recalled a highly descriptive message sent from the 116th's command post back to Hobbs: "Saturating and continuous artillery and mortar fire for three days, with a round falling every three seconds." Maj. James Morris, the 1st Battalion's executive officer, concluded: "I think someone has made Hitler mad since this is the noisiest place I've struck yet. But we don't have any ideas of letting him run us out of the Fatherland."

Some of the German artillery fire came from cannons of super-heavy caliber, yielding shell detonations so massive that no 29er could ever forget them. Once, Burt and some comrades were standing in a Würselen street near a church when a German shell abruptly blasted a large hole in the church's wall. "[There was] noise, but no explosion," Burt recalled. "A soldier said, '[German] 88s are busy today.'" The startled Burt knew, but did not reveal, that the size of the hole, which he estimated at fourteen inches, indicated the source was a gun of much larger size than an 88, probably a huge railroad cannon, and he realized that he likely would have been killed or injured if the shell had not been a dud.

The 116th's action report for October noted, "Artillery and mortar fire was the most severe and continuous ever encountered by this unit." The 29ers and tankers would have no respite from that merciless fire for more than a week. Dawn on October 14 revealed a "clear sky, [with] good visibility"—excellent conditions for American fighter-bombers to make an appearance. Dallas's and Cawthon's battalions, along with their supporting tanks, jumped off at an unusually early hour, 5 A.M., and for a short while, both commanders hoped they had caught the Germans off guard. They did not, despite an exaggerated claim in the 116th's action report that "considerable ground" was gained. Cawthon's battalion journal, written only hours after the events it described took place, told a much more sober and accurate story, noting that at sunset the 2nd Battalion ended up only 250 yards ahead of its morning start line. Hewitt's 30th Division history recorded: "Progress was being made, but it wasn't enough. . . . [It] would continue to depend on trying one technique after another to knock out the key points in the defense— and many of these key points had held out against everything tried against them that day." Burt recalled the Americans' frustration by noting that forward progress was defined by "continuing to get a house or so every day."

Battalion commanders Dallas and Cawthon had relied on one option above all others since Normandy to overcome stubborn enemy resistance—calling for overwhelming supporting fire from nearby artillery. No military force in the world could carry out that support with the speed and power of the U.S. Army, and in Brittany, the 29ers had expertly learned how to add Ninth Air Force fighter-bombers to the mix. At Würselen, however, the 116th Infantry discovered that attachment to an unfamiliar organization put a kink in the routines. Dwyer's men had never before worked with 30th Division artillery forward observer and liaison teams, and as any good infantryman knew, the effectiveness of those teams meant the difference between victory and defeat. Although the teamwork between the 29ers and their new comrades was generally good, friction sporadically erupted between infantrymen and artillerymen over procedural differences.

The commander of the 116th Infantry's Company E, Capt. Robert Garcia, recalled an incident during which his outfit was stalled at a heavily defended objective in open ground just outside Würselen. Under ordinary circumstances, a call from a 111th Field Artillery Battalion forward observer operating with Garcia would have resulted in a deadly volley of shells from the 111th's 105-millimeter howitzers on the enemy position within a few minutes. But this time, the 111th was nowhere near Würselen. "The unit supporting us was from another division and was using 155-millimeter howitzers," Garcia observed. "These guns [possibly from the 30th Division's 113th Field Artillery Battalion] packed a more powerful wallop, and I really felt happy about having them back there to help out." A forward observer team consisting of a captain and a sergeant with a backpack radio accompanied Company E. Garcia promptly asked the captain to place artillery fire on the obstinate strongpoint, but the captain refused, claiming that the chance of short rounds impacting on or near American lines was too great. The captain rebuffed Garcia's plea that Company E was willing to take that chance and then departed. Much to Garcia's astonishment, however, the sergeant returned momentarily and affirmed, "Captain, if you and your men are going to cross that open field, then I'm going to stay here with this radio and call in all the supporting fire you need. You just tell me where you want it, and I'll put it there." According to the grateful Garcia, he did, and eventually, the Germans abandoned their position and pulled back.

Another difficulty affecting Dallas's and Cawthon's ability to get help was the sheer intensity of the Germans' artillery bombardment, which all veterans agreed was the worst they had ever seen. The incessant salvos forced the Americans to hunker down in basements and foxholes for considerable periods, and the thousands of whizzing and screeching shell fragments routinely cut American telephone wire. Dallas and Cawthon knew telephone communication was both more reliable and secure than transmissions of the wireless variety, especially in built-up areas. Intrepid 116th wiremen worked with little or no rest, beneath a rain of shrapnel, to hunt for wire breaks and repair them when found. It was extraordinarily hazardous work. "At times I thought it might be better if my superiors did not have such ready means of passing orders and pressure for progress," Cawthon remarked wryly. "But balancing this was my frequent need for help." In fact, so vital was the ability to call for assistance that battalion and company command posts shifted much closer to the front than normal to minimize the distance wiremen had to lay and repair telephone wire.

In Normandy and Brittany, the wiremen's job was taken for granted; Würselen was different. Wiremen were so essential to the 116th Infantry's job of closing the Aachen Gap that Dwyer eventually took the unusual step of recognizing six particularly noteworthy signalmen by granting them Silver Stars for combat valor. One of those, Pvt. Edward Sexton, was a rarity, a 116th Infantry veteran dating back to the prewar days in the Virginia National Guard. Sexton's Silver Star citation recognized his "unflinching courage" and noted:

During the period October 13–25, 1944, intense enemy artillery and mortar fire necessitated almost constant repair and replacement of telephone lines in order to maintain communications. Private Sexton, a wireman, with complete disregard for his own safety, time after time braved this decimating fire to repair and replace severed lines. On numerous occasions he laid wire in the face of pointblank fire from enemy tanks. During this period Private Sexton rarely slept, for when he was not actually repairing a line, he was out checking or laying new wire.

The work of Sexton and his comrades ensured that however badly the 29ers were being pummeled by enemy fire, the Germans had to endure the same punishment from American artillery.

Which side would crack first? Dwyer had no opportunity to practice tactical brilliance since his 116th Infantry was fighting almost exclusively in the heavily built-up area of northern Würselen. That town was of considerable size, and for days, the Germans had diligently prepared for its defense, establishing dozens of strongpoints in sturdy stone and brick buildings, shored up by well-camouflaged tanks and plentiful mortars whose operators demonstrated an uncanny ability to drop shells exactly where they wanted. It was street fighting at its worst, far more severe than anything the 116th had experienced before. When the regiment had fought the Germans in the streets of Vire and Brest, the demoralized enemy had shown little inclination to stand and fight, but in Würselen, the Germans had issued a challenge and dared the 29ers to come forward and push them out of heavily fortified buildings from which they had vowed not to retreat.

For the men of the 116th, it was on-the-job training, with deadly consequences for anyone who let their guard down for a few seconds or failed to pay heed to the meager number of grizzled veterans who knew how to survive in this grisly new environment. One member of Company B, a private by the name of Eugene Gilmore, noted in the "Lessons" section of the 116th's October action report: "To fight the German in his own backyard and in his own house, you will find that you must go into the cellar and drag him out. The fragmentation grenade is your best bet in this kind of fighting—always have a few with you. Don't go anywhere alone: have a buddy with you always. Stand guard with him. Attack with him. Our famous 'buddy system' pays dividends in street fighting."

Pvt. Emmett Journell, a twenty-three-year-old native of Salem, Virginia, and a prewar veteran of Roanoke's Company D of the Virginia National Guard, offered his own lesson: "Most of your movement will be at night, and that's a hard job. If you once let Jerry hear your movement, he'll thrown so much darn artillery and mortar at you that you will begin to think that Hell is a safer place for you. Take my advice and make as little noise as possible—and if possible, no noise at all." Journell would later be killed in action on April 24, 1945, one of the last 29ers to die in the line of duty in World War II.

Reporter Holbrook Bradley was all over Würselen observing the fighting, which caused Maj. Jim Morris to exclaim, "He certainly takes a lot of chances to get the news." In an October 14 article in the *Baltimore Sun*, Bradley wrote:

> The whole scene reminded one of St. Lô, with the buildings on both sides of the road wrecked and blazing. Small groups of GIs accompanying the tanks crouched in doorways and other sheltered areas as we hurried through the wreckage to find a safe spot for ourselves. We finally dived into the doorway of an apartment building on top of a dead German, who lay face up staring at the ceiling… [Later] we could see 20 or 30 Germans running from the houses. From a three-story building down the street, an American heavy weapons company opened up with machine guns and we watched the Germans drop like tenpins. Some reached the safety of a ditch and an open cellar hole across the street, but by the time the fire had stopped some green-uniformed figures were sprawled on the road where they had been hit.

The Germans had their own reporters to record the Aachen story, and the 29ers would soon learn from a captured October 26, 1944, edition of the notorious Nazi newspaper *Deutsche Allgemeine Zeitung* that the name of the 29th Division had made it into the Nazi press. An article by author Kurt Neher entitled "The Defense of Aachen, City of the Emperors," declared:

> Since October 3, when an American loudspeaker near the German positions in southwestern Aachen demanded the surrender of our grenadiers and announced in a brazen lie, 'Aachen is surrounded,'

bitter weeks have passed for the Americans. They have been weeks of terrible fighting such as these intruders never before have experienced on European soil. During that time, the enemy's dream of bloodless conquest of Germany vanished. . . . October 13 was a difficult day for Aachen's defenders, but it was one which they endured due to their superior grit. The Americans had looked forward to being in possession of the city in a matter of only a few hours. And so it went, day after day. Time and again our grenadiers emerged from cellars and from behind ruins to attack the Americans. They mopped up streets and squares, broke into enemy strongpoints, and interfered with enemy supply. The Americans were terrified by this kind of fighting. . . . It is possible that our adversaries were members of the American 29th Division, which allegedly has assumed the tradition of the 'Maryland Blue and Gray Division' from the last world war.

Since the 116th was a Virginia, not a Maryland, regiment, this latest bit of enemy propaganda in all likelihood elicited the standard reaction from Dwyer's men about anything the Germans said or wrote: those brainless Nazis, as usual, have no idea what they're talking about. One German psychological warfare leaflet did manage to generate a few chuckles among the 29ers. It portrayed an exhausted and disheveled GI with the caption: "Oh, my Aachen back!" At least that portrayal of combat in this devastated corner of the world was fairly accurate.

The 116th suffered a major setback on October 14 when a shell fragment from one of the Germans' constant artillery bursts wounded Major Cawthon in the left leg, forcing his evacuation. The thirty-two-year-old Cawthon had assumed command of the 2nd Battalion on July 30, 1944, when that outfit's redoubtable leader, Lt. Col. Sidney Bingham, had been wounded. Despite Cawthon's lack of confidence that he could adequately replace Bingham, a belief he had shared with an intractable Dwyer in the hopes that someone else would get the job, he had led the battalion expertly for more than two months, guiding it successfully through the frenzied and fierce fighting at Vire and Brest. An experienced and articulate newspaperman in civilian life, Cawthon had enlisted in the Virginia National Guard in 1940 as a private in Company H, 116th Infantry, and gained a commission as a second lieutenant just a few months later. The men of the 2nd Battalion, with whom he had served since the unit's February 1941 mobilization, would greatly miss his quiet, self-effacing leadership. He was replaced by the battalion executive officer, Capt. Eccles Scott, who had landed on Omaha Beach in the first minutes of D-Day as commander of Company G.

Cawthon's wound was of the "million dollar" variety. He recalled it as "narrow and perhaps two inches long; the skin around its edges ragged and dark but barely bleeding. Obviously this was grounds for claim to another cluster to my Great Good Luck Medal, already fairly crowded with clusters. Anywhere other than a leg or arm, it probably would have been fatal. . . . Had my emotions been less self-centered I would have felt sorry for anyone taking over in such a situation." After a long recuperation in Paris and England, Cawthon would return to the 29th Division in April 1945.

The surgeon who patched up Cawthon and sent him on his way to rear-area hospitals was one of the busiest soldiers in the 2nd Battalion. Cawthon characterized the twenty-seven-year-old Capt. Jorge "Doc" Hereter, a native of Caguas, Puerto Rico, as "a cheerful and steadfast asset to the battalion." He had set up an underground aid station just inside the entrance of an abandoned coal mine. As one wounded 29er recalled, it was "situated no more than 1,000 yards to the rear of where the real action was taking place . . . right up there close to where the wounded could not miss it. And when you arrived, you were given immediate attention." In a period of little more than one week, Hereter would treat hundreds of wounded, most of whom could be treated successfully and dispatched to a quieter and safer hospital. Others were beyond help, and instead of a transfer to a hospital, they would ultimately be handed over to graves registration personnel for burial.

One of the wounded brought to Hereter's aid station from Würselen was Captain Garcia, the commander of Company E, who had unwisely peeked around the corner of a house and was the recipient of a shell blast just yards from his face. Garcia described Hereter as "a diminutive Puerto Rican . . . just about 5'3" tall and probably 120 pounds. But all of him was doctor—and a damned good one. He was blond and blue-eyed, liked to have his fun, but was all business when business was what was needed. . . . He quickly and efficiently patched me up, all the time giving me hell for not coming back to him more quickly. . . . 'What did I think I was doing?' I didn't care. All of this cussing out rolled right off my back. He had done his job, excellently, and I just relaxed and let him chew me out. . . . I think he was one of the best."

Captain Burt of the 66th Armor again trekked all over Würselen on October 14, not only guiding his tanks into optimal fighting positions, but also helping Cawthon's beleaguered infantrymen whenever their attacks stalled or leaders became casualties. When Burt learned of Cawthon's wound and imminent evacuation—which could paralyze the entire 2nd Battalion—he darted out of his tank and made his way on foot through a hail of shells to Cawthon's command post to offer help and advice. Furthermore, as related by a citation for valor, "He took great risks to rescue wounded comrades and inflicted prodigious destruction on enemy personnel and materiel even though suffering from the wounds he received in the battle's opening phase."

Good soldiers take initiative when battlefield affairs threaten to swirl out of control, and Burt was obviously an exceptionally good soldier. He remembered:

> By default I took over the team. Even though I commanded a company attached to [Cawthon's] battalion, I then effectively had to take command of the battalion, which was from a different division. But it seemed to work reasonably well. I kept my executive officer in a cellar, and the two remaining battalion [staff] officers likewise, to keep in touch with our rear. . . . Colonel [Hugh] O'Farrell, my battalion commander, had nothing left of his own headquarters because his three tank companies had been assigned out to the 116th. Every night I would go to his headquarters, report what was going on, arrange for supplies (because the 66th still supplied us), and tell him what we were planning for the next day and what our wishes were for artillery, aerial photos, and so forth.

One significant benefit provided to the 116th by Burt's tanks was that the Shermans' steel hulls protected their radios whereas the 29ers' signal equipment frequently malfunctioned or was lost to enemy fire. Burt's secure communication links to the rear generated a resounding response to the Germans' stand-or-die posture in Würselen. The infantrymen appreciated nothing better than giving the Germans a taste of their own medicine, and the American air and artillery bombardment of enemy strongpoints, sometimes less than a block away from friendly lines, provided the 29ers grim satisfaction. "We had air strikes whenever we wanted them," Burt commented. "Fortunately the same unit of P-47s had been with [the 66th

Armor] since Normandy. During rest periods we exchanged personnel to see and talk. They learned what we looked like from the air, and we learned what they could do—such as hit a building across the street from us and use an [effective] bomb setting when the target was an enemy tank so that a near miss would create a crater into which the tank would fall. . . . At least one pilot wanted to stay for the [ground] combat phase, but he couldn't get permission." At Würselen, Burt remembered just how effective the relationship between airmen and tankers could be: "On one occasion we asked for an air strike on a house across the street from a school. I stood in the schoolyard and was showered with metallic links from the airplane's .50-caliber machine guns [and] I was able to read the stenciling on the bomb as it floated by."

Since Würselen was the focal point of the XIX Corps's efforts, Burt could call on plenty of artillery support, including heavy-caliber guns such as 8-inch and 240-millimeter howitzers. Those impressive firepower displays could be decisive against troops in the open, but Würselen's buildings provided such effective cover that only pinpoint artillery fire could dislodge the Germans. No one excelled more at precise artillery fire than U.S. Army cannoneers, and Würselen was the perfect place to practice that science. "One day we were visited by a colonel from [XIX] Corps artillery," Burt commented. "He asked if there were any problems. I said yes; there was a [German] tank: we knew where it was, but we couldn't get any fire on it [because] it was in an alley between houses. He personally set up a 'Long Tom' [155-millimeter long-range cannon] five or six miles away to get a high trajectory and try to clear the roof of the nearest building and come straight down on the enemy tank. He had a lot of fun. He knocked down a few houses, but he never did get the tank."

The Germans, too, were skilled in the use of indirect fire. Several times, Burt witnessed enemy barrages that were undertaken by a "very well-drilled mortar officer [with] incredible precision. The rounds would walk down the street to a corner, turn the corner and walk down the next street." He recalled, however, that the enemy's shells would often arrive at predictable times, and therefore, the Americans could avoid their destructive impact.

The 116th's inability to make significant progress on October 14 triggered an angry exchange between Hodges and Corlett. According to Hodges's aide, Maj. William Sylvan, "General Corlett called before dinner to say that XIX Corps was stopped and he requested more troops and more ammunition. For not the first time, the general reminded him that to obtain more troops and ammunition was at present impossible, and that he was doing everything in his power to see that XIX Corps received more of both. He urged XIX Corps to present whatever alternative or whatever plan they had in mind, but surely they were not admitting that they could go no further."

Corlett had traded harsh words with Hodges several times in the past two weeks, and their relationship was about to take a turn for the worse. Hodges had undeniably been distracted by a series of visits paid to his First Army command post over the course of three days, October 12 to 14, by the likes of George C. Marshall, Dwight D. Eisenhower, Omar Bradley, George Patton, and even His Majesty King George VI of Great Britain. The impression made on those distinguished guests could impact Hodges's job, and protocol demanded that his staff coddle them. At the XIX Corps, however, Corlett had much more grave matters to ponder, and when he phoned the First Army to make his request for reinforcements, Hodges was about to sit down with some of his eminent guests for a mid-day supper, which, according to Sylvan, included "Consommé, Steak with Mushroom Sauce, French Fried Potatoes, Salad, Pie, and Coffee, all fla-vored with the finest of wines and port." That interruption caused Hodges's opinion of Corlett, already low because of his subordinate's astonishing bluntness, to descend even further.

Corlett wanted to close the Aachen Gap just as much as Hodges, and he repeatedly ordered Hobbs to press the 116th's attack on Würselen and allow the Germans no respite. In turn, Hobbs had every right to badger Dwyer to shove his regiment forward, regardless of losses, until either he closed the gap or the 116th wilted from excessive casualties and exhaus-tion. To Hobbs, however, Dwyer was a stranger, a 29er whose time with the 30th Division was strictly temporary. That sort of command relation-ship was awkward for all, but at least for the moment, Hobbs professed confidence that the 116th could do the job. At 7:50 P.M. on October 14, Gerhardt phoned Hobbs and asked, "How's our outfit doing for you?" Hobbs may have had doubts, but if so, he withheld them. "It's pretty tough going, but they are doing all right," he replied. "The army commander [Hodges] thinks they should walk through that place [Würselen], but it just isn't that way. I'm perfectly satisfied with them. They haven't been hurt too badly. They had about fifty-four casualties yesterday, and they'll have a little more today."

Staff officers at Hodges's First Army command post knew that on October 15 the situation at Würselen had reached a point at which something must soon break—would it would be the German defenses, the 116th Infantry's spirit, or even the careers of Corlett, Hobbs, and Dwyer? The situation was critical, and as Hewitt noted, "The plan which took final form on the [30th] Division's G-3 work map on the morning of the 15th was one born of desperation." The 116th had to bull forward yet again through the rubble-strewn streets of Würselen and reach the 1st Division, however many casualties it took. The "desperate" part of the plan would kick in only if Dwyer could still not fulfill his job by nightfall. In that event, Hobbs readied his own 119th Infantry to execute an entirely new scheme of maneuver for the sixteenth, a cunning end run west of Würselen that Corlett had rejected in the past as too risky.

Just an hour into the 116th's October 15 attack, the Germans' unyielding defense of Würselen convinced Corlett that he was eventually going to have to initiate that risky maneuver. Dwyer's exhausted 29ers recommenced their assault at 8 A.M., and in the words of the regimental action report, "The type of resistance encountered on this jump-off was of an extremely heavy nature, and our troops experienced difficult going all the way." Würselen had been transformed into an unearthly place, a mini-Stalingrad, the kind of hideous battlefield the 29ers had innocently thought they would never see again. Recent predictions of Nazi Germany's imminent demise had been premature. Dwyer's orders were clear: the 116th had to drive the Germans completely out of Würselen, if necessary by killing or capturing every defender. As reported by the October 1944 edition of *Le Tomahawk*, the XIX Corps's official newsletter: "The infantry had to slug it out yard by yard."

The men of the 116th were not used to this kind of combat. The Germans were close, often within range of a hand grenade, but were so effectively dug in that they only rarely showed themselves. When they did, even for only a few seconds, the impact on the Americans was usually deadly. The 29ers learned that movement of any kind in the open, even at a dead run, was likely to attract the attention of an invisible German sniper, who was surprisingly skilled at his job. If the 116th were to push the Germans out of Würselen, obviously the only way to do it was to reduce strongpoints by direct assault, one after the other, a process that might eventually succeed but would take time and inflict a number of casualties that could cripple the regiment's spirit for a long time.

The cacophony of battle was so intense that it was difficult for anyone to think clearly. Much of the racket was produced by the incessant barrage of friendly and enemy artillery shells. To that din was added the distinctive ripping blast of German machine guns, the much slower *rat-tat-tat* of American machine guns, the oppressive roar of a tank's cannon, the crack of a sniper's rifle, the *whoosh* of a bazooka, and the sharp pop of hand grenades. Now and then, for reasons no one could fathom, the clamor of battle would abruptly cease, only to resume a few minutes later at even greater intensity. No place was safe, not even the cellars of sturdy stone buildings into which men of both sides commonly took refuge. For the 29ers, proof of that fact came by a simple glance at their surroundings: dozens of once-sturdy buildings had now been flattened; dozens more would soon meet the same fate if the shelling kept up at the current level of intensity. Holbrook Bradley realized the power of German artillery when he made a heartbreaking discovery: "In one basement we found a Maryland sergeant whom we knew very well, who had been killed by a shell that crashed through a cement wall about a half-hour before."

If American tanks and infantry could not do the job, then maybe American artillery could. At one point, the intrepid Burt jumped in his tank, slammed the hatch cover shut, and ordered his driver to maneuver around Würselen several hundred yards beyond enemy lines in a desperate attempt to observe enemy targets for American artillery. Armed with a pair of binoculars, "he dismounted and remained for one hour giving accurate data to friendly gunners. Twice more that day he went on reconnaissance into enemy territory under deadly fire. . . . Twice the tank he was riding was knocked out by enemy action, and each time he climbed aboard another vehicle and continued to fight."

Malfunctioning radios and severed telephone wire created a particularly impenetrable fog of war in Würselen for the 116th Infantry's company and battalion commanders, forcing them repeatedly to shift their command posts forward, in most cases just a block or two behind the front line, to stay in touch with their riflemen. In truth, however, figuring out the actual location of the "front" was nearly impossible. Wherever it was, it was not too far ahead of where it had been the day before, and according to Dwyer's best estimate, which he reported to Hobbs at sunset, the 116th Infantry had gained only about 300 yards on October 15. That was still 1,000 yards short of the Edna phase line and the all-important junction with the 1st Division.

One thousand yards was close enough to dispatch a one-man patrol after dark through enemy lines toward the objective. According to Captain Walker, "The thinking was that if one man could sneak through, a whole battalion could sneak through. Good logic—at least to some." A junior officer from the regimental Headquarters Company, 1st Lt. Robert Clark, volunteered for that seemingly suicidal mission. After blackening his face, 116th staff officers briefed him on what they knew of enemy dispositions, proposed a route around Würselen, and provided him with proper passwords in the event he managed to reach a 1st Division outpost. It was a forlorn hope, and after a few hours wandering in the dark, Clark returned to American lines with no news of the 1st Division. The 116th's monthly action report looked on the bright side when it noted that Clark was "highly successful in that [he] did manage to pass through enemy lines and secure valuable information with regard to German positions."

That was not nearly enough for Hodges. Like all senior U.S. Army commanders in World War II, Hodges grasped that the most important part of his job was to press subordinates relentlessly to achieve positive results regardless of difficulties. According to Corlett and members of the XIX Corps staff, Hodges practiced that technique overzealously. One serious violation of command protocol from Corlett's perspective was Hodges's insistence that failure at Würselen resulted entirely from Hobbs's lack of drive. The 30th Division's commander looked to his immediate boss, Corlett, for instructions, but occasionally during the Würselen fight, Hodges pressed Hobbs directly to close the Aachen Gap. Hodges blurted to Corlett, "I always thought you ought to relieve Leland [Hobbs]." Hodges reasoned, to some extent baselessly, that "[Hobbs] hasn't moved an inch in four days. . . . [He is] either bragging or complaining."

Corlett loyally shielded his subordinate but in turn pressed Hobbs uncompromisingly to close the gap. One day, though, Hodges went too far. As related by Corlett in his autobiography, "[After] a visit to the front, one of my staff officers told me the word from First Army headquarters: 'We couldn't be fighting very hard because we were not having enough casualties.'" That was the wrong thing to say to the touchy Corlett, who recalled: "I saw red. I jumped in my jeep and raced to headquarters. General Hodges was not there, but his chief of staff, Maj. Gen. Bill Kean, and the G-3, Brig. Gen. [Truman] Coursen [actually Thorson], were present. Still at the boiling point, I told them that if they didn't think we were fighting, I would take them down and show them. It would only take an hour and a half. Neither one of them ever showed up at the front." Of course, it was neither Kean's nor Thorson's job to "show up at the front," but it was indeed their job to comment on Corlett's ability to accomplish a mission vital to the First Army. Presently, Hodges would hear of the outburst, and Corlett's job security dropped even lower.

Meanwhile, Hobbs worried that his own job hinged on the success of the 116th Infantry, a unit normally not in his chain of command. Despite his supposed confidence in Dwyer's ability, on the evening of October 15, Hobbs phoned Gerhardt to see if the 29th Division could help prod the 116th to secure Würselen: "Could you make Col. [Leroy] Watson [the 29th's assistant commander] free to go down and check with Colonel Dwyer tomorrow morning? You know what First Army wants on this thing, and I'm afraid [Dwyer] has petered out today. He didn't make very much ground. I know he is trying to do all he can, but I think he needs some of his own people to talk to him."

Brig. Gen. Leroy Watson (pictured as a colonel in October 1944), assistant commander of the 29th Division, next to his jeep, named *Task Force*.

The Würselen situation mirrored almost exactly a highly unfortunate incident in Normandy involving Hobbs and Watson, and both men must have wondered whether history was about to repeat itself. On July 8, 1944, during the opening of the XIX Corps's St. Lô offensive, Watson, then a major general in command of the 3rd Armored Division, had moved—at Corlett's order—a sizable chunk of his division under the command of Brig. Gen. John Bohn across the Vire River into the 30th Division's zone. That maneuver produced so many clogged roads and such command paralysis in the 30th's rear area that Hobbs, Watson's classmate in the West Point class of 1915, complained bitterly to Corlett that Watson had "only a hazy idea" of the tactical situation. Corlett thereupon took the unusual step of removing Bohn from Watson's chain of command and placing him directly under Hobbs. Later, Bohn's supposed inability to reach a critical objective near St. Lô prompted an angry Hobbs to blurt that Bohn was "sitting on his fanny all day—doing nothing!" The following day, Hobbs relieved Bohn of command, an obvious slap at Watson and the entire 3rd Armored Division. Only a few weeks later, Watson himself was relieved and reduced to the rank of colonel.

Was Hobbs about to do the same thing to Dwyer that he had previously done to Bohn? Such a step could generate ripples of shock throughout the First Army and reflect negatively on Gerhardt and the entire 29th Division. But not this time, despite Gerhardt's accommodating statement to Hobbs, "[The 116th] is your outfit, so do what you see fit."

What Hobbs saw fit to do with the 116th on October 16 was to order Dwyer to persist in his Würselen assault, the regiment's fourth straight day of futile frontal attacks. This time, Hobbs would not depend entirely on Dwyer to get the job done, however, for before dawn, he initiated the 119th Infantry's end run around Würselen, his scheme to close the Aachen Gap that only recently had appeared foolhardy, but now represented Corlett's last and best hope of avoiding Hodges's wrath and saving his job.

Even if the 116th could not smash through German lines to reach the 1st Division, a supreme effort at Würselen on October 16 could tie down enemy forces and draw their attention away from the 119th Infantry's audacious flanking maneuver. Dwyer therefore had to try again, although he knew his regiment could not persist for much longer. His 2nd Battalion would make the main effort this time. That outfit was about to get a new commander, Lt. Col. Sidney Bingham, a man whom Dwyer was glad to see because if anyone could achieve results at Würselen, it was Bingham.

The twenty-nine-year-old West Pointer had graduated just four years before and had led the 2nd Battalion on D-Day, gaining the Distinguished Service Cross for heroism on Omaha Beach. His dynamic leadership of the battalion in Normandy had dissolved any doubts in Gerhardt's mind about his maturity, and he promptly became the general's favorite battalion commander, which elicited misgivings in Bingham because wherever the fighting was hottest, the 2nd Battalion invariably was there. Although he served Gerhardt loyally, Bingham did not return Gerhardt's esteem, for like many other 29th Division field-grade officers, he believed Gerhardt's hyper-aggressive leadership style could be coldhearted and, at times, irrational, causing casualties that might have been prevented had more sensible policies been followed. If Bingham wished his 29th Division career to endure, however, he had to entirely repress those critical thoughts for the duration of the war.

Bingham's wound from July 30 had finally healed. Now, misgivings and all, he was back with his old outfit. As he soon discovered, however, the Würselen situation was a tactical dilemma with no solution. Even worse, the battalion to which he returned bore no resemblance to the one

Lt. Col. Sidney Bingham's graduation photo from the U.S. Military Academy's Class of 1940.

he had trained to a cutting edge for D-Day. Turnover among infantrymen in the rifle companies had been virtually 100 percent, and Bingham would need time to familiarize himself with the battalion. More important, the new 29ers would need time to get to know him. The 2nd Battalion was also in appalling condition after three consecutive days of tough street fighting in Würselen. Bingham's executive from Normandy, Major Cawthon, had been wounded, followed shortly thereafter by the battalion operations officer, 1st Lt. Sylvester Johnson, as well as the commander of Company E, Capt. Robert Garcia. The leader of Company F, Capt. Edward Mahaney, had been killed on the attack's first day. One could hardly imagine a more difficult moment to take over command of an infantry battalion.

Bingham recalled:

About noon on October 16, I got to the regimental command post. Colonel Dwyer took me up to my old battalion at Würselen. After talking to Capt. [Eccles] Scott [whom Bingham was replacing], I decided to have a look at the ground. Sergeant Juan Garcia of El Paso, Texas, the platoon sergeant of the battalion's anti-tank platoon (a crackerjack man who was with the outfit in England), said he knew the battalion dispositions and would be glad to show me around. It was very rough. . . . My long tour in the hospital and replacement system hadn't done much toward fortifying me against such a situation. Garcia was an excellent guide; he knew where everyone was and didn't seem to have a nerve in his body. When our excursion was about 45 minutes old, Garcia asked if I wanted to see a Panther tank. I very foolishly said 'yes,' thinking there was a disabled Panther in the vicinity. He led me into a battered house, picked up a remnant of a large mirror, and proceeded to stick this mirror out the front door and said 'Look!' I didn't have time to determine whether it was a Panther or not because almost immediately the mirror disappeared from Garcia's hands in a ripping burst of machine gun fire from said tank. Sergeant Garcia thought the incident very amusing and was laughing heartily when I suggested we *parti* but fast. We did just that and had the pleasure of watching the tank systematically level the house with its cannon immediately after our departure.

Later, a shaken Bingham conversed with Burt to ask him if he could look over an unusual enemy armored vehicle that members of the 2nd Battalion had just knocked out and captured on a Würselen street. "I found that [the 29ers] had used a bazooka from a cellar window on the tank's track, which was very brilliant as that was the only way they could have knocked out the thing. It was not a tank we had seen before. It was not a Mark V Panther, the [enemy's] most typical tank. In fact I told them I thought it was a Jagdpanther [a tank destroyer on a Panther chassis, armed with an 88-millimeter gun], and I wasn't sure we had ever captured one."

Bingham had experienced enough warfare to know that if the Germans in Würselen were using Panthers and Jagdpanthers—some of their most deadly armored vehicles—they did not intend to retreat. Indeed, if the Germans managed to launch an armored attack, the depleted 2nd Battalion would have trouble hanging on. Bingham could do little to improve the situation. He tried to maneuver his 29ers around stubborn resistance nests, but Germans were everywhere. "Heinie infantry holding out in buildings, pillboxes, and World War I-type trenches were sending over more smallarms fire than had been seen in a week," Holbrook Bradley wrote. "Enemy snipers are again active and several American soldiers working from the shelter of nearby buildings cautioned us to keep under cover while moving down the street."

If Bingham ever harbored doubts about the fighting qualities of the current version of the 2nd Battalion and wondered whether they matched the outfit he had brought ashore on Omaha Beach, those doubts evaporated when he observed his men in action over the next few days: "A 60-millimeter mortar squad leader in Company F, the sole survivor of his squad, was firing his mortar, set up in the yard of a house. After firing, he'd run in the house and upstairs, observe the burst, then run down, make corrections, and then repeat the process. A guy like that is a real hero."

The Würselen stalemate was about to crack. Just before sunrise on October 16, the 30th Division's 119th Infantry executed a brilliant flank attack around Würselen, finding a seam in the Germans' defenses and gaining nearly two miles. At 6:15 P.M., the moment Hodges had been anxiously anticipating for weeks finally occurred when GIs of the 1st and 30th Divisions shook hands on a prominent hill south of Würselen. With that accomplishment, the enemy's monumental effort to keep a lifeline open for Aachen, the renowned "City of Emperors," had been defeated. It was only a matter of time now. Field Marshal Gerd von Rundstedt,

Hitler's chief soldier on the Western Front, signaled the commander of the Aachen garrison, Col. Gerhard Wilck, "to remind him, once more, and with the utmost emphasis, that he will hold this venerable German city to the last man, and will if necessary allow himself to be buried under its ruins."

Hardly anyone on the Aachen front was more satisfied about the 119th Infantry's stunning success than the men of the 116th Infantry, for the motivation for their brutal four-day frontal attack had just evaporated. But the two most satisfied American soldiers in that sector were most assuredly Hobbs and Dwyer, whose jobs were now secure, at least until the Germans forced another bloody stalemate somewhere beyond Aachen on the road to the Rhine. Dwyer's 29ers could now hunker down in the cellars of Würselen and wait for the Germans to come to them—a much more desirable state of affairs than a reversal of that relationship. On October 17, clerks in Bingham's 2nd Battalion noted that agreeable change in the unit journal: "1100: Battalion holding defensive positions in our sector; 2000: Day's activities held to a minimum; 2030: Casualties light for the day."

But every 29er knew that such quiet while in direct contact with the enemy could not last. The Germans were certain to take action to rescue their surrounded comrades in Aachen—and they did so the next day, October 18. Happily, when the German counterattack materialized at 2 P.M., near the seam between the 116th Infantry and the 30th Division's 120th Infantry, it was not up to the Germans' usual ferocious standards, a clear indicator that however cruelly the Würselen battle had treated the 116th, the Germans were much worse off. According to Dwyer's action report, the counterattack was "feeble," and it was speedily "nipped in the bud."

One incident in that clash struck the 30th Division's staff as curious but helped to reveal the 29th's unique spirit to their brethren. As German tanks and infantry tried to smash through American lines on the eighteenth, the 30th Division's chief intelligence officer, Lt. Col. Stewart Hall, phoned his 116th Infantry counterpart, Captain Walker, with some urgency. "I could tell he was politely trying to avoid griping at me," Walker wrote. "But he said he was catching hell at 30th Division headquarters because the 30th's troops were reporting a severe counterattack at our common flank."

The word "counterattack" was one that 29th Division staff officers had learned to avoid at all costs for fear of setting off Gerhardt, who believed that the Germans' efforts always had to be belittled. (Fifty-three years later, Walker confessed: "I can say 'counterattack' now—but I still feel queasy about it.") After listening to Hall's anxious assertion, Walker, with all the coolness he could muster, replied: "Counterattack? We're not having a counterattack! We're just having a little enemy activity, and it was broken up by an air strike." Luckily for Walker, the Germans' effort was indeed feeble, and when Hall phoned back later, Walker recalled, "Happiness, relief, and exuberance spilled out of the hand-piece. 'Boy, did you make me look good!' he chortled. 'When I went in to the G-3 and commanding general [Hobbs] with the information you gave me about the counterattack, they were flabbergasted because they hadn't even heard the outcome from their own front-line troops yet!'"

The following week, Hall penned a letter to Gerhardt, announcing that Walker's "work resulted in very accurate, well-evaluated information, of great value to 30th Division headquarters. His personal coolness and presence of mind in many trying and dangerous situations made possible sound and correct operational decisions that might otherwise have not been so successful. I consider Captain Walker's work with us as superior." Dwyer later added, "It is gratifying to have officers of this regiment recognized for their fine work." (Decades after the war, Walker concluded: "Thank you, General Gerhardt, wherever you are, for helping me spread the good word, instead of the wrong word, to our friends in the 30th Division.")

Over the next several days, Hobbs would gather that those Germans trapped in Aachen would strive to break out and those on the outside would strive to break in. As Charles MacDonald wrote in his official U.S. Army history of the campaign, "It was obvious that so long as the enemy's 3rd Panzer Grenadier and 116th Panzer Divisions remained in this sector, a major counterattack to break the encirclement was a logical expectation." It was a tricky tactical situation because the American cordon around Aachen was at its most tenuous in the 116th's Würselen sector. To solidify that cordon and forestall any further German counterattacks, Hobbs resolved to press ahead at Würselen, and he issued orders to Dwyer to renew his attack on October 19. This time, Dwyer decided to give Bingham's depleted 2nd Battalion a break and launch the attack on the 116th's left, on the east side of Würselen, with Dallas's 1st Battalion. Captain James Rabbitt's Company A would be in the lead.

The Germans' Aachen garrison may have been surrounded, but that did not lessen their fighting spirit in Würselen. A deafening American artillery barrage preceded the 116th's attack on the nineteenth, inflicting still more destruction on the unfortunate town, but all Company A members knew that such fireworks had not helped much in the past week and would probably not help much now. They were right. As soon as the 29ers began to climb out of their cellars and rush across the rubble-strewn streets, the Germans' reaction was predictable. The 116th's action report recorded, "The enemy immediately brought to bear considerable fire upon our troops." Company A's executive officer, 1st Lt. Edward Gearing, led a group of his men through that fusillade into a group of enemy-occupied buildings. PFC John Barnes defined the type of fighting that ensued as "not open street fighting, but house-to-house, or rather cellar-to-cellar fighting. Often the enemy was just across the street or in the cellar of an adjacent house. Our guys had to fire out cellar windows, or sometimes blast a hole in the cellar wall to gain access to the next cellar, advancing room by room below ground at all times. It did not go very well. The Jerries brought up self-propelled guns of large caliber to hit our positions."

Gearing, a bona fide Company A hero on Omaha Beach, had been one of only three company officers to survive D-Day. Actually, he had come close to missing the invasion entirely since the Royal Navy landing craft he and his boat team occupied, scheduled to land in the first wave, foundered several hundred yards off Omaha Beach. Rescued by the crew of a passing LCA, the British returned the 29ers, minus their weapons and equipment, to the troop transport *Empire Javelin*. Gearing issued orders to send his team back to England with the object of returning to Normandy in a few days, rearmed and reequipped, but Gearing himself boarded another LCA and headed back to shore, where he joined the desperate fight on and beyond the beach, earning a Distinguished Service Cross.

According to Dwyer, Gearing's leadership at Würselen was worthy of yet another prestigious decoration for valor, this time the Silver Star. Four German tanks roamed the streets of the town, threatening to thwart Company A's attack before it gained momentum, but American artillery fire disabled one, and the 66th Armor's Shermans forced the other three to retire. Gearing's Silver Star citation recorded:

> Despite intense enemy automatic fire at very close range, 1st Lt. Gearing, by his fearless and skillful leadership, succeeded in driving the enemy from the first group of buildings with a minimum of casualties. Shortly thereafter, while leading his men in an

assault against a second group of enemy-occupied buildings, Lt. Gearing was wounded by enemy fire. [Barnes recalled that Gearing was injured when a wall collapsed on his legs.] Undaunted, he continued to direct operations, which resulted in the capture of the buildings and forty of the enemy.

As commendable as was Gearing's action, Würselen was not yet completely under the 116th Infantry's control; in fact, it never would be. As rapidly as the 116th's casualties were mounting, Dwyer knew he would run out of riflemen before he could overrun the town's last enemy enclave. To keep going, Dwyer badly needed reinforcements. That need was met at noon on October 20 when the XIX Corps assigned to the 116th the 99th Infantry Battalion, one of the most unusual U.S. Army outfits of World War II. The 99th, led by Maj. Harold Hansen, was raised in July 1942 to conduct irregular warfare in German-occupied Norway. As the 99th's historian, PFC Howard Bergen, wrote in 1945, the unit was

> composed solely of Norwegians and Americans of direct Norwegian descent [virtually all of whom spoke Norwegian]. . . . They came from far and near, from famous divisions and reception centers, seasoned soldiers and raw recruits, men who had traveled the far reaches of the earth, and boys who had scarcely set foot out of the Norwegian settlements in the great middle West. Day after day they piled out of truck, train, and motor car. . . . The roster of the outfit was typically Scandinavian—Hansen, Johnsen, Petersen, Berg, Andersen, Grunseth, Amundsen and on down the line, but the lives and experiences of these men were as varied as their names were similar. Many were ex-members of the escaped Norwegian merchant marine and victims of ruthless Nazi submarine warfare; many had lived under German tyranny in their native land only to escape and join up to fight with the forces opposing it. All were commonly united in one great resolve: to help to free their country from its oppressor. The feeling was directly transmitted to the American-Norwegians and helped to fuse them together into a vicious and capable combat organization.

In late 1943, the 99th transferred to England and had the distinction of providing the security detail at U.S. First Army headquarters in Bristol when the ultrasensitive Overlord plans for the Normandy invasion took shape. The First Army's staff members ignorant of the differences in Scandinavian ethnicity often referred to the 99th as "The Swedish Guard." Later, after the 99th had been in combat, *Yank* magazine would christen its men the "Fighters from the Fjords," but they would not make it to the land of their ancestors until June 1945, one month after the end of the European war. There they would not conduct the irregular warfare they had trained for, but the much more pedestrian obligation of handling thousands of Germans who had been abruptly transformed from occupiers to prisoners. Prior to that mission, however, the 99th had carried out full-fledged combat duties on the Western Front that were anything but pedestrian, starting on June 21, 1944, when the battalion landed in Normandy, and ending only with the Germans' surrender on May 8, 1945. During its war service, the battalion's penchant for mobility was confirmed by an officer from an armored division working alongside the 99th, who noted, "This is the only damned infantry outfit in the world that tanks have to worry about keeping up with."

But in Würselen, mobility was of no value. As PFC Bergen observed, "The battle of Würselen was, and always will be, a nightmare to the members of the unit who participated in it and were lucky enough to come out of the affair alive." From October 20 to 23, the 99th, the 116th's 1st and 2nd Battalions, and the 3rd Battalion of the 120th Infantry—loaned to Dwyer by Hobbs—battled the Germans for control of an objective whose military value had apparently dwindled to almost nothing. Würselen had practically ceased to exist, yet for every trifling gain of a few houses made by Dwyer's rapidly shrinking force of infantrymen, the enemy struck back with a fierce doggedness that demonstrated to every American that the road through Germany to Berlin would be long and bloody. "In the face of a continual and accurate concentration of artillery, mortar, and point-blank tank fire," Bergen reported, "[we] attacked daily, were counterattacked and outnumbered, driven from [our] hard-won positions, only to surge back and retake them. [The enemy] threw everything in the book at the Americans during this showdown battle."

Neither side had any inclination to back down, and for a time, it seemed as if the brawl would endure until one side or the other ran out of troops. Bergen observed:

> During the entire operation, food, water, and ammunition were extremely difficult to deliver to forward areas because of accurate enemy observation. Even during the hours of darkness, men

bringing up supplies were shelled with amazing accuracy. To the men lying in the cold, sticky mud of their foxholes under constant attack this was but another grim discomfort with which to cope. Sleep was virtually an impossibility . . . and with the cold rain, incessant shelling, lack of food and water, and perpetual counterattacks the growing tension was beginning to tell on the hardiest.

It was the type of savage fighting that writers like Ernie Pyle and men of his caliber had been trying to depict to the American public over the past two years, but except for the *Sun*'s Holbrook Bradley, Pyle and his cohorts had avoided Würselen, a seemingly insignificant place that would never generate headlines on the home front because of more notable events elsewhere. That was a shame, for a truthful depiction of the Würselen fighting would dispel any illusions back home that the end of this monumental war was imminent and reveal to the American public the ruthless realities of human conflict that even Great War veterans of the Meuse-Argonne would find shocking. All 29ers agreed that the war's real heroes were the anonymous frontline soldiers with M1s and BARs and machine guns who engaged the Germans close-up, at places like Würselen, until they became casualties as the inviolable law of averages foretold or until the fighting took such an immense toll on their minds and bodies that they would never be the same men again. Sooner or later, an ordinary man had to break under the pressure, which a disconsolate Pyle himself confessed to a *Life* magazine reporter: "I'd become so revolted, so nauseated by the sight of swell kids having their heads blown off, I'd lost track of the whole point of the war. I'd reached a point where I felt that no ideal was worth the death of one more man."

The members of Dwyer's 116th Infantry had witnessed the deaths of hundreds of their comrades since D-Day, and most had somehow managed to retain faith in that ideal, although they never spoke of it. In all likelihood, a few more days in Würselen would alter that faith. Mercifully, the XIX Corps pulled Dwyer's men out of that ravaged town late on October 23 and, the following day, assigned the regiment back to its rightful owner, the 29th Division. The 116th Infantry would finally get the break from the front it both needed and deserved—minus 500 of its members.

Würselen had been different from anything the 116th had experienced before. The battle did not end happily. For the first time, the regiment had failed to push back the Germans on its front and had not succeeded in seizing an objective that both corps and army commanders had considered essential. The 29ers could take solace in the truth that the 116th had faithfully played its part in the pitiless battle of attrition that every unit involved at Aachen had experienced. That the Americans had won that battle became clear when Col. Gerhard Wilck, the Germans' senior officer in Aachen, finally surrendered at 12:05 P.M. on October 21. Admittedly, American generalship had been poor, and Aachen possessed little more than symbolic value, but the battered Americans had nevertheless emerged victorious. How many more "victories" of this kind could the U.S. Army endure?

The last victim of the Würselen battle was the XIX Corps commander, Maj. Gen. Charles Corlett, the crusty soldier who had dared to respond impertinently to his boss, Lt. Gen. Courtney Hodges, about the First Army's incessant demands that the 116th Infantry and the rest of the 30th Division close the Aachen Gap. As Corlett later observed, final victory at Aachen

> was too late for me. . . . I was sitting with General Hobbs at his command post in a tumble-down building in Germany a few miles north of Aachen, talking over the battle and of future plans, when my chief of staff, Brig. Gen. Hamilton McGuire, called me and said he had an important matter he didn't want to talk about over the phone. He would come up immediately. When he arrived, he handed me a little slip of typewritten paper, an order from General Hodges stating in effect that I had been relieved from command of XIX Corps. . . . When I returned to my command post at Heerlen, I called General Hodges on the phone and told him I had his order. He said he had intended to get down to see me before the order arrived and informed me that my relief would arrive the next day. . . . I parted with my beloved XIX Corps for the last time [October 18, 1944] on the way to army headquarters. My conference with General Hodges was very brief. He told me I was to go up to Luxembourg to see Bradley. On leaving, when we shook hands, he said something about being sorry.

One member of Corlett's staff strove to commiserate with the general about the unjustness of his relief, but Corlett cut him off: "Young man, anyone who sasses the army commander . . . should be relieved. [General Hodges] did exactly the right thing, and I did exactly the right thing, and this is the price one must pay. . . . He should have relieved me—and he did."

The battle for Würselen was over. It was far too early for survivors of that calamitous struggle to place the events of the last eleven days in perspective. For the moment, physical exhaustion and spiritual numbness—sentiments that regularly surfaced in the immediate aftermath of a prolonged battle—precluded logical thought. It would take time to recover, perhaps even longer than at St. Lô, Vire, and Brest, because Würselen was not the kind of battle from which 29ers could derive any pride. What had it all meant? Historians would figure it out later, but one detail was certain: when the annals of this monumental war would be written, the name of Würselen would probably not be mentioned at all. If it would be brought up, it would be a footnote, a place where the Germans established beyond doubt, as they had at dozens of other locales, that if the Allies desired to push into Nazi Germany, they must be prepared to endure the deaths of tens of thousands more of their soldiers. It would also be remembered for the highly esteemed U.S. Army corps commander who lost his job.

Virtually all veterans of Würselen would concur that the battle had not been a model of U.S. Army efficiency. The Americans had achieved their overall purpose—the capture of Aachen—but no one could define what had occurred at Würselen as a triumph. Futile battles of that sort did not provide the top brass with much incentive to dispense laurels to worthy soldiers, but anyone who understood Würselen agreed that one particular soldier, whose prodigious efforts had helped immensely to sustain and provide impetus to the Americans' eleven-day offensive, had performed his duties so dynamically that his feats had to be rewarded.

One eyewitness to the exploits of Capt. James Burt in Würselen asserted: "Anything or everything you ever heard of, or read, or can think of, or imagine—he did." Burt's immediate superiors would soon put him up for the U.S. Army's second highest award for combat heroism, the Distinguished Service Cross, but the submission was quickly returned with instructions to resubmit for a Medal of Honor. It took the Army more than a year to grant that request, but by General Order 95 on October 30, 1945, Capt. James Burt of the 66th Armored Regiment became a recipient of the nation's highest military decoration, the Medal of Honor. His citation concluded: "Captain Burt's intrepidity and disregard of personal safety were so complete that his own men and the infantry who attached themselves to him were inspired to overcome the wretched and extremely hazardous conditions which accompanied one of the most bitter local actions of the war."

Burt's award was highly unusual in that it was issued not for a single combat action, but for many exemplary deeds over the course of eleven days, many of which were performed with members of the 29th Division, not his own tankers. "Almost everything learned or experienced in any activity will

Capt. James Burt, 2nd Armored Division, photographed after the war with his Medal of Honor.
G. BLAKER / J. BURT

almost surely pay off at some future event," Burt noted more than fifty years later. "Be a good watcher, good listener, and when the time is right, a good questioner."

The 29ers fighting in Würselen were the fortunate beneficiaries of Burt's expertise. "Every day in [Würselen], I visited the infantry with whom we worked," Burt recalled. "Maybe a few in this house, a platoon in another place."

Burt concluded: "Treat them like the best—and they will be the best."

SIX

Don't Complicate It

1. STRICTLY OFF LIMITS

October 1944 should have been among the most satisfying periods of Tony Miller's life. Instead, the month was pure hell, a time of almost non-stop strain and dreariness.

The thirty-one-year-old resident of a humble row-house community in west Baltimore had enlisted as a private in the Maryland National Guard at the age of eighteen and, by 1938, had gained a commission in the "Dandy" 5th Regiment, an outfit whose nickname and venerated traditions suggested that only an exceptional enlisted man could hope to join the ranks of its upper-crust officers. Miller had accomplished that feat, and in Normandy, just six years later, he would rise to the command of the 800-man 2nd Battalion, 115th Infantry, known by admiring 29ers in autumn 1944 as "Miller's Maulers" and recognized by General Gerhardt as one of the finest fighting outfits in the 29th Division.

By October 20, Miller should have been riding high. He had only recently detached the gold oak leaves from his collar, symbolizing his rank as a U.S. Army major, and replaced them with the silver leaves of a lieutenant colonel. He had held command of the 2nd Battalion for three months, an impressive record of success and longevity that few battalion commanders could match under Gerhardt's stern and unforgiving

Lt. Col. Anthony Miller, commander of the 2nd Battalion, 115th Infantry.

leadership. And now fame, too, had come his way. He had just learned that the current issue of *Life* magazine on sale on newsstands throughout the United States, featuring the gorgeous young actress Lauren Bacall on the cover, included a story on the 2nd Battalion at the siege of Brest, at the conclusion of which Miller himself had been snapped by a *Life* photographer accepting the surrender of the vast enemy garrison from the haughty German commander.

Miller had the brain of a savvy battlefield leader, but the heart of a dyed-in-the-wool enlisted man. According to GI gossip, he was supposed to have "fought it out man-for-man with a Jerry sniper" in the front lines in Normandy. One 29th Division comrade described him as "a tall, burly guy with all the flavor of a real commander. There's no padded stuff about him. He looks like just what he is: a damned good fighting soldier"—good enough, apparently, that he had gained the admiration of almost every member of the 2nd Battalion. One battalion staff officer, Lt. Robert Henne, described Miller as "the best battalion commander I ever knew: not flamboyant; entirely professional; and most important—he always got the job done."

But the best news of all on October 20 was that Gerhardt had ordered Miller's battalion withdrawn from the front that evening after nineteen straight days in the gloomy Hahnbusch woods, two miles northwest of Geilenkirchen. On October 3, Miller had marked the 2nd Battalion's first full day in Germany by sharing a captured bottle of Scotch with his staff. By now, that seemed to have occurred in a different epoch, one in which Miller and his confident 29ers had expected to punish the Germans, as they just had in Normandy and Brittany, and this time finish them off for good. By October 20, that optimism had vanished, replaced by an overriding struggle for survival.

No one could deny that three weeks in Hahnbusch had devastated Miller's command. Nearly one-fifth of his men had become casualties, which might have seemed slight by the standards of the recent past, but which still exasperated and discouraged his men because the 2nd Battalion had spent that period occupying the World War I–style zigzag trenches at the edge of the woods, striving to endure the enemy's unbearable artillery and mortar bombardments that consistently struck the Americans' positions with uncanny accuracy. Miller's men fought back hard, calling in their own deadly barrages and air strikes on enemy-occupied Waldenrath and launching stealthy nighttime raids to harass the Germans and snatch prisoners. Sgt. Gale Carroll's daring incursion into enemy lines on October 14, which had resulted in the demolition of a prominent tower used by the Germans as an observation post, had been a brilliant achievement, but every 29er grasped that wars were not won by barrages and raids alone—the enemy eventually had to be routed by a conventional infantry attack. Until that occurred, the indecisive warfare in and near Hahnbusch would persist, and the longer it did, the greater the chance attrition would reduce the combat effectiveness of Miller's 2nd Battalion to a dangerously low level.

Almost every facet of existence in Hahnbusch had been dismal. The moderate summer weather of Brittany was a distant memory, now replaced by a chill to which the 29ers were not accustomed and an intermittent rain that soaked shoes and uniforms—neither of which ever seemed to dry out—and left deep pools of mud at the bottom of trenches and foxholes. The only supply line into the woods traveled over routes marked by ominous signposts blaring in large letters: "Road under enemy observation." Reporter Holbrook Bradley observed, "It was difficult to determine directions, or to discern which were enemy troops and which were our own men." According to the 115th's official history, the gloom was oppressive:

> Those nights in and around the Hahnbusch woods were nights that the men of the [2nd Battalion] will never forget. Darkness came early—a darkness so black and so complete that a man venturing outside of his foxhole to relieve himself found it difficult to locate his shelter on the way back. . . . Despite the presence of sentries and wire entanglements, trip wire, and flares, it was possible for Germans to creep unsuspected into the lines of the forward companies. . . . As dark came occasional bullets would come

whizzing through the forest, glancing off trees and sending the men diving into their holes where they spent the remainder of the night in troubled sleep.

The battalion that trudged wearily out of Hahnbusch at 9:30 P.M. on October 20, to be replaced by the 115th Infantry's 3rd Battalion, was certainly not the same outfit that had entered it on October 2. Even Gerhardt would have forgiven the troops' disheveled appearance, for tidy uniforms and personal hygiene could not possibly be maintained under the conditions in which they had lived and fought. Much more vital than their physical image, however, was their spiritual health, which not even a cheerful optimist could define as sound. An observer could readily tell that many of Miller's men were demoralized, which derived from neither defeat nor physical exhaustion, but from the sheer futility of combat over the past three weeks. The Germans, who to a large extent occupied the same positions they had in early October, had not been defeated, and all members of Miller's outfit knew that it would require the efforts of much more than a single battalion to overcome the enemy on their front. As the 115th's historian noted bluntly, all 29ers grasped that "whatever the Allies were to gain inside the Reich would have to be paid for dearly." Furthermore, the proud 29th Division knew how to wage war only one way: with the full fury of all its fighting men and impressive resources. The indecisive struggles around Hahnbusch over the past three weeks revealed a new type of warfare, however, one that all 29ers knew the U.S. Army was fighting on the cheap. As far as the fighting men were concerned, whatever the top brass was asking the 29th Division to do was a lousy way to fight a war.

The members of the 115th had been subjected to unspeakable strains in the past, but this was different. After the prolonged battles for St. Lô, Vire, and Brest, the men had cleared their heads with a few days behind the front, during which they had watched lively USO shows, met a few Hollywood stars, and, more recently at Brest, made all-day outings to the breathtaking beaches of western Brittany. In those glorious days, every 29er knew they occupied a land they had helped to free, whose residents were delighted to have them in their midst.

Not so this time. When the members of Miller's worn-out 2nd Battalion awoke to a typically dreary autumn overcast on the morning of October 21, 1944, they found themselves encamped on the fringe of a godforsaken

German town named Gangelt, whose residents—at least the handful who still remained—were decidedly unhappy about the U.S. Army's arrival. The Americans reciprocated those feelings and assumed that most of the German civilians were spies. No diversions existed in Gangelt to take the 29ers' minds off the war except for a rare Red Cross doughnut wagon and a Sunday church service on October 22. Indeed, at less than two miles behind the front, the misnamed "rest" area was well within range of German artillery. All agreed that no USO show would turn up here, and as for the 29ers' favorite star from Normandy, singer Dinah Shore, surely her handlers would find much better places on the Western Front for a performance than Gangelt.

Although the 2nd Battalion was in division reserve, Miller knew that his commanding general still expected the outfit to strive to improve itself when it eventually returned to battle. As the 115th's history noted, "Following a few days of cleaning up, a training schedule was inaugurated stressing battle critiques, range firing, and small-unit tactics." On the afternoon of October 23, the 2nd Battalion's surgeon gave lectures to the enlisted men on proper field sanitation procedures. Naturally, those dry diversions could hardly lift the apathy and gloom that pervaded the psyches of many 2nd Battalion members. There had to be a way to help the 29ers forget. If the 115th could not get the USO or Dinah, the regiment would have to create its own entertainment, and luckily, Lt. Joseph Dunne, a member of regimental headquarters, came up with the perfect way to do it.

The members of the 2nd Battalion didn't expect much. Most of them were too exhausted to care about Dunne's show, titled *Strictly Off Limits*. How could a theatrical production so close to the front—in *Germany*, for that matter—be any good? Nevertheless, sometime after dark on October 23, Miller's weary men trudged into a ramshackle Gangelt school auditorium, sat down in uncomfortable wooden seats meant for German schoolchildren, and waited skeptically for the curtain to rise. At least the presence of the expert 29th Division band, whose members were tuning up in front of the stage, promised some decent entertainment. Suddenly, an NCO's piercing shout of "'Ten-Hut!" brought the throng to its feet in an instant for the arrival of a surprise guest, none other than Uncle Charlie himself, General Gerhardt, accompanied by his aide, Capt. Bob Wallis. If the general was in attendance, maybe *Strictly Off Limits* might not be too bad.

A 29th Division show in Holland. Note the signs: "Go Boom With the Blue and Gray," "Destruction Since D-Day," and "West Wall Wrecker."

A thunderous version of "The Caissons Go Rolling Along" started the show off on the right foot. Dunne knew that soldiers fresh off the front line were not fans of Shakespeare and did not relish hours of tedious dialogue from the latest Eugene O'Neill play. They were an audience the performers had to grab in the production's first minute and never let go until the final curtain. Dunne would accomplish that goal by providing a revue, a constant barrage of upbeat entertainment interspersed with a little nostalgia for home. According to a late October edition of *29 Let's Go*, Dunne "arranged the performance—took the crew to the location and got things cleared up for the big event. He also negotiated with a troupe of Dutch actors and actresses to participate in the affair. Those people also provided the lighting facilities. They arrived on the scene with full regalia, beautiful costumes and all."

Strictly Off Limits master of ceremonies Howard Brown, a private from the 115th's Service Company and a show business professional in prewar days, enthralled the audience from the moment the curtain went up and threw in some masterful pantomime to boot. The editor of *29 Let's Go* described the show as a "humdinger—the men hadn't been in a theater in a long while, and they just sat there enjoying the fun together. . . . It was the kind of affair you never forget." The 115th's official history added,

"Rarely has a show been greeted with such enthusiastic and spontaneous approval." Private Brown recalled, "The house was jammed. Guys were having the time of their lives—in the aisles all night."

By now, the U.S. Army acknowledged that Gerhardt had molded his division into a first-class outfit, but *Strictly Off Limits* was a revelation to the general, proof that the classic American melting pot that was the 29th Division contained men of superlative talents beyond ordinary soldierly duties. PFC Marty McKenna displayed his vocal skills with several Big Band songs, most notably an unforgettable rendition of Cole Porter's haunting "Night and Day"; an expert accordionist named Steve Fazekas kept the audience mesmerized; and PFC Paul Talley—described by a 115th soldier as "the regiment's Poet Laureate"—recited the kind of verse fighting men could appreciate. One spectator noted that Talley "is an inspired poet. . . . It's a treat to hear him tell about the fightingest men in the Army [in] "The Infantryman" and "A Letter From Dad to Son." His "Ninety-Day Wonder" is one of the best to come out of this war."

But to the audience, the best parts of the show were those featuring the Dutch women, remembered by one observer as "a chorus line of half a dozen buxom beauties." The girls' performed traditional Dutch dances known as *Klompendans*, featuring impressive smacking of wooden shoes on the stage floor with military-style precision. Another charming performer did an energetic sailor's hornpipe, backed up by the rousing music of T/Sgt. Percy Warfield's 29th Division band. But to the enthusiastic 29ers who greeted each act with wild shouts and whistles and applause, much more impressive than the dances were the winsome dancers themselves. The fighting men hadn't seen such attractive women in a long time; moreover, performing so close to the front lines gained the men's respect. The Germans were so close they probably could hear the racket in Gangelt, and a well-aimed artillery shell could have brought the performance to an abrupt and tragic end at any moment. Still, the women came to perform with obvious exuberance—clear evidence that however enthusiastic the 29ers were to watch, the Dutch were even more enthusiastic to flaunt their culture to their liberators, an opportunity they did not have under four years of Nazi oppression. That this exhibition of Dutch pride was taking place not in Holland but on the soil of the reviled enemy epitomized the sudden reversal of fortunes that had brought those four dark years nearly to an end.

According to Brown, "One Dutch doll gave her impression of Gypsy Rose Lee," the legendary American burlesque star known for her consummate skill in removing her clothes discreetly in front of an enraptured male audience. Brown's description of the Dutch woman's act as "pretty cute" indicated that, for obvious reasons, she did not go as far as Miss Lee and maintained a decorum that may have disappointed some, but still captivated most.

The highlight of the evening certainly was the Dutch vocalist who brought the house down with her beautiful rendition of American popular songs. Brown recalled her as a "wow," so extraordinary that the 29ers called her back for "encore after encore." Gangelt was a long way from America, but she transported the men back home with "Carolina Moon," a simple sentimental air that was hardly equal to a Gershwin or Porter ballad, but still did the trick by producing a reverential hush among the audience, at complete variance with its earlier fervor:

> Carolina moon keep shining,
> Shining on the one who waits for me,
> Carolina moon I'm pining,
> Pining for the place I long to be.

By now, everyone knew that no affair of this kind could ever end on a sentimental note, so after the 29ers' ecstatic reaction to "Carolina Moon," the vocalist broke into a bouncy version of "Pistol Packin' Mama," the wildly popular 1943 tune recorded by Bing Crosby and the Andrews Sisters. It was the perfect finale, but the keyed up audience would not let *Strictly Off Limits* end. When the curtain came down, the 29ers stomped and shouted for more. As Brown noted, "The boys, well, they just wouldn't give up. [They] liked it so much they wouldn't go home." The delighted performers obliged, improvising more acts for another ninety minutes.

Not a man left the auditorium disappointed, even Gerhardt. The next morning, he telephoned Miller and declared: "That was some evening! I never had so much fun!" Obviously in an exuberant mood, the general then inquired about Miller's ad hoc rifle range just outside Gangelt and challenged any of his men to a sharpshooting contest. "All it will cost them is twenty marks!" Gerhardt joked. Two hours later, Miller was on his way to Paris for a seven-day leave.

He richly deserved it.

2. BOUNCING BETTY

General Gerhardt had never had a boss who had worked more effectively with the 29th Division than Maj. Gen. Charles Corlett, his late corps commander. In Normandy, Corlett had capably directed the capture of St. Lô and Vire, employing the 29th in a leading role both times. He valued the division's fighting abilities highly and habitually allowed Gerhardt near-total freedom to wield the division's combat power, assuming that power was focused on the XIX Corps's main objective. For the most part, Corlett had displayed remarkable tolerance by overlooking the worst of Gerhardt's occasional lapses of judgment. Gerhardt and Corlett got along famously, but that special relationship had ended because the First Army's commander, Courtney Hodges, had not been willing to overlook Corlett's own lapses of judgment, exhibited in several regrettable incidents during the battle for Aachen.

Gen. Omar Bradley, at Hodges's recommendation, relieved Corlett from command on October 18. Would his successor be tougher on the volatile Gerhardt than Corlett? That issue would not arise if the successor were Gerhardt himself. As the commander of the 2nd Armored Division, Maj. Gen. Ernest Harmon, recalled: "The three division commanders in the corps [Harmon, Gerhardt, and Hobbs], all seasoned veterans, hoped one of us might be promoted to the command. All three of us were disappointed."

Bradley made an unusual choice for Corlett's replacement: fifty-four-year-old Maj. Gen. Raymond McLain, the commander of the 90th Division, currently a component of Patton's Third Army in Lorraine. Unlike most of his peers, McLain was not a graduate of the U.S. Military Academy and reputedly had little formal education beyond the sixth grade. He had spent most of his military career in the Oklahoma National Guard, in which he enlisted as a private in 1912. Commissioned three years later as a second lieutenant, McLain gained much combat experience on the Western Front in World War I as a company commander. When President Roosevelt called the 45th Division into federal service in September 1940, McLain commanded its artillery component, the 70th Field Artillery Brigade, whose Oklahoma City armory occupied the same city in which McLain carried on a successful career as an investment banker. Later, he served brilliantly in combat in Sicily and Italy. As a reward, Bradley assigned him to take over the 90th Division, an outfit that had exhibited severe—and, some feared, uncorrectable—problems when it first entered combat in Normandy.

Maj. Gen. Raymond McLain, commanding general of the XIX Corps.

McLain's selection triggered a disappointed Harmon to remark somewhat caustically, "[Lt. Gen. William] Simpson [commander of Ninth Army] told me later that General Marshall had personally selected McLain for the [XIX Corps] post to silence protests from national guardsmen that too few of their number had received top commands." Actually, McLain was a highly experienced soldier. In early 1937, a time when both Eisenhower and Bradley had been mere lieutenant colonels, McLain had gained a star as a brigadier general, making him an equal to Marshall, who had only recently received a promotion to one-star rank as commander of an infantry brigade. By 1944, Marshall, Eisenhower, Bradley, and many other top U.S. Army soldiers had come to genuinely respect McLain's mature and highly effective leadership style.

Capt. George Forsythe, Corlett's aide-de-camp who stayed on to carry out the same role under the new XIX Corps commander, described McLain as

> one of the finest field generals in the U.S. Army. This guy was a real scrapper. He was really brilliant on the battlefield, and yet he was a very quiet, calm, deliberate sort of man. . . . All three XIX Corps division commanders were West Pointers, and here comes

a national guardsman to take command of the corps. But there was no problem at all because all three of these men realized what a fine soldier McLain was. When he took command of the corps, he never said anything about what had happened in the past. But he had a lot to say about what was going to happen in the future.

One young XIX Corps staff officer who observed McLain regularly at meetings recalled admiringly, "He was a calm man; I never saw him angry."

On August 19 of that year, Eisenhower had written to Marshall, "You will be glad to know that the 90th Division has been transformed into a very effective unit and is now reported by General Patton as one of his best organizations. This is unquestionably due to the outstanding leadership qualities of Brigadier General McLain, a national guardsman." In a postwar interview with his official biographer, Marshall concurred with Eisenhower's assessment: "Few National Guard [general] officers made it. [I] delayed the preparation of the Army a whole year to give them a chance. Finally [I] said we will have to tear them up. . . . Only two or three made it. . . . McLain was one of the best." In 1944, Marshall penned a laudatory Christmas note to McLain: "I have followed your career since the landing in Sicily, particularly in the fighting from the Normandy bridgehead up to the present moment when you are commanding an army corps engaged in one of the world's greatest battles against a desperate foe. Throughout you have displayed outstanding characteristics of a leader, and it is my earnest hope that you will find the same opportunities for your talents in corps command that you did with a brigade and a division."

Lack of confidence in high-ranking National Guard officers among West Pointers, however, was not dead. Corlett reflected:

[McLain] had been a banker and businessman in Oklahoma and prominent for many years as a national guardsman in the southwest. In a few short weeks [after D-Day] he had been promoted very rapidly over the heads of many fine regular army officers like Hobbs, [Ira] Wyche [79th Division], [Clarence] Huebner [1st Division], [Manton] Eddy [9th Division], and [Walter] Robertson [2nd Division], who had spent their whole lives in intensive study of military tactics, strategy, and leadership. They had proved their fine ability on the battlefield as division commanders. In my opinion, McLain, with no reflection on him, was not that good. His appointment, I believe, was a gesture to the National Guard as a whole. If it encouraged and helped that great organization, it was expedient and well worthwhile.

If Gerhardt harbored such negative thoughts, however, he had the good sense to withhold them, at least for the moment, and his behavior toward his new boss when they first conversed on October 18 was entirely correct when he asked, compliantly, "Is there anything special you want from here?" The following day, McLain paid a forty-minute visit to Gerhardt's war room, during which the two generals discussed the 29th Division's secondary role in the ongoing battle for Aachen. For three weeks, Gerhardt had reluctantly accepted his diversionary role, but with the imminent fall of Aachen and the arrival of a new corps commander, he fervently hoped the 29th Division would soon receive a more consequential mission, enabling it to smash through the German line all the way to the Rhine and eventually to Berlin.

But it was not to be. McLain's XIX Corps would not smash through anything until the top brass could address the escalating supply crisis that threatened to shut down virtually all Allied offensive operations on the Western Front. One U.S. Army historian noted that the typical allocation of resources to frontline divisions amounted to "a starvation diet for supplies and left it impossible to build up the necessary stocks for any offensive action." All commanders concurred that now the front had stabilized, their real shortage was no longer gasoline, but ammunition. At least for the foreseeable future, therefore, the 29th Division would have to hold its lengthy eighteen-mile front, from the Meuse River in the west to Geilenkirchen in the east, carrying out operations limited to Gerhardt's obligatory aggressive patrols and large-scale raids. Those methods of war might tie down some German units and keep them alert, but they would yield no decisive benefits to the American side and produce an unceasing toll of casualties. More than 1,000 29ers had become casualties between the close of September and McLain's assumption of command of the XIX Corps on October 18. When the supply emergency evaporated and the Allies resumed their drive to the Rhine, those men would be sorely missed.

The futility of warfare when practiced with scarce resources and inconsequential objectives became obvious to Lt. Col. Randolph Millholland, the commander of the 115th's 3rd Battalion, when Gerhardt directed him to launch a large-scale raid on October 17. The object was merely to destroy a miniscule bridge over Saeffeler Creek just south of the village of Breberen, a locale with which some members of the 175th Infantry and 113th Cavalry Group were entirely familiar because the Germans had reacted with astonishing force two weeks before when those units had traversed that same bridge and attempted to capture Breberen. Any prudent 29th Division battalion commander had long ago learned not to doubt Gerhardt's orders, but this time, Millholland must have wondered whether his commanding general was losing touch with reality. Even if his men were to succeed in their mission, the accomplishment would be of no consequence because Saeffeler Creek was so narrow that German engineers could handily repair the bridge or build a new one. Under Gerhardt's leadership, however, mere lieutenant colonels were advised to avoid pondering matters above their stations, for the general's obvious point was to establish to the enemy that the 29th Division could accomplish anything it wanted, at any time.

With memories of Schierwaldenrath and the earlier Breberen debacles still fresh, 3rd Battalion members could hardly repress ominous thoughts about the upcoming mission. At 7:40 on the morning of October 17, Gerhardt phoned Millholland to discuss the raid and concluded with the warning: "Don't complicate it!" As Millholland would soon learn, what that edict actually meant was that aside from some initial smoke rounds, artillery support would be minimal. Tanks would not be used because rain had fallen nearly continuously for more than two days and the general believed the ground would be too soft. To enhance the element of surprise, no preliminary air strike would take place. Before a concerned Millholland even had a chance to inquire about what kinds of outside fire support would be available, Gerhardt cut him short: "Use your own supporting weapons"—the heaviest of which were six 81-millimeter mortars, not nearly as potent as howitzers of 105-millimeter caliber or greater and the 75-millimeter high-velocity cannon on Sherman tanks.

Nothing went right from the start. From its location as division reserve near Gangelt, the 3rd Battalion moved up across sodden meadows to its jump-off point at Hastenrath about an hour before dark. The raid would take place in the 113th Cavalry Group's sector, and howitzers from the 111th Field Artillery Battalion, currently supporting the 113th, opened the show by dropping smoke rounds in the fields adjacent to Buscherheide, just south of the coveted bridge. If the 29ers hoped to reach the bridge, they would have to move through or around Buscherheide, and if the Germans occupied it in strength, their fire had to be suppressed as Millholland's men crossed the wide-open pastures toward Saeffeler Creek.

Millholland set up a forward command post in a cluster of farm buildings that hardly seemed worthy of a name, although U.S. Army maps called it Kievelberg. The battalion staff had plenty of tasks to occupy their thoughts, but its members could not fail to notice a menacing omen in the nearby fields, a wrecked P-47 Thunderbolt. Companies I and L, commanded by 1st Lt. Alvin Ungerleider and Capt. Earl Tweed, led the attack, which jumped off right on time at 5:45 P.M. The two officers learned to their chagrin that smoke had not suppressed the German fire emanating from Buscherheide. Quite the opposite, in fact, as an action report later recorded: "[The attackers] came under mortar and artillery fire early. Furthermore, as they approached the town, they came under heavy small-arms fire, including machine guns, from prepared positions in trenches and houses. . . . One platoon of infantry managed to get into the town, but it was evident that the enemy was determined to hold stubbornly to his position." The regimental history described the fusillade as "withering" and noted that "the attack staggered and halted as the men sought to escape from the murderous fire."

As Millholland watched in horror from a farmhouse in Kievelberg, the attack evaporated in minutes. Only an hour later, Maj. Al Warfield, the 115th's operations officer, described the chaos to Colonel Witte at division headquarters: "They came under interlocking fire from two flanks, about six machine guns, and were unable to advance from there. Radio control went out. [There were] normal concentrations of artillery by the enemy, and self-propelled guns covered the open spaces, and heavier fire from the left."

The alert Germans had caught the 29ers in the open fields with virtually no cover. Returning to their lines would be just as hazardous as pushing ahead; their only logical option was to wait for the onset of darkness to get away. In desperation, Ungerleider and two radio operators, PFCs William Oakhem and Michael Paster, along with S/Sgt. Andrew Foppe from regimental headquarters, hid behind a haystack. "As the four men waited for the firing to subside, a tracer bullet from a German MG42 [machine gun] burrowed into the haystack, setting it afire and forcing the men to seek another refuge," the 115th's history recorded. "As they

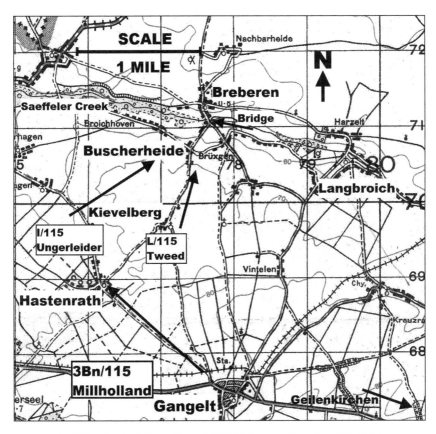

Raid by the 3rd Battalion, 115th Infantry, October 17, 1944.

dashed across the open field to a slight rise in the ground, a shell hit in the center of the group, seriously wounding all of the men except Lieutenant Ungerleider. Oakhem and Foppe died within a few hours, and Paster lost a leg. A short time later the disorganized men moved back through a heavy rain that was falling to the bivouac area around Gangelt."

Millholland's battalion never got close to the bridge, which irritated the commanding general. The next morning, Gerhardt complained to McDaniel, the 115th's commander: "I have been checking on this thing, and they say a company was held down by machine gun [fire]. Now the proper thing to do is to use rifle grenades to knock them out. Another thing: You depended on radio for contact, and it went out. Anybody knows that if you depend just on one, it means it is bound to go out. [Millholland had actually used wire communication as well, but enemy artillery cut it.] I don't think the thing was on a broad enough front."

Millholland needed a long time to get an accurate casualty count because dozens of men were unaccounted for in the darkness and did not return to their units for hours. The final toll turned out to be approximately forty, of whom two died (Oakhem and Foppe) and about fifteen were missing, presumed dead or captured. The number of dead surely would have been much higher had it not been for the laudable work of the 3rd Battalion's medics, who dashed out of the protection of Kievelberg to tend to their injured comrades in the pastures, and the work of vigilant members of Troop A, 113th Cavalry Squadron, under a lieutenant named Lamberson, who drove several armored vehicles out into the fields to evacuate them.

Forty casualties and no gain whatsoever: the pointlessness of pin-prick warfare had become clear to virtually every fighting man in the 29th Division. Gerhardt, the only person whose opinion counted, strove to convince the 29ers that their efforts were anything but futile. Even with his criticism of Millholland's methods on the October 17 raid, Gerhardt later surprised McDaniel by commenting, "I think it turned out fine." With a rare burst of compassion, he concluded, "I think I would give that battalion a break tomorrow."

The general was fixated by one vision: in any sector occupied by the 29th Division, there would be no gentlemen's war, no truces to bury the dead, no mutual understanding between frontline soldiers that they could let down their guard because the war's decisive events were occurring elsewhere. The Germans must come to know the 29th for its aggressive and impulsive attitude, even on a stagnant front. Some raids may have failed to achieve their objects, Gerhardt reasoned, but as long as the division maintained a hard-hitting posture and established that it would always hold the initiative, the German defenders would be forced to sustain a state of perpetual vigilance all across their front that would gradually wear down their spirits. Furthermore, if the German high command hesitated before pulling units away from the 29th Division's front to reinforce the decisive struggle at Aachen, Gerhardt's primary mission, assigned to him by Corlett at the beginning of October, would be fulfilled. Viewed from that perspective Gerhardt fervently believed he was doing exactly what his superiors expected of him.

The 29th's ordinary fighting men could hardly concur with Gerhardt's view, for their world was shaped by a gloomy existence that generals obviously did not understand. As one 29er, T/5 Fred Jesse of the 116th Infantry, wrote bluntly in a letter back home: "The people back in the States I believe are a little premature in their preparations for V-Day. The Germans are plenty tough, and there is a lot of fighting to be done before they will give up. However, it is the opinion of some of our leading generals, and also the Russian big shots, that the war will end over here before the first snow falls. This is the first time in my life that I have wished for the snow to fall as early as this. I never did like cold weather, but if the prediction of these men proves correct, I will accept it gladly."

Even those lucky 29ers who emerged unscathed physically from the pointless struggle paid a heavy psychological toll. Veterans of Brittany and the even more grueling battles that had come before in Normandy had been more than willing to give their all, but more than 16,000 casualties in little over four months had a devastating impact, and after all the triumphs and tragedies of the past, Berlin still lay far beyond the horizon. Only under continuous combat conditions could a period of just four months seem like an eternity. When would it all end? And more to the point, when would the top brass realize that the 29th had already done far more than its share of fighting in World War II? Maj. Jim Morris, a D-Day veteran who currently held the executive officer slot in the 116th Infantry's 1st Battalion, spoke for all weary 29ers when he wrote to his family: "You can bet your boots [the men] are thinking of home. . . . If I get a chance to get out of this scramble now, I'm taking it because I believe I have done my job and could sleep soundly if I got an easier job."

There was nothing to do except carry on in the manner prescribed by Uncle Charlie—and wait for better days ahead. But if the division's situation did not change soon, many 29ers would not live long enough to witness better days. Proof of Gerhardt's unwavering attitude came to McDaniel in a phone conversation on the morning of October 21. "We've been checking, and for three days in a row, your combat patrols haven't accomplished anything," Gerhardt growled. "Send your S-3 [Maj. Al Warfield] with a patrol tonight and pick a mission they can accomplish. Your S-2 [Maj. William Bruning] is to go with a recon patrol."

One of the most treacherous spots in the 115th Infantry's line was the belt of pastureland between the villages of Birgden and Schierwaldenrath. The Germans had doggedly held on to Schierwaldenrath since Company K's disastrous attempt to capture it on October 3; the Americans, with equal resolution, had retained Birgden. It was a highly volatile locale, and both sides were on edge. For nearly three weeks, the antagonists had sparred inconclusively in an effort to gain a tactical advantage. Opposing outposts in the two villages were separated only by 800 yards—too distant for a rifle shot, but close enough that both Germans and Americans could easily observe their adversaries' activities in daylight and drop mortar rounds on them when they demonstrated hostile intent.

A tight cluster of farm buildings situated midway between Schier-waldenrath and Birgden, christened the "Island" by the 29ers, embodied one of those military conundrums that sporadically emerge in war, one that had produced a deadly tactical impasse showing no sign of resolution. The side controlling the Island would obviously hold several significant tactical advantages, which intermittently triggered efforts on both sides to take permanent possession of its buildings. Achieving what one had wished for, however, had proven a curse, for both American and German local commanders had discovered that, short of an abundant supply of troops, which neither side possessed, the Island was virtually impossible to hold on a permanent basis.

On the night of October 20, Lt. Col. Glover Johns, commander of the 115th's 1st Battalion, ordered Company C's executive officer, 1st Lt. George Grimsehl, to select about twenty men from various companies—but mostly Company A—and lead them on a patrol from Birgden to the Island. The intent, according to a 115th patrol logbook, was "to determine enemy positions" and "remain twenty-four hours." The previous evening, a similar Company A mission had gotten nowhere when it ran into mines and booby traps, suffering six casualties. Grimsehl's patrol, however, made it, and as the sun rose on October 21, his men settled quietly into the

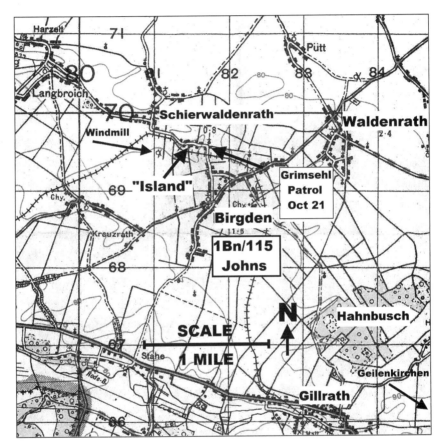

Patrol by the 1st Battalion, 115th Infantry, to the "Island," October 21, 1944.

western periphery of the Island for what the lieutenant hoped would be an uneventful stay that yielded a valuable look at German positions in and around Schierwaldenrath, just a few hundred yards across the flat pastureland.

The alert Germans promptly detected Grimsehl's group and prepared to ensure that the Americans' stay would be much shorter than the twenty-four hours prescribed by orders. Around 8 A.M., they suddenly surged out of Schierwaldenrath and swept around the Island's farm buildings, threatening to envelop and overwhelm Grimsehl's men in one bold rush. The unfortunate Grimsehl was in a predicament and needed to make a hasty decision. He could have ordered an immediate retreat, since fighting a pitched battle against a powerful enemy was not part of a patrol's repertoire. More to the point, by provoking such a response, Grimsehl had already provided valuable intelligence to his superiors about German strength and intentions at Schierwaldenrath.

Grimsehl decided to stay put, but to do so, he would need help. In a radio message back to the 1st Battalion in Birgden, he requested assistance, which Johns granted. For some unknown reason, however, Grimsehl's plea was interpreted by Johns as not particularly urgent. Accordingly, Company A sent out a squad of only twelve men from Birgden to help Grimsehl. The force was entirely inadequate.

For the rest of the day, a concerned Johns learned nothing of the patrol's fate, other than the obvious detail that loud firing within the Island erupted intermittently. At 8:23 that evening, a 115th staff officer reported to the war room euphemistically that Grimsehl's men were "out of communication." It was, in fact, much worse than that: by the morning of October 22, all attempts to contact Grimsehl had failed, and clerks had therefore been forced to list the entire patrol—twenty-seven enlisted men and two officers—as missing in action. For an entire day, Johns did not realize that many of those twenty-nine men, including Grimsehl, were already dead. (The other officer, 2nd Lt. Robert Rose of Company A, survived.)

An anxious McDaniel reported the affair to Gerhardt at 7:34 A.M. on October 22 by announcing "a little [enemy] enthusiasm between Schierwaldenrath and Birgden [and] now we can't find [the patrol]." A frustrated Gerhardt responded, "Get right after that! Were those people in buildings? If they were in buildings and got knocked off, I am going to relieve Johns!" An hour later, the fuming general phoned back McDaniel and snarled, "This is developing like the Company K business [in Schier-waldenrath on October 3]. It's a devil of a state of affairs! Hop on it!"

McDaniel strove to gather details, but "hopping on it" proved diffi-cult. An officer at the 115th's command post reported to the war room that afternoon, "There are thirty men unaccounted for. No one has been in [the Island] since last night, but we are going to send an investigating party out tonight." Unhappily, the "investigating party" failed to return on time, and McDaniel had to send out yet another patrol to ascertain what had happened to the original investigators. How long could this vicious cycle endure?

McDaniel's actions caused Gerhardt's legendary temper to flare. "What's going on? That's a disgrace," he roared. "It's been two days now, and you still know nothing about it! Those things can't happen! There had better not be another one of these things. You'd better get your people together and get something going!" In the course of the general's tirade, he blurted an accusatory word, one he would later regret, to describe why Johns's men had failed. That word, which he had almost never before uttered in reference to his own men, was "cowards."

On October 23, Johns prepared a concise report on the action, but McDaniel reported to Gerhardt, "I'm not satisfied with it." Both McDaniel and Gerhardt would have to let the issue rest with no further comment. In a postwar letter to historian Joe Ewing, Johns unremorsefully, and some-what cryptically, summarized the unfortunate Island incident in a single sentence: "We lost thirty-one men on account of one radio message from Lieutenant Grimsehl, who promptly got himself killed." Whether Johns was implying that Grimsehl should have immediately radioed for more substantive help or that he should have promptly retreated from the Island when the enemy struck remains unclear even today.

According to Gerhardt, and indeed almost every 29er, the best remedy for the humiliation at the Island was revenge. Late on the drizzly after-noon of October 23, in visibility described by the 29th Division's daily G-3 report as "poor," a twenty-five-man patrol from the 115th Infantry's Company B, accompanied by several engineers heavily laden with explo-sives, advanced stealthily out of Birgden to teach the Germans a lesson. The Americans' meaning was clear: as long as Gerhardt's dictum that 29ers had to stay out of buildings still held and the 115th triggered Ger-man "enthusiasm" each time its members endeavored to seize an enemy-held town, the Americans' logical response would be to flatten every building in sight. As Gerhardt reasoned, the division would be better off if the Germans awoke one morning to discover the spot where the Island once stood was now nothing but a pile of rubble.

That was agreeable to the entire American raiding party, which moved to its objective and set out to complete its task with an alacrity motivated by the Germans' inevitable response. The engineers' ensuing success could be judged by several massive explosions reverberating for miles over the gloomy farmland. Those booming detonations, each of which signaled the destruction of a building, were noises Gerhardt, McDaniel, and Johns longed to hear. Unfortunately, they did not hear enough of them, for apparently, the engineers could not haul sufficient explosives to complete the job. Another patrol would have to return later. In the meantime, a few patrol members quietly moved into the adjacent fields just before sunset and for good measure set fire to a huge haystack and placed charges at the base of the prominent windmill southeast of Schierwaldenrath. As related by the 115th's history, "Although the explosion went off as scheduled, the windmill, a suspected Jerry OP [observation post], remained essentially undamaged."

That evening, McDaniel phoned Gerhardt and tried to exit the general's doghouse by proudly announcing, "Major Johns's operations were heroic. We didn't complete all the buildings, but that's another story." Gerhardt, perchance somewhat remorseful over his imprudent portrayal of Johns's men as "cowards" that morning, reassured McDaniel: "That sounds good. Give him a citation for it."

McDaniel elected to hold what remained of the Island overnight with a five-man team so that Johns could send in another infantry-engineer patrol the next day to finish the job. At 6 P.M. on October 24, just minutes before darkness would envelop the landscape, Johns dispatched a fresh patrol, which this time carried enough explosives to dynamite a substantial town to bits. It turned out that the 29ers did not need nearly that much since only five houses still remained standing, all of which disappeared amid crashing explosions and clouds of dust within the next hour. The Island was no more. The only hitch was that a few patrol members suffered minor injuries by setting off enemy booby traps.

While the 29ers were dealing with trivialities that would have no impact on the overall course of World War II, such as demolishing a minuscule bridge or razing the Island, top Allied generals were huddling to devise a plan to bring about Nazi Germany's demise over the next two or three months. Final victory within that time span seemed implausible given the Anglo-American armies' alarming dearth of men and supplies, but Eisenhower and his subordinates resolved to try.

Supreme military efforts of the kind the Allied high command would shortly conduct rarely worked out well for the ordinary fighting men who had to execute them, but this time, the 29th Division would get a much-needed break. The month of October 1944 had been cruel to the 29ers, but as related to Gerhardt by his new boss at the XIX Corps, McLain, on October 30, the 29th Division would be pulled out of that sodden sector of the Rhineland its members had come to detest and head to the friendly confines of Limburg for a rest. No one yet knew how long that rest would endure; in all probability, it would not be long, since the Rhine beckoned and an outfit as experienced as the 29th could not possibly be left out of the next offensive aimed at reaching that mighty river.

As stipulated by McLain, the 407th Infantry, an element of the recently arrived 102nd Division, would assume control of the 29th Division's front between Geilenkirchen and Gangelt at noon on October 30. A few days later, Col. Biddle's 113th Cavalry Group, which had loyally served Gerhardt for a month, would be detached from the 29th Division. Soon, much to the delight of all 29ers—including Gerhardt—the division's entire seventeen-mile front between the Meuse River and Geilenkirchen would be someone else's headache.

To prevent the Germans from taking advantage of the switch, the 29ers needed to indoctrinate the members of the 407th Infantry to the realities of the front in a sector which the Allied high command obviously cared little about but which the Germans valued as a treasured part of their Fatherland. Teaching that lesson to the raw GIs of the 407th—who less than seven weeks before had been waiting for overseas shipment at Camp Kilmer, New Jersey, and had neither fired their weapons in anger nor been on the receiving end of the Germans' weapons—would be a challenge. Ultimately, the rookies' best form of education would be simply to watch the 29ers as they performed their duties, a process that Witte initiated with an 11:22 P.M. phone call to the 115th's operations officer, Maj. Al Warfield, on October 28: "This new organization [the 407th Infantry] would like to send four officers up to you, one to accompany each of your businesses [S-1, S-2, S-3, S-4 staffs]. They are prepared to send their battalion commanders up to your battalion commanders and would like additional officers to accompany the companies."

Lt. Col. William Witte, G-3 of the 29th Infantry Division, referred to by Gerhardt as "my Napoleon."

Unfortunately, the shaken staff members of the 407th would soon emerge from that experience with a sense of what *not* to do to if they wished to survive their tenure in those new and perilous surroundings. Four of Gerhardt's infantry battalions still held the line near Geilenkirchen, and with the 29th's departure set for October 30, the weary members of those frontline units prayed their final hours in their sector would be uneventful. As long as Gerhardt was in command, that hope was not realistic. Late on October 28, word came down from the war room that Gerhardt desired the division to leave the front with a bang. At precisely 4:30 A.M. on the twenty-ninth—little more than thirty hours before the 407th Infantry would take over—each of the four infantry battalions manning the front had to simultaneously initiate a company-size raid on an important strongpoint to its front. Despite the division's imminent departure for another sector, Gerhardt would hold the initiative to the last, leaving the Germans a calling card so that they would never forget the 29th Division. The objective was not to break through enemy lines or to hold territory; rather, Gerhardt desired his men to blow up a few bunkers, kill or capture as many Germans as possible, and leave the enemy with a healthy respect for the Americans' military skills.

Those 29ers who had to carry out Gerhardt's orders would have preferred to leave the raids to the newcomers from the 407th Infantry. But the general's orders were sacrosanct, and the raids had to go forward. The 175th Infantry would carry out two; the 115th would execute the remainder.

The 175th directed its two raids against villages just outside Geilenkirchen, one by the 1st Battalion's Company B on Bauchem, the other by the 2nd Battalion's Company F on Niederheid, but both ran into trouble almost immediately. It was an almost impossible task to sift through the chaos of both nighttime raids and describe them in the official reports Gerhardt demanded, but someone had to try. According to one 175th account,

> Company B passed the line of departure at 0430 hours as planned. They advanced, with two platoons abreast and one in support, toward Bauchem. When they reached the edge of the town, they ran into enemy machine gun fire from a position about 200 yards north of the road. The gun was firing a final protective line across the front of the town. Prompt action resulted in the elimination of the enemy machine gun with rifle grenades. A machine pistol was also silenced in the same operation. During that action the company was halted by heavy fire, and as a result it could not reach the pillbox which was the objective of the raid.

As for Company F's raid on Niederheid, that same report noted that soon after jump-off, the 29ers "were receiving 50-millimeter mortar fire, and enemy flares of all colors illuminated the entire sector as evidence of their frantic call for assistance. . . . Our artillery and 81-millimeter mortars were laid on the wooded area and other registered fires were brought in to cover the withdrawal of the company. At 0547 a smoke screen was laid and on the order of the regimental commander [Purnell], the raiders returned to their company areas." In short, Company F got nowhere.

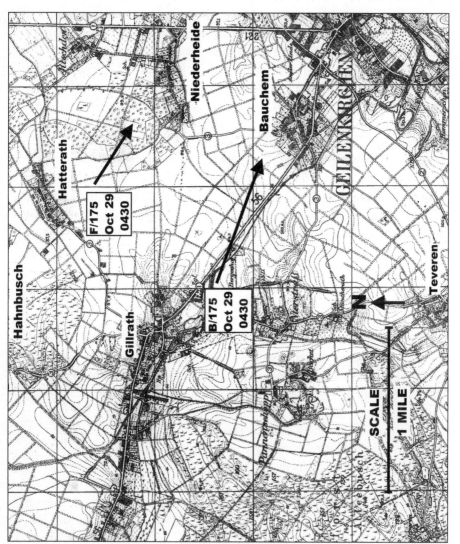

Raids by the 175th Infantry, October 29, 1944.

The failure of both raids to accomplishing their missions would have to be rationalized to Gerhardt, whose reaction could only be imagined. Purnell's staff officers decided that it would help to report the raids' results in a positive light, and their initial report back to the general, delivered just minutes after both companies had returned to American lines, was a blatant obfuscation of reality. "Both companies made their objectives, casualties light, and the only trouble was getting the [attached] engineers up," the report declared. It concluded: "Two prisoners were taken [by Company B], from whom valuable information was gained." That evening, when Gerhardt reviewed the war room transcript, he penned in two underlined words next to the report: "Not so!" The general's cursory investigation of the raids revealed that neither company had accomplished its goals, and both had suffered heavy casualties, amounting to a total of four killed, twenty-five wounded, and eleven missing. That was a high price to pay for the "valuable information" gleaned from just two prisoners.

The unlucky men who had been assigned to accomplish Gerhardt's unworkable raids had done the best they could, and a few had exhibited noteworthy audacity in a hopeless cause. Two Company B non-commissioned officers, T/Sgt. James Lafferty and Sgt. Oscar Tomten, had guided their men toward the Germans' defenses over the dark and dismal no-man's-land pocked with countless shell craters, but they had not progressed far before suffering wounds from German MG42 machine guns. They pressed ahead. According to Tomten's Silver Star Citation, "[He] secured an important position from which his men were able to prevent the enemy from attacking the flanks of the company." Meanwhile, the two prisoners Purnell had categorized as "valuable" were captured by Lafferty, whose Silver Star citation noted that he "advanced and hurled a hand grenade into [an] emplacement, forcing the surrender of two of the enemy crew."

The Company F raiding party had not advanced much beyond its jump-off point when it was stopped cold by the Germans' fusillade, and in the chaotic withdrawal back to American lines in the darkness, two wounded raiders had been left behind in no-man's-land. In a daring act for which he would receive a Silver Star, T/Sgt. Robert Fugini "organized two litter squads and led the group in search of the casualties. Despite having to cross open ground, which was being subjected to mortar fire, Fugini located the wounded and had them evacuated." Unfortunately, one of the casualties, 1st Lt. William Cashin, died of his wounds shortly thereafter. He had joined Company F little more than one month earlier as a replacement officer.

The only one of the four October 29 raids to attain even marginal success was the one run by the 115th Infantry's Company L, temporarily under the command of 1st Lt. John Wilkinson. (Capt. Earl Tweed was on leave.) A tiny patch of woods amounting to no more than a third of an acre—known by the 29ers as the "Frying Pan" because of its distinctive shape on air photos—would be Wilkinson's target. Situated little more than 100 yards from Company L's forward line in Hahnbusch woods—an easy rifle shot—the Frying Pan was reportedly occupied by a German squad of about ten men, who, according to the air photos, were deployed in three cleverly camouflaged machine-gun nests surrounded by barbed wire. The 29ers suspected that those Germans could see and hear almost every action Company L undertook.

A lawyer from Memphis, Tennessee, in civilian life and sometime U.S. Army trial judge advocate, the twenty-four-year-old Wilkinson had come to Company L as a replacement officer shortly after D-Day. As a former enlisted man in the early phase of his military career, he sympathized with the plight of the frontline dogface. Wilkinson picked the 3rd Platoon, thirty-four-men strong and led by 2nd Lt. Frank Silata, and issued orders to "hit the outpost hard and clean it out." Silata's difficulty would be traversing no-man's-land undetected in the predawn darkness. If the raiding party was caught in the flat fields with no cover, bathed in the light of German flares, a few bursts from the enemy's supposed three machine guns could decimate it in an instant. The frosty air was something the 29ers were not used to, and the night sky, with scattered clouds and a moon just two days shy of full, was not as dark as the Americans would have wished. Silata's only advantage would be surprise, which would demand an advance across no-man's-land in complete silence. Would it be possible to preserve that silence when cutting through the belts of barbed wire that surrounded the Germans' machine-gun nests at a range of only fifteen or twenty yards?

Few lieutenants in the 29th Division had more military experience than Silata. His Army career, now four and a half years old, had been sufficiently distinguished for his superiors to grant him an extraordinary tribute, a battlefield commission as a second lieutenant, which he had accepted less than one month earlier. In accepting that promotion,

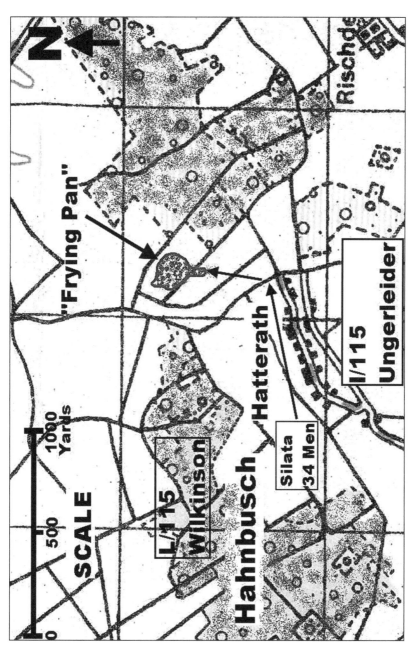

Raid by Company L, 115th Infantry, on the "Frying Pan," October 29, 1944.

however, he had been ordered to depart his unit, Company I, and transfer to the unfamiliar Company L. At twenty-seven, he was older than typical 29th Division lieutenants, including his commander, Wilkinson. Silata recalled:

> The ground was flat and wide open. We weren't discovered. We advanced on our predetermined route [approaching the Frying Pan not from the west, the closest point, but from the south], walking very slowly. . . . The first squad was to clean out and occupy the 'handle' of the Frying Pan. The second squad, splitting into two fire groups, was to silence the two machine gun nests in the southeast and southwest corners of the woods. The remaining squad was to move through the woods and clean out the rest of the patch.

A few days later, while on a three-day pass to Paris, Wilkinson related the story of the Frying Pan raid to a U.S. Army historian in the bar of the famous Hotel George V, a favorite haunt for American soldiers on leave. By coincidence, the historian, 1st Lt. Jack Shea, was himself a former 29er, an aide-de-camp to the legendary Gen. "Dutch" Cota during his tenure as the 29th Division's assistant commander. While Wilkinson recounted the affair, drawing a rough map on a paper napkin, Shea furiously scribbled down notes, which he would eventually transform into a detailed article in the November 1947 issue of *Infantry Journal*. (Wilkinson did not learn of the article's existence for thirty-six years.)

As Wilkinson reported to Shea, when advancing across no-man's-land in the dark, the German weapons the Americans feared above all were mines. Silata's men knew the enemy had sown hundreds of those sinister devices in the open fields adjacent to the Frying Pan, but distinguishing them in the omnipresent stubby cabbage patches in darkness was virtually impossible. Should a 29er set off even a single mine, surprise would be ruined. The sickening realization that Silata's platoon had walked straight into an unseen minefield sank in when one man spotted a typical trip wire designed to detonate a buried mine should a GI snag and pull the wire with his foot. As carefully and quietly as it could, the platoon tried to work its way through that deadly ground without setting off a mine, but a minute or so later, a sharp click resonated over the otherwise hushed landscape. Every 29er knew the meaning of that dreadful sound: some unlucky soul had just triggered the fuse of a "Bouncing Betty," known officially as an "S-mine" (*Schrapnellmine* in German), one of the enemy's simplest and most effective killers, which had killed or wounded countless 29ers over the past month.

The only course of action was to hit the dirt at once, for in just a few seconds, the click would be followed by a sharp bang, then, almost instantaneously, by a considerably louder blast. The nickname "Bouncing Betty" said a great deal about the S-mine's characteristics. Any soldier who accidentally set one off by tripping its wire or stepping directly on its prongs would soon be astonished to observe the cylindrical mine canister actually spring out of the ground about three feet into the air and explode, as if it were some large, nefarious insect. The explosion sprayed dozens of tiny steel balls about twenty yards in every direction.

"Everything broke loose at once," Wilkinson related to Shea. "From my position at the CP [in Hahnbusch], I could see two enemy machine guns in the woods open up. Flares and mortar fire came from the main German positions further east. The scrap was off to a running start." Amid the sudden eruption of fire originating from both sides, Silata's horrified men became aware that the Germans were using some sort of remote control to detonate large mines or howitzer shells buried in shallow holes near the woods. "One American was blown up less than five yards from a companion," Shea's article noted. "The companion insisted that the soldier had been lying on the ground when a sudden explosion burst from the earth near him."

The mines would pose no threat if the 29ers could press forward swiftly into the woods, but somewhere in that thick copse of trees the shadowy Germans lurked, concealed by darkness and thick undergrowth, their locations revealed only when they opened fire. "The men crawled toward the machine gun emplacements," Silata remembered. "They kept flat and worked in as close as possible, then threw hand grenades into the positions. The gun in the southwestern corner of the woods was silenced first. Then they worked on the next one. It, too, was silenced, but we did not actually get in through that high barbed wire to see if we had killed all of the gunners."

The Americans continued to push deeper into the woods, hurling grenades at any spot where a German might be hiding, but eventually, it became apparent that the Germans had departed. If so, the raiders had accomplished one of their goals. Daylight would soon come, and before it did, Silata knew it was time to get out, a realization heightened by the heavy German mortar fire that was beginning to fall among his men. The 29ers would again have to traverse minefields and move across the open ground to return to American lines, and the random enemy machine-gun fire that was currently crisscrossing that space would make the task much more hazardous than the trip in the opposite direction. Silata's radio was not functioning—Wilkinson claimed that the Germans jammed the Americans' frequency—so coordinating the retirement with Company L's main body in Hahnbusch would be difficult. Silata fired a white flare, followed by a green one, signaling Wilkinson that his platoon was heading back. As for the German machine-gun fire, Silata noted dryly, "It was about five feet above the surface of the ground. We just hunched under it and hurried home."

At daylight, the 29ers peered back toward enemy lines and could discern a cluster of German dead lying in the fields near the woods, apparently killed by American long-range machine-gun fire as they attempted to escape Silata's raiders. That was sufficient evidence for McDaniel to phone Gerhardt at 7:02 A.M. and exclaim, "Millholland's [3rd Battalion] raid went off well. Got into the woods and found the positions with a lot of barbed wire. Shot at each other point-blank. Killed a lot of Jerries. [Silata reported ten Germans killed]. Two of our men killed and five wounded." Company L morning reports actually show two men missing, not dead, although both were presumed to have been killed by German mines. Wilkinson soon learned that the two men were indeed dead: Pvt. Frank Boersema from Michigan and Pvt. Charles Rigg from Pennsylvania.

At Waldenrath, the 115th Infantry's Company B undertook the most ambitious, and least successful, of the division's four October 29 raids. That town was no outpost position like the Frying Pan, from which the Germans would retreat if pressed, but a full-fledged part of the Germans' defensive line, one which they did not intend to give up. Had not Hitler himself issued orders that every town and village in Germany "must be a fortress?"

The 1st Battalion's commander, Lt. Col. Glover Johns, had long since learned that the Germans on his front intended to carry out their Führer's order. No longer was Waldenrath a sleepy Rhineland farming village, but a formidable strongpoint from which all civilians had been evacuated, teeming with machine-gun nests and observation posts. Company B, commanded by 1st Lt. Bernard Lipford, had experience in this sort of job as it had successfully participated in a tough October 23 raid against the cluster of buildings in no-man's-land known as the "Island." But Waldenrath would obviously be a much more complex and hazardous operation. Lipford's task, as defined by Johns, was "to kill or capture the enemy holding this position, destroy enemy materiel and weapons found, obtain information of enemy strength and dispositions, and withdraw upon completing mission or on order of battalion commander."

A more ambitious plan for a single rifle company could hardly be conceived. Recent history had established that traversing the 500 yards separating Johns's outposts in the northern fringe of Birgden from Waldenrath—flat and wide-open fields for the most part, heavily mined and crisscrossed with barbed wire—would be an oppressive task, so challenging that only a few 29ers on nighttime patrols had even gotten close. Of those who did, most had not returned. With only about 150 men, Lipford held orders to cross that perilous ground, break into a strongpoint defended by a force equal to or stronger than his own and backed up by artillery and possibly tanks, and withdraw before the Germans could organize an effort to smash his company with a counterattack.

None of the four October 29 raids ordered by Gerhardt was easy, and Company B had drawn the proverbial short straw. Its only chance was to catch the Germans by surprise, moving out in darkness without a word and advancing with sufficient speed to make it back to American lines before daybreak. Lipford's jump-off, at 4:36 A.M., was six minutes late— a delay Johns would later have to explain in writing to his angry commanding general. For ten minutes, the Germans had no clue of their opponents' intent, but even absolute stealth could not prevent what was about to happen. The 29ers had advanced little more than halfway to Waldenrath when their progress was abruptly halted by what Johns later referred to as "the damndest minefield we ever encountered." Two explosions, triggered by soldiers who had caught their feet in unseen tripwires connected to Bouncing Betty mines, shattered the silence and instantly alerted Waldenrath's defenders to the Americans' presence.

Order was thrown into chaos within seconds. In a summary of the action written just hours after the raid, Lipford reported: "Immediately after the burst of the mines, the enemy opened up automatic fire on what was evidently the FPL [final protective line] and covered the area with numerous flares. Upon the illumination of the area, the enemy instantly laid down a concentration from mortars, automatic weapons, estimated as

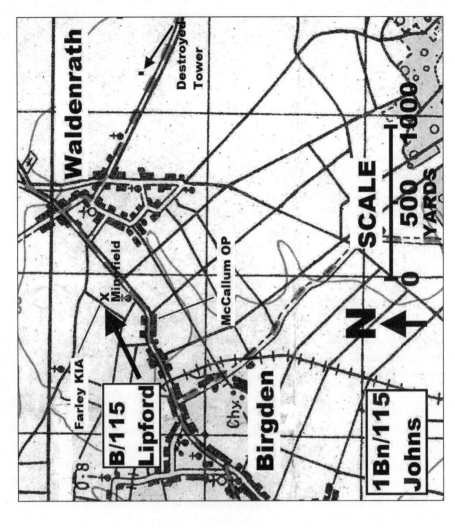

Raid by Company B, 115th Infantry, on Waldenrath, October 29, 1944.

ten to twelve, a large number of which were machine guns, and one SP [self-propelled] weapon. The SP was firing a shell that was identified as being 'white hot metal, but not white phosphorus.'" One alarmed 29er recalled that his reassuring cloak of darkness had instantly vanished, replaced by a radiance courtesy of German flares "as bright as daylight."

Company B hugged the ground, each member striving to remain motionless. Any movement, forward or backward, would be suicide. Was there a way out? The Germans' barrage of flares, bullets, and shells showed no signs of abating. The need for someone in authority to issue orders—any orders—was vital, but no orders came because the initial blast of a Bouncing Betty had wounded a platoon leader, 2nd Lt. Albert Steed, while, nearby, another platoon leader and a senior NCO had been hit by the Germans' ensuing fusillade. One member of Steed's platoon, radioman Pvt. Jack Farley (loaned to Company B from Johns's headquarters), called Lipford's command post, and the tormented tone of Farley's voice, as well as his desperate plea for litter-bearers, intimated to Lipford that the raid had broken down. Presently, Lipford's own radioman, PFC Peter Blackburn, tried to reconnect with Farley, but the only response was static. Blackburn could not know that by then Farley was dead.

Lipford's report greatly understated the predicament his men were in when he later wrote, "There was some disorganization." Based on Lipford's account, Colonel McDaniel later examined the timing of events and observed:

> Some elements of the assault platoons started a withdrawal. Lipford requested the reason for the withdrawal, and was informed that orders were given to withdraw. Lipford immediately countermanded the orders and ordered the men [back] into the line, but in so doing, the lieutenant thought he may have added to the confusion inasmuch as he couldn't lead 'each man to individual positions.' Lt. Lipford then reported his position as untenable because of a large volume of enemy automatic and smallarms fire, and lack of organization of the squads after the loss of the platoon leaders. He was then ordered [by Johns] to withdraw.

German fire was so intense that the act of returning to friendly lines was more dangerous than staying put. Even worse, the retreat would become appreciably more lethal at dawn as German machine gunners could see their targets without the aid of flares. To allow the 29ers to pull back safely, the 110th Field Artillery Battalion, which had been working closely with the 115th Infantry since stateside training at Fort Meade, needed to provide protective fire quickly. Under ordinary conditions, the 110th's expert forward observers could drop rounds on enemy strongpoints with uncanny precision in a matter of minutes. On this featureless German pastureland, however, suitable observation posts from which an observer could watch the fall of American shells and adjust ensuing rounds by radio or telephone were rare. Johns expected the raid to be over before daylight, so the need for dominant observation of Waldenrath hardly seemed necessary. But with the first hints of daybreak showing on the eastern horizon and most of Company B pinned under a murderous enemy barrage, someone from the 110th would have to direct fire on the enemy if Lipford's 29ers were to escape annihilation. Assuming German targets could be located, that support would come in a cascade of 105-millimeter shells, in both high-explosive and smoke varieties.

Standard U.S. Army doctrine mandated that artillery observers be an integral element of any infantry operation, and the Waldenrath raid was no exception. As the difficulties into which Company B had fallen threatened to escalate into a full-blown debacle, the 110th's observer with Lipford, 1st Lt. Will McCallum of Battery A, took decisive action, for which McCallum, a Mississippian, would later gain the Silver Star.

> 1st Lt. McCallum, with complete disregard for his own safety, made his way through intense enemy fire in search of a vantage point. After finding a house [on the northern edge of Birgden], 1st Lt. McCallum established his observation post in the attic and immediately directed artillery fire upon the enemy. Despite the fact that the roof of the house was completely destroyed by enemy fire, 1st Lt. McCallum courageously remained there and continued to direct fire upon the enemy, which permitted the company to withdraw to its former positions.

Withdrawals, however, do not win battles, a point Gerhardt emphasized when he learned of the raid's outcome. Even as Lipford's dazed 29ers made their way back to Birgden, McDaniel reported to the general: "They got halfway to the town. They ran into S-mines and then the Jerries opened up [with] ten to twelve automatic weapons." An enraged Gerhardt roared back: "Those are just excuses! You pick your mission and you do it your way!"

Shortly thereafter, McDaniel strove to do the impossible by filing an official report on the raid, trying to describe ineffable chaos. He had to do it because Gerhardt had demanded an explanation, but his two-sentence summation of the raid would have astonished any Company B member lucky enough to have survived the disaster: "The mission was not completely successful. However, valuable information was obtained of the strength and disposition of enemy defenses of Waldenrath." It was as if Robert E. Lee had announced that Pickett's Charge, although not completely successful, had gained indispensable intelligence of the Union position at Gettysburg. Acquiring McDaniel's "valuable information" had cost Lipford's Company B about twenty-five men, including eleven missing.

One of those 29ers listed as missing at Waldenrath was radioman Jack Farley, a member of Johns's Headquarters Company. His comrades would not learn until February 1945 that Farley had been killed just minutes into the raid and had been buried by the Germans somewhere behind the front. The twenty-six-year-old Farley was hardly an ordinary 29er, and the U.S. Army could have found much better places to use his talents than an infantry battalion. But from the moment he joined the Army in 1943, that is where he wanted to be—and that is where he remained from the moment he joined the 29th as a replacement in August 1944 until his death little more than two months later.

Farley was a bona fide Ivy Leaguer who had earned a bachelor's degree from Yale University in 1939 and shortly thereafter completed a master's degree in business from Harvard. That type of first-rate education typically led to a fast-track career as a business executive, and Farley had already embarked on that path in Detroit with the Ford Motor Company when the United States entered World War II. He could have used his 2-A Selective Service classification, specifying deferment from military service "in support of the national interest," to remain out of uniform—an understandable choice since he was also about to become a father for the first time—but as he told his wife Marjorie, "I have to go. My friends are dying. Anybody can do what I do at the plant. Do you understand?"

Thousands of heartrending exchanges of that kind between husbands and wives were taking place all over America in those troubled times, but whatever anxieties emerged in Marjorie Farley's mind because of her husband's decision surely worsened when she learned how his nascent military career was unfolding. He could have attended an officer candidate school and served in a branch that would have profited from his Ivy League education and business background, such as the Army Service Forces. Even if Jack desired a combat job, it could have been with the engineers or artillery, both of which would be rough, but not nearly as risky as the infantry.

But for Jack Farley, a native of Rochester, New York, infantry was the only choice—as an enlisted man, not an officer. Perhaps he regretted that resolve on August 19, 1944, at the close of the Vire campaign, when he joined his new outfit, Company C of the 115th Infantry, which had been fighting nearly continuously since D-Day. The harrowing stories of combat in Normandy related to him by his new comrades could have readily dismayed even ardent idealists like Farley, crushing any quixotic visions of battle that had survived the depressing replacement depots through which he and thousands of other lonely men had recently passed. It was far too late to get out of it, as tempting as it may have been for a few men to try. The fact that Private Farley, now a member of the storied 29th Division of D-Day fame, was not a man to back out of anything he had willingly started should have been obvious to anyone who knew him. Still, the following day, August 20, someone in authority took pity on this unusually smart, bespectacled young soldier and transferred him from Company C to the somewhat safer confines of the 1st Battalion's Headquarters Company as a radio operator. The new job did not offer much reassurance, as Farley's battalion commander, Johns, had already lost several radiomen over a period of just two months.

On October 29, Jack Farley's name was added to the list of 1st Battalion radiomen who had lost their lives. Members of the British Army's 43rd Infantry Division stumbled upon Farley's grave, dug by the Germans, when they advanced beyond Waldenrath as part of an Allied offensive in mid-January 1945. U.S. Army graves registration personnel would eventually reinter his body at the nearby American military cemetery at Margraten, Holland. When they did, they would forward to Marjorie her husband's personal effects, including his shattered GI eyeglasses and a Bible. The emotional anguish any war widow suffered upon receiving such a package must have been particularly intense because Marjorie herself had presented the Bible to her husband before the Army shipped him overseas. On one of its opening pages was the inscription: "To John A. Farley, from his admiring wife Marjorie."

By about 8 A.M. on October 29, the vortex of violence that had engulfed the rustic pastures between Birgden and Waldenrath the previous night had entirely dissipated. A landscape dotted with shell craters only hinted at the violence that had just transpired, and it did not reflect well on American arms.

Birgden would have an important visitor that day, a detail the 110th Artillery's commander, Lt. Col. John Cooper, had learned when Gerhardt phoned him the previous evening to announce that the new head of the XIX Corps, Maj. Gen. Raymond McLain, would inspect the 29th Division the next morning and wanted to take a close-up look at the enemy lines. Did Cooper have any ideas about an exposed frontline observation post McLain could visit? Cooper knew McLain, a fellow artilleryman and guardsman, from the training period in England and the Normandy campaign and described him as "a prince of a fellow." He protested to Gerhardt that taking a corps commander to an exposed observation post would probably trigger a violent reaction from the alert enemy. The habitually brusque Gerhardt replied, "Well, I want to do it! Now: have you got an exposed observation post or not?"

Cooper reasoned with some reluctance that it would have to be the church steeple in Birgden. He pointed out to Gerhardt in all frankness, however, that to reach the church, McLain's party would have to drive over open farmland, in full view of the Germans. "The land is as flat as a pancake," he advised Gerhardt, "and the instant we start to drive across it, the Germans are going to shell us. They've already gotten two or three vehicles moving out there in daylight. The infantry pretty much moves only at night." Gerhardt's response: "I'll be there [with McLain] at 1000 hours."

At the appointed time, Gerhardt and his new boss arrived at the village of Stahe, and Cooper promptly briefed them on the procedure to follow on the one-mile dash to Birgden. "I took the lead jeep," Cooper recalled. "I told my driver if a mortar shell landed in front, drive like hell; if it landed behind us, slow down. That was because the Germans would systematically bracket you: if the shell hit behind the target, they'd aim ahead; if the shell landed ahead, they'd adjust to the rear." Although the Germans there remained on a high state of alert because of Johns's Waldenrath raid, which had only ended a few hours earlier, much to Cooper's surprise and relief, they did not fire a shot at the procession of American jeeps heading to Birgden. The ancient Birgden church was located near the apex of a large triangular green in the town center, and when the jeeps stopped and their distinguished occupants hopped out, they were greeted by smart salutes from Johns and Capt. Kenneth James, the 110th Field Artillery's liaison officer currently serving in Johns's 1st Battalion command post.

The two generals and their deferential subordinates made the laborious climb up the staircase to the steeple, taking turns peering through the tiny windows near the top at the surrounding landscape, their vision enhanced by an artillery telescope. What they saw was hard to believe. "So help me," Cooper recollected, "The action had died out so completely that not a shot could be heard. . . . All I saw was one German farmer working out in the field with a hoe. Usually there was a lot of movement and activity, and somebody was generally shooting." The peaceful vista was entirely deceptive, for no one in Cooper's group could know that somewhere out in those fields, the bodies of Pvt. Jack Farley and several Company B members killed in the futile Waldenrath raid lay crumpled, unseen in the seemingly infinite rows of moldering cabbage and beet plants.

Lt. Col. John Cooper (at left), commander of the 110th Field Artillery Battalion, next to his jeep, named *Anne* after his daughter.

After McLain's departure, an annoyed Gerhardt turned on Cooper and bellowed, "God damn it! I told you to take us to an exposed observation post! I wanted to give the new corps commander a taste of battle." Cooper could only stammer an apology, although he knew that McLain, a veteran combat soldier who had experienced more than his share of battles in World War I and in the Mediterranean theater during the current war, had witnessed far more combat than Gerhardt himself. "The scenario was very obvious," Cooper mused. "Gerhardt was jealous of this supposed amateur being placed in a superior position to him, especially since McLain had come into Normandy only as a brigadier general and Gerhardt had been a major general."

Cooper, who was, in fact, one of Gerhardt's rare admirers, later had to admit: "I suppose everyone has their human frailties, and this was an instance in which General Gerhardt demonstrated one of his."

3. 1-A IN A 4-F OUTFIT

They were the anonymous men of the 29th Division, those thousands of soldiers like Jack Farley who had been joining the division in a steady stream since D-Day to replace equal numbers of 29ers who had been killed in action or suffered debilitating wounds on the battlefields of Normandy and Brittany. They had been drawn unceremoniously from dismal replacement depots, a process one GI described as like being "pushed out of a place blindfolded," and thrust into a division they knew nothing about other than the somewhat ominous detail that their new outfit had been in combat almost continuously since June 6, 1944. That might have pleased some eager young men who retained a naïve desire to do what soldiers are supposed to do in war—kill the enemy.

A few days in the front lines would cure most of them of that impulse. Indeed, some unfortunate men who had joined the 29th Division while it was actively engaged in its draining efforts to take St. Lô and Vire and Brest did not even live long enough to be cured of their illusion. They died a lonely death in a faraway place just days after entering the front line, before fellow 29ers even had a chance to learn their names. The 116th Infantry's Maj. Charles Cawthon remembered them as "vague shapes, laden with packs and weapons, who were hurried away behind guides to their companies. . . . I felt an ancient among children, knowing and dreading what they were to meet."

Most of those replacements were anonymous, strangers in an outfit populated by cynical veterans who had no desire to befriend them. The veterans' harsh and seemingly callous attitude toward newcomers was in fact a symptom of battle fatigue, for the inviolable law of averages as established in Normandy held that unless the war ended soon, the only means of exiting a typical twelve-man rifle squad was on a stretcher, either wounded or as a corpse. "You give up," one bitter infantryman remarked while recovering from a wound in a hospital. "You feel that you'll never get back anyway. You just try to postpone it as long as possible. . . . All the men have hope of getting back, but most of the hope is that you'll get hit someplace that won't kill you. That's all they talk about."

As the number of 29th Division riflemen who had landed on D-Day dwindled over time to a handful, many of the survivors reacted to the death and wounds of their comrades—with whom they had trained in England and the States for months and even years—with an emotional withdrawal from reality, refusing to allow themselves to get close to new men. Anonymity, it seemed, would help forestall the trauma that had occurred so many times in the past when close friends were lost in combat.

By late October 1944, most of the 29th Division's rifle squads no longer had a single D-Day veteran remaining on their rolls, so among the new replacements, acceptance by old-timers was hardly an issue. Nevertheless, most replacements, who themselves could gain the proud status as "veterans" if they managed to survive a few straight days of intense combat, quickly grasped the message their predecessors had already learned. The turnover of 29th Division riflemen, even in a supposedly quiet sector, was so high that befriending other members of the platoon could routinely turn out to be a devastating experience.

It was one of the supreme paradoxes of World War II infantry combat: solidarity with one's comrades was acknowledged as the best defense against breaking under the strain, but combat shattered that reassuring comradeship with startling rapidity. Since D-Day, the 29th had endured combat at such an intense level—more men had become casualties in four months than had populated the entire division prior to the invasion—that hundreds of men had cracked under the strain, a syndrome so common that it had come to be known on the home front by its World War I classification, "shell shock," or more correctly by the U.S. Army's new, but somewhat euphemistic term, "combat exhaustion." Within the 29th Division—and for that matter all U.S. Army divisions involved in 1944 combat—that affliction was surprisingly common. Throughout its eleven-month period of combat in World War II, for every eight 29ers evacuated from the battlefield due to physical wounds, roughly one man had been withdrawn due to symptoms of combat exhaustion exhibited at various levels of intensity. Actually, that ratio was a vast improvement from the U.S. Army's early 1943 campaign in North Africa, during which approximately a quarter and at times as many as a third of non-fatal battle casualties had been combat exhaustion cases.

Old-school soldiers such as George Patton might still scoff at those soldiers who acknowledged the existence of combat exhaustion—which he categorized as "an excuse for cowardice" and "an easy way out"—but by fall 1944, any 29th Division rifleman who had survived at the front for more than a few days and who understood that his division would probably remain in almost perpetual combat until the war's end, could not fail to recognize that it was a genuine disorder, with such debilitating symptoms, according to the experts, as "tremor, insomnia, startle reaction, and generalized anxiety," which could worsen substantially in a "hyper-reactive stage" to "a general slowing in mental processes and apathy." In one large-scale survey among combat veterans taken in April 1945, the question was asked: "What do you think should be done to a man who 'cracks up' mentally at the front?" Unlike Patton, the respondents expressed overwhelming sympathy for their brothers-in-arms: "Eighty-six percent answered: 'He should be given medical treatment,' whereas only three percent asserted, 'He should be court-martialed' or 'He should be made to go right back into combat.'"

Even such a traditionalist as Gerhardt accepted the Army's official definition of combat exhaustion and would eventually display sincere sensitivity toward those 29ers afflicted with it. He had to: on January 12, 1944, while the 29th was in England preparing for D-Day, the division was authorized a "division neuropsychiatrist," who would specialize in diagnosis and treatment of combat exhaustion. The doctor selected for the job, Maj. David Weintrob, would later report cynically: "[I] prepared to meet, in combat, the problems of combat exhaustion . . . with a sphygmomanometer [to read blood pressure], a set of five tuning forks, a percussion hammer, and an ophthalmoscope [to examine eyes]. . . . [Also] a ward tent, twenty cots, eighty blankets, a staff of five enlisted men, a Coleman heating unit, and an improvised medical chest."

That an arrangement of that kind would be entirely inadequate to treat the 29th Division's combat exhaustion cases became obvious when Gerhardt launched a major assault to capture St. Lô on July 11, 1944. Over the next eight days, the facility admitted more than 500 men, of whom Weintrob could treat only those whose behavior was seriously impaired. The best he could do for everyone else was to sedate them with the turquoise pill known by 29ers as the "Blue-88," whose power—so they said—matched that of the German weapon they feared most, the horrifying 88-millimeter cannon. Sleep would then come to those who had been deprived of it for days, even those men whose nerves were so on edge that they could hardly sit still.

Regrettably, Weintrob got no help. "The [First] Army exhaustion center was unprepared to receive this sudden onslaught of cases and bluntly refused to accept any but the very acute battle psychoneuroses," he reported. "As the great majority of cases were those of extreme physical exhaustion with mild anxiety states, they argued that it was a division administrative problem and must be solved by division."

Gerhardt wanted it that way, since the number of 29ers drawn out of action for psychological reasons at the height of the St. Lô fighting was almost equal to an entire infantry battalion of 800 men. He could not afford to lose so many troops when experience had hinted that a majority of them stood a good chance of a speedy recovery and would eventually return to their units—but just how many? Maj. Herbert Spiegel, a psychiatrist from Washington, D.C., who had entered the Army as an assistant battalion surgeon in the 26th Infantry of the 1st Division and participated in the North African campaign in 1942–43, observed:

> It soon became apparent that a tense, tremulous soldier was not necessarily a psychiatric casualty… A state of tension and anxiety was so prevalent in the front lines that it had to be regarded as a normal reaction to that grossly abnormal situation. Where did ordinary psychological and physiological signs of fear end and where did symptoms of clinical syndrome begin? . . . A critical point of treatment for psychiatric casualties was that fluid, confused period just after the impact of what the soldier experienced as a "crack" or a "breakdown." Almost any influence by a comrade, aidman, or officer that helped suppress fear and guided the man toward quick reparation and reorientation was the psychotherapeutic method of choice.

On July 14, 1944, Weintrob, with Gerhardt's full approval and support, set up a greatly expanded combat exhaustion center that would become known to appreciative patients as the "29th Division Hot Spot Spa." It could accommodate 500 men at once and included a shower, barbershop, and recreation hall. The object was to provide "a program of rest, sedation, psychotherapy, and rehabilitation [that] should return a good percentage to duty within a period of a week." In a postwar report, Weintrob deduced that the number of 29ers actually returning to their companies within that time span was 52.7 percent. Whether that figure was a "good" percentage was open to debate, but it surely was better than what American divisions had achieved early in the war. No U.S. Army field manuals or tables of organization mentioned anything about a "combat exhaustion center," and had it not been for Gerhardt's enthusiastic endorsement, Weintrob could never have initiated it. As Weintrob concluded in an October 1944 paper, using three underlined words and an exclamation mark for emphasis, it was "most, most necessary!"

Gerhardt soon had an even better idea. On August 7, 1944, in the midst of the division's efforts to liberate Vire, he ordered the Hot Spot Spa converted into the much more expansive "29th Division Training Center," an extraordinary effort that reflected how the general's dynamic mind, always brimming with ideas, could occasionally come up with something truly sensible and beneficial. In the new center, treatment of combat exhaustion cases would be just a small part of an ambitious effort to prepare all 29ers for battle, primarily fresh replacements, men returning from hospital, newly joined first and second lieutenants, even men who had been removed from their units due to court-martial offenses.

That Gerhardt's scheme was ahead of its time was related, perhaps, to the fact that no U.S. Army unit had suffered more casualties since D-Day than the 29th Division. Gerhardt therefore already knew what many of his fellow division commanders were just beginning to find out: in the relentless battle to bring down Nazi Germany, the top brass would not have the luxury of giving infantry divisions substantive breaks from combat; every division commander would have to figure out ways to maintain his outfit's high level of combat efficiency, even when casualties had decimated his unit in a matter of days. The cardinal precept of American strategy in the European theater, deriving straight from U.S. Army Chief of Staff Gen. George Marshall's philosophy of war, was to apply continual and overwhelming pressure on the enemy. If a division commander could not keep his unit in a near-constant state of readiness to join that effort, he would soon be a passenger on a forlorn troopship heading back to the States, looking for a new job.

Gerhardt resolved that he would not be one of those unfortunate men. He reasoned that since new soldiers made up the vast majority of his infantry units by the close of the Normandy campaign, the effective trans-formation of those raw soldiers into true 29ers had to be an overriding goal if the 29th was to retain its reputation as a first-class fighting unit. That goal would be tougher than anyone imagined. The cynical nickname disgruntled replacements applied to themselves—"orphans"—hinted at the difficulty Gerhardt would face in the transformation process. Further-more, as Gerhardt had grasped, even if replacements were well trained and energetic, their initiation into combat would be a shock from which many would not recover. As Weintrob noted, of those 29ers suffering from combat exhaustion admitted to Hot Spot Spa, "approximately 50 percent were recent replacements to the division. . . . The frequency with which [I] discovered from [my] personal interviews that a man had been trained as a driver, a mail clerk, a cook, a permanent KP, an officer's orderly, and what have you were truly amazing. These men were thrust into combat insufficiently trained and certainly psychologically unprepared." A late-war study of combat personnel in several U.S. Army divisions in Europe agreed: "Psychiatric breakdowns tended to occur disproportionately among the newest combat men."

What had formerly been a rest area devoted to curing 29ers afflicted with combat exhaustion would now become a thriving rear-echelon train-ing ground with the much more multifaceted object of boosting the com-bat skills of both old and new troops. As Gerhardt had always vowed, defeating the skilled enemy and surviving on the battlefield depended on knowing one's job thoroughly, and if new men joining the division were not trained to the incredibly high standards the 29th Division had achieved in England while preparing for D-Day, then the Training Center had to rectify their shortcomings.

One could hardly imagine soldiers with a more dissimilar frame of mind than a weary fighting man coming out of the front line and a green replacement emerging from a rear-echelon replacement depot. Neverthe-less, those men would come together at the 29th Division Training Cen-ter for the same purpose. Members of frontline units dispatched to the center for a few days of instruction would include not only those dis-tressed 29ers who no longer could tolerate the grotesque sights and sounds of war, but also insubordinate and delinquent soldiers—known as "eight balls"—who required reeducation; junior officers who could profit from the experiences of peers who had fought the enemy in Normandy and Brittany; non-commissioned officers and promising privates and PFCs who would learn tips about the art of low-level leadership on the battlefield; and anyone from a non-infantry branch, such as artillery, who required retraining, voluntarily or involuntarily, as infantrymen. Those 29ers arriving at the Training Center also included fretful replacements— nearly 1,500 in the month of November 1944 alone, 61 of whom were officers—who were about to spend their first day in a combat division near the front, as well as men returning to the division after suffering wounds requiring hospitalization.

Although enthusiastic and apathetic men populated the Training Center, one pervasive theme unified them all: they were members of the 29th Infantry Division. Gerhardt directed the center's commander, Maj. Grat Hankins, to emphasize that point at every available opportunity, a task the twenty-six-year-old Hankins fulfilled with zeal because he himself had been a 29er since he had enlisted in the Maryland National Guard at Bel Air as a private at the age of sixteen in 1934 and remained an enlisted man at a rank no higher than corporal for the next seven years. (He was commissioned shortly after the 29th's February 1941 mobilization.)

If the 29th Division's blue-and-gray insignia did not appear on a soldier's left shoulder and on his helmet, Hankins saw to it that the 29er would soon find himself alone with a cloth division patch, a sewing kit, a small paintbrush, and cans of blue and gray paint to rectify those oversights. As Hankins pointed out, that soldier's family for the foreseeable future would be the 29th Division, and he had to be familiar with its celebrated history going back to its formation in 1917 and know and use the division motto—"29, Let's Go!"—in conversation. The division's sacred "do's and don'ts" list, sometimes known as the "29th Division Bible," catalogued standard procedures that every member of the Training Center had to memorize, although as that list got bigger by the week—by October, it amounted to twenty-eight practices—the likelihood of a 29er reciting them on demand and by heart was low. Nevertheless, he had to try: chin straps always at point of chin; "I don't know, but I'll find out"; a 29th man will "march, shoot, and obey"; proper disposal of cigarette butts; salute at all times; do things cheerfully and with enthusiasm; buttons buttoned, hands out of pockets—and twenty-one more.

They called the Training Center "Uncle Charlie's University," and when the 29th moved to Holland from Brittany at the end of September 1944, the general directed Hankins to set up shop on the beautiful grounds of Kasteel Amstenrade, a 300-year-old brick castle and estate, only five miles behind the front, featuring an impressive swimming pool and a dozen or more greenhouses. According to rumor, during the German occupation, the castle's owner had been visibly sociable with the enemy, and when the Americans arrived, he thought it best to disappear for an indefinite period in fear that local Dutch citizens might seek vengeance.

If almost every Training Center attendee was about to enter or reenter the battle, Kasteel Amstenrade was not a bad place to spend the last few days free of the nerve-wracking sights and sounds of war. Some lucky and incredulous 29ers enjoyed restful sleep inside the locale's various buildings, a rare exception to Uncle Charlie's strict rule that his men must live outdoors throughout the 29th Division's time in combat. Most troops, however, were still housed in tents.

There were hot showers, a pure delight for soldiers who had grown used to living without that luxury. New uniforms and footgear were available in profusion. The food, too, was not bad, prepared in real kitchens with field ranges and captured German stoves using canned or preserved ingredients from B-rations that imaginative mess sergeants could transform into something much tastier than the cold, ready-to-eat C- and K-rations that 29ers had grown tired of. As the Training Center was an unauthorized organization, however, the cooks were always hard-pressed to find enough food to feed everyone, although the general's insistence that they prepare soup twice a day helped to stretch the limited ingredients.

As noted in a Training Center report,

> For entertainment, a large building was secured, which will accommodate 300 men. Stoves have been placed in the building for heat, and a picture show is held every night at 1900 hours. In addition a piano is at hand, and music is furnished by replacements who come through. We have the 29th Division band play twice each week at the noon hour, and a sound truck every day except on days when the band is here. As often as possible a [Red Cross] clubmobile comes to serve hot coffee and doughnuts. Daily, *Stars and Stripes* and *29 Let's Go* are passed out to each house in the area.

The center may have been within range of German artillery, but that sometimes annoying detail could not curtail Gerhardt's determination to inculcate in all attendees the kind of behavior he believed characterized a first-rate soldier. A bugler blew reveille before dawn, as if the division were still encamped at Fort Meade, and each company assembled in full kit for morning roll call. At sunset, regardless of weather, all 29ers attending the Training Center gathered by companies on the improvised parade ground and, upon the barked command of the senior NCO, came to rigid attention and snapped sharp salutes in unison as a bugler blew the tender notes of "Retreat" and two soldiers lowered the Stars and Stripes from the flagpole, carefully ensuring that the color did not touch the ground. "Taps" would follow a few hours later, emanating in the darkness from an unseen bugler, and the call with which even new soldiers had become thoroughly familiar would put exhausted 29ers to sleep in an instant. These were all merely rituals, exasperating to some, but Gerhardt was right: they were unifying and emotional acts that made young soldiers appreciate their small role in helping to cure a world gone mad.

It hardly made sense to mix "eight balls," combat exhaustion cases, junior officers, and the 29th Division's sharpest NCOs in the same group, so Gerhardt segregated attendees into separate companies and schools. The most intractable learners were found in the "Training Company," a euphemistic title for the unit populated by 29ers who had been disciplined for minor and, in a few cases, major disciplinary lapses, such as desertion. Gerhardt believed in redemption, and if any of those men demonstrated a devotion to return to their units, the general would forgive and forget. If not, they would be taken off the division rolls, shipped to an obscure rear-echelon unit in which "eight balls" were the norm, and have nothing more to do with the Blue and Gray Division.

Getting those 29ers who exhibited combat exhaustion back to their units could be an even tougher challenge. Major Weintrob reviewed every case personally and immediately dispatched those displaying severe symptoms, typically bottomless apathy and lethargy rather than outright hysteria, to a rear-area hospital, from which, as Weintrob observed, "the percentage returned to combat duty . . . although treated thoroughly at rear echelons, will be very low." Although in early October 1944, Weintrob estimated that "this type of case forms less then 10 percent" of combat exhaustion patients, evidence from later 29th Division campaigns hinted that the percentage was much higher.

Men presenting milder indicators of combat exhaustion, such as depression, trembling, and insomnia, were given a forty-eight-hour rest period under "very light sedation," during which they would have no military responsibilities beyond cleaning themselves up, donning new uniforms, and reporting to the daily assembly at "Retreat." Assuming the sedation worked and the men could briefly put their minds at rest, most combat exhaustion patients spent that time in the activity they required most—sleeping.

Whether that sleep was blissful or fitful would determine Weintrob's next course of action. If a soldier emerged from his forty-eight-hour rest exhibiting no signs of improvement, or even worsening symptoms, 29th Division policy mandated that Weintrob transfer him out of the division to a hospital. If, on the other hand, a soldier surfaced from a deep slumber as a new man, ready for reassignment to his unit, Weintrob would promptly send him back to the front—a decision that some patients actually welcomed. But Weintrob diagnosed the majority of cases as somewhere in between those two extremes, and any soldier so judged would soon find himself a member of the center's "Rehabilitation Company," commanded by 2nd Lt. Paul McLain. The object, as Weintrob observed, was "to reacquaint himself with his weapon, to gain self-confidence, and become psychologically better prepared for front-line duty."

For worn-out soldiers who worried that Patton, or someone like him, might show up to shame them for their supposed frailties, it was reassuring that McLain and his NCOs imparted poise and self-reliance to the Rehabilitation Company's members rather than humiliating them. A Training Center report noted:

We start a very progressive training program. Lieutenant McLain, who is a veteran of the African, Sicilian, Italian, and French campaigns, and who has served with the 1st and 45th Divisions, is in charge of this group. "Mac" has been wounded five times himself, so the Rehabilitation Company listens to him when he says something. These men have their own [rifle] range, a new one we built especially for them, and little by little, they are getting accustomed to rifle fire and demolition again. It's amazing to see the progress they're making.

Happily, there would be no stigma attached to combat exhaustion within the 29th Division, and McLain's rehabilitative methods were good enough to send about 60 percent of the patients back to their units within five to ten days of their arrival at the center. Compared to the North African and Sicilian campaigns in 1942 and 1943, during which U.S. Army medical personnel returned only a miniscule portion of exhaustion cases to the front, the 29th Division's accomplishment was remarkable. In the 29th's period of combat from D-Day to V-E Day, however, combat exhaustion data indicates that the patients' supposed rehabilitation was not particularly effective. Of the 1,160 29ers returned to combat duty after assignment to the Rehabilitation Company as combat exhaustion patients, almost one third, or 347 men, would eventually be readmitted to that company as a consequence of further bouts of exhaustion.

Despite his reputation as a hard-driving disciplinarian and a stickler for the ways of the old Army, that was not a statistic over which Gerhardt would lose any sleep. Returning a large percentage of combat exhaustion patients to their duties was better than none. Besides, as far as the general was concerned, as long as a soldier acknowledged his duties and made an effort to return to them, the center must be doing good work.

That work, however, had to extend to the replacements, for as important as the rehabilitation of combat exhaustion cases was to the division's efficiency, the center's ability to prepare raw replacements for combat was much more vital. By late October 1944, replacements greatly outnumbered D-Day men in every single one of the 29th Division's infantry companies, and the division could not function if those replacements could not effectively perform the duties of the soldiers whom they replaced. Furthermore, most men passing through the U.S. Army's depressing replacement pipeline were not particularly contented, and 29th Division trainers would face a daunting challenge when they tried to uplift those soldiers' gloomy morale to the high standards Gerhardt expected. One anonymous replacement spoke for thousands when he observed: "Before I got out of the [replacement] pool, I practically got the willies. I was in depots for five weeks. . . . After so long, a man doesn't know whether he's coming or going; he's unsettled and anxious and finally just doesn't give a good goddamn."

Accordingly, from the moment the replacements arrived at the center, they remained busy almost every minute of their two-day stay learning about their new outfit and its occasionally peculiar ways. Of the first two items issued to them, one was entirely practical—a bottle of halazone tablets, the chlorine-based pills that purified drinking water by eliminating deadly parasites and bacteria. The other was wholly spiritual—a single piece of flimsy paper, printed on both front and back by a mimeograph machine, providing "a short history of the 29th Division's glorious achievements." Next, each replacement "had a hot shower, a fresh change of clothes . . . [and] a new M-1 rifle."

Their first full day at the center was signaled by reveille at dawn, followed by a hearty and hot breakfast. The uniform of the day was specified as "ODs [olive-drab uniforms], field jacket, with raincoats on belts, with arms." Starting at 8 A.M. and lasting thirty minutes, they would undertake a vigorous regimen of calisthenics. At 8:30, as a veteran 29er observed, "The curtain rings up. You're sitting out in a bare field with these green replacements, who've been bounced around all over God's creation for maybe a month before they reached this spot. They all look pale—they don't know what's coming up next. Major Hankins, a big, brilliant, good-natured soldier, introduces himself to the crowd." Reporter Lou Azrael described Hankins's theme as a welcome to "the great team that is the 29th Infantry Division."

His pleasantries concluded, Hankins got straight to the point by specifying the rules by which all 29ers lived. Most of the skeptical new men must have suppressed guffaws at those peculiarities, despite repeated warnings by Hankins that they would disregard them at their peril. "Far removed from the realities of battle, you may have gotten other ideas," Hankins began. "But it's chinstraps under your chin! Trousers inside your leggings! Cigarette butts torn up—shredded! Saluting officers! These things are not just a quirk of mind; they are the things we have found that actually pay dividends on the field of battle."

The replacements abruptly sat up and took notice when Hankins announced, "And now we will see a few demonstrations of the way things should and should not be done." Azrael observed: "Hankins blew his whistle, and a squad of soldiers appeared from the next field. They advanced in bad tactical formation, without taking proper precautions against a possible enemy. Suddenly a loud explosion burst, with smoke ahead of them. Some started running to the rear, and their route was blocked by another explosion. . . . [Hankins] explained: 'Squads advance this way in combat, too; they are wiped out just as this one would have been if the shellbursts had been real.'" Azrael noticed that when the demonstration troops exhibited the wrong way to act on the battlefield, they "introduced some humor, some burlesque so spectacular that the replacements got amusement with their lessons." Another observer recalled that the trainers "looked like a bunch of rabbit hunters. The squad leader maintains no discipline. Guys cuss. Want to know where the hell they're going. Got everything in mind but the task for which they were sent over here—to kill Germans."

The trainers returned in a minute, this time with more intensity. The audience watched with a mixture of amusement and gravity as they bellowed, "29, let's go!" and scampered into a field that shook with several mock explosions. Some flopped to the ground and opened fire with blank ammunition. Others kept scampering, crouching low as if it were the real thing, finally coming to a stop in a prone position, lying up against some meager cover. Grenades materialized, and with a few well-aimed tosses, the "enemy" was no more. Actual warfare would not be that easy; as the replacements could plainly see, there was a right way and a wrong way to do it. Furthermore, as Hankins pointed out, if anyone knew the right way, it would be the trainers, all of whom were experienced 29th Division NCOs possessing several Purple Hearts, Bronze Stars, and Silver Stars among them. Azrael concluded, "When they finished the demonstration, several hundred other boys felt much better and knew much more about the ordeal which they were entering."

The entire afternoon was left open for weapons practice. To the replacements' delight, rifle and carbine ammunition was almost limitless, with grenades in equal profusion. There was even time for an hour of bayonet drills, taught by Sgt. Henry Delva of Danville, Illinois, although the likelihood the new men would ever use the bayonet in battle was low. As any good soldier knew, no weapon would be of any value unless it were tenderly cared for and kept clean, and the replacements' lessons for the day concluded with a scrupulous demonstration of the art of maintenance provided by Sgt. Clem Trakeski of Nanticoke, Pennsylvania. By this point in their military careers, all U.S. Army infantrymen could strip and reassemble their M1 rifles in their sleep; what they were about to learn from Trakeski was how life in the mud and rain of a frontline foxhole would necessitate unremitting attention to their rifles if they were to keep them functional, which could eventually save their lives.

The next day, the new men touched up their map-reading skills, learned useful secrets on how to dig and live in a foxhole, and listened to a lecture on chemical warfare. But there was one more thing, a sensitive topic that Hankins saved for last. One of Gerhardt's pet subjects, the behavior expected of all 29ers in the event they were captured, had to be expounded in a half-hour lecture, and even if a replacement failed to absorb it all, a half-sheet handout he tucked inside a pocket for future reference would remind him of its importance. "Subject: Conduct in case of capture. Effective this date the following points will be thoroughly understood by all replacements in this center." Paradoxically, the first of five points was not strictly relevant to suggested behavior as a prisoner of war, for its simple two-word proclamation, typed in capital letters, blared: "AVOID CAPTURE!" The following four points, however, were much more practical: "Give only your name, rank, and Army serial number. Beware of stool pigeons. Be observant. Keep your mouth shut." Simple enough, but by this point, the new men's minds were such a jumble of rules and procedures that it was tough to take in even more dictates. Besides, in the event the Germans captured them, they no longer would be following U.S. Army rules, but those of the Nazis.

No one could deny that the lessons imparted by the Training Center staff to the rookies over two days would help the new men survive their first few days at the front, but the teaching offered no help whatsoever on the question replacements pondered the most. Every new 29er could not help wondering what type of men populated the company he would soon join. Would they accept him—or make him an object of ridicule? One of the 29th Division's "Do's and Don'ts" replacements had just attempted to memorize emphasized: "Use the buddy system." That was reassuring, but at the front, when joining a group of soldiers who had already learned to cope with the terror of war, how likely was it that one could find a "buddy?"

In the weeks immediately following D-Day, the 29th Division had often shoved replacements into their new companies while those outfits were actively engaging the Germans in combat. Under those conditions, befriending anyone was out of the question; the best a terrified new man could hope for was to imitate the veterans and make friends later, assuming he survived his first day. Later, Gerhardt insisted that replacements not be forwarded to their new companies unless those outfits were in reserve, behind the front lines for at least three days. The general called this eminently wise new policy a "get-acquainted period," a chance for the new men to make a few friends or at least get to know the names of their fellow squad members, upon whom they would soon be relying in combat. Initiation to combat would always be a shock some men could not tolerate, but at least 29ers would have a chance to mitigate that shock if they could practice Gerhardt's "buddy system" as the general intended.

And so the replacements departed the center as true 29ers; their new blue and gray shoulder patches and helmet insignia proved that. One veteran 29er who observed the training process perhaps overstated its impact on the fresh replacements: "There's a sparkle coming into their eyes. They are wide awake. You think: If only this rouser course could go on. It is a great benefit to the men." No longer orphans, the new men boarded trucks, took a seat on the uncomfortably hard benches, and bounced and swayed as those trucks roared down the rough country roads of Holland, bringing the men closer to the moment they all feared. Would they ever see home again? At least they were real infantrymen now, members of the storied regiments the men had learned of in Major Hankins's lecture: 115th, 116th, 175th. It really didn't matter which one as long as the men in charge, from squad leaders to the regimental commander, knew their jobs and cared for their flock.

The long-awaited moment came when the new men were dispatched to their companies, the immediate families with which they would remain until the war's end or they became a casualty. Burdened with all their equipment, the fresh 29ers trudged tentatively into company bivouac areas in serene Dutch pastures, lined with endless two-man pup tents, a few latrines, and two or three large tents for the company commander and his entourage. It was a scene with which every replacement was entirely familiar, but there was something more orderly about this arrangement than the typical replacement depot, almost as if the residents here had a greater sense of purpose and dignity than what the neophytes were used to. Perhaps Gerhardt's "Do's and Don'ts," which Training Center NCOs had proclaimed *ad nauseam* to the skeptical learners, were beneficial after all.

Just outside one of the larger tents, reserved for the company commander, a dark blue fork-tailed guidon fluttered on top of a staff, featuring the crossed rifle insignia of the U.S. Army's infantry branch and the regimental number and company letter of the replacement's new outfit emblazoned in white. Presently, the newcomers had to report to that tent and come face-to-face with the officer in command, his gruff "top kick" (the company first sergeant) and a clerk, who would eventually type the newcomers' names, ranks, and serial numbers onto morning reports. It was a moment some men dreaded, a few longed for, and most were simply resigned to. In a few minutes, the first sergeant would dispatch the replacements down the line of pup tents to their new squads. A place in those pup tents was reserved for them, perhaps a spot that had recently been occupied by a 29er who was now dead. At least there would be a couple of days to get used to it all, and even better, squad leaders would keep everyone busy: drilling, exercising, tossing a few live grenades, and firing a few clips from M-1s on makeshift firing ranges. If Gerhardt's "buddy system" were to work, this was the time and place for the replacements to meet their buddies.

If any of the novices had a moment for a breather, perhaps some of them lay in their constricted tents and reached into their pockets to pull out a crumpled half-sheet of paper, one of the dozens handed to them at the Training Center. It read:

> I am pleased to welcome you as a member of the 29th Infantry Division. You are about to enter combat. It is for this that you have spent weeks, and perhaps many months, of hard training. Face the enemy with confidence in yourself and in your weapon. You are a better man than he, and your weapon is the best of its type that can be made. The primary requirements of a combat soldier, which you must always remember, are that he be able to SHOOT, MARCH, AND OBEY. We of the 29th Infantry Division are proud of the record it has made in combat. I am confident that you, too, will be proud to be a member of this division. I welcome you with confidence in your ability and determination to do your part as a member of this division in bringing about the early defeat of the enemy. . . [Signed], C.H. Gerhardt, Major General, U.S. Army, Commanding.

So this was the legendary "Uncle Charlie." As far as encouragement was concerned, the piece of paper wasn't much, but it was better than nothing.

The 29th Infantry Division was good, but it certainly could be better. Even Gerhardt had to admit that, since an alarming number of attacks and raids launched by the division in October 1944 had ended in disaster and had barely dented the German line. Gerhardt himself did not assume the blame for those difficulties; rather, he laid them squarely on the shoulders of his field-grade officers, the regimental and battalion commanders and their senior staff members, who planned and directed the operations, sensible or not, the general had charged them to carry out.

The problem was deeper than that, and Gerhardt knew it, for the heart and soul of the 29th had been ripped out on the battlefields of Normandy and Brittany. The division's low-level leaders—platoon sergeants, squad leaders, platoon leaders, the men who had learned their jobs over months and even years of perpetual training in England and the States and had guided the movement of 29ers in actual combat—were virtually all gone by October 1944. Some good men had taken over for those experienced sergeants and lieutenants, but to learn what their predecessors had learned, the newcomers would need time. Unhappily, that luxury that was in short supply since the law of averages indicated that their battlefield careers would be remarkably short.

How could the 29th Division perpetuate the complex yet vital lessons of training and actual battle if its most effective practitioners did not last long enough to pass the lessons on? According to Gerhardt, the way to do it was to establish at the 29th Division Training Center a "Junior Officers School" and a "Non-Commissioned Officers School." Training Center personnel described those schools as the general's "pets" or "babies," and such words hinted that someone, in all likelihood Major Hankins, would have to put in a great deal of work to ensure they succeeded. Fortunately, they did. In November 1944, nearly 200 fresh lieutenants, as well as a few newly arrived captains, attended the Junior Officers School, while 570 enlisted men took part in classes at the NCO School.

A Training Center report concluded somewhat immodestly that the schools were "a howling success." To demonstrate that, a Training Center action report cover featured a drawing of two 29ers in a humorous "before and after" illustration, like a Charles Atlas ad in a men's magazine displaying a ninety-eight-pound weakling next to a transformed body builder. One slovenly soldier, his uniform in tatters, chin straps dangling, hands in pockets, and wearing no divisional insignia, represented the "before," while an immaculate GI, his uniform and posture perfect in every way, embodied the "after." Cynics might comment that the center's popularity was based on the fact that anything drawing men away from the front for nearly a week, during which students had three hot meals per day and their first restful sleep in weeks, could not fail to be popular. In fact, the schools flourished for the practical reason that their course of instruction, as one attendee wrote, "causes one to have more confidence." Furthermore, what greater motivation could a soldier have than to pay heed to lessons that could save his and his comrades' lives when they inevitably returned to battle?

That attitude was enhanced by the center's educational philosophy, which declared openly that students must not only learn, but also contribute. "All students upon graduation from the Training Center . . . are asked to submit comments on the course of instruction just completed," a report noted. "It is this source of information, direct from the man at the front that dictates the type and nature of training to be followed for the succeeding school. The Junior Officers School was the direct result of a suggestion made by one graduating NCO."

Everyone agreed that the Junior Officers School offered valuable tips on battlefield leadership, although one attendee spoke for all when he concluded, "There is too much material for three days." The highlight for many was the interchange of ideas among officers in classes titled "combat orders," "leadership," and "general discussion," which took up most of the first day. As Gerhardt reasoned, confidence was one of the most vital traits of an effective battlefield leader—Uncle Charlie's own self-assurance never wavered—and if that classroom dialogue helped to instill poise in men who would soon be leading 29ers against a skilled enemy, the instruction would be worth the effort. Some students professed disappointment that practical tips for success and survivability on the battlefield were lacking. One 29er complained on his comment form, "We should have officers with battle experience tell stories of battles: what happened in certain circumstances; how situations were met; and what is the best thing to do against various enemy weapons." Another junior officer, obviously skeptical about the competence of his immediate superiors, wrote: "This school has been very good, but it seems to me that field grade officers [majors, lieutenant colonels, and colonels] could be refreshed." Would anyone dare mention that Gerhardt himself could use some refresher training?

Those who expected classes to be held in a comfortable setting, perhaps even inside a warm and dry Dutch castle, were disappointed. "By order of General Gerhardt all classes were held outdoors, despite rain and mud and numbing cold," one lieutenant remembered. "The men kicked their shoes together to keep their feet warm, while they learned or argued the latest battle facts straight from the front."

On the second day, the students practiced battle drills, compass and map reading, and an unforgettable fifteen-minute exercise designated simply, "Order out of confusion." As related by 2nd Lt. Joe Ewing of the 175th Infantry's Company G, "A group of men would be standing about in no order of position whatsoever, and then some predesignated leader would suddenly call out, for example, 'Form a column of twos on me!' At which point instantly and on the double everyone would have to run to the place of the caller and form up quickly into the ordered formation, seeing how fast they could do it. The big point was the suddenness and the quickness. You didn't drag yourself to the formation. You ran!"

Supposedly, an officer could not graduate from "Uncle Charlie's University" unless he was a conscientious listener. Just to make sure the officers paid attention, on the afternoon of the third day, Hankins gave a one-hour examination. No one is known to have flunked, for most of the examination questions were so absurdly easy that an officer could fail only if his answers were utterly facetious: "Do you consider yourself efficient by requesting more than you need?" "What effect does a missing rifle part have on the weapon?" "Can battles be won by hard fighting alone?"

The thirty-minute graduation ceremony hardly amounted to much, just the presentation of a flimsy graduation certificate and a mimeographed note from Gerhardt welcoming new officers to the 29th Division and concluding for what seemed like the hundredth time, "Bear in mind the primary requirements of a soldier; that he be able to SHOOT, MARCH, AND OBEY." No one would forget those four words anytime soon.

The training of a good non-commissioned officer was infinitely more challenging than that of a lieutenant, for most of those men attending the 29th Division's NCO School had been privates just a few weeks earlier—and some were even still privates. Appalling rates of attrition among 29th Division infantry companies had shoved those men into leadership roles, whether they liked it or not, and on occasion, when a nineteen-year-old private first class with no combat experience suddenly found himself a squad leader, the consequences were usually regrettable. Accordingly, Gerhardt, who often noted that "this is a sergeant's war," would demand six days of instruction for NCOs rather than the officers' three and would have his veteran trainers teach such practical skills as patrolling, infiltration, night operations, demolitions, street fighting, first aid, and field sanitation.

Actually, the NCO School's role as a pivotal component of the Training Center originated from an idea submitted to division headquarters by 1st Lt. Dwight Gentry of the 115th Infantry's Company I. Gentry had joined that unit six days after D-Day and, in the intervening period, had been wounded three times and gained a Silver Star and several Bronze Stars. For much of the month of August 1944, he had been the only commissioned officer in Company I, and during that period, he had witnessed with profound shock how an untrained man could get himself, and many others, killed in the chaos of battle. In one terrible incident in August, when Company I had struggled to push ahead against fierce opposition south of Vire near the village of St. Germain de Tallevende, a young squad leader who had just arrived as a replacement and was thrust into a leadership role because no qualified sergeants were available ordered his equally inexperienced squad members to climb over a hedgerow and advance upright in single file into an open pasture. No Germans were visible, but anyone who had faced enemy bullets in the past would have known immediately that such a maneuver was unwise. Nearby 29ers watched in horror as the men progressed halfway into the field and were felled by a sudden crossfire of German machine guns. The enemy gunners were coldly efficient, and within seconds, every squad member—twelve in number, according to Gentry—was dead, falling in a perfect line as if they had been marching in a parade.

That event prompted the distressed Gentry to tear a piece of paper from a brown bag and jot down suggestions, which, if implemented by the top brass, could save many lives and help make the 29th a better organization. Only a man who grasped the lethality of the modern battlefield, Gentry reasoned, could hope to survive and succeed against such a formidable enemy. It was therefore of the utmost importance to enhance the quality of the division's squad leaders with a special course based on the hard lessons of actual combat. He forwarded his proposal directly to Colonel Witte in the G-3 shop at division headquarters and, five or six weeks later, was pleasantly surprised to receive a favorable reply from Gerhardt himself, who admired initiative and held an identical view on the necessity of quality NCOs.

The general's ability to remember names and faces was renowned, but even so, Gentry was moved when Gerhardt, accompanied by his pet spaniel, named D-Day, passed him in a Dutch field one day and then, when recognition dawned, turned around and approached the young lieutenant. "Gentry, you've certainly done your share of fighting," the general exclaimed. With that thought in mind, Gerhardt had an idea to make the Training Center's NCO school a model of realistic battle training. "[I] was placed on two-week temporary duty, and along with twenty-five of the division's most experienced combat platoon sergeants, was assigned the task of setting up the facility and training the cadre in their roles," Gentry recalled. "Every facet of the training program emphasized squad control and direction. The necessity that the squad leader must follow the directions of the platoon leader or platoon sergeant was driven home at every opportunity." Unfortunately, on November 17, only a short time after Gentry had returned to Company I from his two-week spell at the NCO School, he was badly wounded and never returned to the division he had helped so much to improve.

According to the Training Center's 1st Lt. Gustave Gomory, the NCO course of instruction was "the hottest school we've had." Instructors kept students so busy throughout those six days of learning that one student complained, "There is not enough time to wash and shave." As he surely soon discovered, he nevertheless had to find the time. One factor that nearly all attendees grumbled about was the lack of realistic training with the bazooka, for now that the 29th Division was commonly encountering German tanks, a weapon they had seen little of in Normandy and none of in Brittany, a failure to employ that cutting-edge device properly could lead to disaster.

At the close of the sixth day, 2nd Lt. William Pearce, the head of the NCO School, administered the dreaded one-hour final exam, a much tougher test than the one given to officers. The exam demanded answers, sometimes lengthy, to twenty questions, among them: "Give the sequence of a five-paragraph field order," "List the five things that you as a patrol leader must do in preparation for a night reconnaissance patrol," "List some of the things a squad leader must consider when setting up a defensive position," "Explain how to prepare a pole charge." On his school comment form, one attendee provided a perceptive observation all 29ers certainly would have agreed with: "The course is good and should be given to all combat men." If only there had been time.

One surprising lesson Gerhardt learned about the center was that even a man who helped rehabilitate GIs suffering from combat exhaustion was himself susceptible to that disorder. According to the general, Major Hankins, onetime Maryland National Guard corporal and former commander of the 115th's 3rd Battalion at the height of the Normandy fighting, was displaying symptoms that threatened to cut short his tenure as the Center's leader. Early in the morning of November 4, Gerhardt phoned Maj. James

Ballard, a 175th Infantry staff officer, and announced, "You're too good a bird sitting up there as an assistant S-3. We're going to bring you back to the Training Center. There are excellent possibilities back there. This Hankins is either drunk or disorderly all the time. What it needs is enthusiasm—and he doesn't have it."

Gerhardt shipped Hankins out to a desk job at division headquarters, and Ballard took over the Center on November 5. The exigencies of the November offensive, however, terminated Ballard's role less than three weeks after it started. On November 22, Gerhardt assigned him to the command of the 175th's 3rd Battalion and replaced him with Maj. Charles Custer, one of the general's veteran liaison officers.

All the Training Center's diligent instruction did not always succeed in inculcating its students in the trait Gerhardt valued most in 29ers: a passionate ambition to participate personally in the fight against the Nazis until Hitler was dead and the Allies occupied Berlin. Most of the men who had experienced that fight already and had seen its realities firsthand had discovered that their passions for combat had cooled considerably over time. Nevertheless, the 29th had a dirty job to do, and the general was always on the lookout for men who yearned to fight the enemy. Gerhardt thought he found such a man when he perused an October 1944 issue of *Stars and Stripes*, the wildly popular American armed forces newspaper published in a Paris edition for those hordes of men who had been swept into the United States' main military effort of World War II in western Europe. The section labeled "B-Bag," a column of GI letters usually featured on the left side of page 2, was always a favorite. That soldier-writers could express themselves openly, free of military rigmarole, was made clear by the B-Bag column's subtitle, printed in bold letters next to a caricature of a disheveled GI: "Blow It Out Here." This the writers did with gusto, and it made some of the best reading in *Stars and Stripes*. They did it humorously, irately, sometimes anonymously, but always with a zeal that was a predictable byproduct of the military's mindless routines on men who ached for some sense of rationality in their lives.

Gerhardt sat up and took notice when he read a letter from a "1-A in a 4-F Outfit," featuring a three-word heading: "Wants Combat Job." The anonymous writer observed:

> This might as well be called an application for a job rather than a gripe. I hope the right party sees this so I can get a transfer to an

outfit that's in combat. I've been trying to get a transfer through channels, [but] no dice. I've been in the service for over two years, one year overseas. Never in combat. I've been training and training, and when I was going overseas I thought at last I'd see action, but no! I trained for assaulting beaches and hiked for miles up English hills. For what? Now for the last six months I've been doing guard duty for the Navy. I guess I should be satisfied. . . . I am getting plenty of sleep and food and ample time off for pleasures. Maybe some guys would like to change places with me? . . . I joined the Army to fight, and I trained to fight. I'm not looking for glory. Is it a sin for a guy to want to get into combat? I'd like a chance, too, to prove my worth.

Here was an opportunity Gerhardt could not pass up. In a matter of days, a response from the general appeared on the front page of *Stars and Stripes* under the headline "B-Bag Gets Action for GI." "The undersigned has read with interest a letter by a soldier who desires combat service," Gerhardt wrote. "The 29th Infantry Division can use that soldier and any like him who desire combat. I would be glad to have him as a member of this command. Can you give me his name and present organization?"

Stars and Stripes complied, and Gerhardt soon had the information he needed to contact a private by the name of E. Philip Malin, a twenty-five-year-old Chicago native and prewar veteran of the Illinois National Guard, currently assigned to an obscure rear-echelon service outfit. Much more pleasing to the general was the reaction of hundreds of troops stuck in a dead-end role similar to Malin's, all of whom wrote earnest letters to the B-Bag editor requesting transfer to Gerhardt's fighting division in the naïve hope they would have the chance to come face-to-face with a "Kraut" before the war ended. Gerhardt answered them all with a form letter, and eventually, about 300 managed to secure reassignment to the 29th Division. When he had the chance, Gerhardt welcomed each volunteer to the 29th with a hearty "Mighty fine!"—his standard expression of satisfaction—and the somewhat disquieting greeting, "You're a damned fool, but you've got guts!"

As related by Joe Ewing, himself a newcomer to the 29th in the fall of 1944, the new men "proceeded without ceremony to their new companies, where they were greeted with great curiosity by the front-line soldiers, who found it difficult to understand the logic of anyone's deliberately asking to live at the front which they themselves cursed so easily."

The name of Pvt. E. Philip Malin, however, was never added to the 29th Division's rolls. Gerhardt eventually sent out a captain from the division staff to search for him, but according to Ewing, "Malin was apparently lost in the maze and confusion of the replacement depots, and it wasn't until months later that he was discovered on a limited assignment job with some ASF [Army Service Force] unit near Cherbourg."

He was still a 1-A in a 4-F outfit.

SEVEN

The Democrats Will Win

1. THE MONTH HITLER DREADED MOST

In the proud chronicle of the 29th Division, would the chapter that was about to begin be the last one of World War II?

The bleak days of October, during which the 29th had carried out futile offensives and raids as a diversionary tactic, backed up with meager artillery and air power, were apparently over. The generals had a fresh plan. Starting sometime in early November, when the Allies confidently expected the huge Belgian port of Antwerp finally to open and eventually rectify the supply shortfalls that had severely curtailed offensive operations, the 29th Division would return to its familiar role as one of the U.S. Army's crack divisions, poised for a leading role in the Allied assault into the Reich. If the new attack came off as planned, it would be the beginning of the grand finale of World War II in the European theater. General Gerhardt would be exactly where he wanted to be—in the thick of the fight—and with luck, he would ultimately mount a charger and lead the 29th Infantry Division down Berlin's Unter den Linden to the Brandenburg Gate.

In a vital October 28, 1944, directive to his chief SHAEF subordinates, Eisenhower spelled out his ambitious goals, the topmost of which was straightforward: "the destruction of the enemy forces." According to

Ike, that would best be accomplished by "making the main effort in the north, to defeat decisively the enemy west of the Rhine and secure bridge-heads over the Rhine." The prospect of achieving those objectives before the close of 1944 was boosted by a considerable degree one week later when, according to Eisenhower's aide Harry Butcher, "The good news came in from Monty that the approaches to Antwerp and the Scheldt Estuary are now completely free from enemy interference. Monty said that full and free use of the port of Antwerp is now up to the Navy, which already has minesweepers at work. . . . I have seen Ike several times when he has received good news which normally he has discounted in advance, but on this occasion he could not hide his elation, for on the capture of Antwerp depended all of his future plans to end the war." In short, as the supreme command's official history noted, "[Eisenhower's] chief of intelligence, General [Kenneth] Strong, saw November as the month Hitler dreaded most."

Gen. Omar Bradley now knew with certainty what Eisenhower expected of him. On November 4, he prepared a top-secret "Memorandum for Record" at 12th Army Group headquarters of a conversation that had taken place four days previously at Eindhoven, Holland, between himself and Montgomery. "I told Montgomery that we were set to attack with the First and Ninth Armies. . . . Field Marshal Montgomery questioned our ability to keep pushing to the Rhine in view of the fact that we would have to protect both flanks. I explained to him our plan of attack and, of course, admitted that part of our forces would be used to protect the flanks, but that we felt we could at least go part way and had full confidence we could go all the way." Shortly after the war, Bradley summarized his optimism: "I expected to be on the Rhine in thirty days." An aide to General Hodges witnessed a display of Bradley's confidence and jotted in his diary, "General Bradley believes [the assault] will be the last big offensive necessary to bring Germany to her knees."

In retrospect, Bradley had to admit such goals were much too ambitious, but to him, there was no choice. The alternative was to do nothing and endure a winter campaign on the western frontiers of Germany, which, as Bradley's aide, Maj. Chester Hansen, observed in his diary, "is precisely what we are trying to avoid." Furthermore, in light of the blunt entreaty put forth to supreme headquarters on October 23 by Eisenhower's boss, Gen. George C. Marshall, all senior American leaders on the Western Front agreed the November offensive at least had to be attempted.

The Americans, British, and Canadians must attack unremittingly, Marshall insisted, regardless of logistical and weather difficulties. "We consider that an immediate supreme effort in western Europe may well result in the collapse of German resistance before the heavy winter weather limits large operations and facilitates defensive strategy," Marshall wrote. He justified his aggressive attitude in part by underlining the fickleness of the American public, which in Marshall's view would not tolerate inactivity on the Western Front through four or five months of poor weather. As he would later note pointedly to Eisenhower, "Making war in a democracy is not a bed of roses."

Could Bradley's troops reach the Rhine and beyond by Christmas? The chance of success was slim, as Forrest Pogue, SHAEF's official postwar historian, noted in his 1954 work, *The Supreme Command*: "The proposals to end the war in 1944 by means of an all-out offensive had actually come too late to be effective. Such an attack could succeed only if it were made while the enemy was still disorganized." Despite Eisenhower's joy upon learning of the clearance of the Germans from the approaches to Antwerp on November 3, Allied supply shortages in November 1944 would remain dire. Allied minesweepers did not clear the Scheldt Estuary until November 26, and the French railroad network behind the front was still in disarray.

Bradley's ability to reach the Rhine was even more negatively impacted by the high turnover rate among U.S. Army infantry units on the Western Front, a problem that recent bouts of cold and rainy weather had greatly exacerbated. American infantry and armored divisions would find it increasingly difficult to maintain offensive operations without a steady supply of men to replace battle and non-battle casualties, a flow that so far had been entirely inadequate. Meanwhile, the Nazis had somehow managed to tap their last remaining sources of manpower and produce astonishing numbers of fresh units, which not only filled weak spots in their line, but also established a vast strategic reserve whose purpose the surprised Allies would only discover when the Germans launched their surprise Ardennes counteroffensive on December 16, 1944.

If, as Roosevelt and Churchill had stipulated, the Allies would only accept Nazi Germany's unconditional surrender as a definition of victory, American and British battlefield commanders had since September 1944 absorbed the bleak realization that only a total collapse of German military and civilian morale could lead to that capitulation. The battle for

Aachen, and countless other bitter fights on or near Germany's western frontier in fall 1944 had established beyond doubt that the enemy was far from willing to give up. Even the optimistic Bradley, who was convinced his troops could reach the Rhine in the vicinity of Cologne by mid-December, had to admit he was "shocked" by Marshall's outlook "that he thought these Germans were right on the verge of quitting, and therefore we must just keep up the pressure on them as much as we could."

Rather than launch their November offensive, the Allies could instead have merely waited patiently for a better moment. "There were a lot of good reasons for that [strategy], I suppose," Bradley mused. "To sit back and wait until spring and collect your supplies, build up your railroads, and get ready for a real all-out spring offensive [when] we'll be in a position to deliver an all-out, knock-out blow." According to Bradley, however, "General Marshall was very positive in his belief that we must keep pounding. . . . General Eisenhower thought [that strategy] was right; I thought it was right; and Monty thought it was right." That conviction triggered one of the 29th Division's most intense periods of combat.

Bradley set the offensive to open on November 5, when the U.S. First and Ninth Armies would jump off from the hard-won ground east of Aachen, setting their sights on the Rhine between Düsseldorf and Bonn. A few days later, Patton's Third Army, currently stalled in Lorraine at the gates of the French fortress city of Metz, would join the offensive with high hopes that it could swiftly enter Germany and seize Mainz. It would be the largest American offensive since Operation Cobra. When it peaked in late November, it would exceed Cobra in scale by a large margin. According to Eisenhower's directive, nearly twenty American divisions eventually would be attacking simultaneously, fixated on one objective: the Rhine.

If there was such a thing as a veteran division, the 29th was it. Since D-Day, none of the organizations that would actively participate in the November offensive could claim more combat experience—or casualties—than the 29th. Far too many blunders during the exasperating month of October, however, had established that experience did not count for much when troops were poorly led. Whether the 29th Division's fortunes would improve in November, given more plentiful materiel and sensible objectives, only time would tell.

If Gerhardt craved a pivotal role for his 29th Division, this would be it. This time, however, the general had to be careful not to cross his superiors, for his own status was fragile, and his military career could be in jeopardy should his bosses' moods decline in line with the deteriorating November weather. Gerhardt had been fortunate throughout much of October since his immediate superior at the XIX Corps, Charles Corlett, had exhibited a steady forbearance when it came to the 29th Division's affairs. A more ruthless corps commander could readily have pointed out several major slip-ups in the division's war room that in all likelihood would have effected Gerhardt's relief when the facts surfaced. Unhappily for Gerhardt, some of those unpleasant details had indeed come to the attention of Lt. Gen. Courtney Hodges, commander of the U.S. First Army, whose nephew Sam, a 115th Infantry platoon leader, had been unaccounted for since the debacle at Schierwaldenrath on October 4. Hodges had revealed his uncompromising attitude toward difficult subordinates when he abruptly relieved Corlett on October 18, replacing him with Raymond McLain. Gerhardt would now be working for a corps commander he knew nothing about—a national guardsman at that—as well as an army commander who surely harbored serious doubts about the 29th Division's leadership.

Would Gerhardt be the next to go? Hodges could relieve Gerhardt in an instant should more snafus like the ones that had transpired in October reoccur. But Gerhardt got a lucky break on October 22 when Bradley initiated a major command change on the Western Front, consigning the American sector of the front north of Aachen not to the U.S. First Army, but to the Ninth. The shift was accomplished with the stroke of a pen and a minimal transfer of troops and equipment. McLain's XIX Corps would simply become part of Ninth Army, whose headquarters would be set up at Maastricht, Holland, while the VIII Corps, guarding the quiet Ardennes sector fifty miles to the south, would transfer from Ninth to First.

A reassured Gerhardt would not cross Hodges's path again. Instead, he now had to work for Lt. Gen. William Simpson, the Ninth Army's commanding general, a man Gerhardt had served under and come to admire during the siege of Brest. It would be a welcome change, giving Gerhardt a fresh start under conditions decidedly more favorable than those faced by the 29th Division when it had reentered the line in late September. Actually, almost everyone who worked with Bill Simpson admired him. Eisenhower categorized Simpson's service as "brilliant" and described him as "alert, intelligent, and professionally capable . . . the type of leader that American soldiers deserve." Eisenhower's chief of staff, Lt. Gen.

Walter Bedell Smith, corroborated his boss's opinion when he defined Simpson as "our best prospect: pity he wasn't in [theater] sooner. Bradley agrees with me."

Simpson, a fifty-six-year-old Texan and 1909 West Point graduate (six years ahead of Eisenhower), displayed a humble and unflappable leadership style that was entirely at odds with Gerhardt's high-strung and domineering management of subordinates. As Bradley noted, the Ninth Army was "uncommonly normal" under Simpson's control. That was hardly a trait most military men would apply to Gerhardt's 29th Division. Furthermore, General Smith classified Simpson's staff as "brilliant. . . . You could tell the difference the moment you went from the First Army into the Ninth Army area."

The Ninth Army's chief operations officer, Col. Armistead Mead, depicted his boss with the kind of praise few would apply to Gerhardt: "General Simpson's genius lay in his charismatic manner, his command presence, his ability to listen, his unfailing use of his staff to check things out before making decisions, and his way of making all hands feel that they were important to him and to the Army. . . . I have never known a commander to make better use of his staff than General Simpson." As Mead related, however, Simpson's subordinates who performed their duties carelessly did so at their peril, for there was "an iron fist in the velvet glove."

Unhappily, just a few weeks after Simpson's arrival in Holland, he displayed a little bit of that iron fist to Gerhardt. Early in the morning of November 14, an unfamiliar colonel wearing a Ninth Army patch on his left shoulder strode unannounced into the war room tent and asked to speak with General Gerhardt. He identified himself as Col. Perry Baldwin, Simpson's IG (inspector general). Whatever matter he had come to discuss in all likelihood would not be pleasant, as U.S. Army IGs had full authority to investigate alleged infringements of regulations, even when the investigator had to probe into the activities of much higher-ranking officers. No one in the war room could miss the detail that Baldwin came from Simpson's headquarters and therefore had a powerful backer. Baldwin intensified the mystery by refusing to discuss the reason for his visit until he and Gerhardt were alone. Still worse, when Gerhardt pressed the taciturn IG for an explanation, Baldwin demanded that the general raise his right hand and swear that everything he said would be the truth and nothing but.

An irritated Gerhardt refused to talk and unceremoniously ushered Baldwin out of the tent and sent him on his way. The general promptly contacted his own 29th Division IG, Lt. Col. José Castillo, and inquired angrily about IG powers. "[Baldwin] wanted to get me alone and said that he could direct that he talk to me alone and not in front of a witness. Is that so?" Gerhardt demanded of the astounded Castillo, who responded somewhat uncertainly, "I don't think so." Gerhardt persisted: "He wouldn't tell me what it was about and tried to get me to raise my hand and swear. He wouldn't show me anything in writing. I balked and am going to talk to the Army commander first."

With a few moments to reflect, Castillo responded: "If [Baldwin] has a competent authority indicating an investigation, he has a right to." Gerhardt snapped back, "If I am to be investigated, I want to know what it is about."

Unfortunately, it was about a matter that Gerhardt did not wish the world to know about. Forty minutes later, a more deferential Gerhardt was on the phone with General Simpson. "Your IG came in this morning and said it was a mixture of personal and official, and said I should be alone and wanted me to swear before I was told what it was. . . . Seemed odd that I should get it from a lieutenant colonel [Baldwin was actually a colonel] instead of through command channels," Gerhardt said. Simpson responded impassively: "We got a telegram from General Bradley saying that the Secretary of War [Henry L. Stimson] had received a word through a Jewish-Catholic welfare society that the 29th Division had a house of prostitution for the men somewhere near Brest early in September, and General Bradley directed I report these facts."

So the cat was out of the bag, and even Secretary of War Stimson, a man so eminent that he routinely had the ear of President Roosevelt, now knew of this gross violation of U.S. Army regulations. Gerhardt could hardly deny the accusation: typewritten evidence in the division's war room journal established that the house of prostitution, which he had referred to coarsely as a "riding academy," had been set up at his order. The general had no alternative but to allow Baldwin's investigation to go forward and accept the unfortunate consequences. Obviously, Ninth Army was busy with far more important matters, and if the torpid pace of typical Army investigations held in this case, it would be a long time before Baldwin could prepare an official report on this sordid issue. By then, Gerhardt expected the 29th Division would be on its way to the Rhine and, with luck, might even be across it and heading to Berlin. Such a significant battlefield success could help to overshadow the damaging revelations Baldwin's report would inevitably bring forth. Gerhardt had time on his side; he could not fail to realize, however, that his military career was in jeopardy.

If Simpson were to accomplish Bradley's objective and reach the Rhine opposite Düsseldorf, thirty-five miles away, the Ninth Army's staff would have only two weeks to plan its first major offensive, an operation so weighty that if it achieved its intended result, the Nazi regime might soon collapse. The staff would have to devise troop movements and attacks in Rhineland terrain unlike that sector of the front the Ninth had formerly held, the Ardennes. It would have to cope with late autumn weather that would certainly deteriorate; it would have to issue orders to subordinate units with which it was mostly unfamiliar; it would have to overcome an enemy whose impressive resiliency had wrecked recent Allied plans; and twenty-five miles short of the Rhine, it would have to formulate a complex operation to cross the Roer River, a waterway that could suffer a calamitous flash flood if the Germans wrecked the intake valves on the river's many upstream dams. Supreme skill and some luck would be required to fulfill those challenging missions, but if the Ninth Army's grand scheme worked, the last step, the Rhine crossing, would be the most difficult of all. That goal tantalized the Ninth's staff: if Simpson's men could traverse the Rhine, their triumph would be highlighted in every newspaper in the States.

Simpson's staff had occupied its Maastricht command post for little more than a week when Bradley forced a major change of plans on the Ninth Army. Since the vital Scheldt Estuary had still not been cleared of German mines—the first fully laden Allied supply vessel did not reach Antwerp until November 28—the Americans still had to cope with a severe artillery ammunition shortage that showed little hint of improvement by the offensive's scheduled opening day, November 5. Even worse, two U.S. Army divisions on loan to the British in Holland and Belgium would not return to Bradley's control in time to meet the November 5 deadline. Bradley therefore delayed the start date by six days, to November 11, but even that date was questionable because Eisenhower had committed vast numbers of Allied combat aircraft to support the offensive, and the jump-off date would depend on decent flying weather.

The October fighting had yielded no sign that the Germans would be a pushover, but in matters pertaining to the German Army, any U.S. Army general working for Eisenhower and Bradley could never reveal negativity. The top brass expected the 29th Division and its neighbors would need only five days to reach the Roer River, then bound over that barrier regardless of the flood threat and reach the Rhine opposite Düsseldorf shortly thereafter. Such an accomplishment would represent a magnificent feat of arms, one that would require meticulous planning and smooth teamwork between Simpson and his sometimes peevish subordinates. Unlike October, when the 29th had played a secondary role with inadequate support and limited objectives, Gerhardt's explicit goal in the upcoming offensive would be to gain ground as quickly as possible and with as much fury as his command could muster.

For Gerhardt, that was a welcome change.

2. THE COURAGE OF DESPAIR

Exaggeration was not part of Simpson's repertoire, so when he told his staff during the planning for the November offensive that "I anticipate one hell of a fight," every member of the Ninth Army knew the general's prophecy would come true. Had it not been for a monumental decision made by Adolf Hitler in September 1944, however, that fight would have been infinitely tougher.

That the Germans still possessed a determined will to resist had become obvious to Eisenhower once his armies neared Germany's western frontier. A salient detail that Allied intelligence staffs failed to detect was that by October, Hitler had successfully contained the Allies by committing to the Western Front only a small fraction of the dozens of fresh *Volksgrenadier* and refurbished panzer divisions that had become available since the German Army's disastrous defeat in Normandy. The balance, a vast accumulation of troops amounting to some thirty divisions, was held back at the Führer's strict order as a strategic reserve, to be committed in a great counteroffensive at a time and place of Hitler's choosing.

Such a risky undertaking went against the wishes of all senior field commanders, including the esteemed Field Marshal Gerd von Rundstedt, who argued that his meager army holding back the Allies could not contain its increasingly formidable opponents forever. To yield the strategic initiative to his opponents, however, was unthinkable to Hitler, who declared in a harangue to his senior commanders: "In the end, the one who gains the laurels of victory is not just the most capable one, but most importantly—and I want to emphasize this—the boldest." If the object was victory, not stalemate, Hitler reasoned, "This is never achieved as effectively by a successful defensive as by successful offensive strikes. Long term, then, one can't believe in the principle that defense is the stronger part of the fight."

After the war, Rundstedt revealed to the British military theorist Basil Liddell Hart, "When I received this plan early in November, I was staggered. Hitler had not troubled to consult me about its possibilities. . . . But I knew by now it was useless to protest to Hitler about the possibility of anything." The field marshal's former chief of staff, Gen. Günther Blumentritt, informed Liddell Hart that Rundstedt "was really against any further offensive on our part. His idea was to defend the Roer and hold all the armored divisions in readiness behind the line, as a powerful reserve for a counterattack against a breakthrough. He wanted to pursue a defensive strategy."

If Hitler had agreed to Rundstedt's notion, in all likelihood the Germans would have deployed the bulk of their reinforcements to the Rhineland, where the U.S. First and Ninth Armies intended to launch their November offensive. The Americans had seized a significant chunk of German territory there, including historic Aachen; should they achieve a breakthrough, Rundstedt knew his opponents could be on the Rhine in a matter of days and, even worse, could promptly jump that river and seize Düsseldorf and other cities comprising the industrial heartland of Germany in the Ruhr Valley. In that event, Nazi Germany could not endure for more than a few weeks.

If the Americans launched an offensive from the Aachen area, as Rundstedt expected, the Germans would have little choice but to stand and fight a defensive battle, yielding as little ground as possible in the hope that their opponents would eventually exhaust themselves in a vain struggle of attrition. But lacking the fresh units that Hitler was saving for the Ardennes stroke, Rundstedt presumed an attritional battle would work in the Allies' favor. Consequently, he strove to shift the counteroffensive's focal point from the Ardennes to the Aachen front, a sector not only of greater strategic significance, but also one where the terrain was more suited for offensive operations. The Germans would therefore have a much greater chance of success at Aachen, especially if they limited their objective to encircling and ultimately destroying the American forces thrusting toward the Rhine. Hitler would have none of it: the Ardennes offensive had to go forward, in mid-December, with the highly ambitious goal of reaching Antwerp, 150 miles from the jump-off point. Rundstedt later declared to Liddell Hart: "No soldier believed that the aim of reaching Antwerp was really practicable."

Simpson could not possibly know that Rundstedt's failure to change Hitler's mind had granted the U.S. Ninth Army—and the 29th Infantry Division in particular—a stroke of good luck. If Hitler had bowed to Rundstedt's wish and sanctioned the release of several fresh divisions from his strategic reserve to the Aachen front, the 29th's ability to press forward even at a sluggish pace would have been considerably reduced. Indeed, had the Germans shifted their great counteroffensive from the Ardennes to Aachen, as Rundstedt had suggested, it would have been the 29th Division and adjoining units that would have stood squarely between the Germans and their objective. Gerhardt's command would have been hard-pressed to hold its ground in the face of such an overwhelming onslaught—in which several elite panzer divisions would have participated—and could have suffered the same disastrous fate as those unfortunate U.S. Army divisions that held the supposedly quiet Ardennes sector when the Germans abruptly emerged from the mist and struck westward with such ferocity on December 16, 1944.

The Germans' ability to hold the Anglo-American armies in check on Germany's western frontiers since September 1944 could be ascribed as much to the Allies' supply difficulties and troop dispersion as to a revitalization of German arms. Bradley hoped that his November offensive could commence under much more favorable conditions. Under Bradley's plan, three American armies—the First, Third, and Ninth—would attack simultaneously. All three were in a far superior state of supply and concentration than they had been in October, and to many in the American camp, they seemed unstoppable, at least on paper.

So far, Rundstedt had managed to hold the line, a laudable accomplishment given the battered and, in many cases, green divisions with which he had achieved that goal. All the while, Hitler had for the most part held back the German Army's best trained and most mobile units for the bold stroke he planned for December. If that policy must be adhered to at the Führer's rigid order regardless of Allied intent, could Rundstedt's troops continue to hold when the Americans launched their inevitable November assault?

Bradley had apparently concluded that they could not, and he was eager to bring on the fight. A candid entry in the diary of Maj. Chester

Hansen, Bradley's aide, reflected the pugnacious spirit of the hour in the highest reaches of the American high command: "Brad said . . . it would be good to fight the Germans all the way to Berlin; [to] teach them the lesson of death and destruction they have carried to the rest of the world."

He concluded: "Everyone is in hearty assent."

3. WHERE MY BOYS ARE

If ignorance is bliss, as the maxim goes, dawn on October 30 must have produced thoroughly blissful thoughts in the infantrymen of the 29th Division. As yet, the men knew nothing of how General Bradley planned to use them in his forthcoming offensive designed to reach the Rhine in thirty days. Only one detail mattered that morning: the division's withdrawal from the front lines, scheduled in just a few hours. Every infantryman yearned for that moment, for October had been a remarkably cruel month, which future chroniclers of the division's history would surely depict as a low point in the division's fortunes. It had been characterized by futile combat against a rejuvenated enemy, insignificant terrain gains, miserable weather, trenchfoot, and, worst of all, more than 1,600 casualties. The 29ers had gradually absorbed the disappointing realization that no one would be going home soon, but the next best thing would be a rest to revitalize their spirits, a period that was now imminent.

Dutch towns behind the front beckoned: Heerlen, Brunssum, Kerkrade, Treebeek, Schinveld, and others, all filled with agreeable local inhabitants, most of whom were utterly delighted to have the Americans in their midst. On pay day, 29ers could pick up Dutch guilders from a finance officer and finally spend their hard-earned salaries at shops and restaurants, which one soldier noted carried on a thriving business "just as if no war were going on" and provided a pleasant alternative to drab Army-issue items and GI food. A 29er could also catch a movie at a divisional recreational center; pick up some fresh coffee and first-rate doughnuts, prepared from scratch each morning in the ever-present Red Cross clubmobiles; or, for those whose religious beliefs had been intensified by recent fighting, attend local church services in search of much-needed spiritual comfort. That Holland had much to offer the weary GI fresh off the front line was affirmed by an anonymous 29er who noted in a company newsletter, "Paris passes temporarily out of style, our men buckled down to the job of sweating out four-day passes to Heerlen, where they can forget the war and make friends with the Dutch aided by cigarettes and D-bars."

The soldiers' overriding thought was probably that each Dutch town was populated by plentiful women, many of whom expressed an understandable curiosity about the strangers who had just driven the hated Nazi occupiers from their homeland. Before any 29er would dare to approach a Dutch girl, however, he had to clean himself up, and several ancient coal mines outside Heerlen provided the best place to do it. When the troops emerged from the mines' hot showers, with, as one 29er noted, "the topsoil off their bodies and a good meal under their belts," they were new men, filled with a confidence heightened by an even greater degree if they were lucky enough to receive new uniforms and devote a few minutes for a quick haircut. That process gave them a much greater chance of meeting Dutch members of the opposite sex—although the 29ers could not fail to notice the privations still pervading Dutch society as they watched down-on-their-luck locals scavenging for used soap, cigarettes, or any other item the GIs had disdainfully cast away as no longer useful.

If a combat soldier's efficiency hinged on a sharp focus on the present, while blocking out the past, someone had to help him lock the grisly sights of battle into the deep recesses of his mind, from which they would not emerge for decades, if ever. Gerhardt had entrusted a twenty-nine-year-old major by the name of Thomas Van Arden Dukehart, known affectionately by one and all simply as "Tommy," to do just that. In the unique role at division headquarters known as "Special Service Officer," Dukehart had been providing pleasurable diversions for the 29ers since D-Day, including first-run films, shown in improvised theaters in half-wrecked Norman barns just behind the front; visits by Hollywood stars such as Edward G. Robinson and Mickey Rooney; 29th Division Band concerts; dances; and much more. Dukehart himself sometimes offered a one-man show, exhibiting his amazing wizardry at card tricks.

Dukehart had been forced to practice his craft with a particular energy in October 1944, driven by the recent series of disheartening experiences at the front. If he failed at his job, the 29ers' morale could plummet, which the commanding general would certainly notice, costing Dukehart his job. A 1935 graduate of Johns Hopkins University in Baltimore who had enlisted in the Maryland National Guard's 110th Field Artillery as a private in 1940, Tommy Dukehart had a shrewd ability to judge the needs of ordinary dogfaces when they set off for the rear as lucky recipients of

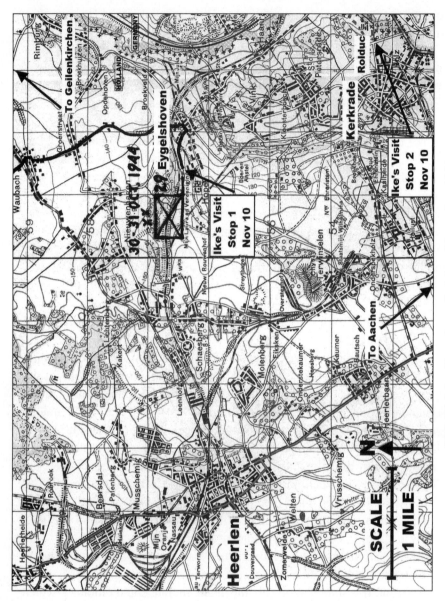

29th Division Rear Area, October–November 1944.

passes of at least forty-eight hours in duration. If all 29ers at the front had to live outdoors at Gerhardt's strict order, even as dismal autumn weather set in, then Dukehart had to provide them with overhead shelter and a real bed. If they endured long periods without conversing with members of the opposite sex, then they had to be given opportunities to meet women. If they griped about constant C- and K-rations, then they must have appetizing food and even beer and wine. If they needed to release pent-up emotions, they would be given some latitude to do so. In short, Gerhardt's conviction that the 29th Division be populated by upbeat soldiers, loyally attached to their unit, was in part dependent on how well Dukehart performed his job.

The core attraction of Dukehart's "Blue and Gray Hotels"—known officially as 29th Division Recreation Centers—was simple, as one 29th Division sergeant pronounced with amazement: "This is the first time I've slept with my trousers off in 140 days." Each recreation center, typically a converted Dutch schoolhouse, could handle 200 29ers at a time on official passes. As a *29 Let's Go* article proclaimed, "It's wide open—there are no rules to break." That was not strictly true—troops had to be off the streets by midnight, for example—but as the anonymous writer concluded somewhat innocently, "In town the men will be given every consideration by the military police."

In matters of food, Dukehart presumed that a well-fed soldier was a happy soldier. He brought fifteen nuns from a local Sisters of Charity congregation into a Brunssum school kitchen to prepare hearty and hot meals of a kind the GIs had not enjoyed for weeks and, in many cases, months. In their ankle-length white habits and enormous headgear spreading over their heads like seagull wings, the nuns provided a memorable reminder that beyond the inexpressible violence of the front, the civility of ordinary life at a level of comfort the troops had almost forgotten must eventually return. When it did, the fighting men hoped to still be alive to enjoy it.

Lt. Chester Bise, a 115th Infantry D-Day veteran, managed the Brunssum establishment. "We've got a beer garden with everything you want," he remarked to a reporter. "Ping-pong, cards, pool table, reading and writing material. We'll have three motion pictures here a day, two different films at the first and third shows." Lieutenant Ewing ventured beyond the recreation center's walls and found Brunssum a charming town, one defined by "bright, red-trimmed doors and windows in the neat brick cottages and apartments, Dutch women scrubbing down their sidewalks, and

An unidentified T/5 from the 110th Field Artillery Battalion poses next to the stairway in a Brunssum photography shop.

Dutch kids running up to hold your hand and walk with you." The recollection of moments such as those would be important to many 29ers, and after cleaning the frontline grime off themselves and their uniforms, they lined up at a popular Brunssum photography shop to have their pictures taken leaning casually against a stairway banister in the entrance hall.

Dukehart's preferred method of putting 29ers and women together in the same room was to arrange dances, although the effort to maintain a one-to-one ratio between sexes was a challenge almost impossible to meet because of the local Dutch matrons' understandable concern for their daughters' welfare. One dance held in Kerkrade for the 175th Infantry's 2nd Battalion, however, would stand out in unit lore for the astounding reason that female attendees greatly outnumbered males. The affair began well enough, despite the usual hesitancy between men and women of different nationalities resulting from language and cultural differences. That timidity would have eventually dissipated, as it always did, but a Company G soldier recalled,

Dutch-American relations were brought to an abrupt an ungraceful conclusion when a large number of beskirted and betrousered Red Cross doughnut girls burst into the room. The situation became increasingly unbearable as some twenty U.S. Army nurses reported for duty. Lt. Col [Claude] Melancon [2nd Battalion CO], hastened about the hall, uniting unattached couples with or without their consent. Most involved in the problem of over-supply was 1st Lt. Hugh Brady, our CO. . . . He found himself inextricably bound up with an excitable lady, a native of South America [but] now a resident of Holland. Later arrival of the U.S. nurses found him paying his respects to them, too. But it wasn't to be that way—that's not the South American way. She cornered our CO: "Come outside where I can talk to you," she said with her low, deep voice, while her eyes flashed. The conclusion of the conference was, "If you stay with me, you don't talk to American girl. You don't dance with American girl."

Men who had already used their passes begged their first sergeants for more, but that effort generally made little headway against the firm top kicks. The only option was to hang about the company bivouac, chatting with old-timers and making tentative approaches to the new men. As Ewing observed: "Hitting the sack was the one bright spot in the soldier's otherwise dismal day. In two-man prone shelters, widened beyond field manual specifications and bedded with straw, one stretched out to full length under OD [olive drab] blankets and forced the war and the clammy November weather from his life. Sleep was the only surcease from the ghastly weather and the full persistent prospect of the new battle."

Normally, Ninth Army policy prohibited troops from seizing food from German farms, but once the 29th Division came out of the line in late October, camp rumors abounded that Gerhardt would not enforce that rule. After all, the U.S. Army had a long tradition of living off the land in enemy territory, a custom that Sherman's men had applied to perfection in the Civil War, and the 29ers, whose attitudes toward German soldiers and civilians alike were decidedly hostile, harbored few misgivings about the procedure known euphemistically as "foraging." The commander of the 116th Infantry's 2nd Battalion, Lt. Col. Sidney Bingham, recalled that yet again, Gerhardt got into trouble with the top brass:

Shortly after the C.G. [Gerhardt] announced that the conquering heroes not only could, but should supplement their rations by relieving the German populace of vegetables and livestock, Sgt. Woodrow Wilson, first sergeant of Headquarters Company [an old-time soldier who had been with that Virginia National Guard outfit in Alta Vista for many years], was leading a foraging party.

He was returned to us by 30th Division MPs, and there was quite a
stink about him stealing chickens. In the course of the investigation, Wilson declared, "We were sent out to get some chickens for
the kitchen. I had three chickens; one got away from me, so I shot
it with my carbine. Just then six Ack-Ack guys came running out
of a house with their hands up. Then a lieutenant showed up and
turned me over to the MPs." And that's that—but our legal looting
was halted.

In the close environment of a military encampment, one phenomenon
every American soldier since Valley Forge had learned to fear was the
effect of rancid food and bad water on the bowels. In World War II, pack-
aged or canned food and Halazone tablets had prevented the kind of
deadly outbreaks of intestinal disease that had wreaked havoc on eigh-
teenth- and nineteenth-century armies, but sanitation in and near the front
was never perfect, and at least once in their military careers, most 29ers
had experienced the unfortunate effects on military readiness of severe
diarrhea, a disease universally referred to by American soldiers simply as
the "GIs." Gerhardt believed that outbreaks of the GIs occurred when soldiers got careless and did not adhere to sanitation principles laid out in
Army field manuals. Even so, that malady struck several 29th Division
units hard in October and November. One member of the 175th Infantry
noted that his company "fought it off with pills or cheese, or just waited
for the foe to expend itself. The ground shook to the thud of running feet
as our men charged to the various company latrines."

The busiest men in the division were surely its chaplains, whose
responsibility for the spiritual welfare of 29ers had intensified by a considerable factor after the division's futile October combat. As related by
Cpl. Jean Lowenthal, the editor of *29 Let's Go*, in an October 29 article,
"We've forgotten who said, 'There are no atheists in foxholes.' But the
truthfulness of that remark is often proved by the large attendance at
church services, when men of the 29th who have been 'through the mill'
are given an opportunity to worship their God." They attended in surprisingly large numbers, even when the chaplain performed the impromptu
service in a muddy pasture, with a jeep hood doubling as a communion
table and empty ration boxes serving as an ad hoc alter, covered by a dark
blue U.S. Army Chaplain Corps flag with a prominent white Latin Cross.
"Servicemen like their religion straight," Chaplain George Metcalf of the

115th Infantry noted. "A GI congregation is the most intelligent and responsive group of worshippers any clergyman could desire to serve. They are in church only because they want to be there to offer God thanks and to receive the peace and strength that he alone can give."

The 29ers also came in throngs to centuries-old Dutch churches, augmenting the local congregation to the point at which the pews could not hold another person, and latecomers had to stand respectfully at the back of the nave. "There's little doubt our presence there convinced the Dutch we came as liberators and not as oppressors," Lowenthal wrote.

The fighting man's ideal chaplain could be a man of any religious persuasion as long as he unhesitatingly offered compassion to all soldiers, weak or strong, who had been touched in one way or another by the close encounters with death so common to the front lines. Such empathy had to be given unreservedly, entirely devoid of judgment, free of a clergyman's customary piousness that might have been applied on the home front, but which was altogether unsuitable in a combat zone. Combat veterans hardly represented an ordinary congregation; only an exceptional man could offer solace to troops whose lives had been overturned by harsh Army training and the cruelties of the battlefield.

The 29th Division had been in combat nearly continuously for five months, and most of its chaplains were entirely sensitive to the impact of that carnage on the soul of the average American soldier. Chaplains who tended to display a sanctimonious distaste for the combat veteran's rough-and-tumble world were rare, but easy to identify, as Ewing noted at a fall 1944 meeting of officers in the 2nd Battalion, 175th Infantry: "I remember our chaplain seemed to have a rather sad countenance and to be preoccupied and was probably not what one would expect a chaplain to be. Once, when he was asked if he had anything to say, he got up and verbally chastised the officers present for using profane language and taking the Lord's name in vain. There was a dead silence after he concluded this admonition. Colonel Melancon thanked him in a formal way and then remarked matter-of-factly: 'You have heard what the chaplain has to say.'"

One 29th Division chaplain who regularly contributed much more inspirational homilies to the fighting men was Capt. Eugene Patrick O'Grady of the 115th Infantry. A graduate of the Pontifical North American College in Rome, O'Grady had found his perfect calling in his hometown as an assistant pastor at a Catholic church in a quaint north Baltimore neighborhood. He performed that job with such ardor, and was

Capt. (Chaplain) Eugene Patrick O'Grady, the beloved "Father Pat."

so highly esteemed by the congregation, that his chief pastor labeled him "the finest priest I have ever known." Despite his vast potential as a parish priest in the Baltimore diocese— the oldest Catholic diocese in the United States— O'Grady left his old life behind in January 1941 when he reported to the Fifth Regiment Armory in Baltimore for a U.S. Army physical. He took that surprising step at the age of thirty-one in response to the War Department's plea to clergymen to support the fresh throngs of young American men in uniform by volunteering for service as military chaplains. On February 3, 1941, as a newly commissioned lieutenant, O'Grady became a 29er and, before long, would travel to Fort Meade to report to his regiment, the historic 1st Maryland, soon to be redesignated the 115th Infantry.

As O'Grady wrote in a letter to a friend, his adjustment to military life "was not exactly a bed of roses, but I'll see it through." He did—from the Carolina pine forests to the bleak English moors and the sands of Omaha Beach, all the way through the Norman hedgerows to the rocky coast of Brittany, and finally to Holland and the enemy's western frontier. He saw his military service through so industriously, with such unflappable poise, that his superiors rewarded him with a Bronze Star for valor in Normandy, an exceptional honor for a chaplain who traveled about the combat zone unarmed. According to his citation, "It may be said without exaggeration that the greatest single contribution to the morale of the personnel of [3rd] Battalion has been the work of Chaplain O'Grady. He epitomizes the militant man of God, and a few words coming from Father O'Grady have on untold occasions, when the going was rough, changed the entire out-look of some individuals—buoyed them and spurred them on to greater efforts. Danger meant nothing to this chaplain. . . . He works untiringly day and night."

O'Grady's modest nickname, "Father Pat," hinted at his lofty reputa-tion among the 115th's rank and file, a standing based on his omnipres-ence at the front, always bearing food and hot coffee, to commiserate with the downtrodden, nurse the wounded, and care tenderly for the dead. One 29er noted, "Never have I seen his face clouded; a smile always beamed new hope into our tormented souls." Another observed, "In the three years I spent under his guidance, I never heard one word spoken against him. . . . Father O'Grady was always with us, and he made some of the toughest marches and went through some of the toughest experiences."

An astonishing number of 29ers in late October 1944 were indeed tor-mented, and when they finally had a chance for a substantive rest in their bivouacs and nearby Dutch towns, Father Pat had to shoulder a workload that might have broken a less devoted man. As one Dutch woman who came to know O'Grady observed, "He always put some heart into the boys. He worked heart and soul." Apparently, so much of Father Pat's heart and soul went into his job that at one point, a Dutch priest noted how fatigued his new American comrade looked. The Dutchman suggested that Chaplain O'Grady could use a furlough, but O'Grady replied, "Yes, that would be fine, but it is impossible: I want to be where my boys are." And where his boys were was exactly where he stayed.

The Ninth Army would begin its next big offensive soon—exactly when, no 29er knew. If the time was short before that offensive jumped off and the 29th Division no longer held a frontline sector, every man yearned for a forty-eight-hour pass or, with luck, one of even greater length. Sadly, some unfortunate 29ers would never receive passes at all. In Bradley's haste to get his November offensive started, he had thrust the 102nd Divi-sion's 407th Infantry into the 29th's old sector near Geilenkirchen before its organic artillery battalion had reached the front from Normandy. Accordingly, to provide fire support for the 407th as it settled into its first combat role in World War II, the 29th Division's 110th and 224th Field Artillery Battalions remained in the same firing positions near the German border they had already occupied for more than a month. Similarly, the 29th's 111th Field Artillery Battalion stayed put in support of the 113th Cavalry Group. The week those 29th Division artillerymen spent at the front before departing on November 6 to prepare for the upcoming offensive was anything but quiet. The most eventful day that week was November 2, when forward observers from the 110th and 224th serving in the front lines with the 407th Infantry called for forty-one fire missions, totaling 463 105-millimeter howitzer rounds.

November 2 was particularly cruel to the 115th Infantry's 2nd Battalion, which Gerhardt had held just two miles behind the front as an emergency reserve in case the green 407th Infantry experienced a case of enemy "enthusiasm" it could not deal with alone. The battalion's encampment, a thick patch of woods just inside the German border, was well within enemy artillery range, but the men agreed the woods offered such effective concealment that the Germans would never notice they were there. According to the 115th's regimental history, this illusion "led many of the men to abandon their holes and sleep in pup tents above ground," a seemingly logical choice as the ground was so muddy that getting any relaxation at all in a foxhole was nearly impossible.

One day, a fighter plane flew directly over the woods at low altitude— a Mustang or Spitfire, the 29ers surmised. It was not. When the sharp-eyed enemy pilot spotted the rows of American pup tents through the canopy of trees, he knew he had a piece of intelligence that any German artillery unit in the vicinity would find invaluable.

If any members of the 2nd Battalion harbored hope that their secluded surroundings and detachment from the front sheltered them from the Germans, that hope was dashed in three minutes on November 2, from 4:52 to 4:55 P.M., when an intense German artillery barrage abruptly descended on the 29ers with uncanny accuracy. The tree bursts caught most of the men outside cover. Since they were concentrated in a tight encampment area, casualties were heavy: three dead and twenty-three wounded, most of whom were from Company F. One of those 29ers killed, a twenty-six-year-old former textile mill worker from the western Maryland mountains, Pvt. Arthur Graham, was an unusual soldier on two counts. First, as a veteran of the Maryland National Guard prior to the 29th Division's February 1941 mobilization, Graham was one of Company F's most senior soldiers. Second, after nearly four years of continuous military service, he was still a buck private, outranked by many draftees with much less time in uniform. (Actually, Graham had been promoted to corporal two days before the United States' entry into World War II, but was busted to private shortly thereafter.)

The 2nd Battalion's losses, its first in nearly two weeks, were particularly heartbreaking because the men were nowhere near the front and had every expectation of spending several tranquil days in the woods. That night, the 2nd Battalion journal noted that "companies were ordered to maintain tactical intervals between men at all times [and] massed battalion formations were to be discontinued." According to the regimental history, which fails to mention the German aircraft that flew low over the woods shortly before the bombardment, the Germans' amazing accuracy led to "speculation as to why that particular piece of woods had been chosen [and] led to a consideration of enemy agents in the vicinity, but further investigation did not particularly bear out that explanation."

Although forty-eight-hour passes among 29ers surged starting on October 30, no company or battery commander would allow more than a small fraction of his men to hold passes at any given time. The rest, at Gerhardt's insistence, were bound to their bivouac areas, most of which were located just west of the German border near the Dutch villages of Kerkrade and Eygelshoven. Those pup-tent villages may have had an impressive military orderliness, but any 29er who yearned for physical comfort would much rather have lived in one of Tommy Dukehart's Blue and Gray Hotels. A nearly incessant rain had yielded thick mud and stagnant pools of water that never dried because the sun almost never made an appearance. Meanwhile, sleeping outdoors on a bed of hay under flimsy canvas and simple GI blankets that provided little warmth sparked many fiery comments among the men concerning Gerhardt's injudicious order that all 29ers on duty had to live outdoors regardless of the weather. Cpl. Arthur Plaut of the 115th Infantry remarked, "For the next few weeks life was about as physically uncomfortable as it ever had been for the men."

Uncle Charlie would also crack down on another aspect of military life that many 29ers had put out of their minds recently. According to Ewing,

> Military courtesy received a strong stimulus in this rear area. The soldier saluted here, buttoned his field jacket, and buckled his chin strap. . . . Sadly, for the man on the line there was no particular significance at all to this burst of garrisonlike atmosphere, but some of the men found a happy explanation: the division was going back to the United States as "demonstration troops." On the other hand, however, the division might be going back to Paris to

guard the railroad yards. These things the men tried hard to believe as they gathered in informal groups in the evenings and talked away the hours till bedtime.

Camp rumors may have had the 29th Division heading away from the front, but in reality, it would soon be heading in exactly the opposite direction. The Ninth Army's top-secret plan book for the November offensive delineated a pivotal role for the 29th, and by the time that assault jumped off, Gerhardt demanded a rejuvenated division, cured of the sloppy practices of October and reinculcated with the unique character he had instilled in his outfit during its yearlong preparation in England for the D-Day invasion.

Looking and acting like a smart soldier was important. Even more vital to Gerhardt, however, was the division's aptitude for beating the Germans, regularly and decisively. The 29ers had utterly failed to accomplish that goal over the past several weeks, and although that could be ascribed more to the commanding general's judgment than the infantry's supposed failings, Gerhardt resolved to take advantage of the 29th Division's break from the front by greatly intensifying its training. In the general's opinion, such a step was essential because the terrain in western Germany where the division had fought, and would soon fight again, was almost exactly the opposite of Normandy and Brittany. Gerhardt's men had taken weeks to get used to those old battlegrounds, but the October fighting had proven that in Germany, the old methods had stopped working. Did the new terrain demand new methods of warfare?

Gerhardt's affirmative answer to that question would be established by rigorous training of a new kind. The 29th Division's operational summary for November 1944 explained some of the general's methods: "Demonstrations were held by all units of the division with a view to clarify, review, and exhibit their ideas and methods for the benefit of all other units. In this way, greater understanding was promoted and new methods and procedures were explained. An intensive training program was also carried on, stressing battle drills with special emphasis placed on tank–infantry–tank destroyer training."

To the ordinary infantryman, all of that dreary language boiled down to more uncomfortable field exercises, several trips to firing ranges to enhance proficiency with weapons, endless calisthenics, even "battle chants" and close-order drill. Cynics wondered how those last two tasks could possibly contribute to the enemy's defeat. As more upbeat veterans remarked, however, seemingly meaningless duties of that kind enhanced morale and, for better or worse, crafted the 29th Division into an outfit other people noticed.

One person who noticed the 29th Division was the supreme commander himself, Gen. Dwight D. Eisenhower. Thankfully, the general's November 10 visit was not unannounced, and when, at precisely 10 A.M., he arrived at the 29th's command post at Eygelshoven, Holland, General Gerhardt was there to greet him with a snappy salute, backed up by the expert Division band, perfectly formed on a wooded hillside alongside regimental and battalion commanders and selected enlisted men from every outfit in the division. Even had Ike not worn on his shoulders the four stars of a full general in the U.S. Army, he would have stood out in any assemblage of American combat soldiers. The 29ers were not used to cheery generals, but Signal Corps films of Eisenhower's November 10 visit to the 29th Division show close-ups of the supreme commander's visage as he unhurriedly walked down long lines of rigid 29ers, looking directly into the eyes of one man after another, and after a simple exchange of only two or three sentences with each, Ike's face invariably broke into a broad grin. That smile had enthralled world-renowned figures such as Franklin D. Roosevelt and Winston Churchill; now the 29ers could see for themselves how easy it was for Eisenhower to work his magic.

The only man among hundreds who was unarmed and whose head was covered not by a steel helmet, but by a simple service cap, Eisenhower, as related by Corporal Lowenthal of *29 Let's Go,*

> went from one [enlisted man] to the other, spoke personally with each man, got his slant on this man's war. The first soldier he spoke with was T/Sgt. George Tyler, Company L, 115th Infantry. [Tyler would soon gain a battlefield commission as a 2nd lieutenant.] George Tyler told General Eisenhower that he was from Crisfield, Maryland. The general asked him what the chow was like—was he getting plenty? George told him, "Most of the time it's good. We get enough." General Ike asked him, "What did you do in civilian life?" The tech sarge told the supreme commander that he was an assistant manager in a motion picture theater. General Eisenhower said, "Good—you look well." And he moved to the next man.

Behavior of that kind came effortlessly to Eisenhower, who explained why in his 1948 book, *Crusade in Europe*: "There is, among the mass of individuals who carry the rifles in war, a great amount of ingenuity and initiative. If men can naturally and without restraint talk to their officers, the products of their resourcefulness become available to all. Moreover, out of the habit grows mutual confidence, a feeling of partnership that is the essence of *esprit de corps*. An army fearful of its officers is never as good as one that trusts and confides in its leaders."

Many 29ers considered Gerhardt the type of autocratic general who could profit immensely from a few hours in Ike's presence, and now that the two men had come together, only good could emerge from it. After chatting amicably with the enlisted men and shaking hands with the officers, Eisenhower was ushered by Gerhardt into a nearby mess tent to sample some typical frontline chow. Food preparation in the U.S. Army had not improved much since a January 1944 study in England concluded that "there were many more messes than there were good cooks," but Mess Sergeant William Craghead of the 29th Division Headquarters Company was one of Uncle Charlie's best chefs. Eisenhower gave Craghead a jovial

Eisenhower meets the 2nd Battalion, 175th Infantry, at Rolduc Monastery, November 10, 1944.

greeting—"What are we giving them, sarge?"—and bantered with the twenty-six-year old former Virginia guardsman from Bedford about the pleasures of corned beef patties and the mysteries of Spam. Eisenhower told Craghead that he was not an enthusiast of the latter, but corned beef prepared in the style of World War I doughboys, known as "corn-willy," was a favorite dish.

Ike's time with the 29th Division was precious, and Gerhardt wanted his boss to see much more of his command than a melting-pot assemblage of 29ers and an austere mess tent. A real fighting outfit, the 175th Infantry's 2nd Battalion, consisting of more than 600 men, was waiting to meet Eisenhower on the grounds of an ancient Dutch seminary named Rolduc, just two miles away, and to keep to the itinerary, the supreme commander presently had to depart. Gerhardt led Ike down a steep embankment and along a short stretch of unused Dutch railroad track. There, parked around a sharp bend in the track, was Uncle Charlie's command jeep, *Vixen Tor*, with T/4 Robert Cuff behind the wheel.

Cuff had painted an impressive list of 29th Division battle honors on *Vixen Tor*'s windscreen, a practice that sticklers for U.S. Army regulations would have objected to, but which was a highly evocative reminder to Eisenhower of the ordeal the division had endured since D-Day. How many more battle honors would have to be entered before Hitler was dead and the war finally ended? No one could guess, but the 29ers suspected if General Ike had anything to do with it, just a few more entries would do the trick. The supreme commander sat in the front passenger seat, smiling as usual for a few snapshots, while Gerhardt took the two-person cushion in the rear, a space to which he was almost entirely unaccustomed since ordinarily he sat in the front, leaving the rear for his aide, Capt. Bob Wallis, and his spaniel, D-Day.

Eisenhower was near the end of a weeklong inspection of the front, and when it would finally end the next day, November 11, he had paid a visit to nearly all the nineteen divisions comprising the First and Ninth Armies. A general less personable than Eisenhower might have found such a trip tedious, and by the time he had to deliver his nineteenth nearly identical speech to members of yet another division of which he surely had difficulty keeping track, it would be tough to muster sufficient sincerity to impress fighting men who desperately needed encouragement. Every member of the 2nd Battalion, 175th Infantry, who watched Ike bound out of *Vixen Tor* at the Rolduc seminary, however, noticed that he never tired of providing such encouragement. He offered it with a humility that was rare in U.S. Army generals, although, in his view, that trait "must always be the portion of any man who receives acclaim earned in the blood of his followers and the sacrifices of his friends."

The 29ers had hastily taken position on a curved hillside, described by T/4 Jack Montrose of 2nd Battalion's Headquarters Company as "a natural amphitheater . . . near a small pond and a large walled building, said to be a monastery." Ever the perfectionist, early that morning, Gerhardt had phoned the battalion commander, Lt. Col. Claude Melancon, and directed him to "have four slit trenches dug in that area just in case."

Montrose noted that "there was little advance notice of Ike's visit," and consequently, aside from the separation of officers in the front and enlisted men to the rear, the jumbled mass of 29ers looked more like a throng at a political rally than a group of disciplined soldiers ready to receive their supreme commander. Gerhardt liked to show off the 29th Division's distinctive character, especially to someone as important as Ike, and he had recently surprised one of Melancon's staff officers by inquiring if the battalion could sing "The Beer Barrel Polka." If the officer was astounded by the question, he did not show it: "Yes; the whole battalion," he asserted. "Sing it as we're coming up," Gerhardt ordered, "and then give the mass command: '29, Let's Go!'" The 29ers had practiced many military arts lately, but singing was not one of them. History does not record the quality of the performance, but without a rehearsal, it was in all likelihood not high. The recital of the 29th's battle cry seemed a simpler matter, although the achievement of perfect unison among hundreds of voices required time for practice that Melancon's men did not have.

As Eisenhower climbed partway up the hillside, he gazed up the slope toward the throng of soldiers waiting expectantly for him. The rough rendition of "The Beer Barrel Polka" and the "29, Let's Go!" chant surely lengthened his trademark smile, for like most American soldiers in the European theater, he had heard through Army scuttlebutt of the July 23, 1944, dedication of the 29th Division cemetery at La Cambe, Normandy. Thousands of 29ers had closed that moving ceremony at Gerhardt's order by roaring "29, Let's Go!" and marching off the field of honor to the strains of "The Beer Barrel Polka," which, like it or not, had now become the 29th Division's official marching song.

Eisenhower came to a halt, put his hands on his hips, and began the kind of conversational address he had performed hundreds of times over the past few years, designed to provide clarity and purpose to the chaotic lives of men who bore the brunt of a terrible war. The supreme commander usually influenced his listeners positively, a result he ensured in this case by bringing up with a surprising familiarity some of their recent accomplishments, the most notable of which was the 2nd Battalion's capture of Fort Keranroux at Brest on September 16, 1944. That achievement had caught the attention of French military officials and would soon gain the battalion a prestigious Croix de Guerre with Silver-Gilt Star.

For his own benefit and that of his audience, Eisenhower kept it short. With a few final words of encouragement and farewell, he began to make his exit. To guard against the omnipresent autumn mud, the general was wearing immense galoshes, each of which was prominently labeled in white near the upper rim with his nickname. Although the galoshes may have protected his shoes from sludge, they were not designed for walking on slippery hillsides, and the result would be remembered by Ike as one of his most embarrassing moments of the war: "I turned to depart. I awkwardly stumbled and sat down solidly and flatly in the deep mud. I think I was more heartily applauded by American soldiers that day than at any other time during the war. . . . I am glad there was no photographer present." (Ike was incorrect. A photographer was present, but he tactfully refrained from snapping any pictures, and Lowenthal did not mention the incident in *29 Let's Go*.)

Sergeant Montrose described the 29ers' reaction to Ike's fall as "similar to the noise at a football game when the home team scores a touchdown. Although thoroughly covered with mud, Ike took the spill very good-naturedly, grinning and waving to the troops as he headed for his vehicle." Before he reboarded *Vixen Tor*, an aide struggled to brush the mud off the general and provided him a GI overcoat for warmth.

The next day, Eisenhower, upbeat as always, cabled the most powerful man in America after the president, George C. Marshall, and declared his immense satisfaction with the 29th Division and several other outfits he had inspected. "Morale is surprisingly high, and the men have succeeded in making themselves rather comfortable," Ike wrote. "There are no signs of exhaustion, and the sick rate is not nearly as high as we would have reason to expect."

Eisenhower also took the time to write a personal letter to his West Point classmate, Col. Leroy Watson, now Gerhardt's second-in-command. Little more than three months in the past, Watson had been senior to

Gerhardt, a major general in command of the celebrated 3rd Armored Division, but he had been relieved of command during Operation Cobra and reduced to the rank of colonel.

> Dear Wop [Watson's West Point nickname], Yesterday I gave a message to Charlie Gerhardt for you which I had hoped to deliver in person. It was that I have recommended you for promotion to brigadier general. . . . Your actions and attitude, following upon your relief from command of the 3rd Armored, have been exemplary. This opinion is fully shared by Brad [Omar Bradley]. I have liked your willingness to jump in and perform efficiently even after suffering the disappointment of losing your own division. . . . I have heard nothing but good reports of you since the day you joined the 29th Division. With best of luck and warm personal regards. As ever, Ike.

Now that the 29th Division was out of the line, Gerhardt's chief subordinates harbored expectations that their commanding general's despotism might soften for a while. It was understandable that in the unpredictability of combat, Gerhardt's temper would now and then flare, but if no 29ers were engaging the enemy and commanding officers were adhering to the general's strict training and discipline regimens, what could possibly go wrong?

But as the 116th Infantry's commander, Col. Philip Dwyer, learned on November 13, even trivial matters could ignite the general's legendary fits of temper. At 7:50 that morning, Dwyer informed Gerhardt that he was granting the 3rd Battalion's commander, Lt. Col. William Puntenney, a well-deserved seven-day leave to Paris. To Dwyer, there was nothing extraordinary about that; similar passes had recently been bestowed to several other worn-out field-grade officers. Dwyer and Gerhardt, both West Point alumni, had even exchanged a few pleasantries the previous day about the recent 59-0 obliteration of Notre Dame by Army's top-notch football team, led by the legendary Doc Blanchard.

Gerhardt held an entirely different outlook on Puntenney's leave, though, a view shaped by the imminent Ninth Army offensive that could begin at any hour at General Bradley's order. The departure of Puntenney, one of Gerhardt's favorites, sparked one of the general's notorious eruptions: "It's on you now. If that battalion has anything on it, it's your neck!"

Beyond those harsh words, the general expressed no desire to make Dwyer's life any tougher than it already was, but Dwyer was about to make the situation much worse.

One could hardly imagine soldiers with more dissimilar personalities than Gerhardt and Dwyer. Gerhardt, the garrulous and flamboyant cavalryman, craved glory and praise. Dwyer, the uncouth former enlisted man, spat tobacco juice and spoke only when necessary. On the rare occasions when Dwyer did speak, he did so gruffly, in tones that cast dread into the hearts of subordinates, but served only to annoy superiors. Dwyer should have known by now not to cross his boss with provocative words. Nevertheless, he did exactly that when he learned of Gerhardt's habitual micromanaging in the matter of Puntenney's temporary replacement.

"I want a field grade officer in charge of the 3rd Battalion and not a captain," Gerhardt announced to Dwyer. "[Lt. Col. Lawrence] Meeks, [Maj. Carleton] Fisher, and [Maj. Asbury] Jackson are available. Do you know who it will be?" When Dwyer grumpily responded that he did not, the general pressed him further, "Who do you want for a commander?"

"Fisher for CO, Jackson for executive," Dwyer replied.

Gerhardt thereupon ignored Dwyer completely: "I'll send Meeks over and leave Fisher where he is."

In another phone call a few minutes later, both men's tempers flared, which Dwyer surely knew would end his 29th Division career. When Gerhardt announced Meeks's imminent arrival at the 3rd Battalion command post, Dwyer snapped a baffling response: "Did I tell you or ask you whether or not Puntenney went on leave? You practically called me a liar!"

Gerhardt's response was predictable: "Those are strong words, and I'll have to relieve you from command."

A notation in the war room journal noted that Dwyer should report to division headquarters "this afternoon," but Gerhardt promptly crossed out those two words and penned in "right away." Less than ten minutes later, Gerhardt phoned McLain to explain Dwyer's relief. "He's very stubborn and contentious," to which McLain replied, "I think you're doing the right thing."

Gerhardt selected Lt. Col. Harold Cassell, the regimental executive, as the 116th's new commander, announcing to him that "we made this change because I haven't been satisfied [with the command relationship] since before St. Lô, and neither was Dwyer. You'll do a good job and give it all you have." The general's closing remark, however, was guaranteed not to fill Cassell with confidence: "Don't figure [on the command] as permanent." He was right: Cassell was replaced in less than three weeks.

The 29ers maintained a vested interest in the politics of command as it related to the 29th Division, but politics on the home front held a decidedly low standing in the 29ers' minds as the big November offensive loomed. In American newspapers, politics had recently overshadowed war news because on Tuesday, November 7, 1944, American voters would determine whether President Franklin D. Roosevelt would be elected to a fourth four-year term. In no previous presidential election in American history had so many citizens been away from home, a quandary the War Department had to address if the vote would be perceived as a valid exercise in participatory democracy. In the 29th Division, absentee ballots had been issued after the fall of Brest. Within each battalion, "voting officers" explained to their men their responsibilities as good citizens to choose between FDR and his opponent, Thomas Dewey, the Republican governor of New York. These voting officers did not make much of an impression. Their jobs, according to Ewing, "proved to be not especially burdensome, for a relatively small number of 29th Division soldiers took advantage of this opportunity to vote. Domestic politics was of slight concern to them at this time. The United States was a 'foreign' world, and the things that concerned them most were the battle lines on the western front and the Russian front, and the bombing raids on Germany."

The youngest of 29ers could hardly remember when Roosevelt had first been elected president in 1932, a detail that emphasized how millions of Americans in 1944 could not picture a world in which FDR was not chief executive. Lt. Bob Henne, the voting officer in the 115th Infantry's 2nd Battalion, was in fact so young—he had recently turned twenty—that someone pointed out he had not yet reached the minimum voting age of twenty-one years. Accordingly, the battalion commander, Lt. Col. Tony Miller, appointed the slightly older Lt. Nestor Browne to replace Henne as voting officer.

To those millions of Americans who had become thoroughly accustomed to Roosevelt as president could be added one essential Briton, Winston Churchill, who sent the president a cable on November 8, the day of his victory over Dewey: "I always said that a great people could be trusted to stand by the pilot who weathered the storm. It is an indescribable relief to me that our comradeship will continue and will help to bring the world out of misery." Despite Churchill's congratulations, Roosevelt's victory in the 1944 election established that his reign of unparalleled duration was an affront to a significant portion of the American voting public, for Roosevelt's tally of 53 percent of the popular vote was the lowest percentage of any of his four presidential elections, down from nearly 61 percent in 1936.

None of this monumental home-front news made any impression on the 29th Division. On November 8, *29 Let's Go* featured a one-paragraph story of just sixty-six words, concluding, "The reelection of President Roosevelt is certain." And that was that—never again in the newsletter did the election appear. Meanwhile, the same November 8 issue featured a three-paragraph, 117-word article stating, "1944 will be remembered in baseball as the 'End of the Jinx' year. . . . The Athletics had never beaten Ernie Bonham of the Yankees until this April. Nor had the Cubs been able to beat Al Gerheauser of the Phillies until they did it behind Paul Derringer in May."

Why hadn't Frank Capra's renowned *Why We Fight* films addressed the real topics that stirred American soldiers' passions?

4. RIGHT INTO BERLIN

For eight consecutive and unquestionably glorious days, starting on October 30 and lasting through most of November 6, 29th Division infantrymen could finally strive to release the pent-up tensions that had tormented them so cruelly over the past month. There would be no "aggressive patrols," no prisoner snatches, no clearance of enemy minefields, no foxholes filled with frigid, brown water. Those unpleasant details of frontline life were now some other poor dogface's responsibility. Good luck to him—he would need it.

Still, every member of the 29th Division knew that the Germans would not yield unless the Allies undertook at least one more great offensive. "Everyone sensed it," according to Ewing. Precisely when that moment would occur, however, was anybody's guess.

That the 29th Division would be drawn into that monumental effort became clear at 7:38 P.M. on November 4, when the XIX Corps's General McLain contacted Gerhardt by phone. "All quiet up this way," Gerhardt reported. McLain's response revealed that he did not yet understand the 29th Division and its hard-hitting commander: "You don't have much trouble keeping quiet, do you? I don't care if you don't do anything at all for a couple of days. Take it easy; because when you go again, it will be a long drive. Right into Berlin." That was a city to which Gerhardt longed to pay a visit.

If concentration of strength was one of the core prerequisites of any successful military operation, Simpson's Ninth Army would certainly begin the November offensive with a major advantage over the Germans. The Ninth would launch its attack across a frontage of less than ten miles, shorter by far than the sector held by the 29th Division alone for most of October. McLain planned to crowd three divisions into that zone: the 2nd Armored Division in the north, the 29th Division in the center, and 30th Division in the south—all veteran organizations that had been fighting side-by-side in the XIX Corps under Generals Corlett and McLain for more than a month and, before that, in Normandy. As the U.S. Army's official historian of the campaign, Charles MacDonald, later wrote, "Nowhere along the western front in the fall of 1944 were so many troops and installations jammed into such a narrow sector."

After spending late summer in the glorious climate of Brittany, October in Germany had been a shock to the 29th Division. No 29er could fail to note that November's arrival had turned the weather not only more frosty, but more glum as well, as difficult as it was for the troops to imagine that October's gloominess could worsen. In light of Uncle Charlie's cardinal rule that no 29er could live or fight inside a house, life at or near the front would severely challenge the troops' survival skills, even if the Germans remained uncharacteristically passive.

The nature of the challenge would be revealed soon enough. McLain had issued the inevitable order that the 29th end its rest period and take its spot in the XIX Corps' line late on November 6. Snow fell that day for the first time since the division had entered combat, and although the flakes signaled winter's approach, the men at first welcomed the change—anything was better than the incessant drizzles and downpours of October.

The 29th Division's new sector was three miles long, a frontage that three infantry battalions—or even four or five—would have held under normal conditions. But Gerhardt resolved to keep as many of his infantrymen as possible out of the front lines, resting and training for the impending offensive. Intelligence reports implied that the Germans could not possibly mount a serious counterattack, so if it was not essential, why pile troops into soggy foxholes and trenches? Instead, the general would hold the front only with minimal force and leave plenty of troops in reserve,

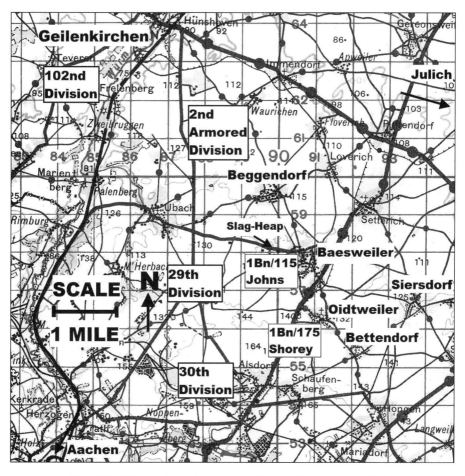

The 29th Division's Return to the Front, November 6, 1944.

who could spend their time more productively by practicing their craft and revitalizing their worn-out bodies.

Some unlucky units would have to occupy the front, and for that disagreeable task, Gerhardt selected the 115th Infantry's 1st Battalion, led by Lt. Col. Glover Johns; and the 175th Infantry's 1st Battalion, under the command of Lt. Col. Miles Shorey. At 10:45 P.M. on November 6, Shorey's unit took over a section of the line in and around the village of Oidtweiler from the 1st Battalion, 405th Infantry, an element of the 102nd Division. Forty-five minutes later, a few hundred yards to the north, Johns's battalion traded places with units of the 2nd Armored Division's Combat Command B at Baesweiler. With those two troop rotations, which a pleased Gerhardt noted were executed flawlessly and without loss, the 29th was back in the fight again.

Nearly a month earlier, the 116th Infantry had captured both Oidtweiler and Baesweiler, but the front line in that locale had not budged one yard since. Veteran infantrymen winced at the thought of storming strongpoints across no-man's-land that German troops had labored to perfect over a thirty-day span. For most of the 29ers, however, the static battle line actually made the return to the front a little less jarring, as forward outposts, machine-gun nests, mortar positions, and communication trenches had already been thoroughly prepared thanks to the copious time available and the Germans' relative passiveness. Frontline dugouts and foxholes hardly provided sumptuous lodgings, but they were much better than what the 29ers had been used to near Geilenkirchen. Even so, life would be infinitely more comfortable if Gerhardt rescinded his ludicrous order that 29ers stay out of buildings. Some brave soul who was willing to risk his military career should talk to the general about that . . .

In the meantime, Johns and Shorey ordered their men to use their GI shovels energetically to upgrade their field positions. One day, Johns phoned the Company B command post on the fringe of Baesweiler and was amused to receive the following salutation: "Baker Construction Company . . . ditches our specialty . . . field superintendent speaking." That type of warfare—so the men thought—was supposed to have ended at the Meuse-Argonne.

One positive detail of which Johns surely took note was his battalion's commanding observation of the Germans. That essential tactical advantage was sure to come in handy sometime soon, for any position American observers could see would swiftly become the target of pinpoint 105-millimeter howitzer fire from the 115th Infantry's direct support unit, the 110th Field Artillery Battalion. Achieving superior observation of that kind on the typical flat pastureland near Baesweiler seemed impossible, but members of the 110th always managed not only to locate first-class observation posts, but also to survive in them despite the Germans' efforts at eradication. Although Baesweiler was hardly a large town, like most Rhineland settlements, it featured one or more impressive churches, generally Catholic or Lutheran. In this case, the twin spires of Baesweiler's St. Petrus Catholic church would work nicely for the 110th's purposes. Even better was the giant coal-slag pile of the Karl-Alexander mine, which loomed two hundred feet high just west of town. Climbing that grimy pile of debris was an ordeal, but 29ers faced an even greater trial at the top. John Cooper of the 110th Field Artillery described it:

> A corps artillery battalion previously had established an observation post [at the top] only to abandon it as "too hot." Indeed, German artillery drove the 110th's first party from the "slag pile," as the cannoneers quickly dubbed the rubble. Under the cover of darkness, however, the intelligence and survey sections, working under Maj. Asa B. Gardiner and Capt. Frank Steele, succeeded in excavating, reinforcing, and concealing an observation post near the top. . . . In good weather, observers could see to and beyond the Roer River, nine miles to the front. . . . Soon the slag pile post became such a favorite target for German artillery that the observers had many close calls.

For the ordinary riflemen in Johns's and Shorey's battalions, reentry into the front indicated that sometime soon, they would again have to participate in those hazardous and frustrating endeavors known to the general as "aggressive patrols." Soldiers populating the bottom of the 29th Division's hierarchy valued those tasks far less than those at the top. Gerhardt not only expected patrols to be carried out daily, but also demanded that they accomplish significant results. Shorey's men got lucky in their first day in the line when, much to the general's delight, they captured a German prisoner and promptly forwarded him back to division for interrogation. Shorey failed to admit that his patrols could not take credit for the accomplishment since the enemy soldier had walked into the American lines as a deserter. Still, no matter how the prisoner was captured, his *Soldbuch* would provide modest intelligence. If he talked freely, his information could be priceless. Ultimately, the prisoner did not talk much, and the best the Americans could do was to determine that he was a member of the 689th Infantry Regiment of the 246th *Volksgrenadier* Division, a unit with which U.S. Army intelligence officers were entirely familiar, since it had been fighting on the Aachen front since September.

Both Johns and Shorey routinely forwarded their patrol results to their regimental commanders, who in turn sent them on up to Gerhardt at the war room. One typical patrol run by the 175th's Company A after dark on November 11 provided the kind of knowledge that satisfied the general. "Patrol drew machine gun fire from 928562 [a map coordinate, southwest of Siersdorf]," noted the war room transcript. "It went further, heard talking and working, estimated fifteen to twenty men laying barbed wire; tried to get close, but drew machine gun fire from vicinity of the railroad. Heard a tracked vehicle and was fired on by a machine gun from vicinity of the underpass. No casualties. Mission accomplished."

Learning the locations of three German machine-gun nests was indeed valuable intelligence, but patrols occasionally paid a high price for such information. On the night of November 10, one patrol by Company C, 175th Infantry, worked toward the enemy-occupied village of Bettendorf and soon found itself in a perilous spot. At 8:07 A.M. the following day, Purnell reported to Gerhardt, "Our patrols developed evidence that the Jerries have spruced things up a little in front of us. We had a lieutenant killed last night [2nd Lt. MacMurtry Walsh]. The patrol said they got in a bad spot and couldn't bring his body back." (Company C morning reports listed Walsh as missing in action since American medical personnel could not verify his death.) The general at first offered a sympathetic response with a simple, "That's bad luck." But two hours later, he phoned Purnell back to probe him further: "I've been thinking over this patrol business. Did they run away and leave him?"

Purnell did the best he could to defend his men's honor: "No, sir. The sergeant who was with him went over to him and tried to move him, but couldn't. They were under pretty close fire, and he didn't want to bring up any more men because he was afraid they might get shot."

Gerhardt never mentioned the affair again.

5. A SORRY OUTLOOK

If the 29th Division was to contribute materially to the Ninth Army's forthcoming offensive, the top brass could help by informing the 29ers precisely when they were expected to attack. Unfortunately, when the division reentered the line on November 6, not a single 29er, not even Gerhardt, knew when that attack would come. Even the Ninth's commander, General Simpson, held no power to select a jump-off date.

At 9 o'clock sharp on the morning of November 8, Gerhardt convened a special meeting in the war room tent to explain to his chief subordinates those details of the plan that had filtered down to him from McLain and Simpson. Armed with a pointer, the general stood in front of a wooden easel with an enormous map of the Rhineland, covered with clear acetate film. Countless sandbags, piled higher than a man's head, served as a reminder to all that Gerhardt's preferred location for a divisional command post was close to the front. As always Gerhardt commanded deference from the audience, for his ramrod posture, assertive mannerisms, and smart uniform—spruced up with a non-regulation cavalryman's neckerchief—signaled to all that he was a boss to whom no subordinate could become overly familiar. He was not wearing his usual helmet, and the onlookers could not help noticing that he seemed a little older and less intimidating than he did in full battle regalia in the field.

The meeting lasted nearly three hours, which energetic soldiers used to living outdoors would ordinarily have found taxing; in this case, however, Gerhardt's elucidation of the military situation in the European theater undeniably captivated those field-grade officers who typically knew little more of the big picture than a civilian on the home front. Gesticulating at the map with his pointer and rambling in his distinctive upper-crust accent, the general, as expected, dominated the room, but the meeting could have been boiled down to one simple directive: the 29th Division, along with its left- and right-hand neighbors, the 2nd Armored and 30th Infantry Divisions, held orders to crack the German line on the offensive's opening day and reach the Rhine River as swiftly as possible. They would then wheel to the left and drive northward down the Rhine valley to meet the British and Canadians under Montgomery, thereby pocketing 100,000 or more Germans on the river's west bank. As Gerhardt pointed out with his inborn flair, if the 29th Division and its neighbors could attain their objectives in a timely manner, Hitler would not be in power much longer, and the folks back home in the States would be reading in local newspapers of a military triumph even grander than D-Day.

As for the pressing question—when the attack would begin—Gerhardt established that the 29ers would not learn the answer until just hours before they were expected to launch the offensive. Furthermore, the decision would be made not by a ground soldier on the scene, but by an Eighth Air Force general back in England, based on a prediction from his weathermen of clear weather over the front lines, thereby allowing warplanes, including unprecedented numbers of strategic bombers, to open the offensive with a spectacular air bombardment. Gerhardt had nothing against heavy air support—the more, the better—but to attain decisive results, it had to be carried out with an expertise Allied infantrymen knew had almost never been achieved. Time was also precious; each day the Allies postponed their assault provided the Germans with more time to prepare their defenses and, more critically, brought winter weather closer. Waiting for a clear, sunny day in western Germany in mid-November, Gerhardt surmised, would not be much better than waiting for the proverbial blue moon.

Gerhardt (right) addresses reporters prior to the November offensive. Standing next to Gerhardt is his aide, Capt. Bob Wallis. Next to Wallis is the 29th's chief of staff, Col. "L. G." Smith.

By this stage of the war, senior Anglo-American ground commanders had become inextricably bound to their air force brethren when planning major offensive operations. During the preparation for the Normandy invasion, Gen. Bernard Montgomery had defined that relationship to his subordinates by declaring with his usual conviction, "Before the army staff initiates or takes any action, the first question must always be: 'How will this affect the air?' . . . Formation and unit commanders, and regimental officers and men, must be taught to realize that without the help of the air, they cannot win the land battle."

Indeed, since D-Day, the veracity of Montgomery's theory had been established, but in light of the many notable failures that had occurred when strategic air power had been employed in a tactical role, could the ground soldiers take their reliance on air power too far? By autumn 1944, many senior Allied military leaders thought so. On October 23, however, a man who harbored profound faith in air power's decisive role on the battlefield, Gen. George Marshall, suggested to Eisenhower that "employing strategical air in all-out tactical operations wherever and whenever the advance of ground troops can thus be facilitated" should be a guiding principle if the Allies hoped to bring the war to a victorious conclusion by early 1945. Although Ike maintained a thoroughly deferential attitude toward his boss Marshall, he pointed out with candor, "All of our heavy bomber work [in direct support of ground operations] has had to be done through overcast with special technique, and this technique is not—repeat not—suitable for tactical work."

In a letter to RAF chief Sir Charles Portal, Eisenhower's deputy, Sir Arthur Tedder, presented an even blunter view, one he could have applied just as readily to the Americans as the British: "The British Army have for months now been allowed to feel that they can, at any time, call on heavy bomber effort, and it will be laid on practically without question. . . . I am sure you will realize that, the Army having been drugged with bombs, it is going to be a difficult process to cure the drug addicts."

The 29th Division's appalling experience with heavy bombers on D-Day, however, warded off addiction. Bradley had famously promised first-wave men of the 116th Infantry "ringside seats for the greatest show on earth" courtesy of the Eighth Air Force's cascade of bombs that were supposed to have saturated Omaha Beach minutes before H-Hour. Packed into their landing craft, the hopeful infantrymen had peered into the sky looking for the incessant waves of B-24 Liberators scheduled to stream over Normandy from the north. Then nothing—no eruption of flame and smoke from bomb hits, no bomb craters, no dead or dazed German soldiers. The "greatest show on earth" had been an utter flop.

If the November offensive's air support plan, code-named Operation Queen, could not substantially improve upon the abysmal results achieved by the heavy bombers on Omaha Beach, delaying the opening of the 29th Division's assault until perfect flying weather materialized made little sense. Gerhardt knew that the 29th had succeeded many times in the past with little or no air support, and if necessary, it could do so again. Nevertheless, as Bradley noted, "We would hitch our plans to the heavy bombers," revealing yet again his faith that the Eighth Air Force would this time wield its immense military power more effectively on the battlefield than it had in the past. Defined by the U.S. Army Air Force's official history as "the largest air-ground cooperative effort yet undertaken by the Allied air forces," Operation Queen would determine once and for all whether B-17s, B-24s, and Lancasters could help the infantry punch a hole in the enemy's line.

And so, at the November 8 commander's conference in the spartan 29th Division war room tent, Gerhardt's minions listened with hushed amazement as the general explained how the division in time would receive orders to commence its long-awaited assault. On the evening of November 10, the commander of the Eighth Air Force, the legendary Lt. Gen. Jimmy Doolittle, would consult with his chief meteorologist to determine whether the Eighth's heavy bombers would have the clear skies they needed to take off from their English airfields the next day and saturate the German lines in the Rhineland with bombs. A prediction of good weather would trigger Operation Queen the following morning. An unfavorable forecast, however, would force postponement, in which case, on the evening of November 11, Doolittle would again decide whether his aircraft could undertake precision bombing on a massive scale the next day. Yet another poor forecast would compel a second postponement, giving Doolittle just one more chance, on the evening of November 12, to determine if B-17s and B-24s could support the ground attack on the thirteenth. Ultimately, if the Eighth Air Force could not bomb for three consecutive days, responsibility for the decision to initiate the offensive would shift to U.S. First Army, and it would then be the turn of its commander, Gen. Courtney Hodges, to scan the skies and his meteorologist's reports to determine the attack's jump-off date.

Gerhardt could not help noting that his boss, Simpson, did not have a voice in the decision-making process. Instead, the pronouncement to commence or postpone originating from the Eighth Air Force (or later, First Army) would not reach Simpson's Ninth Army headquarters until late at night. In turn, it would eventually filter down the chain of command to McLain at the XIX Corps and finally to Gerhardt at his command post near Eygelshoven. As all 29ers would soon realize, that drawn-out process was not a particularly rational method to prepare men for battle. If the men of the 29th Division were to be ready for the big attack, as Gerhardt fully expected them to be, they had to assume it would begin on November 11, its earliest possible start date, and they therefore had to steel themselves mentally and physically for the tough task ahead. The letdown of one or more postponements, however, would invariably slacken the men's focus and generate frustration over the apparent vacillations of the top brass. Even worse, repeated delays would give the alert Germans the opportunity to pick up signals that their opponents were ready to launch a big attack, thereby enabling them to deploy reinforcements to the endangered point and enhance their defensive preparations. In short, for each day the American high command put off the offensive, the forthcoming job would become tougher. An effective aerial assault could offset difficulties caused by repeated postponements, but regrettably, recent history did not provide much evidence to support the hope that air power would make a substantive difference.

As always, Eisenhower was optimistic. On the morning of November 10, a careful scrutiny of Eighth Air Force weather maps yielded what Ike described in a letter to Marshall as "a rather favorable prediction," but that forecast grew grim by evening. It was not until shortly before midnight that Gerhardt received a call from McLain, during which the XIX Corps commander uttered only a single sentence of seven words: "You can go back to bed now." The general promptly informed Witte, "She's cancelled—the whole works. For tomorrow anyway. Notify the units. On second thought, I'll do that."

The Eighth Air Force perceived no improvement in the weather over the next two days, obliging McLain on both November 11 and 12 to repeat his late-night communication to Gerhardt, this time shortened to a simple "no-go." A frustrated Ike observed to Marshall: "The [weather] predictions now give us a sorry outlook." According to his aide Harry Butcher, "Ike said he thought the abominable weather was a secret weapon of

Hitler's and, as I have heard him and seen him do many times before, he paced the living room, pausing now and then to look out the window to judge the weather." Gerhardt's fervent hope that the weather would soon clear probably drove him to pace as well. "I think we're all set, but we don't want to delay it too long," he grumbled to McLain at 8:08 P.M. on November 11.

After three consecutive postponements, the man who now had to analyze the weather and judge its impact was not an airman, but First Army commander Courtney Hodges. The gloomy skies persisted. In the 29th Division war room, the scenario of the previous three days played out in identical fashion over the next two, November 13 and 14. Twice more, the staffers had to postpone the offensive, prompting an annoyed Gerhardt to inquire of McLain, "Any telling how long this weather will keep on?" McLain's confession that he had no idea induced Gerhardt to blurt: "You know how you felt about [the plan], and we felt the same way. I guess it hinges on the other people." McLain concluded wearily: "That's about it."

Only one thing could assuage Gerhardt's mounting frustration, and that was for the sun to make a prolonged appearance over the next day or two. But the apparent rarity of that kind of weather in this corner of the world at this time of year had started to fray the nerves of American soldiers, from privates to generals, who at any moment were about to be thrown into one of the most crucial offensives undertaken by the U.S. Army in World War II. One soldier whose nerves were acutely frayed, the First Army's chief meteorologist, was described by Hodges's aide as "the most harassed, worried, and hard-working officer on the continent at the present time, and should the present situation last beyond the 16th, he would undoubtedly be fair meat for a Section VIII discharge." (Section VIII was a part of U.S. Army regulations detailing conditions of mental unfitness mandating discharge from military service.)

The Germans eavesdropped expertly on their opponents' conversations, and consequently, the U.S. Army demanded that users of its famously cutting-edge communications network refrain from divulging sensitive information when using the radio or telephone. American soldiers strove to baffle German listeners by talking in slang and using prearranged code words to signify various units, leaders, places, or missions. So regularly did Gerhardt communicate with McLain about the initiation of the upcoming offensive that XIX Corps staffers thought it best for the two generals to disguise their language when they interacted by phone, just in case the Germans were eavesdropping. According to the plan, the topic of Gerhardt's conversations with McLain would involve not military operations, but the outwardly innocuous subject of home-front American politics, specifically the recent presidential election between Democrat Franklin D. Roosevelt and Republican Thomas Dewey. If overcast skies had forced the offensive's postponement, McLain would call Gerhardt to discuss the Republicans, using phrases like "Dewey is winning" or "It looks like a Republican victory." On the other hand, if the weather permitted the assault to begin the following day, McLain would initiate a dialogue concerning the Democrats, such as "It's a Democratic landside" or "The Democrats are ahead."

The routine was patently absurd, as the entire world knew Roosevelt had already won the November 7 election. Accordingly, the likelihood of fooling any clever eavesdropper was low. As long as the scheme forced the Germans to wonder for a few days what the gibberish meant, however, the Americans hoped their offensive would commence before the enemy figured it out.

For several days running, Gerhardt and McLain limited their standard late-night conversation to the Republicans. Simple, repetitive banter such as "Dewey is gaining" and "Dewey is still gaining" carried with it a secret and disheartening meaning to the two generals: the weather in western Germany might not improve until spring.

Late on November 15, an impatient Gerhardt, clipboard in hand, waited in his folding chair near the war room phone for McLain's nightly call, which usually came shortly before midnight. Strange: no call this time, even when midnight had passed by several minutes. In fact, the 29th Division duty officer, Capt. Charles Gendler, whom Gerhardt habitually referred to erroneously as "Genzler," noted that not a single radio or telephone message from anyone had come in for the past two hours, a decidedly unusual state of affairs in the war room, since, even in the middle of the night, the tent bustled with busy clerks and staff officers striving to handle an incessant flow of incoming and outgoing communications.

Finally, at thirty-eight minutes past midnight on November 16, a light on the war room switchboard flashed. Gendler took the call: General McLain for General Gerhardt. The adroit operator promptly thrust a telephone cord into an empty switchboard jack and pulled back on a key to buzz the general's phone. Meanwhile, a nearby clerk scrambled to place earphones on his head so he could listen in on the call and make a steno-graphic record of the conversation for the war room journal. The first few words the clerk scribbled on a pad in shorthand as the generals conversed smacked of triviality. Was there a hidden meaning?

General McLain declared, "The Democrats will win."

References

The following citations provide the bibliographic or archival sources from which the historical information in this book was derived. The following examples demonstrate how to read citations:

13   *"To most of the men"*: Ewing, *29 Let's Go*, 289.

Thus, on page 13, the source for the quote beginning "To most of the men . . ." is Ewing's book, *29 Let's Go*, page 289. For more details on *29 Let's Go*, consult the bibliography. Here is another example:

83   *"So quit calling"*: 29ID, WRJ, 10/3/44, 1230.

Thus, on page 83, when General Gerhardt states, "So quit calling up here and asking if you can do so and so," the source is the 29th Infantry Division Archives, specifically the division's War Room Journal (WRJ) for October 3, 1944, at 12:30 P.M. See below for a full list of abbreviations.

Most of the historical information provided in this book was derived from the 29th Infantry Division Archives, managed by the Maryland Military Department and housed in the Fifth Regiment Armory, 29th Division Street, Baltimore, Maryland 21201. The abbreviation "29ID" is used in citations to indicate historical details drawn from this source, followed by more specific information detailing the precise location in the archives where those details can be found. For example, "Holland" indicates that the information can be located in the archival boxes pertaining to the 29th Division's movement to Holland and entry into the line in September–October 1944. "Personnel" means that the information can be found in the archival boxes containing files on individual 29th Division soldiers. When newspaper articles are quoted, dates are indicated with the byline provided by the reporter, which was not necessarily the date in which those articles appeared in the paper.

For further information on the history of the 29th Infantry Division, please join the "29th Infantry Division Archives" page on Facebook or consult our websites at www.29div.com or www.angelfire.com/md/29division/. To contact the author, e-mail him at 29division@gmail.com.

The following abbreviations are used in the citations:

29ID: 29th Infantry Division Archives, Fifth Regiment Armory, Baltimore, Maryland; **29LG**: 29th Division newsletter *29 Let's Go*; **AAR**: After-action report; **113CG**: 113th Cavalry Group; **CI**: Combat Interview files, 29th Division (part of NA RG 407); **DEL**: Dwight Eisenhower Presidential Library, Abilene, Kansas; **DEP**: Dwight Eisenhower Papers, Johns Hopkins University Press; **FM**: Field Manual; **FRA**: Fifth Regiment Armory, Baltimore, Maryland; **FRUS**: Foreign Relations of the United States, U.S. State Department publications; **GO**: General Orders; **G3J**: 29th Division G-3 Journal; **IDPF**: Individual Deceased Personnel File; **LOC**: Library of Congress Veterans Project oral history interview; **MHI**: Military History Institute, Carlisle Barracks, Pennsylvania; **MDNG**: Maryland National Guard; **MR**: Morning Reports; **MS**: Manuscript; **NA**: U.S. National Archives and Records Administration, College Park, Maryland; **NG**: National Guard; **NYT**: New York Times; **RG**: U.S. National Archives Record Group; **TC**: 29th Division Training Center; **USMASC**: U.S. Military Academy Library Special Collections, West Point, New York; **WRJ**: 29th Division War Room Journal.

INTRODUCTION
xii   *"32,000 battle deaths"*: Stanton, *World War II Order of Battle.*

ONE: AN AMERICAN ART OF WAR
1. Hold or Die
2   *"the sorry plight"*: Cooper, *History of the 110th Field Artillery,* 168.

3   *"I thought they might quit"*: MHI, Bradley Papers, Hansen note-cards, "The Optimistic Phase of Sept."

3   *"The retrograde movement"*: USMASC, Dickson Papers, First Army G-2 Estimates, 9/5/44.

3   *"the vital factor is time"*: Pogue, *Supreme Command*, 290.

4   *"The affairs of the United Nations"*: FRUS, *Conference at Quebec, 1944*, 312–13.

4   *"The German working man"*: FRUS, *Conference at Quebec, 1944*, 318.

4   *"still not quite possible"*: FRUS, *Conference at Quebec, 1944*, 316.

4   *V-2 rockets*: Hinsley, *British Intelligence in the Second World War*, vol. III, pt. 2, 565.

5   *"considered proposals"*: Churchill, *Triumph and Tragedy*, 50.

5   *"The decline in morale"*: USMASC, Dickson Papers, G-2 Estimates, 9/26/44.

5   *"from the military point of view"*: Blumentritt, *Von Rundstedt: The Soldier and the Man*, 248.

6   *"It was my duty"*: Blumentritt, *Von Rundstedt: The Soldier and the Man*, 242.

6   *"My Führer"*: Barnett, *Hitler's Generals*, 201.

6   *"Germany will go on fighting"*: USMASC, Dickson Papers, G-2 Estimates, 10/31/44.

6   *"The appointment of Field Marshal von Rundstedt"*: USMASC, Dickson Papers, G-2 Estimates, 9/26/44.

6   *"In the west"*: U.S. Army, Führer Directives, 1942-1945, 9/16/44.

6   *"The whole organization"*: Wilmot, *The Struggle for Europe*, 480.

8   *"fog, night, and snow"*: Heiber, *Hitler and His Generals: Military Conferences, 1942–1945*, 481.

9   *"The men had somehow"*: Ewing, *29 Let's Go*, 284.

2. Sound Off

9   *"I speak with an emphasis"*: Pogue, *George C. Marshall: Organizer of Victory*, 351.

10   *"During recent months"*: Bland, *Papers of George C. Marshall*, vol. 4, 589–92.

11   *"The operation at Brest"*: 29ID, Personnel, John Jones.

15   *"To most of the men"*: Ewing, *29 Let's Go*, 289.

16   *"I knew he could not be a 29er"*: 29ID, Personnel, Henry Green, Mar. 2007 interview.

16   *"It is those superficial things"*: DEL, Gerhardt Papers, 1943 visit to Mediterranean theater.

17   *"March, Shoot, Obey"*: DEL, Gerhardt Papers, 1943 visit to Mediterranean theater.

17   *"Personnel must have chin strap"*: Ewing, *29 Let's Go*, 160.

3. A Very Dangerous Place to Be

18   *"The rush seems"*: 29ID, WRJ, 9/21/44, 0845.

18   *"The general is now"*: MHI, Bradley Papers, Hansen 9/21/44 diary entry.

21   *"[Trucks] can drive with lights"*: 29ID, WRJ, 9/21/44, 1936.

23   *"how very impressed I was"*: 29ID, Personnel, Gerhardt memoir.

24   *"The English started"*: MHI, Corlett Papers, "Cowboy Pete" ms, 287.

24   *"damned nuisance"*: MHI, Bradley Papers, Hansen notecards, "Evaluation of Results of Arnhem Drop."

24   *"one of the most arrogant"*: MHI, Bradley Papers, Hansen note-cards, "Evaluation of Results of Arnhem Drop."

24   *"This is no longer a Normandy"*: DEP, *The War Years*, vol. 4, 2,222.

24   *"[We] may get a nasty"*: DEP, *The War Years*, vol. 4, 2,185–86.

25   *"completely destroying Germany"*: *New York Times*, "Morgenthau Plan on Germany Splits Cabinet Committee," 24 September 1944.

25   *"not unnaturally"*: Stimson, *On Active Service in Peace and War*, 569.

25   *"All industrial plants"*: FRUS, *Conference at Quebec, 1944*, 102.

25   *"The standard of living"*: FRUS, *Conference at Quebec, 1944*, 97.

25   *"All schools"*: FRUS, *Conference at Quebec, 1944*, 103.

25   *"No person in Germany"* : FRUS, *Conference at Quebec, 1944*, 104.

25   *"OK . . . in agreement"* : FRUS, *Conference at Quebec, 1944*, 467; FDR and Churchill stated their agreement on September 15, 1944.

26   *"The Jew Morgenthau"*: Wilmot, *The Struggle for Europe*, 549.

26 *"A stronger weapon"*: Ellis, *Victory in the West*, vol. II, 147.
26 *"Perhaps the most important news"*: Sylvan, *Normandy to Victory*, 132.

TWO: A PLACE CALLED LIMBURG
1. Hommes 8—Chevaux 40
28 *"Entraining point"*: 29ID, WRJ, 9/23/44, 1330.
29 *"The Red Cross"*: Binkoski, *The 115th Infantry Regiment in World War II*, 170.
29 *"It was possible to shade"*: Cawthon, *Other Clay*, 148.
30 *PFC Allen Levin*: 29ID, Personnel, Levin.
31 *"The boxcar riders"*: Ewing, *29 Let's Go*, 149.
31 *"little children"*: Binkoski, *115th Infantry*, 171.
32 *"Paris from the railroad yards"*: Binkoski, *115th Infantry*, 170.
32 *"only in their dreams"*: Binkoski, *115th Infantry*, 170.
33 *"I was heating a cup of coffee"*: 29ID, Personnel, Van Roosen.
33 *"heroes who left the train"*: 29ID, WRJ, 11/11/44, 1115.
34 *"The bonjour changed"*: 29ID, 29LG, 10/2/44.
35 *"the first beer"*: Cooper, *110th Field Artillery*, 170–71.
37 *"lining the road"*: Cooper, *110th Field Artillery*, 170–71.
37 *"The Blue and Gray cavalcade"*: 29ID, 29LG, 9/30/44.
38 *"A city of beauty"*: 29ID, 29LG, 10/2/44.
38 *"Children and adults flocked around"*: Cooper, *110th Field Artillery*, 170–71.
38 *"Paris may not be"*: *Baltimore Sun*, "Marks of War Few in Paris," byline 30 September 1944.
39 *"I am informed that the dress"*: DEP, *The War Years*, vol. 4, 2,153–54.
39 *"Efforts to break the Paris fever"*: Ruppenthal, *Logistical Support of the Armies*, vol. II, 32.
39 *"It appeared that practically an entire unit"*: Eisenhower, *Crusade in Europe*, 316. For more detail on racketeering, see Bykofsky, *The Transportation Corps: Operations Overseas*, 351; and *The Administrative and Logistical History of the ETO*, Pt. XI, "Basic Needs of the ETO Soldier," vol. II, 128–39.
39 *"partly because of the need"*: Cooper, *110th Field Artillery*, 171.
40 *"The ever-changing countryside"*: Cooper, *110th Field Artillery*, 171.

40   *"The church steeples on the horizon"*: 29ID, 29LG, 9/30/44.

41   *"[We] felt at home"*: Cooper, *110th Field Artillery*, 172.

42   *"Drivers began to encounter"*: Cooper, *110th Field Artillery*, 172.

43   *"The continual flashes"*: Cooper, *110th Field Artillery*, 172.

43   *"Our division got its elementary education"*: Baltimore News-Post, "Maryland Troops Fighting in Germany," byline 23 October 1944.

45   *"pleased the old man"*: 29ID, Personnel, Cooper, 1/14/47 letter to Ewing.

45   *"You have another rendezvous"*: 29ID, 29LG, 9/30/44.

2. Either You Get It or You Don't

48   *"she [spoke] in some strange tongue"*: Baltimore News-Post, "Azrael Outlines Yank Soldiers' Money Troubles," no date (probably October 15, 1944).

48   *"Almost everyone [in Holland]"*: 29ID, Personnel, Gerhardt memoir, 50.

49   *"We've got money troubles"*: Baltimore News-Post, "Money Troubles," no date (probably October 15, 1944).

50   *"deeply pleasing"*: MHI, Corlett Papers, "Cowboy Pete" ms, 288.

50   *"very wonderful people"*: MHI, Forsythe oral history, 216.

50   *"the hospitality and kindness"*: U.S. Army, XIX Corps, *Normandy to the Elbe*, 28.

50   *"three cheers for the U.S. Army"*: MHI, Corlett Papers, 10/15/44 correspondence.

50   *"of collaboration with the Germans"*: MHI, Corlett Papers, "Cowboy Pete" ms, 289.

50   *"Holland is again a democracy"*: MHI, Corlett Papers, "Cowboy Pete" ms, 289.

51   *"attracted scores of Dutch"*: Cooper, *110th Field Artillery*, 173.

3. Volksgrenadier

54   *"adapt the whole of public life"*: Wilmot, *The Struggle for Europe*, 380.

55   *"I believe that the war"*: Nash, *Victory Was Beyond Their Grasp*, 325. See also pages 6–13 for a description of the establishment of *Volksgrenadier* divisions. Himmler speech given in Posen August 3, 1944, to Nazi Party district chiefs.

55   *"the cause of this toughness"*: U.S. War Department, *Handbook on German Military Forces*, 2.

56   *"One twenty-one-year-old lieutenant"*: *New York Times*, "Ninth Army Also Slowed," 25 November 1944, 6.

56   *Volksgrenadier divisions*: U.S. War Department, *German Military Forces*, 90, 92, 97.

57   *"For the most part [the enemy]"*: 29ID, 115th AAR Nov. 1944, "Forces Engaged," 6.

THREE: SCHIERWALDENRATH
1. Patrolling and That Kind of Business

59   *"German cities and villages"*: U.S. Dept. of the Army, *Führer Directives, 1942–1945*, 9/16/44, 9/30/44. Copy in USMA History Dept. Library, West Point, NY.

59   *"the Führer Directive"*: NA RG319, MS A-991 Koechling, "The Battle for the Aachen Sector," 12/9/45.

60   *"German SS troops"*: 29ID, WRJ, 9/30/44, 1313, statement by Maj. Custer.

60   *"The maneuver plan"*: DEP, *The War Years*, vol. 4, 2,137.

60   *"thrust, so far as current resources"*: DEP, *The War Years*, vol. 4, 2,201.

60   *"first mission"*: DEP, *The War Years*, vol. 4, 2,212.

60   *an argument voiced by his aide, Captain Forsythe*: MHI, Forsythe oral history, 211.

61   *"delight that Charlie Gerhardt"*: MHI, Corlett Papers, "Cowboy Pete" ms, 288.

61   *"One of the results"*: Sylvan, *Normandy to Victory*, 134.

62   *"Ike told me"*: MHI, Corlett Papers, correspondence.

62   *"loved every man and officer"*: MHI, Corlett Papers, "Cowboy Pete" ms, 300.

62   *"to inform all commanders"*: Butcher, *My Three Years With Eisenhower*, 678.

63   *"to chase the SOS out of Paris"*: Sylvan, *Normandy to Victory*, 139.

63   *"Our mission now"*: MHI, Bradley Papers, Hansen 9/29/44 diary entry.

63   *"prepare to exert pressure"*: 29ID, 29th Division AAR, Oct. 1944.

63   *"patrolling and that kind of business"*: 29ID, WRJ, 9/28/44 1535.

65   *"[A]relief is preceded"*: War Dept., *FM 7-40 Rifle Regiment (1942)*, Section X, 178, Paragraph 275.

65   *"Achtung!"*: *Baltimore Sun*, "Bradley Describes Army Push From Holland Into Germany," byline 2 October 1944.

65   *Battery B, 110th*: Cooper, *110th Field Artillery*, 173–74.

2. Indian Fighting

68   *"Want to let you know"*: 29ID, WRJ, 10/1/44, 0658.

68   *"a very smart individual"*: 29ID, Personnel, Laborde.

68   *"Your patrol activities"*: 29ID, WRJ, 10/1/44, 0722.

68   *"We are going to begin to push"*: 29ID, WRJ, 10/1/44, 0858.

69   *"I don't think there are many [Germans]"*: 29ID, WRJ, 10/1/44, 0722.

69   *"I understand you occupied fourteen"*: 29ID, WRJ, 10/2/44, 0715.

70   *"was unlike any"*: Cooper, *110th Field Artillery*, 174.

70   *"like giant parade grounds"*: Ewing, *29 Let's Go*, 153.

71   *"The only possible cover"*: 29ID, Personnel, Cooper, 2/26/47 letter to Ewing.

71   *"a washout today"*: 29ID, WRJ, 10/1/44, 0840.

72   *"had the dubious pleasure"*: Johns, *The Clay Pigeons of St. Lô*, dust jacket, Johns biography.

72   *"no junior officer"*: Johns, *The Clay Pigeons of St. Lô*, 37.

72   *"gutty, pushy, arrogant"*: 29ID, Personnel, Johns, letter to R. Hawk.

73   *"plush diplomatic assignment"*: Johns, *The Clay Pigeons of St. Lô*, dust jacket, Johns biography.

73   *"as complete and accurate"*: U.S. Army, *Breaching the Siegfried Line: XIX Corps, 2 Oct. 1944*, 9.

73   *"couldn't get through"*: 29ID, WRJ, 10/1/44, 1940.

73   *"It is bare ground"*: 29ID, WRJ, 10/1/44, 1907.

74   *"The Germans made it evident"*: 29ID, Holland, file 28.

74   *"The Krauts were going to do a job"*: 29ID, Holland, file 28.

75   *2nd Lt. Hull*: 29ID, Personnel, Hull.

75   *"By this time"*: 29ID, Holland, file 28.

76   *"For thirty-six hours"*: 29ID, Holland, file 28.

76   *"put pressure on Geilenkirchen"*: 29ID, WRJ, 10/3/44, 0740.

76   *"What became of those fourteen"*: 29ID, WRJ, 10/3/44, 0737.

76   *"The pine trees were so close"*: Baltimore Sun, "Indian Tactics Used by Yanks," 9 October 1944.

78   *"One lieutenant found"*: Baltimore Sun, "Indian Tactics," 9 October 1944.

78   *Maj. Miller and scotch*: Baltimore Sun, "Bradley Describes Army Push From Holland Into Germany," byline 2 October 1944.

78   *"The enemy sensed"*: Binkoski, *115th Infantry*, 179.

78   *"A German machine gun"*: Baltimore Sun, "Indian Tactics," 9 October 1944.

79   *"having difficulty maintaining control"*: 29ID, 2/115 Journal, 10/3/44, 0930.

80   *"The two companies banged their way"*: 29ID, Holland, file 28.

80   *"They came out of the woods"*: 29ID, Holland, file 28.

80   *"vicious close-in fighting"*: Binkoski, *115th Infantry*, 183.

81   *"The Germans kept coming"*: 29ID, Holland, file 28.

81   *"The Krauts didn't even know"*: 29ID, Holland, file 28.

81   *"As war goes"*: 29ID, Holland, file 28.

3. Decisive Action

82   *"Two prisoners taken"*: 29ID, 115th S-2 Journal, 10/3/44, 0415.

83   *176th Infantry Division*: Tessin, *Verbände und Truppen der deutschen Wehrmacht und Waffen-SS im Zweiten Weltkrieg, 1939–1945*, vol. 7, 186–87.

84   *"the significance of the Volksgrenadier division"*: U.S. War Department, *German Military Forces*, 90.

84   *Volksgrenadier divisions*: U.S. War Department, *German Military Forces*, 90, 92, 97.

85   *"mediocre. . . . Because it is largely constructed"*: "Machine Carbine Redesignated," *Tactical and Technical Trends*, vol. 57, April 1945.

85   *"The main battle area must be organized"*: Condell, *On the German Art of War*, 122.

86   *"The optimal situation"*: Condell, *German Art of War*, 121.

86   *"to think and act independently"*: Condell, *On the German Art of War*, 18 (Paragraph 10 in original 1933 *Truppenführung* manual).

86   *"The first criterion in war"*: Condell, *On the German Art of War*, 19. To emphasize its importance, this sentence was italicized in the original 1933 *Truppenführung* manual.

86 *German POW comments*: 29ID, 29th Division AAR, Sept. 1944, "Summary of POW Interrogations Concerning Enemy Reaction to Our Combat Efficiency."

4. Captain Schmitt

87 *"lit the countryside for miles"*: Binkoski, *115th Infantry*, 173.

87 *"clear and cold"*: *Baltimore Sun*, "Maryland Men Play Big Role in Battle on German Soil," byline 8 October 1944.

88 *"Colonel, this town is too damn big"*: Binkoski, *115th Infantry*, 175.

89 *Sgt. Pietz*: Binkoski, *115th Infantry*, 175.

89 *"German machine guns opened up"*: Binkoski, *115th Infantry*, 175.

90 *"Company K reports"* : 29ID, WRJ, 10/2/44, 1027.

90 *"I don't want any more reports like that"*: 29ID, WRJ, 10/2/44, 1100.

91 *"Companies I and L"*: 29ID, WRJ, 10/2/44, 1456.

91 *"probably has killed as many"*: 29ID, 29LG, "Red Head," 10/14/44.

91 *"He's so good"*: 29ID, 29LG, "Red Head," 10/14/44.

91 *"Get on your initial objectives"*: 29ID, WRJ, 10/2/44, 1906.

91 *"The tanks were then kept"*: DEL, Overlord Papers, 747th Tank Battalion, Box 180.

93 *"The terrain was as flat as a table"*: Wilkes, *APO230: The 747th Tank Battalion*, 139.

93 *"This fellow Bruning"*: 29ID, WRJ, 10/3/44, 0954.

93 *"You are the commander"*: 29ID, WRJ, 10/3/44, 1020.

93 *"Get on that objective"*: 29ID, WRJ, 10/3/44, 1157.

94 *"General Gerhardt was definitely not the kind"*: 29ID, Personnel, Laborde.

95 *"to get Company K going"*: 29ID, Holland, file 5, "Capture of Lt. Samuel Hodges," 10/19/44.

95 *"a very risky undertaking"*: 29ID, Holland, file 5, "Capture of Hodges," 10/19/44.

95 *"covered with heavy logs"*: *Baltimore Sun*, "Bradley Goes With Army Into Germany," byline 2 October 1944.

95 *"advised against further advance"*: 29ID, Holland, file 5, "Capture of Hodges," 10/19/44.

95 *"The regimental CO agreed"*: 29ID, Holland, file 5, "Capture of Hodges," 10/19/44.

95 *"Colonel Smith followed orders"*: 29ID, Personnel, Laborde.

96 *"It was agreed that the attack"*: 29ID, Holland, file 5, "Capture of Hodges," 10/19/44.

96 *"We all bitched about it"*: 29ID, Personnel, Hodges.

96 *"The company officers expressed doubt"*: NA, RG 407 CI, K/115 Surrounded and Captured at Schierwaldenrath, Box 24036, 2.

96 *"Schierwaldenrath was surrounded"*: Johns, "Raid on Schierwaldenrath," *Infantry Journal (Overseas)*, May 1945.

96 *"Capt. Schmitt admitted it would be rough"*: NA, RG 407 CI, K/115 Surrounded, Box 24036, 2.

96 *Captain Schmitt career*: 29ID, MDNG Service Cards, Schmitt.

97 *Captain Schmitt commission*: 29ID, Personnel, McCool, 6/6/08 interview.

98 *"He had the pallor"*: 29ID, Personnel, Leary (questionnaire, Cornelius Ryan collection, Ohio Univ. Library, Special Collections, Athens, OH; box 6, file 33).

98 *"We all thought of Capt. Schmitt as tops"*: 29ID, Personnel, Cheatham.

98 *"I want to go on record"*: 29ID, Personnel, Wilch.

98 *"Without question, he was a man"*: Cottrill, "29th Division POWs," *Twenty-Niner*, Nov. 1989.

98 *"about six feet"*: 29ID, Personnel, McCool, 6/6/08 interview.

98 *Dr. Waldo LaSalle Schmitt career*: Blackwelder, *The Zest for Life: The Life of Waldo LaSalle Schmitt*, 90.

98 *"Doctor Schmitt was such a success"*: Rosenman, *The Public Papers and Addresses of Franklin D. Roosevelt: The Continuing Struggle for Liberalism*, 503.

99 *"a damned good platoon leader"* : DEL, Hodges Papers, "First U.S. Army Memorabilia," Box 25.

99 *"Everything worked smoothly"*: NA, RG 407 CI, K/115 Surrounded, Box 24036, 2.

99 *"traveled in front of the infantry"*: NA, RG 407 CI, K/115 Surrounded, Box 24036, 2.

99 *"did not think it advisable"*: DEL, Overlord Papers, 747th Tank Battalion, Box 180.

100   *"Enemy fire split the company"*: NA, RG 407 CI, K/115 Surrounded, Box 24036, 3.

100   *"My platoon ended up in a house"*: 29ID, Personnel, Hodges, LOC, 13.

100   *"A POW reports"*: 29ID, WRJ, 10/3/44, 1740.

101   *"Capt. Schmitt decided to dig in"*: NA, RG 407 CI, K/115 Surrounded, Box 24036, 3.

101   *"they had reached their assigned objectives"*: Ewing, *The 29th: A Short History of a Fighting Division*, 49.

101   *"He described the situation"*: NA, RG 407 CI, K/115 Surrounded, Box 24036, 4.

101   *"At about 2100 hours"*: NA, RG 407 CI, K/115 Surrounded, Box 24036, 4.

102   *"so foggy"*: Wilkes, *APO230: The 747th Tank Battalion*, 139.

102   *"Carbaugh saw a German tank"*: NA, RG 407 CI, K/115 Surrounded, Box 24036, 6.

103   *"We're receiving lots of small arms"*: NA, RG 407 CI, K/115 Surrounded, Box 24036, 8.

103   *"The captain was on the radio"*: Binkoski, *115th Infantry*, 181.

103   *"Germans were everywhere"*: 29ID, Personnel, Hodges, Cox interview.

103   *"upon hearing this"*: Wilkes, *APO230: The 747th Tank Battalion*, 140.

104   *"Several times the Germans attempted"*: Cottrill, "29th Division POWs," *Twenty-Niner*, Nov. 1989.

104   *"About one hundred yards"*: DEL, Overlord Papers, 747th Tank Battalion, Box 180.

104   *"Company K getting repeated counterattacks"*: 29ID, 3/115 Journal, 0700 and 0830.

104   *"The regimental CO was kept advised"*: 29ID, Holland, file 5, "Capture of Hodges," 10/19/44.

104   *"Had Colonel Smith chosen to disobey"*: 29ID, Personnel, Laborde.

105   *"The Germans were so close"*: 29ID, Personnel, Hodges, LOC, 13.

105   *"Will I get more men"*: NA, RG 407 CI, K/115 Surrounded, Box 24036, 8.

105   *"He didn't do it"*: 29ID, Personnel, Tawes.

105   *"Hearing a tank"*: Cottrill, "29th Division POWs," *Twenty-Niner*, Nov. 1989.

105   *"A tank poked its nose"*: 29ID, Personnel, Hodges, Cox interview.

106   *"[Schmitt] kept talking"*: Binkoski, *115th Infantry*, 182.

106   *"Capt. Schmitt and I"*: 29ID, Personnel, Hodges, Cox interview.

106   *"After the attack is launched"*: War Dept., *FM 100-5 (15 June 1944)*, 118–19.

106   *"Going to get anywhere"*: 29ID, WRJ, 10/4/44, 0742.

106   *"They're having some trouble"*: 29ID, WRJ, 10/4/44, 0840.

107   *"Don't stick your necks"*: 29ID, WRJ, 10/4/44, 1016 and 1811.

107   *"humble and somewhat meek"*: 29ID, Personnel, Laborde.

107   *"very unmilitary"*: 29ID, Personnel, Tawes, 6/7/08 interview.

107   *"a nice man"*: 29ID, Personnel, Henne.

108   *"Col. [Edward] McDaniel is coming down"*: 29ID, WRJ, 10/5/44, 0720.

108   *"The 115th had a bad day"*: 29ID, WRJ, 10/5/44, 0818.

108   *351st Regiment*: 29ID, 29th Division AAR, Oct. 1944 G-2 Narrative.

108   *"Military intelligence"*: War Dept., *FM 100-5*, 48, 117.

108   *"he did not wish to have blame"*: 29ID, Personnel, Tawes, 6/7/08 interview.

109   *"should be avoided"*: 29ID, 29th Division AAR, Sept. 1944, "Battle Lessons and Conclusions."

109   *"There was no reason"*: 29ID, WRJ, 10/5/44, 0755 to Purnell.

109   *"Anyone who wants to get in trouble"*: 29ID, WRJ, 10/5/44, 0926 to Lowenthal.

109   *"example of very bad security"*: 29ID, 29th Division AAR, Oct. 1944, "Battle Lessons and Conclusions."

110   *"not to do a 'Schmitt'"*: 29ID, Personnel, Laborde.

110   *"They were in a house"*: 29ID, WRJ, 10/25/44, 0901.

110   *"Gen. Gerhardt made a fool of himself"*: 29ID, Personnel, Laborde.

110   *"The headquarters boys"*: 29ID, Personnel, Leary (questionnaire, Cornelius Ryan collection, Ohio Univ. Library, Special Collections, Athens, OH; box 6, file 33).

111   *"As they marched us"*: Cottrill, "29th Division POWs," *Twenty-Niner*, Nov. 1989.

111   *"A small [American] sergeant"*: 29ID, Holland, file 5, "Condensation of POW Interrogation."

111   *"The ten of us"*: 29ID, Personnel, Hodges, "Return to Hell" memoir.

111   *"a German soldier took"*: Cottrill, "29th Division POWs," *Twenty-Niner*, Nov. 1989.

111   *"We were aligned"*: 29ID, Personnel, Hodges, LOC, 14.

112   *"Many of us were abused"*: Cottrill, "29th Division POWs," *Twenty-Niner*, Nov. 1989.

112   *"I will be gone when you get back"*: 29ID, Schmitt IDPF.

113   *"I think I acquired"*: MHI, Robert Ploger oral history, Sept. 1978.

113   *"[Commanders] must be resolute"*: War Dept., *FM 100-5*, 28.

113   *"highly acceptable to me"*: DEP, *The War Years*, vol. 2, 951.

114   *"[Gerhardt's] enthusiasm"*: Bradley, *A Soldier's Story*, 236.

114   *"obtain the complete story"*: Sylvan, *Normandy to Victory*, 152.

115   *"Col. Millholland said"*: DEL, Hodges Papers, "First U.S. Army Memorabilia," Box 25.

116   *"a very risky undertaking"*: 29ID, Holland, file 5, "Capture of Hodges," 10/19/44.

116   *"A good commander"*: War Dept., *FM 100-5*, 28.

117   *"with sorrow"*: 29ID, Schmitt IDPF. All details of Dr. Schmitt's search for his son's remains and their subsequent return to the U.S. are derived from this file.

117   *"I will return to Europe"*: 29ID, Personnel, Hodges, LOC, 21.

5. Red Horse Cavalry

120   *"Concentration of superior forces"*: War Dept., *FM 100-5*, 33, 110.

120   *"The Command and General Staff School"*: 29ID, Personnel, Gerhardt memoir, 22.

121   *"slightly nuts"*: U.S. Army, XIX Corps, *Normandy to the Elbe*, 18.

122   *"demonstrated beyond question"*: MHI, Biddle Papers, 3/8/74 Simpson letter.

123   *"I was greatly honored"*: MHI, Biddle Papers, 3/8/74 Simpson letter.

123   *"spoiled boy"*: Balkoski, *From Beachhead to Brittany*, 257.

123   *"Colonel [Leroy] Watson"*: 29ID, WRJ, 10/1/44, 0752.

123   *"[Watson] soon made it clear"*: MHI, Biddle Papers, 113CG Operations, Oct. 1944, 2.

124   *"We are not going to give you"*: 29ID, WRJ, 10/1/44, 0752.

124   *"Mechanized cavalry units are organized"*: War Dept., *FM 100-5*, 9–10.

124   *"[Cavalry] suffered"*: MHI, Biddle Papers, "Mechanized Cavalry" report for ETO General Board, 2.

127   *"The terrain did not favor"*: MHI, Biddle Papers, 113CG Ops, Oct. 1944, 2.

128   *"The whole thing hinges"*: 29ID, WRJ, 10/2/44, 0719.

128   *"I think the [enemy line]"*: 29ID, WRJ, 10/2/44, 0723.

128   *"The advance met stiff opposition"*: MHI, Biddle Papers, 113CG Ops, Oct. 1944, 6.

130   *"I understand the stream"*: 29ID, WRJ, 10/2/44, 1015.

130   *"terrain difficulties"*: MHI, Biddle Papers, 113CG Ops, Oct. 1944, 6.

130   *S/Sgt. Smith, PFC Romanik Silver Stars*: Rose, *The Saga of the Red Horse.*

131   *"They are short of ammo"*: 29ID, WRJ, 10/2/44, 1838.

131   *"The captain reported"*: 29ID, WRJ, 10/2/44, 1915.

131   *"beyond [Chappell's] control"*: 29ID, WRJ, 10/3/44, 0850.

131   *"less than satisfactory"*: MHI, Biddle Papers, 113CG Ops, Oct. 1944, 8.

131   *"The continuous use of tanks"*: 29ID, Holland, file 15, 12/4/44 "Recommendations for Tank Operations."

131   *"I received a report"*: 29ID, WRJ, 10/3/44, 1230.

131   *"[The engineers] are taking"*: 29ID, WRJ, 10/2/44, 1915.

132   *"the stream runs pretty close"*: 29ID, WRJ, 10/2/44, 2017.

132   *"Read manual"*: 29ID, WRJ, 10/2/44, 1915.

132   *"was pretty heavily held"*: 29ID, WRJ, 10/2/44, 2017.

132   *"very well coordinated"*: 29ID, WRJ, 10/3/44, 0215.

132   *"I understand the Krauts"*: 29ID, WRJ, 10/3/44, 0728.

133   *"[The attack] proceeded"*: MHI, Biddle Papers, 113CG Ops, Oct. 1944, 8.

134   *"visibility was too bad"*: 29ID, WRJ, 10/3/44, 1220.

134   *"At [Gerhardt's] direction"*: MHI, Biddle Papers, 113CG Ops, Oct. 1944, 9.

134   *"How're you doing"*: 29ID, WRJ, 10/3/44, 1305, 1926.

134   *"[Blandford] is stretched"*: 29ID, WRJ, 10/4/44, 0756.

135   *"How far are you across"*: 29ID, WRJ, 10/3/44, 1153, 1200.

136   *"This cavalry on the left"*: 29ID, WRJ, 10/3/44, 0730.

138   *"enemy was displaying"*: 29ID, WRJ, 10/3/44, 1907.

138   *"I would like to be careful"*: 29ID, WRJ, 10/4/44, 0756.

138   *"Having then a bridgehead"*: 29ID, Holland, file 12, 2/11/47 Blandford letter to Ewing.

138   *"The cavalry is about wound up"*: 29ID, WRJ, 10/3/44, 2020.

138   *"[Gerhardt] explained"*: MHI, Biddle Papers, 113CG Ops, Oct. 1944, 10.

139   *"not designed for offensive"*: War Dept., *FM 2-20: Cavalry Reconnaissance Troop*, 4.

139   *"was received with enthusiasm"*: MHI, Biddle Papers, 113CG Operations, Oct. 1944, 9.

139   *"unskillful use"*: 29ID, WRJ, 10/3/44, 0740.

139   *"revealed that those losses"*: MHI, Biddle Papers, 113CG Ops, Oct. 1944, 9.

139   *"a confused fight"*: 29ID, Holland, file 12, 2/11/47 Blandford letter to Ewing.

139   *"enthusiastic"*: 29ID, WRJ, 10/4/44, 2224.

140   *"The arrival of [Portwood]"*: MHI, Biddle Papers, 113CG Ops, Oct. 1944, 12.

140   *"The [Panther] was well protected"*: MHI, Biddle Papers, 113CG Ops, Oct. 1944, 12.

140   *"The enemy holds the town"*: 29ID, WRJ, 10/5/44, 0336.

141   *Forty-five L/175 casualties*: 29ID, L/175 MR, 10/5/44 and later.

6. Sergeant Humphrey

141   *"sergeant's war"*: Balkoski, *Beyond the Beachhead*, 80.

142   *Sgt. Ned Humphrey*: 29ID, Personnel, Humphrey. All details on Humphrey's life and military career from this file, provided mostly by Humphrey's descendants.

148   *"3rd Platoon"*: 29ID, 121st Engineer Journal, 0930.

149   *"Capt. Smith reports"*: 29ID, 121st Engineer Journal, 1600.

152   *Sgt. Humphrey's death, burial*: 29ID, Humphrey IDPF.

FOUR: NOTHING WILL BE HELD BACK
1. As Quickly as Humanly Possible

155   *"I went through five armies"*: Bland, *Papers of George C. Marshall*, vol. 4, 629.

156   *"The Combined Chiefs of Staff direct"*: Bland, *Papers of George C. Marshall*, vol. 4, 636.

156   *"the wonderful telegram"*: Danchev, *War Diaries: Field Marshal Lord Alanbrooke*, 615.

156   *"I was very optimistic"*: MHI, Bradley Papers, Hansen notecards, "The Optimistic Phase of Sept..."

156   *"We would be lucky"*: Bradley, *A General's Life*, 338.

157   *"Plans of both"* : DEP, *The War Years*, vol. 4, 2,212.

157   *"In the battle for Aachen"*: Weigley, *Eisenhower's Lieutenants*, 364.

157   *"fooled the German division"*: MacDonald, *Siegfried Line Campaign*, 267.

159   *"to be set to go"*: 29ID, WRJ, 10/4/44, 1220.

159   *"our long extended front"*: 29ID, WRJ, 10/4/44.

160   *"Aachen had little military significance"*: Collins, *Lightning Joe*, 271.

160   *"the best we could hope"*: Bradley, *A Soldier's Story*, 426.

160   *"[He] released us"*: 29ID, WRJ, 10/6/44, 1200.

160   *"I told Harmon"*: 29ID, WRJ, 10/6/44, 1445.

2. Red Raiders

162   *"Massacre every Kraut"*: 29ID, WRJ, 10/5/44, 1130, 1958.

163   *"I requested the works"*: "Raid on Schierwaldenrath," *Infantry Journal*, May 1945.

163   *"A properly trained battalion"*: Ewing, *29 Let's Go*, 285.

163   *"What do they get"*: 29ID, WRJ, 10/5/44, 1936.

163   *"The terrain in front of Kreuzrath"*: 29ID, Holland, file 4, 10/10/44 Johns report "Raid on Schierwaldenrath." All Johns quotes in this section are drawn from this source.

164   *Paragraph 2, Mission*: War Dept., *FM 101-5 Staff Officers' Field Manual (1940)*, 43.

167   *"The Germans never really got going"*: *Baltimore News-Post*, "Azrael Tells of Avenging Maryland Yanks," byline 7 October 1944.

168   *"Most of the windows"*: 29ID, Personnel, Burkert, memoir, 30.

168   *Pvt. Gass*: "Battalion Raid on Schierwaldenrath," *Military Affairs*, Summer 1947, 85.

168 *"No single house"*: 29ID, WRJ, 10/7/44, 1035.

169 *"Tiger tanks were very common"*: 29ID, Holland, file 22, "War Memoirs of James Burt."

170 *"But sir, [we] can't"*: "Battalion Raid on Schierwaldenrath," *Military Affairs*, Summer 1947, 86.

171 *Lt. Huff, Capt. Hays Silver Stars*: 29ID, GO, 150, 11/7/44; 153, 11/11/44.

172 *"There were none"*: 29ID, WRJ, 10/7/44, 1050.

173 *Sgt. Young Silver Star*: 29ID, GO, 177, 12/8/44.

173 *"Now there's something"*: 29ID, WRJ, 10/7/44, 0916.

173 *"Johns needs a rest"*: 29ID, WRJ, 10/10/44, 1725.

174 *"Red Raiders"*: Ewing, *29 Let's Go*, 160.

3. Are You with Me?

174 *"go into one of these towns"*: 29ID, WRJ, 10/6/44, 0906.

174 *"Activity was [now confined]"*: 29ID, 175th Infantry AAR Oct. 1944, 2.

176 *"This woods had been a source"*: Baltimore News-Post, "Azrael Tells of Avenging of Maryland Yanks," byline 7 October 1944.

176 *"some oil bombs"*: 29ID, WRJ, 10/6/44, 0913.

176 *"We are going in"*: 29ID, WRJ, 10/6/44, 1251, 1755.

176 *"The plan was"*: 29ID, 175th AAR Oct. 1944, 2.

176 *"The woods are burning"*: 29ID, WRJ, 10/7/44, 0125.

176 *"We exploded the gas"*: 29ID, WRJ, 10/7/44, 0155.

177 *"Good going"*: 29ID, WRJ, 10/7/44, 0155.

178 *"[The platoon's] leading squad"*: 29ID, WRJ, 10/8/44, 0104.

178 *"[The patrol] reached the edge"*: 29ID, WRJ, 10/8/44, 0504.

179 *"Darkness was absolute"*: Binkoski, *115th Infantry*, 189.

179 *"I'm going to stress"*: 29ID, WRJ, 10/7/44, 0731, 0734.

181 *"I guess it was the German"*: 29ID, 29LG, 10/16/44.

181 *"a good show"*: 29ID, WRJ, 10/9/44, 0742.

181 *"I have been thinking"*: 29ID, WRJ, 10/9/44, 1550.

181 *"Farinholt administered first-aid"*: 29ID, Personnel, Farinholt.

182 *"often had a foot of water"*: 29ID, 1944 Unit Histories, 29th Division Medical Activities.

183 *"securing information and prisoners"*: 29ID, 2/115 Journal, 10/9/44, 1217-1220.

183 *"Company commanders"*: 29ID, 2/115 Journal, 10/9/44, 1840.

184   *"an old tower"*: Binkoski, *115th Infantry*, 193.

184   *"The artillery and tank destroyers tried"*: 29ID, 29LG, 10/17/44.

185   *"good progress"*: 29ID, 2/115 Journal, 10/13/44, 2200.

185   *"Impossible to accomplish mission"*: 29ID, 2/115 Journal, 10/13/44, 2340.

186   *"Company G 'Big Boy'"*: 29ID, 2/115 Journal, 10/14/44, 0012.

186   *"Regimental order for battalion"*: 29ID, 2/115 Journal, 10/14/44, 1415.

186   *"famous for his fighting talks"*: 29ID, 29LG, 10/17/44.

188   *"Sgt. Carroll, at the point"*: Binkoski, *115th Infantry*, 193.

188   *"The men bent low"*: Binkoski, *115th Infantry*, 193.

188   *"We headed straight for the tower"*: 29ID, 29LG, 10/17/44.

189   *"Patrol accomplished mission"*: 29ID, 2/115 Journal, 10/15/44, 0051.

189   *"The group had gone about 200 yards"*: Binkoski, *115th Infantry*, 194.

189   *"We wriggled"*: 29ID, 29LG, 10/17/44.

190   *S/Sgt. Mowery Silver Star*: 29ID, Holland, file 11.

190   *"I am reading the report"*: 29ID, WRJ, 10/15/44, 0840.

191   *"immediate decrease"*: Binkoski, *115th Infantry*, 194.

191   *"Two POWs captured"*: 29ID, 115th S-2 Journal, 10/16/44.

192   *"Our 1st Battalion has four"*: 29ID, WRJ, 10/9/44, 2300.

192   *"This business of sharpshooters"*: 29ID, WRJ, 10/10/44, 0849.

193   *Pvt. Moon, sniping*: 29ID, Personnel, Moon.

FIVE: WÜRSELEN
1. An Oversupply of Fighting

196   *"This is the last time"*: 29ID, WRJ, 10/16/44, 0912.

197   *"There was an oversupply of fighting"*: Walker, *Vierville to Victory*, 98B.

198   *"It was demonstrated"*: 29ID, 29th Division AAR, Oct. 1944, "Battle Lessons and Conclusions."

199   *"Orders [were] simply"*: 29ID, 116th Infantry AAR, Oct. 1944, "Phase 1," 1.

200   *"The greatest infantry soldier"*: Barnes, *Fragments of My Life*, 94.

200   *"raised him like one of my own boys"*: 29ID, Personnel, Nash.

201   *"We have a hole"* and *"The job is finished"*: MacDonald, *Siegfried Line Campaign*, 279, 294.

201 *"In the nine days that followed"*: MacDonald, *Siegfried Line Campaign*, 294.

201 *"A platoon firing demonstration"*: Cawthon, *Other Clay*, 152–53.

202 *"The Germans put up ferocious"*: Harmon, *Combat Commander*, 212–13.

203 *"so fat there is no place"*: Wilson, *Maneuver and Firepower*, 184.

204 *"All I wanted to do"*: 29ID, Personnel, Puntenney, memoir.

205 *"As the columns crossed the bridge"*: 29ID, 116th AAR, Oct. 1944, "3/116 Actions When Attached to the 2nd Armored Division."

207 *"We are now fighting"*: 29ID, K/116 MR, 10/6/44.

207 *"Along the road"*: *Baltimore Sun*, "Battle Turns Into Gun Duel," byline 8 October 1944.

209 *"withering"*: 29ID, 116th AAR, Oct. 1944, "3/116 [with] 2nd Armored Division."

209 *"T/4 Sneed"*: 29ID, Holland, file 7, Sneed Silver Star Citation.

209 *"To reach the town"*: Snipas, *How It Happened*, 32.

210 *PFC Mesa Silver Star*: 29ID, GO, 163, 11/7/44.

210 *"five civilians"*: 29ID, K/116 MR, 10/6/44.

211 *"very heavy"*: 29ID, 116th AAR, Oct. 1944, "3/116 [with] 2nd Armored Division."

211 *Maurice McGrath, details*: 29ID, Personnel, McGrath, provided by Katherine Cranney (sister) and Sally McGrath (niece).

213 *"The guns of an American battery"*: *Baltimore Sun*, "Battle Turns Into Gun Duel," byline 8 October 1944.

215 *"badly in need"*: 29ID, WRJ, 10/9/44, 1703.

215 *"are pretty tired"*: 29ID, WRJ, 10/9/44, 0827.

216 *"nailed a German steer"*: 29ID, K/116 MR, 10/26/44.

2. Treat Them like the Best

216 *"It is hoped that the circle"*: Sylvan, *Normandy to Victory*, 144.

216 *"appeared to be a relatively easy task"*: Hewitt, *Workhorse of the Western Front*, 126.

217 *"I considered our small crew"*: Cawthon, *Other Clay*, 153.

217 *"We are being attacked"* and *"Gen. Hodges tells me"*: Hewitt, *Workhorse of the Western Front*, 134, 137.

218 *"During this period"*: MHI, Corlett Papers, "Cowboy Pete" ms, 297.

218   *"entrusted with the mission"*: 29ID, 116th AAR, Oct. 1944, "Phase II."

218   *"involved too many unknowns"*: 29ID, Holland, file 6, 6/20/47 Hewitt letter to Ewing.

219   *"If the 116th Panzer"*: MacDonald, *Siegfried Line Campaign*, 301.

219   *"The reason for the Würselen attack"*: 29ID, Holland, file 6, 6/20/47 Hewitt letter to Ewing.

219   *"The action called"*: Hewitt, *Workhorse of the Western Front*, 138.

219   *"It would be our first experience"*: Walker, *Vierville to Victory*, 96–97.

219   *"The roads were littered"*: *Baltimore Sun*, "German Towns Lie in Ruins in Wake of Fight for Aachen," byline 13 October 1944.

220   *"It was Friday the 13th"*: Barnes, *Fragments of My Life*, 98.

220   *"extremely heavy"*: 29ID, 116th AAR, Oct. 1944, "Phase II."

220   *"It was evident"*: Walker, *Vierville to Victory*, 97.

220   *"The [2nd] Battalion had much experience"* and *"The tankers were aggressive"*: Cawthon, *Other Clay*, 155.

222   *"We had encountered"*: 29ID, 116th AAR, Oct. 1944, "Lessons," 3.

222   *"When infantrymen ran into"*: U.S. Congress, *Medal of Honor Recipients*, 118.

222   *"There was no hospitalization"*: 29ID, Holland, file 22, Burt Memoirs, 4.

223   *"Going in right behind"*: Cawthon, *Other Clay*, 155.

223   *"bitterly heavy"*: Hewitt, *Workhorse of the Western Front*, 138.

223   *"saturating and continuous artillery"*: Walker, *Vierville to Victory*, 97.

223   *"I think someone has made"*: Stapleton, *Out in Front All the Way*, 62.

223   *"[There was] noise"*: 29ID, Holland, file 22, 2/5/95 Burt letter to Blaker.

223   *"Artillery and mortar fire"*: 29ID, 116th AAR, Oct. 1944, "Phase II," 7.

223   *"clear sky"*: 29ID, G3J, 10/14/44.

224   *"considerable ground"*: 29ID, 116th AAR, Oct. 1944, "Phase II."

224   *250 yards ahead*: 29ID, Holland, file 6, 2/116 Journal, 10/14/44.

224   *"Progress was being made"*: Hewitt, *Workhorse of the Western Front*, 138.

224   *"continuing to get a house"*: 29ID, Holland, file 22, Burt Memoirs, 2.

224   *"The unit supporting us"*: Garcia, "The Unknown Artillery FO," *Twenty-Niner*, Mar. 1997.

225   *"At times"*: Cawthon, *Other Clay*, 153.

225   *"unflinching courage"*: 29ID, GO, 175, 12/6/44.

226   *"To fight the German"* and *"most of your movement"*: 29ID, 116th AAR, Oct. 1944, "Lessons."

227   *"He certainly takes a lot"*: Stapleton, *Out in Front*, 62.

227   *"The whole scene"*: *Baltimore Sun*, "Battle for Escape Road From Aachen Still Rages," byline 14 October 1944.

227   *Deutsche Allgemeine Zeitung*: 29ID, Holland, file 6.

229   *"narrow and perhaps two inches"*: Cawthon, *Other Clay*, 157.

229   *"a cheerful and steadfast asset"*: Cawthon, *Other Clay*, 126.

229   *"situated no more than 1,000 yards"* and *"a diminutive Puerto Rican"*: Garcia, "Dear Old Comrades," *Twenty-Niner*, Nov. 1995, 27.

230   *"He took great risks"*: U.S. Congress, *Medal of Honor Recipients*, 118.

230   *"By default I took over"*: 29ID, Holland, file 22, 2/92 Burt letter to Blaker; Burt Memoirs, 2, 12–13.

230   *"We had air strikes"* and *"On one occasion"*: 29ID, Holland, file 22, Burt Memoirs, 2.

231   *"One day we were visited"*: 29ID, Holland, file 22, Burt Memoirs, 13–14.

231   *"very well-drilled"*: 29ID, Holland, file 22, Burt Memoirs, 25.

231   *"Gen. Corlett called"* and *"Consommé"*: Sylvan, *Normandy to Victory*, 149.

232   *"How"s our outfit doing"*: 29ID, WRJ, 10/14/44, 1950.

233   *"The plan which took final"*: Hewitt, *Workhorse of the Western Front*, 139.

233   *"The type of resistance"*: 29ID, 116th AAR, Oct. 1944, "Phase II."

233   *"The infantry had to slug"*: 29ID, Holland, file 24, *Le Tomahawk*, Oct. 1944, no. 6, "Aachen Encircled."

234 *"In one basement we found"*: Baltimore Sun, "Würselen Fight Still Heavy," byline 17 October 1944.

234 *"he dismounted"*: U.S. Congress, *Medal of Honor Recipients*, 118.

235 *"The thinking was that"*: Walker, *Vierville to Victory*, 98.

235 *"highly successful"*: 29ID, 116th AAR, Oct. 1944, "Phase II."

235 *"I always thought"*: MacDonald, *Siegfried Line Campaign*, 303.

235 *"[After] a visit"*: MHI, Corlett Papers, "Cowboy Pete" ms, 297.

236 *"Could you make Col. [Leroy] Watson"*: 29ID, WRJ, 10/15/44, 1935.

237 *"only a hazy idea"* and *"sitting on his fanny"*: Blumenson, *Breakout and Pursuit*, 110–18.

237 *"[The 116th] is your outfit"*: 29ID, WRJ, 10/16/44, 0755.

239 *"About noon on Oct. 16"*: 29ID, Holland, file 6, 2/6/47 Bingham letter to Ewing.

240 *"I found the [the 29ers] had used"*: 29ID, Holland, file 22, Burt Memoirs, 14.

240 *"Heinie infantry"*: Baltimore Sun, "Würselen Fight Still Heavy," byline 17 October 1944.

240 *"A 60mm mortar squad leader"*: 29ID, Holland, file 6, 2/6/47 Bingham letter to Ewing.

241 *"to remind him, once more"*: MacDonald, *Siegfried Line Campaign*, 314.

241 *"1100: Battalion holding"*: 29ID, Holland, file 6, 2/116 Journal, 10/17/44.

241 *"feeble"*: 29ID, 116th AAR, Oct. 1944, "Phase II."

241 *"I could tell he was politely trying"*: Walker, *Vierville to Victory*, 98E–98G.

242 *"It was obvious"*: MacDonald, *Siegfried Line Campaign*, 313.

243 *"The enemy immediately brought"*: 29ID, 116th AAR, Oct. 1944, "Phase II."

243 *"not open street fighting"*: Barnes, *Fragments of My Life*, 99.

243 *"Despite intense enemy automatic fire"*: 29ID, GO, 164, 11/24/44.

244 *Details on 99th*: Bergen, *History of 99th Infantry Battalion*.

246 *"I"d become so revolted"*: Lincoln Barnett, "Ernie Pyle," *Life*, 2 April 1945, 106.

247   *"was too late for me"*: MHI, Corlett Papers, "Cowboy Pete" ms, 298–300.

247   *"Young man, anyone who sasses"*: MHI, Forsythe oral history, 211.

248   *"Anything or everything you ever heard"*: 29ID, Holland, file 22, 2/92 Burt letter to Blaker.

249   *"Capt. Burt"s intrepidity"*: U.S. Congress, *Medal of Honor Recipients*, 118.

249   *"Almost everything learned"*: 29ID, Holland, file 22, 2/4/95 Burt letter to Blaker.

249   *"Every day in [Würselen]"*: 29ID, Holland, file 22, Burt Memoirs, 24.

249   *"Treat them like the best"*: 29ID, Holland, file 22, 2/4/95 Burt letter to Blaker.

SIX: DON'T COMPLICATE IT
1. Strictly Off Limits
251   *Lt. Col. Miller career*: 29ID, MDNG Service Cards, Miller.

252   *"fought it out"*: 29ID, 29LG, 9/14/44.

252   *"best battalion commander"*: 29ID, Personnel, Henne, 3/5/10 interview.

253   *"It was difficult"*: *Baltimore Sun*, "Indian Tactics Used by Yanks," 9 October 1944.

253   *"Those nights in and around"* and *"whatever the Allies were to gain"* and *"Following a few days of cleaning"*: Binkoski, *115th Infantry*, 196, 199, 197.

256   *"arranged the performance"* and other details on *Strictly Off Limits*: 29ID, 29LG, 10/27/44.

257   *"Rarely has a show"*: Binkoski, *115th Infantry*, 198.

258   *"That was some evening!"*: 29ID, WRJ, 10/24/44, 0720.

2. Bouncing Betty
259   *Maj. Gen. Harmon comments on McLain*: Harmon, *Combat Commander*, 216.

259   *Maj. Gen. McLain, details*: *National Guard Register, 1939*, 1,037.

260   *"one of the finest field generals"*: MHI, Forsythe oral history, 215–16.

261   *"He was a calm man"*: 29ID, 3/19/09 Thomas Hope e-mail to author.

261   *"You will be glad to know"*: DEP, *The War Years*, vol. 4, 2,080.

261   *"Few National Guard [general] officers"*: Bland, *George C. Marshall: Interviews and Reminiscences*, 578.

261   *"I have followed your career"*: Bland, *The Papers of George Catlett Marshall*, vol. 4, 702.

261   *"[McLain] had been a banker"*: MHI, Corlett Papers, "Cowboy Pete" ms, 299.

262   *"Is there anything special"*: 29ID, WRJ, 10/18/44, 1345.

262   *"a starvation diet"*: Parker, *Conquer: The Story of Ninth Army*, 59.

263   *"Don't complicate it!"*: 29ID, WRJ, 10/17/44, 0740.

264   *"[The attackers] came under mortar"*: MHI, Biddle Papers, 113CG Operations, Oct. 1944, 20.

264   *"withering"*: Binkoski, *115th Infantry*, 195.

264   *"They came under interlocking fire"*: 29ID, WRJ, 10/17/44, 2020.

264   *"As the four men waited"*: Binkoski, *115th Infantry*, 196.

266   *"I have been checking"*: 29ID, WRJ, 10/18/44, 0930.

266   *"I think it turned out fine"*: 29ID, WRJ, 10/17/44, 2133.

267   *"The people back in the States"*: 29ID, Personnel, Jesse (courtesy Kelly Morel).

267   *"You can bet your boots"*: Stapleton, *Out in Front All the Way*.

268   *"We've been checking"*: 29ID, WRJ, 10/21/44, 0825.

268   *"to determine enemy positions"*: 29ID, *115th Patrol Summary*, Oct. 1944.

270   *"out of communication"*: 29ID, WRJ, 10/21/44, 2023.

270   *"a little [enemy] enthusiasm"*: 29ID, WRJ, 10/22/44, 0734, 0743.

271   *"There are thirty men"*: 29ID, WRJ, 10/22/44, 1409.

271   *"What's going on?"*: 29ID, WRJ, 10/23/44, 0717.

271   *"We lost thirty-one men"*: 29ID, Holland, file 4, 1946 Johns letter to Ewing.

272   *"Although the explosion went off"*: Binkoski, *115th Infantry*, 195.

272   *"Maj. Johns's operations"*: 29ID, WRJ, 10/23/44, 1819.

273   *"This new organization"*: 29ID, WRJ, 10/28/44, 2322.

275   *B/175 and F/175 Oct. 29 raids*: 29ID, 175th 1944 Unit History, "Operational Narrative Supplement," 26-27.

277   *"Both companies made their objectives"*: 29ID, WRJ, 10/29/44, 0655.

277   *Sgt. Tomten Silver Star*: 29ID, GO, 189, 12/20/44.

277   *T/Sgt. Lafferty Silver Star*: 29ID, GO, 191, 12/22/44.

277   *T/Sgt. Fugini Silver Star*: 29ID, GO, 191, 12/22/44.

278   *L/115 "Frying Pan" raid*: Shea, "Raid on the Frying Pan," *Infantry Journal*, Nov. 1947.

278   *Lts. Silata and Wilkinson*: 29ID, Personnel, Silata, Wilkinson.

282   *"Millholland's [3rd Battalion] raid"*: 29ID, WRJ, 10/29/44, 0702.

283   *"to kill or capture the enemy"*: 29ID, Holland, file 26, 10/29/44 "Report on Night Raid of B/115 on Waldenrath."

283   *"the damndest minefield"*: 29ID, Holland, file 4, 1946 Johns letter to Ewing.

283   *"Immediately after the burst"*: 29ID, Holland, file 26, 10/29/44 "B/115 Raid."

285   *"as bright as daylight"*: St. George, "Enlistee Finds Parallels to Past," *Washington Post*, 17 December 2002, A17.

285   *"There was some disorganization"* and *"Some elements"*: 29ID, Holland, file 26, 10/29/44 "B/115 Raid."

286   *"1st Lt. McCallum"*: Cooper, *110th Field Artillery*, 177.

286   *"They got halfway"*: 29ID, WRJ, 10/29/44, 0754.

287   *"The mission was not completely successful"*: 29ID, Holland, file 26, 10/29/44 "B/115 Raid."

287   *Pvt. Farley*: St. George, "Enlistee Finds Parallels," *Washington Post*, 17 December 2002, A17; and 29ID, MR, C/115, 8/20/44.

289   *McLain visit*: Cooper, *110th Field Artillery*, 177; and 29ID, July 1984 interview with author.

3. 1-A in a 4-F Outfit

291   *"pushed out of a place blindfolded"*: Stouffer, *The American Soldier*, vol. 2, 273.

291   *"vague shapes"*: Cawthon, *Other Clay*, 81.

292   *"You give up"*: Stouffer, *The American Soldier*, vol. 2, 88.

293   *Ratio, physical wounds to combat exhaustion*: 29ID, Holland, file 2, "Combat Exhaustion," 1/13/45; and Glass, *Neuropsychiatry in World War II*, 8.

293   *"an excuse for cowardice"*: Patton, *War As I Knew It*, 294, 326.

293   *"tremor, insomnia, startle reaction"*: Swank, "Combat Neuroses: Development of Combat Exhaustion," *Neurology and Psychiatry*, 1946, vol. 55, 236–47. Abstract in *Psychoanalytic Quarterly*, 1947, vol. 16, 287.

293   *"What do you think should be done"*: Stouffer, *The American Soldier*, vol. 2, 198–99.

293   *"[I] prepared to meet"* and *"The [First] Army exhaustion center"*: 29ID, Holland, file 2, "Meeting the Problem of Combat Exhaustion," 10/2/44.

294   *"It soon became apparent"*: Glass, *Neuropsychiatry in World War II*, 118–20.

295   *"a program of rest"* and *"most, most necessary"*: 29ID, Holland, file 2, "Problem of Combat Exhaustion," 10/2/44.

295   *52.7 percent*: 29ID, Holland, file 2, "Annex XV."

296   *"approximately 50 percent"*: 29ID, Holland, file 2, "Problem of Combat Exhaustion," 10/2/44.

296   *"Psychiatric breakdowns"*: Stouffer, *American Soldier*, vol. 2, 452.

297   *Maj. Hankins*: 29ID, Personnel, Hankins.

297   *"I don't know, but I'll find out"*: 29ID, TC AAR, Oct.–Dec. 1944.

298   *"For entertainment"*: 29ID, TC AAR, Dec. 1944.

299   *"the percentage returned"*: NA, RG 407, 10/3/44 Shea interview with Weintrob, Box 24035.

300   *"to reacquaint himself"*: 29ID, Holland, file 2, "Problem of Combat Exhaustion," 10/2/44.

300   *"We start a very progressive training"*: 29ID, TC AAR, Dec. 1944.

301   *347 readmissions for combat exhaustion*, 29ID, Holland, file 2, "Annex XV."

301   *"Before I got out"*: Stouffer, *The American Soldier*, vol. 2, 276.

302   *"short history of the 29th Division's glorious achievements"*: 29ID, TC AAR, Nov. 1944, S-3 Summary.

302   *"The curtain rings up"* and *"Far removed from the realities"*: 29ID, 29LG, 10/10/44.

302   *"the great team"* and *"And now we will see"*: *Baltimore News-Post*, byline 13 October 1944 (title unknown).

304   *"Subject: Conduct in case of capture"*: 29ID, TC AAR, Oct.–Dec. 1944.

304   *"get-acquainted period"*: Balkoski, *From Beachhead to Brittany*, 91.

305   *"There's a sparkle"*: 29ID, 29LG, 10/10/44.

306   *"I am pleased to welcome you"*: 29ID, TC AAR, Oct.–Dec. 1944.

307   *"a howling success"*: 29ID, TC AAR, Nov. 1944.

307   *"causes one to have more confidence"*: 29ID, TC AAR, Dec. 1944.

308   *"All students upon graduation"*: 29ID, TC AAR, Nov. 1944, "Lessons."

308   *"There is too much material"*: 29ID, TC AAR, Dec. 1944.

308   *"By order of General Gerhardt"*: Ewing, *29 Let's Go*, 166.

308   *"A group of men would be standing"*: Ewing, *The 29th*, 51.

309   *"this is a sergeant's war"*: Balkoski, *Beyond the Beachhead*, 80.

309   *Lt. Gentry*: 29ID, Personnel, Gentry, Jan 2010 interview; also Gentry, "29th Division School for Squad Leaders," *Twenty-Niner*, Mar. 1993, 9.

311   *"the hottest school"*: 29ID, TC AAR, Nov. 1944.

311   *"There is not enough time to wash"*: 29ID, TC AAR, Dec. 1944.

312   *"You're too good a bird"*: 29ID, WRJ, 11/4/44, 0754.

312   *"1-A in a 4-F Outfit"*: 29ID, Holland, file 27, *Stars and Stripes*, Oct. 1944, "Wants Combat Job."

313   *"Mighty Fine!"*: Ewing, *29 Let's Go*, 282.

314   *"Malin was apparently lost"*: Ewing, *29 Let's Go*, 282.

SEVEN: THE DEMOCRATS WILL WIN
1. The Month Hitler Dreaded Most

315   *"the destruction of the enemy"*: DEP, *The War Years*, vol. 4, 2,258.

316   *"The good news came in"*: Butcher, *My Three Years With Eisenhower*, 698.

316   *"[Eisenhower's] chief of intelligence"*: Pogue, *Supreme Command*, 306.

316   *"I told Montgomery"*: USMASC, Bradley Papers, 11/4/44 and 11/19/44, "Memorandum."

316   *"I expected to be on the Rhine"*: MHI, Bradley Papers, Hansen notecards, "Nov. Offensive Turns Into a Slugging Match."

316   *"General Bradley believes"*: Sylvan, *Normandy to Victory*, 175.

316 *"is precisely what we are trying"*: MHI, Bradley Papers, Hansen 9/23/44 diary entry.

317 *"We consider that an immediate"*: Bland, *Papers of George C. Marshall*, vol. 4, 636.

317 *"Making war in a democracy"*: Pogue, *George C. Marshall: Organizer of Victory*, 552.

317 *"The proposals to end the war"*: Pogue, *Supreme Command*, 309.

317 *Scheldt Estuary cleared Nov. 26*: Ruppenthal, *Logistical Support of the Armies*, vol. II, 110.

318 *"shocked . . . that he thought these Germans"* and *"There were a lot of good reasons"*: MHI, Bradley Papers, Hansen notecards, "Confused by Marshall's Attitude;" "Replacement Problem Goes Back to Marshall Visit;" "Nov. Offensive: The Choice."

319 *"brilliant . . . alert, intelligent"*: Eisenhower, *Crusade in Europe*, 376.

320 *"our best prospect"*: MHI, Pogue Papers, Pogue 5/13/45 interview with Smith.

320 *"uncommonly normal"*: Bradley, *A Soldier's Story*, 422.

320 *"brilliant. . . . You could tell the difference"*: MHI, Pogue Papers, Pogue 5/8/47 interview with Smith.

320 *"General Simpson's genius"*: Stone, "Gen. William Hood Simpson: Unsung Commander of U.S. Ninth Army," *Parameters*, vol. xi, no. 2, 1981, 47.

320 *Col. Baldwin visit to war room*: 29ID, WRJ, 11/14/44, 0940.

321 *"Your IG came in"*: 29ID, WRJ, 11/14/44, 1020.

2. The Courage of Despair

323 *"I anticipate one hell of a fight"*: U.S. Ninth Army, *Offensive in November*, pt. 1, 8.

323 *"In the end the one who gains the laurels"*: Heiber, *Hitler and His Generals*, 538–39.

324 *"When I received this plan"* and *"was really against"*: Liddell Hart, *The German Generals Talk*, 275–76.

325 *"No soldier believed"*: Liddell Hart, *The Germans Generals Talk*, 275.

326 *"Brad said . . . it would be good to fight"*: MHI, Bradley Papers, Hansen 9/21/44 diary entry.

3. Where My Boys Are

326 *"just as if no war were going on"*: Ewing, *29 Let's Go*, 167.

326 *"Paris passes"* and *"topsoil off their bodies"*: 29ID, *Chin Strap*, G/175 newsletter, Nov. 1944 (Ewing file).

327 *Maj. Thomas Dukehart career*: 29ID, MDNG Service Cards, Dukehart; Personnel, Dukehart.

329 *"This is the first time I've slept"*; *"It's wide open"*; and *"We've got a beer garden"*: 29ID, 29LG, 10/20/44.

329 *"bright, red-trimmed doors"*: Ewing, *29 Let's Go*, 167.

330 *"Dutch-American relations"*: 29ID, *Chin Strap*, G/175 newsletter, Nov. 1944 (Ewing file).

331 *"Hitting the sack"*: Ewing, *29 Let's Go*, 166.

331 *"Shortly after the C.G. announced"*: 29ID, Holland, file 6, 2/6/47 Bingham letter to Ewing.

332 *"fought it off with pills"*: 29ID, *Chin Strap*, G/175 newsletter, Nov. 1944 (Ewing file).

332 *"We've forgotten who said"*: 29ID, 29LG, 10/29/44.

332 *"Servicemen like their religion"*: Metcalf, *With Cross and Shovel*, 57–58.

333 *"There's little doubt our presence"*: 29ID, 29LG, 10/29/44.

333 *"I remember our chaplain"*: 29ID, Personnel, Lott, 12/29/90 Ewing letter to Lott.

333 *Captain (Chaplain) O'Grady*: Balkoski, "Father Eugene Patrick O'Grady," *Maryland Historical Magazine*, vol. 102, no. 1, Spring 2007.

336 *"led many of the men to abandon"*: Binkoski, *115th Infantry*, 202.

336 *fighter plane flew directly over the woods*: 29ID, Personnel, Moon, 2/3/10 interview with Moon.

336 *Pvt. Graham career*: 29ID, MDNG Service Cards, Graham.

337 *"companies were ordered to maintain"*: 29ID, 2/115 Journal, 11/2/44.

337 *"speculation as to why"*: Binkoski, *115th Infantry*, 201–2.

337 *"For the next few weeks"*: Binkoski, *115th Infantry*, 201–2.

337 *"Military courtesy"*: Ewing, *29 Let's Go*, 165–66.

338 *"Demonstrations were held"*: 29ID, 29th Division AAR, Nov. 1944, "Phase X, The Battle for Jülich, 1.

339   *"went from one [enlisted man] to the other"*: 29ID, 29LG, 11/12/44.

340   *"There is, among the mass of individuals"*: Eisenhower, *Crusade in Europe*, 314.

340   *"there were many more messes"*: Ross, *The Quartermaster Corps: Operations in the War against Germany*, 524.

342   *"must always be the portion"*: Bartlett, *Familiar Quotations*, 14th ed. (1968), 1,016.

342   *"a natural amphitheater"*: Montrose, Letter to Editor, *Twenty-Niner*, Nov. 1989.

342   *"have four slit trenches dug"* and *"The Beer Barrel Polka"*: 29ID, WRJ, 11/10/44, 0910.

343   *"I turned to depart"*: Balkoski, *Maryland National Guard*, 76 (8/18/65 Ike letter to Gen. Archibald Sproul).

343   *"similar to the noise"*: Montrose, Letter, *Twenty-Niner*, Nov. 1989.

343   *"Morale is surprisingly high"* and *"Dear Wop"*: DEP, *The War Years*, vol. 4, 2,297–98.

344   *"It's on you now"*: 29ID, WRJ, 11/13/44, 0750.

345   *"Did I tell you or ask you"*: 29ID, WRJ, 11/13/44, 0840.

345   *"we made this change"*: 29ID, WRJ, 11/13/44, 0937.

346   *"proved to be not especially burdensome"*: Ewing, *29 Let's Go*, 166.

346   *"I always said that a great people"*: Kimball, *Churchill and Roosevelt: Complete Correspondence*, vol. 3, 383.

347   *"The reelection of President Roosevelt"*: 29ID, 29LG, 11/8/44.

4. Right into Berlin

347   *"Everyone sensed it"*: Ewing, *29 Let's Go*, 169.

347   *"All quiet up this way"*: 29ID, WRJ, 11/4/44, 0738.

348   *"Nowhere along the western front"*: MacDonald, *Siegfried Line Campaign*, 521.

350   *"Baker Construction Company"*: 29ID, Personnel, Johns.

351   *"A corps artillery battalion"*: Cooper, *110th Field Artillery*, 182.

352   *"Patrol drew machine gun fire"*: 29ID, WRJ, 11/12/44, 0115.

352   *"Our patrols developed evidence"*: 29ID, WRJ, 11/11/44, 0807.

5. A Sorry Outlook

355   *"Before the Army staff initiates"*: Brooks, *Montgomery and the Battle of Normandy*, 97–98.

355   *"employing strategical air"*: Bland, *Papers of George C. Marshall*, vol. 4, 636.

355   *"All of our heavy bomber work"*: DEP, *The War Years*, vol. 4, 2,247.

355   *"The British Army have for months"*: DEP, *The War Years*, vol. 4, 2,248.

356   *"We would hitch our plans"*: Bradley, *A Soldier's Story*, 439.

356   *"the largest air-ground cooperative effort"*: Craven, *The Army Air Forces in WWII*; vol. 3, 631–32.

357   *"a rather favorable prediction"*: DEP, *The War Years*, vol. 4, 2,297.

357   *"You can go back to bed now"*: 29ID, WRJ, 11/10/44, 2318.

357   *"The [weather] predictions"*: DEP, *The War Years*, vol. 4, 2,297.

357   *"Ike said he thought"*: Butcher, *My Three Years with Eisenhower*, 702.

358   *"I think we're all set"*: 29ID, WRJ, 11/11/44, 2008.

358   *"Any telling how long this weather"*: 29ID, WRJ, 11/13/44, 0800.

358   *"the most harassed"*: Sylvan, *Normandy to Victory*, 172.

360   *"The Democrats will win"*: 29ID, WRJ, 11/16/44, 0038.

Bibliography

Balkoski, Joseph. *Beyond the Beachhead: The 29th Infantry Division in Normandy*. Harrisburg, PA: Stackpole Books, 1989.

———. "Father Eugene Patrick O'Grady: A Legendary Twenty-Niner and Baltimorean." *Maryland Historical Magazine*, vol. 102, no. 1 (Spring 2007).

———. *From Beachhead to Brittany: The 29th Infantry Division at Brest*. Mechanicsburg, PA: Stackpole Books, 2008.

———. *The Maryland National Guard: A History of Maryland's Military Forces*. Baltimore: Maryland Military Historical Society, 1991.

Barnes, John. *Fragments of My Life with Company A, 116th Infantry*. New York: JAM, 2000.

Barnett, Corelli, ed. *Hitler's Generals*. New York: William Morrow, 1989.

Barnett, Lincoln. "Ernie Pyle." *Life* (2 April 1945).

Bergen, Howard. *History of 99th Infantry Battalion*. Oslo, Norway: U.S. Army, 1945.

Binkoski, Joseph, and Arthur Plaut. *The 115th Infantry Regiment in World War II*. Nashville: Battery Press, 1988.

Blackwelder, Richard. *The Zest for Life, or Waldo had a Pretty Good Run: The Life of Waldo LaSalle Schmitt*. Lawrence, KS: Allen Press, 1979.

Blaker, Gordon. *Iron Knights: The 66th Armored Regiment in WWII*. Mechanicsburg, PA: Stackpole Books, 2008.

Bland, Larry, ed. *The Papers of George Catlett Marshall*. Vols. 3 and 4. Baltimore: Johns Hopkins University Press, 1991.

————. *George C. Marshall: Interviews and Reminiscences*. Lexington: Marshall Foundation, 1996.

Blumenson, Martin. *Breakout and Pursuit*. Washington: Office of the Chief of Military History, 1961.

Blumentritt, Günter. *Von Rundstedt: The Soldier and the Man*. London: Odhams Press, 1952.

Bradley, Holbrook. *War Correspondent*. Lincoln: iUniverse, 2007.

Bradley, Omar. *A Soldier's Story*. New York: Henry Holt, 1951.

Bradley, Omar, and Clay Blair. *A General's Life*. New York: Simon and Schuster, 1983.

Brewer, James. *History of the 175th Infantry (Fifth Maryland)*. Baltimore: Maryland Historical Society, 1955.

Brooks, Stephen, ed. *Montgomery and the Battle of Normandy*. Gloucestershire: Army Records Society, 2008.

Butcher, Harry. *My Three Years with Eisenhower*. New York: Simon and Schuster, 1946.

Bykofsky, Joseph. *The Transportation Corps: Operations Overseas*. Washington: Office of the Chief of Military History, 1957.

Cawthon, Charles. *Other Clay*. Niwot: University Press of Colorado, 1990.

Chandler, Alfred, ed. *The Papers of Dwight David Eisenhower: The War Years*. Baltimore: Johns Hopkins University Press, 1970.

Churchill, Winston. *Triumph and Tragedy*. Boston: Houghton Mifflin, 1953.

Collins, J. Lawton. *Lightning Joe*. Baton Rouge, LA: Louisiana State University Press, 1979.

Condell, Bruce, and David Zabecki, eds. *On the German Art of War*. Mechanicsburg, PA: Stackpole Books, 2009.

Cooper, John. *History of the 110th Field Artillery*. Baltimore: Maryland Historical Society, 1953.

Craven, Wesley, and James Cate. *The Army Air Forces in WWII*, vol. 3, *Europe: Argument to V-E Day*. Chicago: University of Chicago Press, 1951.

Danchev, Alex, and Daniel Todman, eds. *War Diaries: Field Marshal Lord Alanbrooke, 1939–1945*. Berkeley: University of California Press, 2001.

Eisenhower, Dwight. *Crusade in Europe*. New York: Doubleday, 1948.

Ellis, L. F. *Victory in the West*. Vol. 2. London: HMSO, 1968.

Ewing, Joseph. *29 Let's Go!* Washington, DC: Infantry Journal Press, 1948.

———. *The 29th: A Short History of a Fighting Division*. Paducah: Turner, 1992.

Garth, David. "Battalion Raid on Schierwaldenrath." *Military Affairs* (Summer 1947).

Glass, Albert, ed. *Neuropsychiatry in World War II: Overseas Theaters*. Washington, DC: Office of the Surgeon General, 1973.

Harmon, Ernest. *Combat Commander*. Englewood: Prentice-Hall, 1970.

Heiber, Helmut, ed. *Hitler and His Generals: Military Conferences, 1942–1945*. New York: Enigma Books, 2004.

Hewitt, Robert. *Workhorse of the Western Front: The Story of the 30th Infantry Division*. Washington: Infantry Journal Press, 1946.

Hinsley, F. H. *British Intelligence in the Second World War*. Vol. 3, pt. 2. London: HMSO, 1984.

Hoffman, David, ed. *I'll Be Home For The Christmas Rush*. Bennington: Merriam, 2009.

Hogan, David. *A Command Post at War: First Army Headquarters in Europe, 1943–1945*. Washington, DC: Center of Military History, 2000.

Houston, Donald. *Hell on Wheels: The 2nd Armored Division*. New York: Ballantine, 1995.

Johns, Glover. *The Clay Pigeons of St. Lô*. Harrisburg, PA: Military Service Publishing Co., 1958.

———. "Raid on Schierwaldenrath." *Infantry Journal (Overseas)* (May 1945).

Kimball, Warren, ed. *Churchill and Roosevelt: The Complete Correspondence*, vol. III, *Alliance Declining*. Princeton, NJ: Princeton University Press, 1984.

Liddell Hart, Sir Basil. *The German Generals Talk*. New York: Morrow, 1948.

MacDonald, Charles. *The Siegfried Line Campaign*. Washington, DC: Office of the Chief of Military History, 1963.

Maryland National Guard. *Historical and Pictorial Review of the National Guard and Naval Militia of the U.S., State of Maryland, 1940*. Baton Rouge, LA: Army and Navy, 1940.

Metcalf, George. *With Cross and Shovel*. Cambridge: Riverside, 1960.

Mitcham, Samuel. *German Order of Battle*. Vols. 1–3. Mechanicsburg, PA: Stackpole Books, 2007.

Nash, Douglas. *Victory Was Beyond Their Grasp*. Bedford, PA: Aberjona, 2008.

Ninth U.S. Army. *Ninth U.S. Army Operations: Offensive in November*. Holland: 4th Information and Historical Service, 1945.

Parker, Theodore, and William Thompson. *Conquer: The Story of Ninth Army*. Nashville: Battery Press, 1993.

Patton, George. *War As I Knew It*. New York: Pyramid, 1966.

Pogue, Forrest. *George C. Marshall: Organizer of Victory, 1943–1945*. New York: Penguin, 1993.

———. *The Supreme Command*. Washington, DC: Office of the Chief of Military History, 1954.

Rose, Ben. *The Saga of the Red Horse*. Holland: Thieme, 1945.

Rosenman, Samuel. *The Public Papers and Addresses of Franklin D. Roosevelt: The Continuing Struggle for Liberalism*. New York: Macmillan, 1941.

Ross, William, and Charlse Romanus. *The Quartermaster Corps: Operations in the War against Germany*. Washington, DC: Office of the Chief of Military History, 1965.

Ruppenthal, Roland. *Logistical Support of the Armies*. Vol. 2. Washington, DC: Office of the Chief of Military History, 1959.

Shea, Jack. "Raid on the Frying Pan." *Infantry Journal* (November 1947).

Snipas, Ben. *How it Happened: War Stories from a Replacement Infantry Lieutenant*. Private, n.d.

Stanton, Shelby. *World War II Order of Battle*. New York: Galahad, 1984.

Stapleton, Gregory. *Out in Front All the Way: Lt. Col. James Morris*. Kentucky: Private, 2006.

St. George, Donna. "Enlistee Finds Parallels to Past." *Washington Post* (17 December 2002): A17.

Stimson, Henry, and McGeorge Bundy. *On Active Service in Peace and War*. New York: Harper, 1947.

Stone, Thomas. "Gen. William Hood Simpson: Unsung Commander of U.S. Ninth Army," *Parameters*, vol. 11, no. 2 (1981).

Stouffer, Samuel, et. al. *The American Soldier: Combat and Its Aftermath*. Princeton, NJ: Princeton University Press, 1949.

Swank, Roy, and A. Marchand. "Combat Neuroses: Development of Combat Exhaustion." *Neurology and Psychiatry*, vol. 55 (1946).

Sylvan, William. *Normandy to Victory: The War Diary of Gen. Courtney Hodges and the First U.S. Army.* Lexington, KY: University Press of Kentucky, 2008.

Tessin, Georg. *Verbände und Truppen der deutschen Wehrmacht und Waffen-SS im Zweiten Weltkrieg, 1939–1945.* Osnabrück: Biblio-Verlag, 1973.

Tobin, James. *Ernie Pyle's War.* Lawrence, KS: University Press of Kansas, 1997.

Twelfth U.S. Army Group. *Effect of Air Power on Military Operations in Western Europe.* Germany: Twelfth Army Group, 1945.

U.S. Army. *The Administrative and Logistical History of the ETO*, part 11, *Basic Needs of the ETO Soldier*, vol. II. Washington: Office of the Chief of Military History, 1946.

U.S. Army. *Breaching the Siegfried Line: XIX Corps, 2 October 1944.* Germany: XIX Corps, 1945.

U.S. Army. *Normandy to the Elbe: XIX Corps.* Germany: XIX Corps, 1945.

U.S. Army. *U.S. Army Order of Battle: ETO, 1943–1945.* Germany: ETOUSA, 1945.

U.S. Congress. *Medal of Honor Recipients, 1863–1963.* Washington, DC: Government Printing Office, 1964.

U.S. Dept. of the Army. *Führer Directives, 1942–1945.* Washington, DC: Government Printing Office, 1948.

U.S. Dept. of State. *Foreign Relations of the United States: The Conference at Quebec, 1944.* Washington, DC: Government Printing Office, 1972.

U.S. Military Academy. *Roster of Graduates and Former Cadets, 1982.* West Point, NY: Association of Graduates, 1982.

U.S. Military Intelligence Service. "Machine Carbine Redesignated." *Tactical and Technical Trends*, vol. 57 (April 1945).

U.S. War Dept. *FM 100-5, Field Service Regulations: Operations.* Washington, DC: Government Printing Office, 15 June 1944.

U.S. War Dept. *Handbook on German Military Forces.* Washington, DC: Government Printing Office, 1945.

Virginia National Guard. *Historical and Pictorial Review of the National Guard of the Commonwealth of Virginia, 1940.* Baton Rouge, LA: Army and Navy, 1940.

Walker, Robert. *From Vierville to Victory: With the Stonewallers of the 116th Infantry*. Los Angeles: Private, 1998.

Weigley, Russell. *Eisenhower's Lieutenants*. Bloomington, IN: Indiana University Press, 1981.

Wilkes, Homer. *APO230: The 747th Tank Battalion*. Scottsdale, AZ: Private, 1982.

Wilmot, Chester. *The Struggle for Europe*. London: Collins, 1952.

Wilson, John. *Maneuver and Firepower: The Evolution of Divisions and Separate Brigades*. Washington, DC: Center of Military History, 1998.

Acknowledgments

The task of naming every 29er who provided assistance to me during the research and writing of this book is manifestly impossible, for thirty years have now elapsed since those generous men first began to correspond and converse with me about their World War II experiences in the 29th Infantry Division. All interested parties wishing to discover the extent of the 29ers' generosity should visit the Fifth Regiment Armory in Baltimore, Maryland, and consult the voluminous collection of the 29ers' correspondence and memoirs preserved over the years.

I feel obligated, however, to single out several 29ers and their descendants who were of immeasurable assistance as I prepared *From Brittany to the Reich* for publication. Raymond Moon of Company F, 115th Infantry, never failed to provide answers—no matter how tough the questions. Similarly, Maurice Dana Tawes (115th Infantry), Lucien Laborde (115th and 29th Headquarters), Robert Minor (29th Headquarters), Dwight Gentry (115th), Nick Demond (29th Headquarters), Victor McCool (115th), Robert Henne (115th), Thomas Hope (XIX Corps), Noel Dube (121st Engineers), and Sidney Smith (121st Engineers) freely provided their perspective on numerous issues pertinent to this book. I offer profound appreciation to Holbrook Bradley, the *Baltimore Sun* reporter who spent months with the 29th Division during its combat period, for his recollection of the events he witnessed and the people he knew.

Numerous descendants of 29ers offered valuable insight that contributed heavily to the research process. Among them are Gene and

Joyce Cox, Cassi Cardiel, Fran Sherr-Davino, Kay Gutknecht, Kelly Morel, Walter Carter, Sue Schlereth, James and Katherine (McGrath) Cranney, Sally McGrath, John Wilkinson, and Orman Kimbrough. Again, I am obliged to single out Chris Sorenson and his wife, Fissa, of Shropshire, England, for their crucial input concerning Chris's uncle, Sgt. Ned Humphrey of the 121st Engineer Combat Battalion. Sergeant Humphrey, who gained two Silver Stars for valor in two months of combat, was one of the most notable soldiers in 29th Division history. Without Chris and Fissa's contribution, I never could have understood the personality of that dedicated fighting man. Similarly, Sergeant Humphrey's grandson, the late Christopher Humphrey of Salt Lake City, was extraordinarily generous in supplying me with essential information on his grandfather.

Beyond the 29th Division family, I am exceedingly fortunate to maintain friendships with some brilliant World War II historians and archivists. First among them is Dr. Simon Trew, a lecturer at the Royal Military Academy at Sandhurst, who imparted to me invaluable research advice and many rare documents related to the German Army on the Western Front in late 1944. At the Military History Institute at Carlisle Barracks, Pennsylvania, David Keough and Dr. Richard Sommers yet again offered indispensable advice and insight. Tim Nenninger, chief of modern military records at the National Archives, helped guide me through the significant official documents pertinent to my subject. Capt. James Burt of the 2nd Armored Division, who gained a Medal of Honor while operating with his tanks in conjunction with the 116th Infantry at Würselen, was a soldier with whom I had to become familiar to tell the Aachen story accurately, and thanks to Gordon Blaker, director of the U.S. Army Artillery Museum at Fort Sill, Oklahoma, I did indeed come to understand Burt. Likewise, the 113th Cavalry Group, commanded by Col. William Biddle, played a key role in October 1944 during its attachment to the 29th Division, and I profited immensely from Harry Yeide's knowledge of American cavalry operations in World War II. Too, Arno Lasoe of Heerlen, Holland, graciously made available information and photos related to General Corlett and Colonel Biddle. I must also express thanks to Rick Atkinson for sharing with me some fascinating insights on the wartime U.S. Army he has presented so brilliantly in his Liberation Trilogy.

Finally, I would like to thank all my historically minded comrades in the Maryland and Virginia National Guard, active and retired, who maintained a perpetual enthusiasm for 29th Division history and helped to make the task of researching and writing this book thoroughly enjoyable.

I am privileged to have friends as loyal and virtuous as those listed above. In the words of the famous wartime song, Bless 'em all.

Index

403